Texas Politics

Constraints and Opportunities

Fifth Edition

Texas Politics

Constraints and Opportunities

Fifth Edition

Wilbourn E. Benton
TEXAS A&M UNIVERSITY

Nelson-Hall Publishers nh Chicago

WILBOURN E. BENTON, PH.D., is professor of political science at Texas A & M University. He received his doctorate from the University of Texas at Austin in 1948 and taught at Southern Methodist University and the University of Houston. He has written books and articles on state government and law and has participated in official studies of governmental problems in both Dallas County and the Houston-Harris County area. He is a member of the Southwestern Political Science Association, the Southwestern Social Science Association, and the American Society of International Law.

LIBRARY OF CONGRESS CATALOGING IN PUBLICATION DATA

Benton, Wilbourn E.
    Texas politics.

    Includes bibliographical references and index.
    1. Texas—Politics and government.   I. Title.
JK4816.B46   1984   320.9764   83-26458
ISBN 0-8304-1092-9 (cloth)
ISBN 0-8304-1108-9 (paper)

Manufactured in the United States of America

10 9 8 7 6 5 4 3 2 1

To my mother and father

and

Josephine, Cindy, and Ronnie

Contents

1836—1986

In Commemoration of the
Texas Sesquicentennial

WE, THEREFORE, THE DELEGATES, with plenary powers, of the people of Texas in solemn convention assembled, appealing to a candid world for the necessities of our condition, do hereby resolve and declare that our political connection with the Mexican nation has forever ended; and that the people of Texas do now constitute a free sovereign and independent republic, and are fully invested with all the rights and attributes which properly belong to independent nations; and, conscious of the rectitude of our intentions, we fearlessly and confidently commit the issue to the decision of the Supreme Arbiter of the destinies of nations.

Texas Declaration of Independence, March 2, 1836.

Preface

APART FROM ITS COMMITMENT to democracy and to the improvement of state government, *Texas Politics: Constraints and Opportunities* attempts to analyze Texas politics in a direct and candid manner. In short, an effort is made to "tell it like it is," politically speaking.

In addition to presenting the necessary factual information about governmental structure and procedures, I have tried to portray the realities of government at work in the states—the pressures, the obstacles, the conflicts. From this the student may be able to understand what the government is trying to do and judge how well it *is* doing it.

Wherever practical, the text presents conflicting viewpoints on controversial subjects. Various observations and conclusions have been included to give students a touchstone against which they can test the manner in which government operates as well as test their own beliefs and experiences. It is hoped that this approach may create more student interest and encourage participation in politics.

Government and politics are, indeed, dynamic—especially so in the space "revolution" with its "aerospace" politics. It could not be otherwise, for mobility and change are important considerations in an evolving democratic society. The changes in Texas politics give ample evidence of the dynamic nature of government. To observe the political changes and developments, as well as intelligently interpret them, is no easy matter; but on the other hand it does offer a challenge and an opportunity for those concerned with government in action.

I wish to express my sincere thanks to the state and local public officials who provided information. Some of the information was secured by personal interview and other information was obtained by letter or from agency reports. To friends and other persons who freely gave of their time and energy, I am deeply grateful. Also, I wish to thank Mr. B. H. Dewey, Jr., Justice of the Peace of Bryan, and former member of the Texas legislature, for his kindness and invaluable help. Thanks also to the editors of Nelson-Hall, Elizabeth Rubenstein, Dorothy Anderson, and Kristen Westman, for their contributions in the preparation of the manuscript.

Finally, I wish to express my sincere gratitude to my wife, Josephine, who typed and retyped the manuscript, as well as offered assistance in many other ways. Without her sympathy, understanding, and forbearance, this book would not have been possible.

For any errors, the author assumes full responsibility.

Part One

Background

---

1 From Coahuila and Texas to an Urban State

TEXAS, LIKE THE FORTY-NINE other states, is a product of its history and experience. Out of this experience there evolved, in varying degrees, a distrust of government and politicians, fear of centralized government, opposition to a strong executive, distrust of the legislature, strong support for the Democratic Party, and a negative and individualistic rather than positive and constructive attitude toward government. One may observe some or all of these attitudes in Texas state and local government today. "The past is not something that we have left behind us . . . it is something that moves along with us."

Coahuila and Texas jointly were a state within the Mexican nation. Consequently, Texas was a district of the State of Coahuila and remained such a district until the Republic of Texas was established. Texas could have been de-attached to become a separate state. Leaders of the Texas district petitioned for separation but the Mexican authorities refused to grant permission for the establishment of a separate state.

The State of Coahuila and Texas were divided into three departments for the convenience of local administration: The Department of Bexar, the largest geographically; the Department of Brazos; and the Department of Nacogdoches. The Mexican headquarters were in San Antonio and each department had a political chief who was nominated by the officials of the municipalities and appointed by the governor. The congress of the Republic of Texas—after Texas independence—and the Texas state legislature, after annexation by the United States, authorized the creation or organization of new counties from land formerly located in these departments or districts. Some new counties were created or organized from one or more existing counties.

The Classic or Golden Era of Texas History

The period 1835–1845, which included the Texas revolution, independence, the Republic of Texas, and annexation by the United States, is considered by some as the classic, golden, or glorious phase of Texas history. Certainly the period is writ large with the deeds of courageous men and women. Such drama and gal-

3

lantry left an ineradicable imprint upon the life of the state and nation and made Texans sensitive and proud of their heritage.

The first battle in the struggle for Texas independence from Mexico was the battle of Gonzales, October 2, 1835. Since this was the first military confrontation between Texas and Mexican troops, the battle of Gonzales is known as the "Lexington of the Texas revolution." As the first shots of the Texas revolution, it was a minor skirmish. The Texas volunteer army assembled at Gonzales, under the command of Stephen F. Austin, later marched to San Antonio to participate in the siege of Bexar. The first Texas soldier killed in the Texas revolution was during the battle of Concepcion which was fought around Bexar on October 28, 1835.

The siege of the Alamo by Mexican troops under the command of General Antonio López de Santa Anna lasted thirteen days—from February 23, 1836, to March 6, 1836. For Texans, the siege was considered "thirteen days of glory." When Santa Anna and the first of his troops arrived in San Antonio on February 23, 1836, there were approximately 145 Texans within the walls of the Alamo under the joint command of William B. Travis and James Bowie: Travis was in command of the regulars and Bowie in command of the volunteers. Dissension developed between the two commanders. However, on February 24, 1836, Bowie became ill with typhoid-pneumonia, and Travis assumed full command of all troops within the Alamo.

The "Travis line" has been a part of the proud Texas revolutionary history ever since the battle of the Alamo. Although it is not certain that Travis drew such a line; such a gesture was characteristic of Travis and well within the nobility and courage of all the men who died in defense of the Alamo against overwhelming odds. This is the line which Travis is said to have drawn on the floor of the Alamo; across which all of Travis's comrades joined him in defense of the Alamo. There comes a time in the lives of free men and women when the maximum sacrifice must be made. Evidently, those within the walls of the Alamo must have resolved—in one form or another—that this was the time.

On February 24, 1836, Travis wrote his famous letter addressed "To the People of Texas and All Americans in the World." If not the most heroic document in American history, the letter must be ranked among the greatest. Again, this letter illustrates the dramatic and courageous nature of Travis the man. Such characteristics and leadership traits must have had a profound influence on the men under Travis's command. All great historic events must have, in varying degrees, a touch of the dramatic, courage, and nobility.

During the siege of the Alamo Travis made an appeal for reinforcements. The only reinforcements received by Travis were thirty-two volunteers from Gonzales under the command of Captain Albert Martin who broke through the Mexican lines and entered the Alamo on March 1, 1836. The thirty-two volunteers from Gonzales were killed with the other defenders of the Alamo.

The Alamo fell on March 6, 1836, following the storming of the mission on all sides by the Mexicans and the building to building—and room to room—fighting. Bowie died on his cot. But the Texans had made a courageous and noble stand in defense of liberty. Travis had approximately 187 men who confronted Santa Anna's army of more than 5,000 men. The survivors of this epic shoot-out included about 15 noncombatants, mostly women and children. All other Texans in the Alamo were killed and their bodies burned on order of Santa Anna. Mexican losses have been estimated at between fifteen to sixteen hundred men. "Remember the Alamo" became a symbol of all liberty-loving people everywhere and the courage of the defenders of the Alamo has been recorded in song, literature, the movies, and on television.

One of the most tragic events that occurred during the Texas revolution was the massacre of Colonel James W. Fannin and his men at Goliad, March 27, 1836, by order of General Antonio López de Santa Anna—the Goliad Massacre. The exact number of men who were executed, or who escaped, has never been established. However, it has been estimated that 342 of Fannin's men were executed; 28 escaped; and 20 were not executed because they were physicians, nurses, interpreters, and mechanics.

During the Texas revolution the Texans lost all the important battles except the last one. In the battle of San Jacinto, April 21, 1836, in which the major confrontation lasted but eighteen minutes, Sam Houston and his men defeated the forces of Santa Anna. There is little doubt that this battle was one the most significant military engagements in North American history. Indeed, it was a decisive military victory for the Texans and their supporters.

At San Jacinto the Texans charged with the battle cry, "Remember the Alamo!" "Remember Goliad!" With this decisive military victory—including the capture of General Santa Anna—the military phase of the Texas revolution was concluded.

Among the inscriptions on the San Jacinto monument are these words:

> Measured by its results, San Jacinto was one of the decisive battles of the World. The freedom of Texas from Mexico won here led to annexation and to the Mexican War, resulting in the acquisition by the United States of the states of Texas, New Mexico, Arizona, Nevada, California, Utah, and parts of Colorado, Wyoming, Kansas, and Oklahoma. Almost one-third of the present area of the American nation, nearly a million square miles of territory, changed sovereignty.

The unanimous Texas Declaration of Independence was approved by the delegates of the people of Texas in general convention at the town of Washington, March 2, 1836. Thus, the declaration was approved four days before the fall of the Alamo on March 6, 1836, and prior to the battle of San Jacinto on April 21, 1836. The indictment or "bill of particulars" against the Mexican government was, as one might expect under the conditions, drafted with considerable emotion. Some of the charges were as follows:

> The Mexican government, by its colonization laws, invited and induced the Anglo-American population of Texas to colonize its wilderness under the pledged faith of a written Constitution that they should continue to enjoy that constitutional liberty and republican government to which they had been habituated in the land of their birth, the United States of America. In this expectation they have been cruelly disappointed, inasmuch as the Mexican nation has acquiesced in the late changes made in the government by General Antonio Lopez de Santa Anna, who, having overturned the Constitution of his country, now offers us the cruel alternative either to abandon our homes, acquired by so many privations, or submit to the most intolerable of all tyrrany [sic], the combined despotism of the sword and the priesthood.
>
> It has sacrificed our welfare to the state of Coahuila, by which our interests have been

continually depressed through a jealous and partial course of legislation carried on at a far distant seat of government, by a hostile majority, in an unknown tongue; and this too, notwithstanding we have petitioned in the humblest terms, for the establishment of a separate State Government, and have, in accordance with the provisions of the national Constitution, presented to the general Congress a republican Constitution which was, without just cause contemptuously rejected. . . .

It has failed and refused to secure on a firm basis, the right of trial by jury; that palladium* of civil liberty, and only safe guarantee for the life, liberty, and property of the Citizen.

It has failed to establish any public system of education, although possessed by almost boundless resources (the public domain) and, although, it is an axiom, in political science, that unless a people are educated and enlightened it is idle to expect the continuance of civil liberty, or the capacity for self government.

It has suffered the military commandants stationed among us to exercise arbitrary acts of oppression and tyrrany [sic], thus trampling upon the most sacred rights of the citizen and rendering the military superior to the civil power.

It has dissolved by force of arms, the State Congress of Coahuila and Texas, and obliged our representatives to fly for their lives from the seat of government; thus depriving us of the fundamental political right of representation.

It has demanded the surrender of a number of our citizens, and ordered military detachments to seize and carry them into the Interior for trial, in contempt of the civil authorities, and in defiance of the laws and the Constitution.

It has made piratical attacks upon our commerce, by commissioning foreign desperadoes, and authorizing them to seize our vessels, and convey the property of our citizens to far distant parts for confiscation.

It denies us the right of worshipping the Allmighty [sic] according to the dictates of our own conscience; by the support of a national religion calculated to promote the temporal interest of its human functionaries rather than the glory of the true and living God. . . .

It has through its emissaries, incited the merciless savage, with the tomahawk and scalping knife, to massacre the inhabitants of our defenceless frontiers. . . .

We, therefore, the delegates, with plenary powers, of the people of Texas in solemn convention assembled, appealing to a candid world for the necessities of our condition, do hereby resolve and declare that our political connection with the Mexican nation has forever ended; and that the people of Texas do now constitute a free sovereign and independent republic, and are fully invested with all the rights and attributes which properly belong to independent nations; and, conscious of the rectitude of our intentions, we fearlessly and confidently commit the issue to the decision of the Supreme Arbiter of the destinies of nations.

Richard Ellis, president
of the Convention

The Republic of Texas, 1836–1845

The constitution of the Republic of Texas was framed by a convention which assembled at Washington, on the Brazos River, March 1, 1836; proclaimed a dec-

---

*A sacred statute or image; any safeguard, as of a city or institution; the statute in Troy on the preservation of which the safety of the city was supposed to depend.

laration of independence March 2; and approved an ordinance establishing a government *ad interim*. The convention completed its labors on March 17, 1836.

The congress of the republic consisted of a house of representatives and a senate. House members were chosen annually, "on the first Monday of September each year, until congress shall otherwise provide by law, and shall hold their offices one year from the date of their election." Each county was entitled to at least one representative, and a house member must have resided in the county or district six months next preceding his election. The senators were "chosen by districts, as nearly equal in free population (free Negroes and Indians excepted) as practicable"; and each district was entitled to only one member. Senators were chosen for a term of three years. The vice-president of the republic was president of the senate, but could not vote on any question, unless the senate was equally divided.

The executive authority of the Republic of Texas was vested in the president. According to the constitution,

> The first president elected by the people shall hold his office for the term of two years, and shall be ineligible during the next succeeding term; and all subsequent presidents shall be elected for three years; and be alike ineligible; and in the event of a tie, the house of representatives shall determine between the two highest candidates by a *viva-voce* vote.

The judicial powers of the Republic of Texas were vested in one supreme court, and such inferior courts as the congress might, from time to time, ordain and establish. Judges of the supreme and inferior courts held their offices for four years, and were eligible for reelection. The judges of the supreme and district courts were elected by joint ballot of both houses of congress. The supreme court consisted of a chief justice and associate judges; the district judges composed the associate judges. Also, the constitution provided for county courts and justices of the peace—the latter were commissioned by the president.

The constitution of the Republic of Texas provided for a vice-president, "chosen at every election for president, in the same manner, continue in office for the same time, and shall possess the same qualifications of the president."

A majority of the members elected to the house and senate could propose constitutional amendments which were required to be referred to the congress next to be chosen. If the latter congress approved the amendment or amendments by a vote of two-thirds of all the members elected to each house, the constitution required their submission to the people. Such amendments became a part of the constitution when approved "by a majority of the electors qualified to vote for members of congress voting thereon." No amendment or amendments could be referred to the people more than once in three years.

A declaration of rights, as the concluding section of the constitution of the Republic of Texas, enumerated the rights of the people that could "never be violated on any pretence whatever."

Since the Republic of Texas was a sovereign nation, the president could, with the advice and consent of two-thirds of the senate, make treaties; and, with the consent of the senate, appoint ministers and consuls to represent the republic in the United States and other countries. Ministers and consuls of the United States and other countries were accredited to the Republic of Texas.

The presidents of the Republic of Texas were honored when the counties bearing their names were created:

- David G. Burnet, provisional president of the Republic of Texas—Burnet County (central Texas).
- Sam Houston—Houston County (east Texas). The city of Houston was named in honor of General and President Houston.
- Mirabeau B. Lamar—Lamar County (northeast Texas on the Oklahoma border).
- Anson Jones, last president of the Republic of Texas—Jones County (west central Texas).

The Continuing Conflict with Mexico

General Sam Houston's victory over Mexican forces at San Jacinto in 1836 did not end Mexico's efforts to stymie Texas's push for independence. Mexican soldiers made several forays back into Texas after San Jacinto and once even recaptured San Antonio. Although the Battle of San Jacinto, April 21, 1836, concluded the military phase of the Texas revolution, the conflict between Texas and Mexico continued for a period of time. The continuing conflict took the form of raids and counter raids—attack and counter attack—by both Texans and Mexicans.[1] The period was replete with atrocities and brutality committed by both Texans and Mexicans.

One phase of the continuing warfare between Texans and Mexicans during the days of the Republic of Texas, 1836–1845, was the Mier expedition of 1842, which was an attempt to challenge Mexican raids into Texas. The expedition to Mier, a small city just over the Rio Grande, was one of the raids by Texans across the Mexican border. This was the last and most disastrous of the raiding expeditions from Texas into Mexico.[2]

The Mier episode developed out of the Somervell expedition. The purpose of the latter was to engage the Mexican army, as well as seize and plunder Mexican towns. The Mexican army was not engaged, and there was little opportunity for seizing and plundering by the Texans. On December 19, 1842, Alexander Somervell realized his expedition had been a failure and ordered his troops to return home by way of Gonzales. Only 189 officers and men under the command of Somervell obeyed the order to return to Texas. Those who opposed the order to return home decided to separate from the command, select their own commander, cross the Rio Grande River, and attack Mexican settlements in order to secure cattle and horses. Thus was organized the Mier expedition.

Some of those who participated in the Mier expedition wanted revenge and retaliation against the Mexicans; others sought adventure. The leaders of the expedition, for the most part, were political opponents of Sam Houston.

At the Mexican town of Mier, the Mexican commander sent a white flag to the Texans of the Mier expedition and demanded they surrender. The Texans claimed later they surrendered as prisoners of war and should have been treated as such. The capitulation, which was not signed until the Texans had been relieved of their arms, declared the Texans would be treated with "consideration" rather than as prisoners of war. Since President Houston later declared the men of the Mier expedition had acted without authorization of the government of the Republic of

Texas, the Mexican government was under no legal obligation to treat the Texans as prisoners of war. The Texans alleged their surrender had been secured by a ruse.

The Texans who surrendered at Mier were sentenced to be executed; however, the order was reversed. On February 11, 1843, the Texas prisoners escaped from the Mexican authorities and headed toward the Rio Grande River with the hope of crossing over into Texas. Many of the Texans became separated and lost, and later, after extreme suffering, they surrendered to Mexican troops individually and in small groups. Only three members of the Mier expedition made good their escape to Texas.

One hundred seventy-six members of the Mier expedition were recaptured and Antonio López de Santa Anna ordered they be executed. However, Francisco Mexia, governor of the State of Coahuila, refused to carry out the order. As a result of the governor's refusal to carry out the order, and because of the intervention of ministers of foreign governments in Mexico, the execution order was amended to provide only every tenth person be executed. To select those to be executed, a black and white bean lottery was devised: those who drew the black bean would be executed; those who drew the white bean would not be executed. Seventeen men drew the black bean and were blindfolded and shot. Although the leader of the attempted escape by the Texans, Ewen Cameron, drew a white bean, he was executed by special order of Santa Anna. The selection of the seventeen men for execution is known as the "black bean episode" in Texas history.

Some of the members of the Mier expedition who did not draw the black bean later escaped and returned home; many died while held captive in Mexico; and some men were released at the request of the United States and other foreign governments. By order of Santa Anna, the last captives were released September 16, 1844.

The Spanish and Mexican Periods in Texas History

Mexican municipalities *(municipalidad),* which were somewhat similar to the New England towns since they usually included several surrounding villages and towns, performed various governmental functions. One Spanish influence after Texas counties were created during the days of the Republic of Texas (1836–1845), and after Texas became a state, following annexation by the United States, was the partial use of Spanish and Mexican names and their system of land division. Among the twenty-three original Texas counties created in 1836—the first counties—some were created or organized from, or named for, Mexican municipalities.

"The Mexican influence was greatest in the legal system that resulted from the hybridization (crossing of different varieties) of the civil and common law. There was a blending of the English common law and the civil law."[3] The common law jury system was introduced in Texas. The failure of the Mexicans to provide the jury system was among the grievances included in the Texas Declaration of Independence. The right of trial by jury was considered "that palladium of civil liberty, and only safe guarantee for the life, liberty, and property of the citizen." The civil law, derived from the Roman law and introduced in Texas by way of the

Spanish and Mexican law, and the civil law of Louisiana, exerted its greatest influence on civil procedure.

The Mexican influence on the Texas legal system is also observable in the matter of property and land law, water rights, the land system, and community property. Also, in the tidelands controversy, Texas lawyers argued the state's boundary extended ten and one half miles seaward (historic boundaries)—and that this claim was based upon old Spanish and Mexican law.

Of course, the Spanish-speaking people of Texas have made a substantial contribution to the state and nation. Many fought and died in the Texas independence movement, and in wars in which the United States was involved. Their deeds of courage have been recorded in the life of the state and nation, many received the highest award for valor, for which the nation is grateful. Also, they have made significant contributions in art, literature, music, dancing, athletics, education, and in the political system, among other endeavors. Their fiesta and celebrations in San Antonio, as well as other Texas cities, have won wide acclaim and have been enjoyed by thousands of people. The Spanish-speaking in Texas have endeavored to create their own customs and traditions in the state for which they have justifiable pride, rather than merely accept the cultural patterns of Mexico. Indeed, the state has been enriched by their many contributions.

The Post-Republic of Texas Period: Problems and Conflicts between Mexico, the United States, and Texas

The most serious confrontation between Mexico, Texas, and the United States occurred during the Texas revolution and during the time of the Texas Republic, the annexation of Texas by the United States, followed by the war between the United States and Mexico. However, there have been a multitude of problems and conflicts involving Mexico, Texas, and the United States over the years. There has been considerable controversy involving the Rio Grande River, such as water rights and territorial claims, as well as other controversies due to changes in the flow of the river. These issues have been resolved by agreements and treaties, for the most part, for example, the Chamizal tract of 437 acres north of the Rio Grande adjoining El Paso, Texas, originally in Mexico, later in the United States because of change of the course of the Rio Grande. After long controversy the tract was ceded to Mexico by the United States in 1963.

Treaties have been negotiated regulating fishing in American and Mexican waters by Mexican and American fishermen, and some of these treaties have been renegotiated or terminated. There has also been evidence of "gunboat diplomacy" when American shrimpers have been forced out of Mexican waters, and Mexican shrimpers forced out of American waters.

Offshore oil wells, some of which are owned by the Mexican government, have produced oil spills along the shoreline of South Padre Island and other areas of the Texas coast. Such operations came under attack especially by coastal Texas cities because of the damage to the environment and the possible loss in tourist trade. The cleanup of the Texas beaches required considerable effort and funds on the part of the federal, state, and local governments in the United States and Texas. Such an occurrence does not tend to promote better American-Texas-Mexican relations, which have been rather difficult to maintain at times.

Acting under a Mexican law, President Cárdenas nationalized most of the properties of British and U.S. oil companies in 1938, valued at $450 million. U.S. Secretary of State Hull admitted the right of expropriation, but insisted on fair compensation for the oil companies. The United States terminated the purchase of Mexican silver at a price above the world level, which threatened Mexico's financial stability. A joint commission reached a settlement on certain aspects of the controversy, and payments by the Mexican government began in 1939. Other matters in disagreement were settled by agreement between the United States and the president of Mexico.

In 1916, a revolutionary group in Mexico, led by Pancho Villa, operated in northern Mexico, in opposition to the Carranza regime. Villa was responsible for the deaths of Americans on both sides of the border, and made repeated raids into Texas and New Mexico. There was considerable pressure in Congress for intervention, and President Wilson abandoned his policy of "watchful waiting." With Carranza's reluctant consent, President Wilson ordered General John J. Pershing to pursue Villa into Mexico. This American action antagonized Carranza and intensified anti-American feeling south of the border. Joint commissioners of the United States and Mexico favored withdrawal of United States troops and joint, but independent, policing of the border. Early in 1917, when war with Germany became imminent, President Wilson withdrew the expeditionary force from Mexico. A new constitution of Mexico was proclaimed, and Carranza was elected president. The United States recognized the new government as *de jure* (the legal government in power).

Also, the Zimmermann Note, a code message, January 19, 1917, created fears and doubts concerning American-Texas-Mexican relations. The code message was sent to the German minister in Mexico by the German foreign secretary in Berlin, Alfred Zimmermann. In the event of war between Germany and the United States, the German minister in Mexico was instructed to propose an alliance with Mexico, as follows: "That we shall make war together and together make peace. We shall give generous financial support, and it is understood that Mexico is to reconquer the lost territory in New Mexico, Texas, and Arizona." Also, Mexico was to urge Japan to support Germany. British naval intelligence intercepted and decoded the message and gave it to the U.S. ambassador in London who transmitted it to the U.S. State Department, which released the note to the American press.

Mexican workers have come to Texas by the thousands seeking work, and this has created serious problems for the United States, Texas, Mexico, and the workers. The United States and Mexico have entered into agreements in regard to the number of workers that may enter for temporary employment. In the past some Texas farmers and ranchers have not provided sufficient wages or living conditions, and have been disqualified for employing these workers. Texas labor unions have complained that the employment of these nonunion workers has been to the disadvantage of Texas labor unions and labor union members, that nonunion laborers that are paid lower wages compete with the higher wages paid to union members. Sometimes the temporary Mexican workers are employed rather than the Spanish-speaking Texans, thereby increasing the number of the latter unemployed. And in the border towns especially, the unions complain that union members are disadvantaged because of the Mexican laborers that work in Texas and live in Mexico, the commuter-workers.

The federal border patrol has attempted to prevent the Mexican workers from swimming or wading across the Rio Grande River, and there have been complaints by Mexico of the mistreatment of such individuals on occasion. The border patrol attempts to prevent the illegal aliens from entering the United States.

Despite all the problems, the Mexican workers desire to enter the United States and Texas where they can find work and possibly a better living than in Mexico. Yet, there has been evidence of worker exploitation.

Certainly there are other developments that illustrate the multitude of difficult and sensitive problems that have confronted the United States, Mexico, and Texas dating from the period when Texas was a part of Mexico. On the other hand, the United States and Mexico have entered into a number of treaties and agreements, and matters have been settled by joint commissions and peaceful negotiations. And there are no fortifications or large armies stationed between the two countries. Two sensitive and proud nations have had their problems. Yet, there have been significant successes in their historic relationship.

The Annexation of Texas—1845

The joint resolution to annex Texas was passed in the U.S. House of Representatives by a vote of 120 to 98, February 25, 1845, and in the U.S. Senate, by a vote of 27 to 25, March 1, 1845, and approved by President Polk, March 1, 1845.

The president of the United States has the power "by and with the Advice and Consent of the Senate, to make Treaties, provided two-thirds of the Senators present concur" (Art. II, Sec. 2, U.S. Constitution). Considering the close vote on the joint resolution in the U.S. Senate (27 for, 25 against), it would have been impossible to have annexed Texas by the treaty method. The joint resolution in the U.S. Congress required only a majority vote in both houses.

Joint Resolution of the U.S. Congress for Annexing Texas

Resolved by the Senate and House of Representatives of the United States of America in Congress assembled, That Congress doth consent that the territory properly included within, and rightfully belonging to, the Republic of Texas may be erected into a new State, to be called the State of Texas, with a republican form of government, to be adopted by the people of said republic, by deputies in convention assembled, with the consent of the existing government, in order that the same may be admitted as one of the States of this Union.

Sec. 2. And be it further resolved, That the foregoing consent of Congress is given upon the following conditions, and with the following guarantees, to wit: First. Said State to be formed, subject to the adjustment by this Government of all questions of boundary that may arise with other governments, and the constitution thereof, with the proper evidence of its adoption by the people of said Republic of Texas, shall be transmitted to the President of the United States, to be laid before Congress for its final action on or before the first day of January, one thousand eight hundred and forty-six. Second. Said State, when admitted into the Union, after ceding to the United States all public edifices, fortifications, barracks, ports, and harbors, navy and navy-yards, docks, magazines, arms, armaments, and all other property and means pertaining to the public defence belonging to said Republic of Texas, shall retain all the public funds, debts, taxes, and dues of every kind which may belong to or be due and owing said republic, and shall also retain all the vacant and unappropriated lands lying within its limits, to be applied to the payment of the debts and liabilities of said Republic of Texas, and the residue of said lands, after discharging said debts and liabilities, to be disposed of as said State may direct, but in no event are said debts and liabilities to become a charge upon the Government of the United States. Third. New States, of convenient size, not exceeding four in number, in addition to said State of Texas, and having sufficient population, may hereinafter, by the consent of said State, be formed out of the territory thereof, which shall be entitled to admission under the provisions of the Federal Constitution; and such States as may be formed out of that portion of said territory lying south of thirty-six degrees thirty minutes north latitude, commonly known as the Missouri compromise line, shall be admitted into the Union with or without slavery, as the people of each State asking admission may desire; and in such State or States as shall be formed out of said territory north of said Missouri compromise line, slavery or involuntary servitude (except for crime) shall be prohibited.

As provided in the Joint Resolution of Congress for the annexation of Texas, "the deputies of the people of Texas in convention assembled, in their name and by their authority, do ordain and declare that we assent to and accept the proposals, conditions, and guarantees contained in the first and second sections of the resolution of the Congress of the United States aforesaid." Texas officially gave its consent to annexation on July 4, 1845.

By the terms of the Joint Resolution of Annexation, Texas had to cede to the United States "all public edifices" and "all other property and means pertaining to the public defence" of the Republic. This transfer of the military property of the Republic of Texas strengthened the military establishment of the United States, and made it unlikely that Texas could successfully wage war against any state or country.

As part of the compromise, under the terms of the Joint Resolution, the state of Texas retained "all the public funds, debts, taxes, and dues of every kind" which belonged to or owed the Republic of Texas. Also, the state of Texas retained "all the vacant and unappropriated lands lying within its limits, to be applied to the payment of the debts and liabilities" of the Republic of Texas. The United States refused to assume any of the debts and liabilities of the Republic of Texas. At the time of annexation, the Republic of Texas had a $10 million debt which the United States refused to assume. Thus, one notes the compromise agreed to in the annexation agreement.

Also, as stipulated in the annexation agreement, a maximum of four new states, in addition to the state of Texas, could be formed out of the territory of the Republic of Texas. A bill or resolution passed by the Texas legislature could create the four additional states, but this is not very likely to be done. The one, two, three, or four new states, in the words of the annexation agreement, "shall be entitled to admission under the provisions of the federal Constitution" which provides in Article IV, Section 3, "New states may be admitted by the Congress into this Union."

If Texas as it currently exists were composed of Texas and four additional states, it would increase the total electoral votes of the area by eight, since each state has as many electoral votes as it has U.S. senators and congressmen, assuming the total number of congressmen currently assigned to Texas are distributed among four new states. Each state, of course, is entitled to at least one congressman regardless of population, or a minimum of three electoral votes. The annexation agreement provides that the new states must be of "convenient size" and have "sufficient population."

In addition to retaining all the public funds, debts, taxes, and dues which belonged, or was due the Republic of Texas, the state of Texas, according to the annexation agreement, retained "all the vacant and unappropriated lands lying within its limits, to be applied to the payment of the debts and liabilities of said Republic of Texas." One may seriously doubt that in 1845 the lands covered for miles by the sea off the coast of Texas were considered vacant and unappropriated lands in the sense that individuals would be interested in purchasing or homesteading such land for agricultural or ranching purposes. "Tidelands" included the coastal areas that were covered and uncovered by high and low tides, rather than a large expanse of land extending seaward for several miles.

The "historic" seaward boundaries of Texas did not become a political and legal issue until the 1940s when it was discovered that within such coastal boundaries there was a great potential for the production of oil and natural gas. On the basis of early Spanish and Mexican law, as well as the annexation agreement of 1845, Texas claimed her seaward boundaries were as follows: a line drawn from the mouth of the Sabine River (on the Louisiana border) at low tide, and extending seaward for ten and one-half miles; a line drawn from the Rio Grande River at low tide, and extending seaward for ten and one-half miles; and a line drawn connecting the outer points of these two lines. Revenue from rentals, leasing, and producing natural gas and crude oil would provide billions of dollars for either Texas or the federal government. The stakes were very high in this extraordinary political and legal confrontation between Texas and the federal government.

In *United States* v. *California* (332 U.S. 19, 1947), the U.S. Supreme Court declared that the federal government, rather than the state of California, had control of the sea bed underlying territorial waters. Justice Douglas, who authored the majority opinion, believed that the acquisition of dominion and control over a three-mile belt of territorial waters resulted from action taken by the federal government after the independence of the United States; in consequence, "not only has acquisition, as it were, of the three-mile belt been accomplished by the national government, but protection and control of it has been and is a function of national external sovereignty." Although Louisiana had extended its boundary out to twenty-seven miles from shore, the U.S. Supreme Court decided against Texas. Again, Justice Douglas for the court declared "if . . . the three-mile belt is in the domain of the nation rather than that of the separate states, it follows a *fortiori* (for a stronger reason) that the ocean beyond that limit also is. The ocean seaward of the marginal belt is perhaps even more directly related to the national defense, the conduct of foreign affairs, and world commerce than is the marginal sea." (*United States* v. *Louisiana,* 339, U.S. 699, 1950.)

Texas claimed that while an independent republic her boundaries extended ten and one-half miles from shore, and that upon annexation by the United States in 1845 Texas retained its public lands. In a four to three decision, with Justice Douglas writing the majority opinion, the U.S. Supreme Court decided against Texas (*U.S.* v. *Texas,* 339 U.S. 707, 1950). The decision was based primarily upon the fact that Texas was admitted to the Union on an "equal footing" with the other states. Therefore, Texas had no greater rights over her marginal seas and the lands beneath them than did the other states. In 1947 the Texas legislature extended the state boundary to the edge of the continental shelf (the submerged shelf of land that slopes gradually to the point where the steep descent to the ocean bottom begins). Enactment of the law made no difference as far as the U.S. Supreme Court was concerned.

In the 1952 presidential campaign, the Republican nominee, Dwight D. Eisenhower, supported the Texas position in the off-shore controversy, while Adlai Stevenson, the Democratic nominee, rejected the Texas position. Texans, by a comfortable majority, voted for Mr. Eisenhower in 1952. His support of the Texas position was an important factor in his victory in the state.

To carry out the campaign pledge of Mr. Eisenhower, Congress passed the Submerged Lands Act in 1953 (67 Stat. 29) which released to the states all rights to the lands beneath navigable waters out to the three-mile limit *or the boundary of the state in the Gulf of Mexico if more than three miles.* Thus, Congress has authority to override a U.S. Supreme Court decision, if the federal law itself is not unconstitutional or if not contested in the courts.

Also, in 1953 Congress passed the Outer Continental Shelf Lands Act (67 Stat. 462) which relates to the sea bed and subsoil of the continental shelf outside the boundaries of the states or the three-mile limit. The United States has jurisdiction over such lands. However, the waters above such lands are considered as high seas. The federal government receives bids for oil leases of such lands.

The Submerged Lands Act, passed by Congress in 1953, which released to the states all rights to the lands *beneath navigable waters* out to the three-mile limit or the boundary of the state in the Gulf of Mexico if more than three miles, was a federal quit-claim law. In other words, the federal government relinquished to the coastal states its claim to the property or right in the Continental Shelf. The federal law has been very profitable for Texas by the deposit of millions of dollars in the Texas Permanent School Fund (PSF). In fact, the latter is the largest educational endowment fund in the world.

The Texas PSF, which was created by the writers of the Texas constitution, finances part of the cost of primary and secondary public education in the state. Money deposited in the PSF comes primarily from oil and gas leases made on state lands. Money in the fund is invested in a variety of bonds, treasury bills, and other investments. In 1981, the fund had increased to more than $3 billion, due in large measure to the increase in energy prices and aggressive state leasing policies.

The rapid growth of the PSF is largely attributable to leasing policies that have allowed the state to increase its royalty revenues as oil and gas prices increased. Leases on many of the state's best oil and gas tracts have gone to producers willing to give the state the highest royalty payments. The average royalty paid to the state has increased from one-sixth of the producer's revenues to one-fifth and one-fourth. At one time royalty payments were fixed and leases were let according to who would pay the largest bonus to the state for rights to drill.

In addition to the conflict between Texas and the federal government over the rights to minerals off the Texas coast, a controversy developed between Texas coastal cities and the state. This controversy arose over offshore annexation by some coastal cities. In 1979 Port Arthur annexed a mile-wide strip of land stretching ten miles out from the coast. The state instituted suit to void the annexation.

Galveston and Corpus Christi officials have contended they should have the right to annex submerged land as far as ten miles seaward in order to regulate off-shore drilling, protect the environment, and broaden the tax base of the municipalities. In 1979 the Texas legislature passed a law that prohibits general law cities (cities which do not operate under a locally adopted city charter) from annexing submerged land more than one mile seaward. The oil companies have opposed any additional taxes and regulations by municipalities. The conflict between the state and coastal cities has not been resolved finally.

The Election of President Andrew Jackson in 1828—
The Impact of Jacksonian Democracy

Andrew Jackson became a national hero by his defeat of the British at New Orleans. However, in this operation it was the incompetence of his opponents rather than his own military skill that carried the day. Nevertheless, Jackson got credit for the victory and, almost overnight, became the best known American general of his time.

Like many Americans, Andrew Jackson lacked patience and tact. He was a fighter by instinct and temperament. His life was spent in conflict and in waging war—against the Indians, the British, the congressional caucus, the bureaucracy, nullification, the bank, and the aristocratic spirit.

Andrew Jackson was the product of his military experience and his bucolic (rural, rustic) surroundings.

> There was no suavity [polish, urbanity] or spirit of compromise in his rather ungainly [without grace or ease] frame. He wore shabby clothes, chewed tobacco, and went about unshaved. He told stories that would have shocked Boccaccio [Italian poet, diplomat, and author, 1313–1375]. . . . His opponent in the election of 1828, John Quincy Adams, called him "that brawler from Tennessee" and not without reason, for Jackson was far from being the embodiment of gentility. He was neither studious nor teachable, and hence during his few terms at school never learned to use the English language correctly. His grammar was a law unto itself and his spelling likewise. Adjectives and adverbs he regarded as having been created free and equal. On the other hand, his thought was clear, and his ideas clean-cut, hence his style was very effective in spite of its formal blemishes.
>
> Jackson's inauguration set a record. Never before had Washington seen such a spectacle. The great unwashed came to the capital by the thousands, most of them looking for a prompt articulation with the public pay roll. They swarmed into the White House, where they drained the punch bowls and then stood with their cowhide boots upon the upholstered chairs to get a glimpse of their own Sir Galahad (a knight who was successful because of his purity and nobility of spirit), the first frontier President, the first American chief executive who had made his hands horny [callous and tough] by toil, and the first since Washington who was not a college graduate.[4]

Jacksonian Democracy gave impetus to the spoils system, long ballot, the election of administrators and judges, short term and rotation in office, expansion of manhood suffrage (by abolition of property, tax, and religious qualifications for voting), the abolition of property qualifications for officeholding, and the practice of nominating candidates for office by conventions rather than by legislative caucuses. Andrew Jackson declared war on "King caucus" since he realized there could be no popular election without a more democratic system of nomination.

These and other ideas of Jacksonian Democracy had a significant impact upon government in the United States.

Jacksonian Democracy had an influence long beyond the life of Andrew Jackson. Even today a lingering Jacksonian Democracy, with twentieth century, and in time twenty-first century, innovations, is, and no doubt will be, observable. There was, in a sense, a blending of the reaction against Mexican rule, the revolutionary and frontier spirit, and Jacksonian Democracy. This blending encouraged a strong desire for more popular control of government to prevent the emergence of a "squirearchy" (government by country gentry or large landowners).

The American Civil War and Reconstruction

As might have been expected with the downfall of the southern confederacy, general confusion and disorder prevailed in the states that had seceded from the Union. The immediate task was to establish a quasi-civil or some other type of government in each of the southern states and to appoint the officials to operate the governments. On June 17, 1865, Andrew Johnson, president of the United States, appointed A. J. Hamilton provisional governor of Texas and instructed him to call a constitutional convention; the members or delegates to the convention were to be elected by the loyalists of the state. The provisional governor invited local groups to advise him with regard to eligible persons that he might appoint to the various county offices. In many counties it was necessary to appoint "rebels," instead of "loyalists," to some of the local offices since Union applicants were not available, or were insufficient.[5] Hamilton's authority was shared with the military and was, therefore, very limited; however, both were anxious to avoid conflict.

As a phase of the presidential policy of Reconstruction, Governor Hamilton issued a proclamation which set the date for the election of delegates to the constitutional convention which met in Austin from February 7 to April 2, 1866. J. W. Throckmorton was elected governor under the new constitution, and was sworn in August 9, 1866. Eleven days later, U.S. President Johnson issued a proclamation declaring the rebellion terminated and civil government reestablished.

Texas adopted two Reconstruction constitutions, the constitutions of 1866 and 1869. Civil government, as it operated under the Texas constitution of 1866, was of short duration. The radicals—or vindictive element—secured control of Congress and enacted the first Reconstruction act, March 2, 1867. The congressional Reconstruction policy went far beyond the presidential Reconstruction policy. The act of Congress was based on "the conquered province theory." Civil governments in the southern states were retained for the sake of convenience, but were rendered powerless, and thus insufficient for the protection of life and property. The law superimposed a military government upon the existing civil governments of the conquered states. The southern states were divided into military districts; Texas and Louisiana constituted the fifth military district. An army officer for each district, who was responsible for protecting personal and property rights, suppressing disorders, and punishing criminals, was designated by the president. Local courts could try offenders or, at the discretion of the military commander of the district, they could be tried before military commissions. Before sentences affecting the life or property of any person could be carried out, they had to be approved by the district commander.

Various conditions were stipulated for the southern states to regain their full political rights in the Union*: (1) delegates to a state constitutional convention had to be chosen by universal manhood suffrage. Those disfranchised for participation in the rebellion, or for conviction of a felony, or ineligible to hold public office, could not vote to select convention delegates; (2) the state constitution could not be in conflict with the national constitution; (3) the state constitution had to be ratified by the people of the state and approved by Congress; and (4) the Fourteenth Amendment had to be ratified by the state legislature.

The purpose and effect of the congressional acts of Reconstruction were "to paralyze the state governments that had been restored since the war, to place the whole South under potential martial law, to disfranchise the leading whites, and to enfranchise the blacks."[6]

During presidential reconstruction, Governor Hamilton of Texas appointed all civil officers of the state. As a result of the Reconstruction acts passed by Congress, the military authority was supreme. Among other things, the military authorities had to approve the appointment of all civil officers. On July 8, 1867, Governor Throckmorton of Texas was forced out of office and E. M. Pease was appointed by General Sheridan to succeed him as governor of the state.

The Texas constitution of 1869 was the second and last of the Texas reconstruction constitutions. On April 16, 1870, General Reynolds, military commander of the district, issued a proclamation reestablishing civil authority within the state. At this point in Texas history, the notorious administration of Governor E. J. Davis was inaugurated.

Governor E. J. Davis of Texas

E. J. Davis was the Republican governor of Texas from 1870–74, and was the last Republican governor of the state until William P. Clements Jr. was elected in 1978. Davis owed his office, his power in Texas, and his hopes for reelection to U.S. President Grant.

> Governor Edmund J. Davis was what most Southerners of that Reconstruction period called a "scalawag," a Texan who attained power by siding with the North.† He had been a brigadier general in the Civil War, commanding a regiment of Unionist Texans who the rebels called "The Texas Traitors." After the war he had returned to lead the Radical Republican element, proposing disenfranchisement of all former Confederates and unlimited Negro suffrage.[7]

The Democrats did not nominate a candidate for governor in 1869. Considering the military supervision of elections and the disenfranchisement of so many Democrats, it would have been fruitless for the Democratic party to have nominated a candidate. Consequently, E. J. Davis, a member of the radical wing of the Repub-

---

*In *Texas* v. *White*, 7 Wallace 700 (1869), the U.S. Supreme Court declared, "The [U.S.] Constitution, in all its provisions, looks to an indestructible Union, composed of indestructible States. When, therefore, Texas became one of the United States, she entered into an indissoluble relation."

†A carpetbagger was a northerner who went to the South after the Civil War and took advantage of the unsettled conditions for political or financial gain. A carpetbag was an old-fashioned kind of traveling bag made of carpet fabric.

lican party was elected governor and a legislature in sympathy with Davis was elected.

Although there have been some myths and exaggerations concerning reconstruction and the Davis administration in Texas,[8] there was ample evidence of misrule and corruption.

The injustice, oppression, and extravagance in government, which resulted from action taken by Governor Davis and the "radical" state legislature, increased the popular prejudices against the existing regime.[9] The state debt and state taxes were increased greatly; a vast political and partisan arrangement under the pretence of operating free public schools was established in the state; an expensive and irritating system of voter registration was placed in operation, as well as a vicious, partisan, and mercenary state police; a multitude of partisan and useless government officials harassed the people; the legislature voted millions of dollars in subsidies to the railroads; martial law was declared and the writ of habeas corpus suspended. The twelfth legislature, 1870–1872, if measured in terms of responsibility and statesmanship, was, undoubtedly, the worst in the history of the state. There appeared to be little or no limits on legislative corruption.

A number of acts passed by the radical state legislature applied to local governments; for example, the act creating a state police under the control of the governor. All local peace officers, including the sheriffs and constables in the counties, were made a part of the state police, and were subject to the command of the governor. "Some of the worst desperados in the state took service in the (state) police, and under the shield of authority committed the most high-handed outrages: barefaced robbery, arbitrary assessments upon helpless communities, unauthorized arrests, and even the foulest murders were proven against them."[10]

Another obnoxious legislative act, which affected local government, gave the governor control over registration of voters and elections. Registrars in each county were appointed by the governor to supervise the registration of voters. A board of appeals, the members of which were appointed by the governor, was established in each county. Nearly all Negroes were permitted to register while the white persons who opposed the Davis regime were denied the privilege of voter registration. Voting was burdensome for many since elections were held at the county seats for a period of four days. In view of the fact that travel was slow and difficult, voting was inconvenient for those that lived some distance from the county seat. Elections were postponed by the governor to stave off defeat at the polls.

The legislative act which authorized the governor to appoint formerly elected local officials was considered obnoxious to those out of power. Under new charters, the governor could appoint mayors and aldermen in some cities and towns. The radical politicians in the local areas were fearful they could not elect their friends in the municipal elections under the broadened suffrage then existing. Local supporters of Davis nominated persons for the governor to appoint; other cohorts of the governor requested persons be removed from office. It was estimated the governor had power to appoint 8,538 persons. Such enormous patronage was not overlooked by the Democratic state convention, meeting in Austin in January 1871, which declared:

The legislature has by enactment, in violation of a plain constitutional provision, autho-

rized the governor to remove officers elected by the people, and appoint men of his own choice in their place, which power he has repeatedly exercised.

The Democratic state convention was indeed indignant of this violation of the constitution, as well as of misrule and corruption; however, the Democratic party and state convention were unable to do anything other than complain at the time.[11] The Davis administration was, in effect, a continuation of the congressional policy of reconstruction.

Some of the charges against the policy of reconstruction and the Davis administration were exaggerated and played upon the popular prejudices. To some extent Texas conservatives and reactionaries, by their attack upon reconstruction and the Davis regime, were, in effect, attacking northern liberal nationalism. Many reactionaries wished to return to the Texas constitution of 1845 (the first state constitution in anticipation of annexation) and once again assume the leadership and control of state and local government.

The Civil War, the defeat of the South, Reconstruction, and the Davis administration had a significant influence upon Texans and their state and local political systems. The distrust of arbitrary and centralized government, and the negativist view of government were promoted by the pre- and post-Civil War developments. The present constitution of Texas provides for a constitutionally weak executive in which the Governor has inadequate budgetary, fiscal, and appointive and removal powers, and the long or "jungle" ballot places too great a burden on the people for intelligent voting. Also, numerous procedural and substantive limitations were placed on the legislature in various parts of the state constitution, as well as on the courts, education, and local government. And only in recent years has the long tradition of a one party (Democratic) state begun to change by voting Republican in the presidential election, by electing a Republican governor in 1978, and by electing more Republicans to the Texas legislature and to Congress.

The Populist Movement in Texas—
The People's Party[12]

Populism and the People's party in Texas sprang from the soil, and was based upon the ideological concept of the equality of man. "Not only were men created equal; they had certain equal and inalienable rights," of which one could not be deprived. This concept was as old in America as the Declaration of Independence: for the Populists, "Equal rights to all, special privileges to none." Yet, despite the natural equality of man, certain economic inequalities did exist which adversely affected all working men—especially the agricultural classes. And justice could not become a reality unless these inequalities could be eliminated. However, the elimination of economic inequalities could be accomplished effectively only through government assistance and regulation. In the event such governmental intervention was not adequate, the government would assume public ownership of all industries "affected with the public interest"—but such action would be taken only as a last resort.

The Populists were concerned with the great inequality of land ownership. Men, as the Populists spokesmen declared, "come upon the earth not by any law of government, but by nature's laws, the laws of God, and have a perfect right to the use of the earth, free and unencumbered.'' According to Populist theory, every man had a natural right to acquire as much land as necessary to provide a decent living, and it was the responsibility of government to see that men could secure as much land as they needed, at a reasonable price. The Populists considered land the source of all wealth, and while the farmers created the wealth, they had little or no voice in its distribution. Members of the People's party were concerned that the state should establish an equitable system of landholding. Such a state policy was necessary since the railroads and other corporations, as well as aliens, owned thousands of acres of land in the state. Therefore, all public lands that remained, and all that could be recovered, should be reserved as homesteads for actual settlers; no corporation should own more land than actually needed in its business operation; and aliens should not be allowed to own land in the state.

The matter of adequate transportation facilities was important for the men of the soil; otherwise they would not receive maximum benefit from the money crops. However, the farmers were convinced the railroads were not operating in their best interest; in fact, they believed the "iron horse" had conspired against them, and the situation required drastic action. Since regulation of the railroads had not been adequate, the People's party supported public ownership of the railroads. In fact, the party platform of 1892 favored state construction, ownership, and operation of a railroad from "the deepest water on the Gulf to the most eligible point on the Red River.'' In 1894, the party declared telephone and telegraph lines should be owned and controlled by the government.

Assuming the critical land and distribution problems were solved in a way acceptable to the People's party, there remained the important matter of finance. Everybody, so it seemed to the farmers, had money except the men of the soil. It was a rather common occurrence that farmers found prices at the lowest exchange rate when agricultural commodities were moved to market and that many farmers had only a subsistence income—just enough to keep the family going until the next year. The reason for this dilemma, as far as the Populists were concerned, was that not enough money was in circulation. Also, the government had abdicated its powers by the establishment of national banks with authority to issue money, and such banks had become too powerful as a result of the privileged position they enjoyed.

The People's party offered a number of proposals pertaining to the currency problem. They felt that the money system was too inflexible, and therefore perceived a need to get more money in circulation with greater flexibility. The party declared that the national banks should be abolished and the government itself assume full responsibility for the nation's fiscal system; that there be free and unlimited coinage of silver and the issuance of legal tender treasury notes "in sufficient volume to transact the business of the country on a cash basis"; and that the amount of paper money in circulation be increased. Also, the party supported the imposition of a graduated tax on incomes.

Governmental expenditures were another important aspect of the general problem of finance so important to the People's party in Texas. The party advocated public retrenchment, economy in government, honest public administration, governmental reform, and a reduction in the salaries (as much as 50 percent in one party platform) of all national and state officers. The reforming zeal of the Populists extended to the county governments by indicating maximum salaries for county officials and elimination of the fee system which was subject to so much abuse. The party platforms criticized the abuses of the appropriation power, and identified individuals in their charges of corruption and indiscretion by public officials. With vigor, the Populists attacked and counterattacked the existing governmental order; for them it was, indeed, a time for change.

During the period of Populist concern, the railroads were the greatest monopolies, and they, as well as trusts and combinations in general, were denounced by the faithful party leaders and followers. "We declare the People's party to be an antimonopoly party." Quite naturally the party supported the cause of labor, including the enactment of laws providing for an eight-hour day for laborers, a charge or liability against property worked on until the services were paid (a lien provided by law rather than by contract), the establishment of a state bureau of labor and a state board of arbitration, the protection of free labor from competition with convict labor, and the nonenforcement of antivagrant laws against those unemployed through no fault of their own. Thus, the Populist program was based upon egalitarian assumptions, and the principles of equality and justice as articulated by party spokesmen.

In addition to the various programs designed to promote the economic betterment for its adherents, the Populists were anxious to provide greater popular control of government. This could be accomplished by a number of innovations: the direct election of the president, the vice-president, U.S. senators, and federal judges. They believed all public officials should be elected, that no official should be allowed to serve for a long term, and the number of terms should not exceed two, because repeated reelection would result in monopoly in office. Also, they favored limiting the salaries of public officials to a definite maximum amount and the abolishing all fees of office. They included in their platform a demand for proportional representation, direct legislation, and recall. Through these propositions the Populists sought to enhance the influence of the common man in public affairs, wherein every man had an equal voice with every other man. Thus, the government would be strengthened and in a better position to make the Populist program operational.

The various programs of the Populist party were not of a novel nature since the party incorporated the programs of the Grange, the Greenback party, various labor groups and parties, and the Alliance; however, some variations were introduced by the party. Some of the original issues of the Populist party disappeared from the political scene, some were forgotten, and some appropriated by rival parties. When third party programs gain sufficient popular support, some, or all, of their issues and programs will be taken over by one or both major parties. In the area of national politics, the Democratic party nominated Bryan on a free silver platform and renounced the leadership of Cleveland. The national and Texas Democratic parties included the Populist program in their platforms. Thus, the Democratic party, both nationally and in Texas, was recast.

The Populist movement sprang forth as the champion and spokesman for the common man, and once this cause had been brought to the forefront, the party had served its purpose.

Populism, as symbolized by the People's party in Texas, was alive and robust in 1896, but by 1900 its power and influence faded away.

Of the various acceptable explanations of the phenomenon called Populism none is more attractive than that which characterizes the movement as a child of the Frontier. . . . Professor Frederick Jackson Turner [*The Frontier in American History,* New York: H. Holt & Co., 1921] . . . pointed out how the staunch individualism of the pioneer shades off gradually into a demand for protection and assistance by the government; how the rugged equality originally enforced by the conditions of frontier life thus becomes a legal equality guaranteed by law; and how the changed attitude is evidenced by agitation for free silver and greenback money, trust regulation, popular election and short terms for all officials, direct legislation and the recall, and other dogmas too numerous to record. This authority indeed has gone further: he has analyzed the ideology of Populism and has so correlated it with the geographical distribution of Populist strength as to leave little doubt of the fundamental correctness of his conclusions. Nor do they suffer when applied to the People's Party in Texas. There is much to be said for the proposition that this State in the [1890s] . . . was yet frontier territory. Without pressing that point, there is no question but that its western and west-central portions were in the frontier stage of development. And, supporting Professor Turner's thesis, it was precisely in the west-central counties that Populism had its greatest vogue in Texas. It was those counties which furnished the staunchest leaders of the Third Party; it was there that men talked most about equality, that they revolted first, fought hardest, and surrendered last. The Populist movement, in Texas and elsewhere, was a complex of many forces, not least among which were the conditions and the state of mind bred of frontier life.[13]

The Grange in Texas was a phase of the Populist movement and had considerable influence upon the government and politics of the state. The present Texas constitution of 1876 is a Grange constitution since members of the Grange were dominant in the drafting and ratification of the basic law. The Grange program of "Retrenchment and Reform" served as a guide for the work of the constitutional convention. Such Grange and Populist concepts as economy in government, limited public salaries, short terms and rotation in office, the long ballot, and the election of judges and administrators were included in the constitution. By the long ballot the Grange sought to enhance the influence of the "common man" in public affairs—a lingering common man philosophy of government. However, at least in a sense, by the very nature and complexities of man, then, as today, the so-called common man is most uncommon.

There are elements of similarity in the philosophy of Jacksonian Democracy, the Populist movement, and the Democratic revolt in the early twentieth century.

2 An Overview

EVERY STATE HAS BEEN affected by its past. Some are careless about their heritage, some apologetic, but Texas is determinedly Texan. From the time Moses Austin and his son Stephen caught the vision of an Anglo-American colony in Texas, a past worthy of record has been unfolding. This past, composed of both history and legend, has been extraordinary, to say the least. The drama, gallantry, triumph, vicissitude, and tragedy have left an ineradicable imprint upon the life of the state and nation. Stories of the early settlers, living under the six flags of Spain, France, Mexico, the Republic of Texas, the southern Confederacy, and the United States, as well as the emotion-charged Battle of the Alamo, and the defeat of the forces of Santa Anna at San Jacinto by Sam Houston's troops were more than enough action to create a proud heritage—part history, part legend, filled with sensitivity, sentimentality, and an awareness of the past.

With the professional Texan, whether native born or recently arrived from out of state, these qualities may lend expression to worn-out exaggerations and braggadocio. Yet a mature understanding of a state's successes and failures has its own value. Of course, astute politicians and commercial public relations firms, among others, frequently trot out the Texas heritage, or some version of it, and exploit it for their own purposes. It is probably true that in no other state does one find so much exploitation of the state's heritage or of local pride and sentiment.

One-Party Dominance

Texas, in most elections, has been a one-party state, electing Democratic candidates to the U.S. Senate and the U.S. House of Representatives, voting Democratic in presidential elections, and electing Democrats to state and local offices. On occasions, the Democratic party of Texas has suffered some major setbacks: Hardin R. Runnels was defeated for governor in 1859 by Sam Houston, who had the support of the Know-Nothing party and insurgent Democrats. In 1978, William P. Clements, Jr., a Republican was elected governor of Texas—the first Republican governor of the state in 105 years. In the 1928 presidential election, Texas voted for the Republican nominee, Herbert C. Hoover, instead of Alfred E. Smith, the Democratic candidate. Dwight D. Eisenhower carried Texas in the

1952 and 1956 presidential elections. John G. Tower, a Republican, was elected U.S. senator from Texas in a special election in 1961 and reelected in 1966, 1972, and 1978. And Richard M. Nixon carried Texas in the 1972 presidential election, as did Ronald Reagan in 1980.

In large measure, history explains the dominance of the Democratic party in Texas. The state was settled primarily by immigrants from the Old South, and it was the national Democratic party that favored the annexation of Texas as a slave state. Furthermore, the issue of Texas's annexation was settled with the election of James K. Polk, the Democratic nominee for president, in 1844.

Secession, war between the states, defeat, carpetbag, and military rule following the war, and in general the policies of Reconstruction are associated with the Republican administration. Consequently, the bitterness engendered by the Civil War and Reconstruction made the Republican party very unpopular in Texas and in the South in general. Also, because Texas for many years, like other southern states, depended upon the export of cotton and had little manufacturing, she opposed the high tariff policies of the Republican party.

Despite the dominance of the Democratic party in Texas, there is considerable evidence of increased strength and power of the Republican party in the state. It is no longer a sure thing that Texas will vote Democratic in presidential elections, and more Republicans are being elected to the Texas house of representatives and senate. Party fund raising, as well as the vigor and activity of the Republican state and local party organization, is stronger than ever before in the state. Some Texans—including ex-Texas Governor John Connally—have joined the Republican party. Many Texans vote Republican in presidential elections and Democratic in state, district, and local elections.

States' Rights

Those who support the doctrine of states' rights advocate a strict interpretation of the U.S. Constitution with regard to the limitation of federal powers and the extension of the autonomy of the state to the greatest possible degree.

The doctrine of states' rights, in Texas and other southern states, is intimately associated with history,[1] not just as a doctrine for, by, and of the southern states. For example, the New England states invoked the states' rights argument against Jefferson's embargo; it is reflected in the resolutions passed by the Hartford convention of December 1814; Massachusetts, Vermont, Ohio, and Connecticut argued it in opposition to the annexation of Texas as a slave state. Certain northern states fell back on the states' rights argument in their reaction to the passage of the Fugitive Slave Act of 1850. Coastal and southern states invoked the states' rights argument in regard to offshore oil lands and public school integration.

Northern, southern, and various other states have invoked the states' rights argument to support nullification, secession, or to declare that the federal government has exceeded its constitutional powers. In actual practice the doctrine of states' rights—that Arthur M. Schlesinger, Sr. referred to as "the states' rights fetish"—has been used by the states, north and south, to promote the economic and political interest of a particular state or region. For this reason, "scratch a Wisconsin farmer and you find a Georgia planter!"

In Texas, the fear of strong central government and support of states' rights was influenced by the arbitrary rule of the central government while Texas was a part of the Republic of Mexico and by the carpetbag and military rule in Texas during Reconstruction. Yet one may imagine that the magical formula or slogan would be utilized today and in the future even if these events were not a part of the Texas heritage.

If "states' rights" is a state slogan—as is often the case—then it may be exploited by interest groups for their own purposes. It is good public relations if the interest groups can tie in the promotion of their own interests with those of the public in general. Oil interests were able to do this quite successfully over the issue of the offshore oil lands. (There was no conflict over the tidelands, since the lands between high and low watermark, or that portion of the shore covered and uncovered by the ebb and flow of the tide, were considered to be within the state.) If the states owned the minerals in the maritime belt from low water to ten and one-half miles (historic boundaries), Texas would secure additional revenue from taxes, leases, royalties, and fees that would become a part of the permanent school fund. On the other hand, federal ownership would mean the loss of this revenue and would force the state to find new sources of income.

The oil people feared the loss of millions of dollars in state revenue to the federal government, and, in the event new taxes were necessary, an effort to increase taxes on natural resources. Also, the oil companies had an effective and well-located lobby in the Texas legislature, but they questioned their ability to maintain a comparably effective lobby in Congress. Therefore, state ownership of the offshore oil resources was best not only for the state but also for the oil companies.

Some corporation lobbyists have greater influence in state legislatures than in Congress. To expand existing state programs or assume additional governmental responsibilities will, in most instances, require the levying of more taxes; hence, the corporate interest may support the governmental minimum or status quo. When this approach is not feasible, the corporate interest may support more regressive state taxes. The influence of the interest groups is reflected in the types of state tax programs. Corporations and their lobbyists frequently oppose the expansion of powers of the federal government because it taxes them more heavily than do the local governments.

In theory, at least, the federal income tax is a *progressive tax,* since those in the higher income brackets pay a larger proportion of their wealth in taxes than do those in the lower income brackets. The opposite of a progressive tax is a *regressive tax,* which is a considerable tax burden for those in the low income brackets. An example of a regressive tax is a sales tax. Although all persons pay the same tax, it takes a larger part of a poor person's money to pay it. For this reason some argue that the federal tax system should be used more to finance services administered by local governments. If this position is well taken, federal taxes, through the mechanism of federal grants-in-aid to state and local governments, as well as other federal programs, tend to redistribute the wealth of the nation downward, whereas a shift of financial responsibility to the states redistributes the wealth upward. Whether federal taxes are more equitable than state taxes, the tax question and the influence of interest groups are major considerations in the issue of states' rights versus expansion of federal powers.

States' rights, at least to some, approaches inalienable rights, natural laws, or the fixed and unchangeable laws of Euclid, despite the fact that our federal system, which divides the powers and obligations of government between nation and states, is in constant flux. Thus, all too frequently the individual does not understand more than the *slogan* of states' rights. For despite the dynamic nature of our society and government, the allegation of states' rights is seldom subjected to a careful analysis of what is best for the state and nation over the long haul. Our federal system today is *not* the federalism of 1787; if it were, the nation and states would find it difficult indeed, if not impossible, to meet the challenges of today.

Many Texans view states' rights in their negative context—as a means of retaining title over offshore minerals, preventing or delaying integration of the public schools, or opposing further extension of federal powers. One might interpret states' rights to mean state obligations. In this sense, the states' rights doctrine would be invoked in support of administrative reorganization, judicial reform, and adequate funds for education, public health, law enforcement, the prison system, hospitals, and special schools, among other things. A negative concept of states' rights frequently leads to the "perpetuation of states' wrongs" or a political environment that makes possible corruption and misrule. The time is at hand when the states can ill afford this type of luxury in government. Inefficiency, corruption, and inadequate state services are an open invitation for more federal intervention in the affairs of the states.

To promote the welfare of the nation, as contrasted to that of the economic and political interests of various groups, some persons contend that the question of nationalism and states' rights should be determined in each particular case in the light of reason and experience, rather than on the basis of an inflexible dogma. This view, it is argued, is said to be in the best interest of the nation as a whole and is more flexible and dynamic than rigid support of either national power or states' rights.

Today, when a state invokes the states' rights argument through the doctrine of interposition—wherein the state interposes its sovereign authority between the federal government and the people, or attempts to nullify a federal court decision by delay or state legislation—the state is following a historical pattern of promoting what it conceives to be its own interest against the onslaught of the federal government. The states' rights position of today is not based upon a deliberately conceived philosophy of government, but is a means of protecting interest groups as well as the economic and political interest of the state in a particular crisis. Looking back over the issues of nullification and secession in the Civil War period and the expansion of federal powers down through the years, one must conclude that efforts to promote states' rights have not been very successful, although it could be argued they have been a delaying factor or a counterbalance that has added stability to our federal system. If this is true, a synthesis or, more correctly, a counterbalance between the extreme views of the "nationalists" and "states' righters" has evolved.

Ambiguity

Local inhabitants are aware of more than one Texas and of the fine gradations of opinion in Texas. In speaking with each other or with non-Texans, Texans frequently ask, "Do you mean east, west, north, south or central Texas?" In like manner one speaks of national, state, liberal, conservative, middle-of-the-road, and reactionary Democrats. The state, politics, and the weather are changeable and unpredictable. As a consequence, Texas Democrats—of whatever classification—may nominate a conservative for governor and a liberal for U.S. senator at the same primary. Such was the case in 1958 when Price Daniel, Sr. and Ralph Yarborough were nominated for these two offices in the first primary. Texans "love that dichotomy" or "love that trichotomy" in their politics.

The political proliferation within the Democratic party in Texas has produced a multifactional arrangement within a predominately one-party state. This means there is a constant political realignment by factional leaders in the never-ending struggle for power within the party. Terms like "harmony" and "compromise" make good fillers for speeches. However, such strategy, if ever successful, is only briefly so. To view politics in Texas, one must observe as if from a revolving door. No doubt this factionalism leads to party irresponsibility, since it is difficult to hold the party, factions, and leaders accountable for political action or inaction.

Part of this ambiguity in Texas politics is due to the independent political temperament of the people. Yet, certain unanswerable questions remain. What is the political complexion of the state? How does one determine the public opinion of Texas when a proper query would be, "Of what public and of what opinion do you inquire?" And the government and politics of Texas are further complicated by developments in population and economic activity.

Population Trends and Urbanization in Texas

The population growth in Texas since 1870 is illustrated by table 2.1. The population growth rate of Texas between 1970 and 1980 increased 27 percent as compared to 11 percent for the nation as a whole. Only one state, California, added more people. Texas ranks third among the states in total population (California, 23,668,562; New York, 17,557,288; and Texas, 14,228,383).[2] Texas, on the basis of the 1980 census, has approximately 14.2 million citizens—one out of every sixteen Americans—and the growth of the 1980s may well make that one out of every twelve Americans.

A number of factors explain the rapid population growth in Texas. Certainly industrialization in the state has been a significant factor in both economic and population growth. The diversity of Texas industry and the rate of industrialization have been phenomenal. Oil production, one of the state's outstanding industries, exemplifies this rapid growth. Until around 1900, the search for water in Texas was more important than the search for oil; attempts were made to case off the "nuisance" oil when a driller struck oil in the search for water. The automobile, paved streets, and better roads soon made their appearance as the twentieth century ushered in the "Motor Age" and with it an increased demand for oil. No longer was oil considered a nuisance. Oil companies rose to meet the demand for crude oil by bringing in fields such as Spindletop, Beaumont (1901), Petrolia (1904), Wagoner or Electra (1911), Ranger (1917), Luling, Mexia, and Powell areas (early 1920s), the East Texas oil field (1930), and the explorations and discoveries in the Inner- and Outer-Continental Shelf in the Gulf of Mexico off the coast of Texas. And wells continue to be drilled in the state.

Table 2.1. Population growth in Texas, 1870–1980.

Census year	Rank among states	Population	Increase over preceding census Number	Percent	Population per square mile
1870	19	818,579	214,364	35.5	3.1
1880	11	1,591,749	773,170	94.5	6.1
1890	7	2,235,527	643,778	40.4	8.5
1900	6	3,048,710	813,183	36.4	11.6
1910	5	3,896,542	847,832	27.8	14.8
1920	5	4,663,228	766,686	19.7	17.8
1930	5	5,824,715	1,161,487	24.9	22.1
1940	6	6,414,824	590,109	10.1	24.3
1950	6	7,711,194	1,296,370	20.2	29.3
1960	6	9,579,677	1,868,483	24.2	36.4
1970	4	11,198,655*	1,618,978	16.9	42.7
1980	3	14,228,383†	3,029,728	27.1	54.3

*Final census count, as of April 1, 1970. This figure did not include 102,057 Texans abroad in 1970, including servicemen, federal employees, and their dependents.

†This figure did not include Texans abroad in1980, including servicemen, federal employees, and their dependents.

Source: *Texas Almanac, 1982–83* (Dallas Morning News), p. 166.

Shipbuilding, petroleum refining, the manufacture of oil field machinery and tools, the production of nonferrous metals, the milling of flour and other grain-mill products, the expansion of the bakery and dairy industries, the production of chemicals, the mechanization of farming, and cotton figure prominently in the continuing industrial development in the state. In fact, the extended coastal area, as well as other parts of the state, have evolved into a vast industrial complex.

With an abundance of natural resources and the facility of coastwise shipping, the industrial potential was ever present; yet it took World War II and government contracts to awaken local and out-of-state capital to the vast industrial potential in Texas. During the war, North American Aviation built a plant at Hensley Field near Dallas to manufacture military aircraft, and a bomber assembly plant was established in Fort Worth. Shipbuilding facilities were expanded at Beaumont, Orange, and Houston during the war, and a huge smelter was located in Texas City to refine tin ore imported from Bolivia. These and other defense plants, along with the huge government contracts and spending, attracted out-of-state labor and capital, much of which remained in the state following the war.

With the location of the Manned Spacecraft Center (MSC) in Houston and the millions of dollars the federal government is spending in Texas on space research, the "Space Age" also represents an era of economic activity in Texas. Each epoch of economic activity—cattle and ranching, cotton, oil, and diverse industrialization—left its imprint upon the life and politics of the state.

The extensive coastal area of Texas encouraged the expansion of maritime commerce to and from the state. Also, the labor force, augmented by skilled and unskilled laborers from out-of-state, provided the necessary human resources for economic growth. There has never been a serious shortage of workers in the state. Generally speaking, and with some exceptions, weather conditions have been favorable for construction and business operations.

Texas has a very favorable tax structure for business and corporations, and local chambers of commerce have included this consideration in their efforts to attract businesses to Texas. The state has no personal or corporate income tax; there is undertaxation of crude oil (4.6 percent of market value), natural gas (7.5 percent of wellhead value), and sulfur ($1.03 per long ton). Also, the unemployment tax on business is very modest due to a high rate of employment in the state, and very limited payments to those who become unemployed. The tax is paid only by the employer.

According to a study by the Tax Foundation, a nonpartisan research organization, Texas ranked forty-fifty among the states in 1980 in the per capita *state taxes* collected. In 1980, the national average of state taxes collected for every person in the United States was $607. In Texas the per capita tax collection for 1980 from state taxes was $475.

With the rapid industrialization of the state, organized labor became an important fact of life in the process. As Texas moved into the industrial stage, labor unions had limited input; in fact, the state was known as a weak labor union state with limited popular support of unions, due in part to the pioneer spirit and individualism of the people, as well as their conservative nature. In the 1940s and 1950s there was considerable conflict between business and labor unions, with the people, for the most part, opposed to unionization. The struggle was not good for unions or business. Indeed, it was a significant period of readjustment for the state.

Labor unions in Texas do not have the influence of organized labor in the other industrial states. As a result, there have been only a limited number of prolonged management-labor confrontations, and corporate boards took note of this in considering whether or not to locate in the state. There has been an adequate labor force in Texas for years, and, with some exceptions, a relatively peaceful relationship between labor and management.

In addition to the favorable conditions for industrialization described above, the Texas climate has not discouraged industrialization, although the state has had hard winters, summer heat and droughts, as well as hurricanes, tornadoes, and floods.

Traditionally, Texas has had a larger number of people moving into the state (in-migration) than leaving the state (out-migration). The volume of net migration to the state has been accelerating, particularly in the 1970s and 1980s. The in-migration includes various types of people: workers (skilled and unskilled), professionals and semiprofessionals, technicians, and retirees (both military and nonmilitary). Consequently, the increase in the net migration to the state has been a significant consideration in the total state population increase in these two decades.

	Annual net in-	*Percent of population*
	migration increase	*increase*
1950–1960	11,400	6
1960–1970	21,400	13
1970–1980	170,000 plus	58

Population Growth in Texas Counties

The population increase in Texas's 254 counties was larger between 1970 and 1980 than between 1960 and 1970. Only 108 (42.5 percent) of the counties in Texas increased in population between 1960–1970; while 210 counties (83 percent) increased in population between 1970–1980. As might be expected, the counties with large cities had the greatest increase in population in the 1970–1980 period. Harris County (Houston) had a population increase of 668,000 which accounted for 22 percent of the state's population increase in the 1970–1980 decade. Dallas County (Dallas) population increased 229,000 from 1970–1980. Five other counties in Texas (Bexar, Tarrant, Travis, El Paso, and Hidalgo) each had population increases of more than 100,000. Fifty-one percent of the increase of the population in Texas from 1970–1980 was recorded in the above seven Texas counties.

Composition of the Texas Population

As is true of the other American states, the Texas population is comprised of people of various nationalities and ethnic backgrounds. As a result of the 1980 census, "Anglos" (all whites *excluding* Hispanics) comprised 66 percent of the state's population; Hispanics 21 percent; and Negroes 12 percent. Texas ranks third among the states in Negro population, and second in the number of Hispanics.

An interesting aspect of population growth in Texas since 1960 has been the predominance of females in numbers as compared to males. On the basis of the 1980 census the females widened their margin of predominance in numbers to 232,000. The birth rates of males and females in the state, life spans, accidents and health, as well as other considerations, determine the female-male ratio in the general population.

The Political Impact of Population Growth in Texas

The dramatic increase in population in Texas, as well as in other states, has had far-reaching consequences in government, economics, and social adjustment. Politically it has enlarged the electorate, altered the method of campaigning, increased the cost of seeking the nomination and election to office, and brought to the fore political issues that were nonexistent when Texas was a state with a much smaller population. More persons in the state are eligible to register and vote (although a large percentage of those eligible neither register to vote nor, if registered, actually vote in the primaries and general elections).

As a consequence of the increase in population, Texas elects more members to the U.S. House of Representatives. As a result of the 1980 federal census, the number of U.S. congressmen elected from Texas was increased from twenty-four to twenty-seven, which also increased the electoral vote of Texas for president and vice-president from twenty-six to twenty-nine, since each state has as many electoral votes as the state has members in the House of Representatives and Senate in Washington. Also, the increase in population and electoral votes in the state, among other considerations, has increased presidential campaigning in the state every four years, as well as campaigning for nomination and election to the U.S. Congress. And of course, the candidates and the parties spend vast sums of money in Texas.

Since they have large populations, the states of California, New York, and Texas have a large representation in the national House of Representatives. Thus, these states and other large population states have considerable influence in Congress and its regional coalitions—the Frost Belt-Sun Belt coalitions. These coalitions, the Frost Belt (members of Congress from the north and northeastern states) and Sun Belt (members of Congress from the south and southwest), are interested in securing legislation favorable to their particular region, especially in the matter of federal funds. Various federal programs provide a formula or basis for making federal funds available to the states, and each coalition seeks favorable treatment in the distribution of federal funds—the "politics of Frost Belt versus Sun Belt."

The number of delegates and alternates each state and territory select to attend the national conventions of the Democratic and Republican parties every four years is determined by the national committee of each party, and the delegate formula may, or may not, be altered from that used in the last convention. Hence, California, New York, Texas, and other large populated states are allotted a large block of the convention delegates and alternates. The candidates for the presidential and vice-presidential nominations, and their supporters, spend considerable time and money campaigning in these states prior to the national conventions. And the votes of these states on the convention floor are very important in determining the presidential and vice-presidential candidates to represent the party in the November election. Also, the popular and electoral votes in these states are very important in determining the outcome of the presidential election.

After each federal decennial census, most, or all, of the states must enact legislation providing for the redistricting of the House and Senate of the state legislature; Nebraska has a unicameral or single legislative chamber. Also after the release of the federal census the states must pass legislation providing for congressional redistricting. In Texas, if the state legislature fails to redistrict the House of Representatives and Senate in Austin, the redistricting will be done by the Legislative Redistricting Board, which is an arm of the legislature. Congressional redistricting in Texas is a responsibility of the state legislature since the Legislative Redistricting Board is not involved in this activity.

Nothing could be more political in a state than redistricting since the manner in which the state legislative and congressional districts are drawn will either promote or hinder the reelection of incumbent legislators, as well as promote or hinder the interest of the Democratic and Republican parties in the state in electing party members to the state legislature and Congress. The protection of the incumbents and the interest of the party are of major concern.

Legislative redistricting may be tested in the courts if it is alleged the state legislature did not "make an honest and good faith effort to construct districts, in both houses of its legislature, as nearly of equal population as is practicable" (one person, one vote principle).

Legislative incumbents and the political parties are not the only groups with a vested interest in legislative redistricting. Minorities are also included, e.g., the Negroes and Spanish-speaking in the state. The manner in which the state legislative and state congressional districts are drawn may restrict or erode the political influence of the minority group in the state; that is, the minority might not receive their fair representation in the state legislature and in Congress.

Since redistricting involves political boundaries, elections, voting procedures, political influences, etc., there must be, as required by the Federal Voting Rights Law, preclearance or prior approval by the U.S. attorney general before redistricting becomes operational for state legislative and congressional districts, the four districts in each county from which one county commissioner is elected to the county commissioner's court, as well as for the redrawing of districts from which members of city councils are elected. In some cases the federal courts have upheld elections to city councils in Texas in which some members of a particular city council are elected at-large, and the remaining members elected from individual council or ward districts. Hence, the population trends in Texas, the federal census, and the diverse practical, political, and legal problems involved in redistricting are closely interrelated. This is very evident when the Texas legislature meets in regular session, and, if need be, in a special session, in the odd year following the preliminary and other federal census reports.

Population growth has created a need for more governmental services, such as sewage disposal, garbage collection, fire protection, law enforcement, airports, education, public welfare, highways, transportation, parks and recreation, public health, regulation of labor and business, promotion of agriculture, protection of the environment, conservation of human and natural resources, and provision of water for human and commercial purposes. The expansion of these and other governmental services has required greater expenditure of public funds and has increased taxes at all levels of government. Hence, government has become more complex, more bureaucratic, more paternalistic, and of course, more expensive. Individualism has had to give way to more government regulation, which becomes necessary as people live in larger groups and in closer contact with each other.

The rapid increase of population, among other considerations, has been a factor in the increase of juvenile delinquency, crime, divorce, use of illegal drugs, and venereal disease.

The movement of the population into urban centers has created a large labor market necessary to attract and sustain industry. With industrialization has come an expansion of organized labor and the growing involvement of labor in Texas politics.

Political communication within each large urban area in Texas has experienced great change. Tremendous sums are spent on campaigning in Dallas, Fort Worth, Houston, and San Antonio. If a candidate can poll a large vote in these four cities, the candidate is well on the way to winning nomination and election to statewide office. The large daily newspapers in these cities, although they cannot dictate candidates or assure winners, have great influence in molding public opinion; otherwise, there would be no need for candidates to aggressively seek their support.

Besides the urban newspapers, other communications media have political implications, for example, radio, TV, billboards, use of public parks and public auditoriums for political gatherings, distribution of handbills, parades, and public address systems. Well-financed and highly organized public relations firms, as well as peer and pressure groups, influence the communication of ideas and the molding of opinion in the urban centers. And of course, the professional and well-paid pollsters release their polls to the candidates to indicate areas where they are weak or strong—and the polls may be released to the public if to the advantage of the candidate. The emphasis of the newspapers, public relations firms, and pollsters may depend on the position taken by the so-called power elite, for example, corporation executives, labor union leaders, and bankers, among other individuals and organizations within the urban area.

The institutionalizing of public opinion on a large scale in support of candidates and public propositions (bond issues, city charter amendments, etc.) is expensive. Much public opinion in the urban areas is "public" only in the sense of its mass distribution and consumption, not in its formulation at the grass roots.

Metropolitan Statistical Areas

Metropolitan Statistical Areas were developed primarily for federal agencies to use in producing, analyzing, and publishing data on metropolitan areas. The standards for MSAs took the place of those previously used in defining Standard Metropolitan Statistical Areas (SMSAs).

To qualify for recognition as an MSA, an area must either have a city with a population of a least 50,000 within its corporate limits or it must have a Census Bureau urbanized area with a population of at least 50,000 and a total MSA population of at least 100,000. A few MSAs that do not meet these requirements are recognized because they qualified under past standards.

For the past ten years, the Dallas-Fort Worth area had been designated as an eleven-county Standard Metropolitan Statistical Area (SMSA). Effective June 30, 1983, the federal Office of Management and Budget revised this region to a nine-county Consolidated Metropolitan Statistical Area (CMSA). This decision was based on a year's review by the federal Committee on Metropolitan Statistical Areas. During this process, which occurs every ten years, all metropolitan area definitions were reconsidered and certain terminology changes were made as a result. Based on these new definitions, another consideration for geographic groupings was added: "economic interdependence" among the cities and counties, involving 1980 Census information such as commuting patterns, population density, migration characteristics, and economic involvement.

The previous term "SMSA" was shortened to "Metropolitan Statistical Area" (MSA). An area with more than one million population and meeting other specified requirements is termed a "Consolidated Metropolitan Statistical Area" (CMSA). The latter consist of major components designated as "Primary Metropolitan Statistical Areas" (PMSAs). For example, the Dallas-Fort Worth area had been designated as an eleven-county Standard Metropolitan Statistical Area (SMSA). In 1983, the Office of Management and Budget revised the region to a nine-county Consolidated Metropolitan Statistical Area (CMSA). In addition to the nine-county CMSA, two Primary Metropolitan Statistical Areas (PMSAs) have been designated. The Arlington-Fort Worth PMSA includes three counties—Johnson, Parker, and Tarrant—and Arlington and Fort Worth are designated as the two central cities. The city of Dallas was designated as a PMSA, as part of the nine-county Consolidated Metropolitan Statistical Area (CMSA) composed of Collin, Dallas, Denton, Ellis, Kaufman, and Rockwall counties and the cities of Dallas, Irving, and Denton were designated as central cities.

The standard metropolitan definitions were developed to help federal statistical agencies use the same geographic definitions to study metropolitan characteristics. Statistical information is made available for individual metropolitan areas (MSAs, PMSAs, and CMSAs) on population, housing, industry, trade, employment, local housing markets, payrolls, and labor markets. Also, state and local governments, as well as private organizations, may use the federal definitions in comparing their own metropolitan data with federal statistics. The federal designations are also key planning areas for many of the councils of governments activities, for example, the preparation of regional housing surveys and population estimates.

Metropolitan statistical areas are designed to facilitate the presentation and analysis of data on large concentrations of the metropolitan population. Chamber of commerce groups are very interested in the expansion of statistical areas as an aid in attracting new industry and securing government grants. There is much competition for airline routes, since new routes generally are based on potential markets. When a statistical area is expanded, an increase follows in various statistical categories, including population, retail sales, effective buying income, nonagricultural employment, and bank deposits. As a result of the growth of the population-industrial complex in Texas, one notes the competition and politics involving chambers of commerce, local officials, and the statistical areas. And indeed another dimension is added to the politics of an industrial society.

The metropolitan areas continue to become more mobile—the commuting population flowing daily in and out of the central city—for shopping, visiting, or work. This population movement and the problems created thereby have been referred to as the disease of "suburbanitis," "fringitis," "scatterization," and "sprawl." The "metropolitan age," at least thus far, has shown no signs of receding.

The metropolitan age has produced acute governmental and social problems, some of which are summarized briefly.

1. Commuters and their families have forced the central cities to expand municipal services, though these people contribute little to the treasury of the central city.
2. The decentralization of residential areas has created a traffic flow that has almost strangled urban life.
3. The central cities are faced with serious financial problems and increased evaluations of property for tax purposes.
4. Annexation and incorporation to avoid annexation have created rivalry among municipalities and made intermunicipal cooperation more difficult.
5. Expansion of governmental services and limited municipal taxing powers

Table 2.2. Population, migration.

Locality	1980 pop. tsnds	1970 pop. tsnds	Chnge	Pct chnge	New arriv
State of Texas	14229	11199	3030	27.1	11.0
Metro areas					
Dallas-Ft. Worth	2975	2378	597	25.1	12.7
Houston	2905	1999	906	45.3	13.8
San Antonio	1072	888	184	20.7	10.9
Austin..................	537	360	176	48.9	13.1
El Paso................	480	359	121	33.6	13.0
Beaumont area	375	348	28	8.0	7.0
Corpus Christi	326	285	41	14.5	8.8
McAllen-Pharr-Edin	283	182	102	56.0	6.8
Killeen-Temple	215	160	55	34.3	29.5
Lubbock...............	212	179	32	18.0	10.6
Brownsville area	210	140	69	49.4	7.2
Galveston-Texas City	196	170	26	15.4	9.7
Amarillo...............	174	144	29	20.3	12.0
Waco	171	148	23	15.7	7.7
Longview-Marshall......	152	121	31	25.7	9.9
Abilene................	139	122	17	13.9	11.3
Wichita Falls	131	129	2	1.6	15.4
Tyler..................	128	97	31	32.2	9.3
Odessa	115	93	23	24.5	9.5
Laredo	99	73	26	36.2	3.6
Bryan-College Sta	94	58	36	61.4	11.4
Sherman-Denison	90	83	7	7.9	11.8
San Angelo.............	85	71	14	19.3	10.5
Midland	83	65	17	26.3	11.9
Texarkana	75	69	6	9.3	11.8
Victoria	69	54	15	28.0	6.7

Source: *Houston Chronicle*, March 13, 1983. Copyright Houston Chronicle.

have encouraged the creation of numerous special districts, which levy taxes and provide limited services. This has resulted in the duplication of governmental services and made more difficult the integration of government. The result has been a system of "fractionated administration"—the multiplicity of governmental and taxing units.

6. Land utilization, planning, and the withdrawal of land for parks, playgrounds, schools, and other purposes have created controversies and serious problems.

7. The exigencies of twentieth-century living have outrun an eighteenth-century governmental structure. Yet the deep roots of local government make the ab-

Table 2.3. Age of population.

Locality	Med age	Under 5yrs	18 to 65-yrs	65-yrs & over
State of Texas	28.2	8.2	60.1	9.6
Metro areas				
Bryan-College Sta	22.9	6.8	70.8	6.8
Laredo	23.6	10.5	52.1	8.4
McAllen-Pharr-Edin	24.1	10.5	51.5	9.2
Killeen-Temple	24.2	9.5	64.1	7.2
El Paso................	25.0	9.4	58.2	6.6
Brownsville area	25.0	10.4	52.1	9.6
Lubbock...............	25.5	8.4	63.3	7.9
Austin.................	26.6	7.3	65.7	7.8
Corpus Christi	26.9	9.3	58.0	.4
Odessa	27.1	9.3	61.9	7.0
Victoria	27.3	9.2	59.1	8.5
San Antonio	27.4	8.4	59.2	9.0
Houston	27.5	8.5	63.3	6.2
Midland	28.4	8.8	62.5	7.4
Amarillo...............	28.6	8.5	61.6	9.7
Dallas-Ft. Worth	28.6	7.7	62.5	8.3
Abilene................	28.7	8.0	59.8	12.4
San Angelo.............	28.9	7.6	60.6	12.1
Wichita Falls	29.2	7.6	61.3	11.8
Galveston-Texas City	29.3	8.1	61.2	9.1
Beaumont area..........	29.3	8.1	59.9	10.3
Waco	29.3	7.4	60.1	13.2
Longview-Marshall	29.5	8.1	58.3	12.2
Tyler..................	30.0	7.7	58.5	12.5
Texarkana	31.3	7.9	57.0	13.3
Sherman-Denison	32.9	6.8	58.0	15.6

Source: *Houston Chronicle*, March 13, 1983. Copyright Houston Chronicle.

olition, consolidation, or administrative reorganization of local units difficult, if not impossible.

8. Counties in the metropolitan areas have assumed functions they are ill-prepared to perform. This has been due to the operational features of county government as provided in the Texas constitution and state laws, as well as lack of adequate fiscal resources.

9. Suburbanites have little interest in the problems of the central city in which many earn their living. Many people live outside the corporate limits of the central city, and therefore are not qualified to vote in it. Thus, they have no responsibility as voters for the policies of the central city. Economically, they are members of a metropolitan community; yet, most choose to remain aloof from its problems.

Table 2.4. Ethnic characteristics.

Locality	Anglo	Black	Span. origin	Orient	Amer Indian
State of Texas	65.9	12.0	21.0	0.8	0.3
Metro areas					
Abilene.................	82.2	5.4	11.6	0.6	0.3
Amarillo...............	85.2	4.9	8.6	0.9	0.4
Austin.................	71.9	9.4	17.6	0.9	0.3
Beaumont area..........	73.8	21.8	3.4	0.8	0.2
Brownsville area	22.3	0.3	77.1	0.2	0.1
Bryan-College Sta	77.5	11.1	10.1	1.2	0.2
Corpus Christi	46.8	4.0	48.5	0.4	0.3
Dallas-Ft. Worth	76.3	14.1	8.4	0.8	0.4
El Paso................	33.2	3.8	61.9	0.8	0.3
Galveston-Texas City	68.3	18.5	12.0	0.9	0.3
Houston	65.2	18.2	14.6	1.8	0.2
Killeen-Temple	70.1	17.1	10.3	2.1	0.4
Laredo	8.2	0.1	91.5	0.1	0.1
Longview-Marshall	75.0	22.6	1.9	0.3	0.3
Lubbock...............	71.9	7.5	19.6	0.8	0.3
McAllen-Pharr-Edin	18.3	0.2	81.3	0.1	0.1
Midland	75.9	8.6	14.9	0.3	0.3
Odessa	73.2	4.5	21.5	0.4	0.5
San Angelo.............	74.0	4.0	21.2	0.5	0.3
San Antonio	47.3	6.8	44.9	0.7	0.2
Sherman-Denison	90.6	7.0	1.5	0.2	0.7
Texarkana	76.3	21.9	1.3	0.3	0.2
Tyler..................	74.4	22.0	3.1	0.3	0.2
Victoria	62.3	6.8	30.4	0.3	0.2
Waco	74.8	16.0	8.8	0.3	0.2
Wichita Falls	84.1	8.4	6.0	1.0	0.5

Source: *Houston Chronicle*, March 13, 1983. Copyright Houston Chronicle.

10. Area-wide resources are not utilized to deal with area-wide problems.

Reporting the News—TV and Newspapers

Newspapers are only one of several communications media. Nevertheless, they provide an essential link between government and the governed; and their political influence, although it cannot be measured accurately, is significant.

In a sense, the urban newspapers are in competition with the local and national TV news that is reported daily in early evening broadcasts. There has been some discussion on the reporting of TV news, that is, whether or not the officeholders, candidates, political issues, and other news are presented in a fair and balanced manner. The TV news does not endorse issues or candidates, which is common

Table 2.5. Education, English.

Locality	Don't speak Eng. at home	Speak poor Eng. 5-17	Speak poor Eng. 18-up	High school grads
State of Texas	21.8	15.6	22.5	62.6
Metro areas				
Laredo	92.8	20.7	29.8	41.5
McAllen-Pharr-Edin	80.4	20.2	35.0	41.1
Brownsville area	76.7	19.0	33.4	43.8
El Paso	62.4	17.0	28.3	59.5
Corpus Christi	45.4	10.4	18.2	57.7
San Antonio	42.3	12.5	16.4	62.7
Victoria	28.8	14.1	14.6	58.4
San Angelo.............	21.5	8.4	16.3	59.8
Odessa	21.0	14.4	22.9	61.1
Lubbock	20.0	6.9	13.3	66.4
Austin..................	18.8	12.1	12.7	73.1
Houston	16.6	19.0	23.0	69.7
Midland	15.1	16.7	20.8	72.5
Killeen-Temple	13.5	9.3	11.2	68.2
Bryan-College Sta	13.0	12.1	9.8	69.1
Abilene................	12.1	11.2	13.8	61.2
Galveston-Texas City	11.9	15.0	14.6	65.3
Dallas-Ft. Worth	9.7	16.1	20.2	70.0
Amarillo...............	9.6	19.1	12.6	69.4
Waco	9.2	11.0	13.5	58.5
Wichita Falls	7.2	12.4	12.7	64.1
Beaumont area..........	6.6	12.6	12.0	62.5
Tyler..................	4.2	17.5	22.3	65.1
Longview-Marshall	3.5	11.3	26.7	62.3
Sherman-Denison	2.4	14.7	8.8	60.5
Texarkana	2.4	9.6	11.3	59.9

Source: *Houston Chronicle*, March 13, 1983. Copyright Houston Chronicle.

practice among newspapers, although on occasion a newspaper may not make an endorsement—especially if the public issue or candidate(s) appears somewhat equally divided among the voters. If the TV did support and endorse a candidate or political issue, equal time would have to be made available for those who requested it (as provided by regulation of the Federal Communications Commission). Also, there is a practical consideration that influences the reporting of the local and national evening TV news, i.e., competition between, for example, NBC and CBS for the viewing public. Many Americans have a favorite TV news station, while others may view both of the major networks.

Among the criteria for rating newspapers, the following might be listed: com-

Table 2.6. Income, transportation.

Locality	Med fam inc	Per cap inc	Below pvty level	Poor over 65	Poor under 18
State of Texas	19.6	7.21	14.7	13.4	38.9
Metro areas					
Houston	24.4	8.90	10.1	9.6	37.6
Midland	24.2	10.1	8.6	9.0	38.9
Galveston-Texas City	22.9	7.89	10.6	13.3	34.9
Dallas-Ft. Worth	21.9	8.28	9.9	13.3	36.1
Beaumont area	21.7	7.42	12.4	14.1	37.7
Odessa	21.1	7.75	11.2	9.2	39.2
Victoria	20.9	7.12	13.1	13.4	42.7
Austin.................	20.6	7.31	14.2	9.2	28.1
Amarillo...............	20.2	7.71	9.8	14.1	35.1
Tyler..................	19.2	7.12	13.4	16.8	36.2
Longview-Marshall	19.1	6.78	14.3	18.3	36.7
Corpus Christi	19.0	6.51	17.0	10.1	43.8
Lubbock	18.7	6.93	14.3	8.5	36.6
Sherman-Denison	18.4	6.93	9.7	32.9	25.6
Bryan-College Sta	18.1	5.90	22.3	6.9	16.4
Wichita Falls	18.0	7.04	12.3	18.0	34.4
San Angelo.............	17.6	6.80	12.5	17.6	30.7
Abilene................	17.3	6.68	12.5	19.4	32.8
San Antonio	17.2	6.17	18.1	10.5	44.4
Texarkana	17.2	6.25	16.2	20.1	39.2
Waco	17.0	6.24	17.2	15.8	32.0
El Paso................	15.4	5.31	21.7	6.6	47.8
Killeen-Temple	14.7	5.60	15.7	10.8	40.2
Brownsville area	12.9	4.34	31.8	7.6	49.9
Laredo	12.2	3.98	33.1	8.6	48.4
McAllen-Pharr-Edin	12.1	4.04	35.2	7.3	50.1

Source: *Houston Chronicle*, March 13, 1983. Copyright Houston Chronicle.

plete news, comprehensive treatment; unbiased, objective treatment of news; judgment in selection of news; layout, typography; good writing style; accuracy; balance among syndicated columnists with different views; integrity; public service; depth, analytical perception, and interpretive and feature articles; absence of hysteria; "cultural tone"; "lively without being frothy, solid without being stuffy"; vigorous and courageous editorial expression; absence of editorializing in the headlines; manner in which controversial issues are presented; balance and fairness in selecting and editing letters to the editor; equal coverage and use of best photos of all candidates; and the absence of views quoted out of context.[3] Applying these standards, how would one rank newspapers in Texas? Thus far, no newspaper in Texas has been ranked among the first ten newspapers in the United States.

Table 2.7. Housing occupancy.

Locality	No. in home	Own home	5 or more units	Moved Jan 79 Mar 80
State of Texas	2.82	64.3	18.4	29.1
Metro areas				
Sherman-Denison	2.58	71.0	8.1	25.1
Bryan-College Station	2.60	48.0	26.1	44.8
Austin..................	2.61	55.0	24.4	38.3
Wichita Falls	2.63	66.8	13.1	29.5
Amarillo................	2.64	67.5	13.5	28.7
Waco	2.65	63.3	13.3	26.2
San Angelo.............	2.67	64.4	18.0	28.2
Abilene................	2.68	68.2	8.3	28.0
Texarkana	2.70	72.0	9.8	22.3
Dallas-Ft. Worth	2.72	62.2	23.1	31.3
Tyler..................	2.73	69.0	11.6	25.4
Longview-Marshall	2.75	69.8	10.0	26.9
Lubbock...............	2.76	60.8	19.2	35.3
Midland	2.77	71.0	14.7	29.5
Galveston-Texas City	2.79	64.8	16.3	26.6
Houston	2.79	58.8	29.8	34.1
Beaumont area..........	2.81	71.9	10.0	22.8
Odessa	2.83	67.2	15.4	31.8
Killeen-Temple	2.85	53.8	16.7	41.0
Victoria	2.96	65.6	12.4	28.0
San Antonio............	2.97	64.0	17.5	26.8
Corpus Christi	3.08	62.2	17.1	28.4
El Paso................	3.32	59.4	23.1	29.2
Brownsville area	3.56	64.7	15.8	23.9
McAllen-Pharr-Edinburg .	3.71	69.6	13.9	22.9
Laredo	3.79	62.0	11.7	22.1

Source: *Houston Chronicle*, March 13, 1983. Copyright Houston Chronicle.

The newspapers have a tremendous ethical responsibility. A free press depends, in large measure, upon willingness of newspaper owners to maintain high standards. The press is no stronger than the maintenance of this code.

In an earlier period, many Texas newspapers, by actual word count, were unfair in reporting the candidates for public office. Some candidates were given considerably more coverage, by ninety to ten, for example, on an actual word count. Also, unflattering photos of candidates were included in the paper, and sometimes statements of candidates were quoted out of context. And it was not uncommon for a larger percent of the letters to the editor that were published to reflect the position of the newspaper on a particular issue—and letters to the editor were unfairly edited and published.

Fig. 2.1. Per capita income for twenty-five metropolitan areas in Texas.
Source: *Houston Chronicle*, May 11, 1983. Copyright Houston Chronicle.

Texas had the richest and the poorest of 305 metropolitan areas in terms of 1981 per capita income, according to statistics released by the Commerce Department. The Houston area, with a per capita income of $13,303, ranked 10th. Per capita income for the United States was $10,495, up from $9,483 in 1980.

The number under the name of each area is its ranking among 305 metropolitan areas of the country.

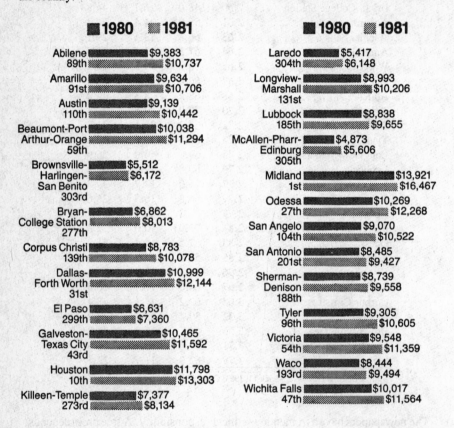

■1980 ▒1981

Area	1980	1981
Abilene / 89th	$9,383	$10,737
Amarillo / 91st	$9,634	$10,706
Austin / 110th	$9,139	$10,442
Beaumont-Port Arthur-Orange / 59th	$10,038	$11,294
Brownsville-Harlingen-San Benito / 303rd	$5,512	$6,172
Bryan-College Station / 277th	$6,862	$8,013
Corpus Christi / 139th	$8,783	$10,078
Dallas-Forth Worth / 31st	$10,999	$12,144
El Paso / 299th	$6,631	$7,360
Galveston-Texas City / 43rd	$10,465	$11,592
Houston / 10th	$11,798	$13,303
Killeen-Temple / 273rd	$7,377	$8,134

■1980 ▒1981

Area	1980	1981
Laredo / 304th	$5,417	$6,148
Longview-Marshall / 131st	$8,993	$10,206
Lubbock / 185th	$8,838	$9,655
McAllen-Pharr-Edinburg / 305th	$4,873	$5,606
Midland / 1st	$13,921	$16,467
Odessa / 27th	$10,269	$12,268
San Angelo / 104th	$9,070	$10,522
San Antonio / 201st	$8,485	$9,427
Sherman-Denison / 188th	$8,739	$9,558
Tyler / 96th	$9,305	$10,605
Victoria / 54th	$9,548	$11,359
Waco / 193rd	$8,444	$9,494
Wichita Falls / 47th	$10,017	$11,564

Texas newspapers have shown considerable improvement over past practices. Of course the state's newspapers have the privilege of endorsing candidates and propositions on their editorial pages or elsewhere. However, it has become rather common practice to devote approximately equal word space to various candidates and issues; if it were otherwise, especially in the large metropolitan areas, there could be a serious reaction on the part of newspaper customers. Also, in the large cities with two major newspapers, each may support different candidates and propositions. And Texas newspapers today show greater balance as regards the syndicated columnists who may present different views on candidates and issues and have a more liberal or more conservative view. At an earlier period in Texas, it was not uncommon for the large newspapers of the state to include only the syndicated columnists with the more conservative view, which was more likely to be the position of the newspaper.

Cultural Diversity in Texas and the Nation

In any democratic society there is a degree of unrest which may result from a variety of factors; for example, protest against the corruption and evils of society; criticism of the establishment; concern over computerized rules and regulations; an awareness of the dehumanization of life; a feeling of alienation; and the desire for greater numbers of persons to participate in the policy making of such organizations as banks, corporations, labor unions, and schools. However, in contrast to this drive toward participatory democracy, a large number of people may prefer a nonparticipatory lifestyle—for example, a withdrawal of interest in the political system.

In a free society, individuals have the right to dissent, to express opposition to practices that they consider unjust. This freedom does not include the use of violence in attacks upon persons and property. Such action is not only antiestablishment but antiintellectual as well. Groups and individuals, in resorting to violence, may exploit persons for their own advantage, and those exploited may suffer injury. This is especially true of professional agitators, who may assume a safe rearguard role. And violence may lead to repression.

To quote Mr. Justice Brandeis,

> The greatest menace to freedom is an inert people;. . . public discussion is a political duty; . . . order cannot be secured merely through fear of punishment for its infraction; . . . it is hazardous to discourage thought, hope and imagination; . . . fear breeds repression; . . . repression breeds hate; . . . hate menaces stable government; . . . the path of safety lies in the opportunity to discuss freely supposed grievances and proposed remedies.[4]

In the words of Mr. Justice Roberts,

> To persuade others to his own point of view, the pleader, as we know, at times, resorts to exaggeration, to vilification of men who have been, or are, prominent in church or state, and even to false statement. But the people of this nation have ordained in the light of history, that, in spite of the probability of excesses and abuses, these liberties are, in the long view, essential to enlightened opinion and right conduct on the part of the citizens of a democracy.[5]

Perhaps the challenge is for a confrontation of ideas instead of a confrontation of physical power; a need for the rationally committed rather than the emotionally committed. In this country there is room for intellectual and emotional individualism, cultural diversity, and eccentricity.

No doubt there will be a continual conflict between the *aspirations* of the people—regardless of one's station in life—and the *realization* of one's abilities.

3   The Constitution of 1876

MR. JUSTICE MILLER OF the U.S. Supreme Court on one occasion gave a rather concise definition of the organic or constitutional law as the terms are used in this country. "A constitution in the American sense of the word," according to Justice Miller, "is a written instrument by which the fundamental powers of government are established, limited, and defined, and by which those powers are distributed among several departments for their more safe and useful exercise for the benefit of the body politic." In a sense, a constitution—which may be both written and unwritten in part—establishes, defines, distributes, and limits the fundamental powers of government.

The American Constitution consists of not one but three constitutions: (1) the constitution of liberty, or Bill of Rights; (2) the constitution of government, or those articles and sections that establish the principal departments of government; (3) the constitution of sovereignty, or the provisions relating to the suffrage, elections, amending, and revising of the Constitution, in which the people play a vital role. Hence, there has evolved in this country a theory of a constitutional or organic law, a fundamental or higher law, as contrasted with statutory law.

The tendency to glorify and adore constitutions in this country has made them as symbolic for the American people as the kingship and royal family are for other nations. The veneration of Americans for constitutions has made us a rather conservative and legalistic people. One must admit, though, that the attitude of Americans toward the federal Constitution is a much deeper veneration than that exhibited toward state constitutions, many of which need to be adapted to the spirit of the times and the spirit of the people.

The Relationship between the U.S. Constitution and the State Constitutions

Article VI (2) of the U.S. Constitution provides as follows:

> This Constitution, and the Laws of the United States which shall be made in Pursuance thereof and all Treaties made, or which shall be made, under the Authority of the United States, shall be the supreme Law of the Land; and the Judges in every State shall be bound thereby, any Thing in the Constitution or Laws of any State to the contrary notwithstanding.

Members of Congress and the state legislatures, as well as all executive and judicial officers of the United States and of the several states, are bound by oath or affirmation to support the American Constitution.

The above "supremacy statement" incorporated into the American Constitution, as drafted in 1787, illustrates the perception of the founders of the nation. As a result of this provision, it was not necessary to revise or amend any of the original thirteen American state constitutions that were operational prior to the drafting of the U.S. Constitution.

In the original U.S. Constitution, the supreme law of the land consists of three elements: the federal Constitution, valid laws passed by Congress, and treaties. In the event a provision of a state constitution or state law conflicted with the federal Constitution, federal law, or treaty, the federal courts, in the final analysis, would uphold the supremacy clause of the U.S. Constitution. In a sense, the supremacy provision of the American Constitution is the king-pin of the governmental system.

As a result of federal court decisions, executive agreements constitute a fourth element that is a part of the supreme law of the land in this country. The presidents of the United States have negotiated numerous executive agreements with the leaders of various foreign states. Unlike a treaty, these agreements need not be ratified by the U.S. Senate. However, the president may consult with members of Congress; Congress may pass a concurrent resolution authorizing the president to negotiate such an agreement; and the appropriation of funds or other legislation by Congress may be necessary for the agreement to be carried out by the United States. Thus, there are checks on the president in this area of American foreign relations. However, in times of military necessity, the president must have the power to act quickly and decisively by executive agreement rather than by the slower process of treaty-making.

In *U.S.* v. *Belmont* (1937) the U.S. Supreme Court held that the "external powers of the United States are to be experienced without regard to state laws or policies. The supremacy of a treaty in this respect has been recognized from the beginning." And it added that "all international compacts and agreements" are to be treated with similar dignity for the reason that "complete power over international affairs is in the national government and is not and cannot be subject to curtailment or interference on the part of the several states." Thus, treaties and executive agreements under the supremacy clause (Art. VI, Cl. 2) are the "Law of the Land." The decision in *U.S.* v. *Belmont* (1937) was affirmed by *U.S.* v. *Pink* (1942). As a result of U.S. Supreme Court decisions, state constitutions and state laws that conflict with the U.S. Constitution, valid federal laws, treaties, and executive agreements would be held unconstitutional by the courts.

The Texas Constitution of 1876 as a Product of the Times

Constitutions are seldom, if ever, "dashed off" at a given time. They are more the product of environment and history. Certainly this is true of the existing constitution of Texas. Upon examining the major developments of the nineteenth century, one may doubt seriously whether it would have been possible to draft a constitution adequate for the age. An examination of the nineteenth century—

especially the post-Civil War phase—will illustrate the stream of history out of which evolved the organic law of the state.*

Of considerable significance in the nineteenth century was the period of Jacksonian democracy (1820–1840). In this period impetus was given to the spoils system, long ballot, short term, rotation in office, expansion of manhood suffrage (by abolition of property, tax, and religious qualifications), the abolition of property qualifications for office holding, and the use of nominating conventions. These and other ideas of the Jacksonian period influenced constitution making and governmental practice long beyond the life of Andrew Jackson. Even today a lingering Jacksonian democracy, with twentieth-century innovations, is still with us. The Texas constitution of 1876 shows the imprint of these Jacksonian concepts.

Another development in the nineteenth century was the noticeable decline in the power and prestige of state legislatures. In the early 1800s the state legislatures were still considered the guardians of the liberties of the people. This respect for state legislative bodies befitted the descendants of the colonial legislative bodies that had stood their ground against encroachments upon local government by the British crown. They were given a favored position in the newly formed states, notwithstanding the widespread belief that governmental powers should be distributed and the authority of each department restricted. The results of several decades of legislative supremacy were disappointing, since the spirit of localism dominated state legislatures. Members showed more interest in the affairs of their local communities than in the welfare of the state as a whole.

The abuse of legislative power was common in the nineteenth century and provoked popular reaction against legislative corruption. When the Texas constitution of 1869 was amended in 1873, an article was included prohibiting the passage of local and special bills over a variety of subjects. The present Texas constitution, in Article III, Section 56, contains a list of twenty-nine prohibited subjects that cannot be covered by local or special law.

The general trend has been toward an increase of constitutional restrictions, both substantive and procedural, on state lawmaking bodies. While the governor was gaining in power and prestige, the legislature was becoming more and more fenced-in by constitutional restrictions.

During the latter part of the nineteenth century the influence of the legislature suffered a still further decline. To the sin of localism, legislators added venality which, in time, led to more constitutional restrictions on state legislatures.

Following the period of Reconstruction, state government became increasingly corrupt and inefficient. The concept of "spoils" was broadened to include the granting of franchises and special privileges to various interest groups. For a time the railroads were seeking favors from the state, and their lobbyists were very active at the state capitals. In fact, the railroad lobbyists were so successful that they were able to secure almost complete control over many state legislatures.

---

*Previous constitutions of Texas include the following: 1827—for the State of Coahuila, Texas, which was under the Mexican constitution of 1824; 1836—the constitution of the Republic of Texas; 1845—The first state constitution in anticipation of annexation; 1861—the constitution of Texas while a member of the Confederacy; and 1866 and 1869—Reconstruction constitutions.

Later the "trolley crowd" and the "gas combine," by their success in securing franchises, privileges, and exemptions, ushered in a period of legislative corruption in public utilities.

Throughout the post-Civil War period, bribery, direct and indirect, was a potent factor in state legislative practice. The reaction that followed made a serious effort to end corruption in state government. State constitutions were amended or revised to include matters such as regulation of corporations and other businesses (with special attention focused on public utilities, banks, and insurance companies); structure and control of local government; educational organization and methods; protection of labor; and taxation and finance. Hence, state constitutions were becoming more statutory, more similar to a legislative code than to a fundamental law. These matters might well have been left to the legislature, but many people felt the legislature had forfeited the public trust, a trend that explains in part the greater length of state constitutions. It was in this period (1850–1900) that the present constitution of Texas was drafted and inevitably influenced by this distrust of the legislature.

In addition to Jacksonian democracy and the general decline of state legislatures, a third factor that had tremendous influence on state constitution-making in the nineteenth century, especially in the South, was the Civil War and Reconstruction. The Civil War and its aftermath brought forth Confederate constitutions and their alternation in order for the southern states to regain privileges of the Union. Southern reaction to carpetbag rule, corruption, and Reconstruction played a vital role in constitution-making in the South, and the Texas constitution offers concrete evidence of this reaction.

Texas Politics in the Preconvention Era

Because of the military supervision of elections, as well as the disfranchisement of so many party members, the Democrats did not enter a candidate for governor in the election of 1869. E. J. Davis, a member of the radical wing of the Republican party, was certain to be elected with a legislature friendly to his views.

There was ample evidence of misrule and corruption in the executive and legislative branches. For example, "some of the worst desperados in the state took service in the [state] police, and under the shield of authority committed the most highhanded outrages: barefaced robbery, arbitrary assessments upon helpless communities, unauthorized arrests, and even the foulest murders were proven against them."[1] The Twelfth Legislature, for the biennium of 1870 to 1872, has never been equaled in corruption throughout the legislative history of Texas. The senate membership included sixteen radical Republicans, and the house contained fifty from the radical wing of the Republican party. Included in the radical membership of both houses were eleven Negro legislators, two in the senate and nine in the house.

> The worst measure of the session, and perhaps the worst ever passed by any Texas legislature, was one granting to two parallel railroads, the Southern Pacific and the Memphis, El Paso, and Pacific, $6,000,000 of thirty-year 8 percent state bonds, under the sole condition that the roads unite at a point about halfway across the state. It was provided that these bonds might later be exchanged for public land at the rate of twenty-

four sections for every mile.* Since the roads were already claiming sixteen sections under an old act, they ran a good chance of getting a total gift of over 22 millions of acres.[2]

In less than six months, the state debt increased from $400,000 to more than $800,000. Furthermore, the rate for state taxes "had risen from fifteen cents in 1860 and in 1866" to two dollars and seventeen and one-half cents on the one hundred dollars valuation, exclusive of that levied to pay interest on the bonds donated to the International and the Southern Pacific railroads, which would equal about sixty cents additional, and exclusive also of a two-dollar poll tax."[3]

As a result of misrule, radicalism, and corruption there was a persistent demand for an overhauling of the "radical" constitution of 1869 and a return of the state to Democratic control. Texans had decided it was "time for a change" and time to clean up the "mess" in Austin. Even though the constitution of 1869 was, in some respects, superior to the one drafted in 1876, to Texans of the period it symbolized radical, carpetbag, and Negro domination; for these reasons the state had to be swept clean of all the remains of Reconstruction and corruption. Obviously the constitution of 1876 was to reflect the fears, disgust, and prejudices of the period.

Call for Constitutional Convention

In 1875 the Texas legislature passed a joint resolution that provided for the calling of a constitutional convention to meet in Austin on the first Monday in September. An election was held and the voters were asked to vote either "for a convention" or "against a convention." Under the terms of the joint resolution, ninety delegates—three from each senatorial district—were to be elected by the voters. After a lively campaign in the summer of 1875, the voters approved the calling of a constitutional convention and selected delegates to represent them in the convention. The legislature appropriated $100,000 for convention expenses.

Influence of the Grange

The Texas Grange, organized in Dallas in October 1873, had a membership of almost 50,000 in 1876.† The organization and its members played an important role in the selection of delegates, as well as in the drafting and ratification of the constitution. Besides their program of "Retrenchment and Reform" to be followed by the convention, the Grangers secured the election of nearly half of the delegates. The constitution, as it evolved from the convention, represented a severe reaction against the notorious extravagances and corruption of the E. J. Davis administration. In a sense the Texas constitution of 1876 was a form of reprisal against carpetbag rule.

---

*A section of land is 640 acres or a square mile.

†The Texas Grange supported the various programs of the National Grange, that is, abolition of the protective tariff, establishment of an interstate commerce commission, elevation of the Bureau of Agriculture to cabinet rank, correct labeling of adulterated food, reduction of postage and express rates, lower interest rates, issuance of more fractional currency, establishment of land-grant colleges, and popular election of U.S. senators. These agrarian "crusaders" or "reformers," at both state and national level, had a tremendous influence on political developments during the latter part of the nineteenth century.

The frame of mind of the delegates may be illustrated by the decisions concerning their pay and manner of operation. In their determination to reduce the cost of government, the delegates set their own per diem at $5 for each day in attendance, and mileage was set at $5 for every twenty-five miles. This was below the $8 per diem and mileage of $8 for each twenty-five miles established for the legislators under the constitution of 1869. The delegates also decided against employing a stenographer. However, in their zeal for economy, the delegates spent some $900 per diem debating the question of employing a stenographer, whose services would have cost only $500 to $600.

The Grangers' program of "Retrenchment and Reform," which was in harmony with the demands of the majority of voters at the time, served as a guide for the work of the convention. In a qualified sense, the leaders of the Grangers constituted the unofficial rapporteurs of the convention, or those responsible for the preparation of ideas for the delegates. The Grangers' demands for "Retrenchment and Reform" found expression in the provisions decreasing salaries, terms of office, and the appointive power of the governor.

Other influences of the Grange upon the constitution of 1876 include those sections that relate to the homestead of a family. According to these sections:

Article XVI, Sec. 49. The legislature shall have power . . . to protect by law from forced sale a certain portion of the personal property of all heads of families, and also of unmarried adults, male and female.

Article XVI, Sec. 50. The homestead of a family shall be . . . protected from forced sale, for the payment of all debts except for the purchase money thereof . . . the taxes due thereon, or for work and material used in constructing improvements. . . ; nor shall the owner, if a married man, sell the homestead without the consent of the wife, given in such manner as may be prescribed by law. . . .

Article XVI, Sec. 51 [as amended in 1983]. The homestead, not in a town or city, shall consist of not more than two hundred acres of land, which may be in one or more parcels, with the improvements . . .; the homestead in a city, town, or village, shall consist of a lot or lots amounting to not more than one acre of land, together with any improvements on the land . . . provided also, that any temporary renting of the homestead shall not change the character of the same, when no other homestead has been acquired. [The amendment applied to all homesteads in the state, including those acquired before the adoption of the amendment on November 8, 1983.]

The influence of the Grange was reflected in the provisions relating to public and higher education. A well-organized group in the state at the time opposed maintaining any public school system whatever. A compromise was reached, however, at the convention, and a system of public free schools was established. Nevertheless, the constitution of 1876, unlike that of 1869, did not require the legislature to pass a compulsory school-attendance law. A board of education, composed of the governor, comptroller, and secretary of state, replaced the office of state superintendent. There was no provision in the constitution for local school taxes. Separate schools were to be provided for the white and Negro children and impartial provision was to be made for students of both races (Art. VII, Sec. 7). Some concern for the financial support of the public schools was indicated by the fact that there was "to be set apart annually not more than one-fourth of the general revenue of the State, and a poll-tax of one dollar on all male inhabitants [of the]

State between the ages of twenty-one and sixty years, for the benefit of the public free schools" (Art. VII, Sec. 3). Also some 45 million acres of public lands were set aside as a permanent endowment for the schools. In the matter of higher education the legislature was directed to establish a state university "of the first class" and the Agricultural and Mechanical College of Texas, established by an act of the legislature, April 17, 1871, was made "a branch of the University of Texas, for instruction in Agriculture, the mechanic arts, and the natural sciences" (Art. VII, Secs. 10, 13). The 3,200,000 acres of land previously set aside for a state university were reduced later to 1 million acres, and no tax could be levied and no appropriation made from the general revenue for purposes of erecting university buildings. The restrictions on education have required considerable amending of the constitution in order to provide a system of public and higher education in the state.

The Grange influence at the convention was noticeable in provisions relating to railroads. The railroad problem had not become as serious for the farmers of Texas as for those of other western states; nevertheless, anticipating the possibility that it might become serious, the Grange delegates used their influence to place ample power in the legislative body to regulate railroads. The Grange was also in favor of limiting the state debt: the debt which the state might incur to supply deficiencies was limited to $200,000.

The most striking features of the program of "retrenchment and reform" were the limitations on the executive and legislative branches. Laws passed by the Twelfth Legislature had given Governor E. J. Davis almost unlimited power. For example, both the state militia and state police were placed under the control of the governor, who did not hesitate to declare martial law and suspend the writ of habeas corpus in an effort to make his position more secure and to carry out the policy of national Reconstruction. The governor had complete control over the registration of voters. In some cities, which had drafted new charters because their radical politicians feared they could not carry the municipal election under the unrestricted suffrage then existing, he appointed the mayor and board of aldermen. Another law authorized the governor to designate in each judicial district a newspaper to do the public printing for the district and to serve as the official organ for the radical regime in the district. On occasion, the governor postponed elections to stave off defeat at the polls. As a result of the broad grant of power given the governor by the constitution of 1869 and the augmentation of his power by legislative enactment, plus a misuse of powers granted, limitations were placed on the governor in the constitution of 1876. These limitations took the form of a long ballot and restrictions upon his appointive power, among others.

The most important changes were those relating to the legislature.

Of the fifty-eight sections of the chapter dealing with this branch of the government, over half of them placed limitations upon its authority. Minute provision was made for the procedure to be followed by the Legislature in its work. The time of meeting, the size of the quorum, the amount of mileage and per diem were definitely determined. The manner of framing, passing, and amending bills was carefully prescribed. The power to levy taxes was limited; the pledging of the State's credit was forbidden; local and special laws on a long list of subjects were prohibited.[4]

Other restrictions on the legislature are found elsewhere in the constitution.

Ratification of the Constitution

The convention completed its work on November 24, 1875, with approval of the constitution by a vote of fifty-three to eleven. The governor, submitting the new constitution to a vote of the people, was requested to issue a proclamation for the election. The election was held on the third Tuesday in February 1876. Between November 24, 1875, and February 15, 1876, a lively campaign, both for and against adoption, was carried on throughout the state. Many people, including numerous newspapers, were vigorous in their criticism of the new constitution. The criticism centered on the provisions dealing with the courts, education, and internal improvements, and on the excessive limitations upon the executive and legislative branches. The supporters of the constitution countered that the new constitution was more adequate than the obnoxious instrument of 1869, which had been forced upon the people of Texas. Furthermore, the supporters argued, the admitted defects of the new constitution could be corrected by amendment. The campaign boiled down to the choice between two evils: retain the 1869 constitution or approve the inadequate new constitution which, of necessity, would have to be strengthened by amendments. It appears that the voters voted more *against* the 1869 constitution than they did *for* the 1876 instrument. Nevertheless, of the 150 counties reporting election returns, only 20 counties showed an unfavorable vote, and the constitution was adopted by a vote of 136,606 to 56,652.

As might be expected, the rural sections of the state voted overwhelmingly for ratification, since many of the constitution's provisions were in their interest. Most of the larger towns and cities, including Dallas, Galveston, Houston, and San Antonio, voted against adoption. The counties that gave large majorities in favor of the constitution were rural and white. Many of the eastern counties, having a dense Negro population, voted for the Republication candidates and against adoption of the constitution. Some of the counties with large German populations, notably those of Comal and Kendall, voted against the constitution.

Since the new document was a Granger product, it was natural that almost all of the Grangers would support adoption. The influence of 50,000 Grangers and their friends was no small consideration in ratification. Since five-sixths of the delegates at the convention were Democrats, the new constitution was primarily the work of the Democratic party. Richard Coke, the Democratic candidate for governor, took a strong stand in support of adoption. Coke won the election over his Republican opponent by more than 100,000 votes, and it was only natural that, aided by the Grange influence, almost 80 percent of the Coke majority voted for adoption.

Under the constitution of 1869 (Art. VI) only male citizens of the United States, "without distinction of race, color, or former condition," being twenty-one years and upwards, and not laboring under the disabilities named in the constitution, were eligible to vote, provided they were residents of the state at the time of the adoption of the constitution or had resided in the state one year and in the county sixty days preceding the election. The 1876 constitution was adopted under limited suffrage requirements.

Defects of the Texas Constitution

Excessive Length

The Texas constitution, consisting of seventeen articles and numerous sections, is one of the longest state constitutions, a "Texas-size" document. Since the states' governments have reserved or undefined powers, their constitutions, of necessity, must be of greater detail than the federal Constitution. However, there is no need for the state constitution to be five or six times longer than the national instrument.

Numerous Amendments

In the period from 1876 to November 8, 1983, the people have approved 262 constitutional amendments. When compared with the 26 federal amendments, the Texas constitution is a patchwork of amendments. So many amendments illustrate poor draftsmanship of the original document and point up its rigidity. The constitution has been made adaptable more by formal amending than through judicial interpretation and statutory elaboration, as has been the case of the federal Constitution.

Repetition

Repetition of various concepts in the Texas constitution can be found throughout the document. For the sake of brevity these repetitive sections should be eliminated.*

Ambiguities

The Texas constitution contains a number of ambiguities and is in need of clarification.

Poor Arrangement

The arrangement of the material in the Texas constitution is quite inadequate. For example, the office of lieutenant governor, pensions and retirement funds for public servants, teachers, veterans and their widows, as well as grand juries, are dealt with in a number of different articles and sections. Material concerning an office, particular problem, or concept should be codified under an appropriate article.

Legislative Code Rather Than a Constitution

If a constitution means a flexible, written instrument by which the *fundamental powers of government* are established, limited, defined, and distributed among several departments, one may doubt whether Texas has a constitution. Many items in the constitution could be incorporated into statutes, making it easier to distinguish between constitutional and statutory law. Statutes should include a

---

*For example, the underlying idea of Article I, Section 7, is repeated in Article VII, Section 5, and therefore is superfluous.

considerable amount of the material found in the sections dealing with the following matters:

education	courts and judges
asylums	Social Security
the state university	State Building Commission
county seats	retirement for municipal employees
private corporations	college building program
public lands and land office	countywide hospital districts
legislative redistricting	community property
teachers' retirement	local option
rural fire prevention districts	public printing
veterans' land program	homestead
fence and stock laws	water conservation

The constitution is a hodgepodge of legislative rules, statutory material, and a limited amount of fundamental law. All but fundamental material should be eliminated from the existing constitution. Once this is done, a manageable constitution for intelligent revision might present a less difficult task.

Long Ballot

Every four years the voters elect a governor, lieutenant governor, attorney general, state treasurer, comptroller of public accounts, commissioner of the general land office, and agriculture commissioner. In addition to those officials, 150 house members and one-half of the senate members are elected biennially. Also, a member of the railroad commission and some members of the state board of education are elected every two years.* All the judges are elected for four- and six-year terms. As if the election of all these state officials were not enough, the voters must elect members of Congress, members of city and county governments, as well as officials to operate the schools and special districts. The "jungle" or long ballot is confusing for the voter and discourages popular participation in the electoral process. The short-ballot reform movement has had little or no influence in Texas.

Disintegration

There is disintegration in the legislative, executive, and judicial branches. The legislature is fenced-in by many procedural and substantive limitations that have made necessary many amendments. Legislative leadership is also lacking, since it is divided among the governor, lieutenant governor, and the speaker of the house, who may or may not be in agreement on policy. The long ballot and inadequate appointive and removal power do not place the governor in a position to control administration. Other than the secretary of state, those who would nominally compose the governor's cabinet are elected by, and responsible to, the people. This has led to administrative irresponsibility and approaches a headless system. With two supreme courts (one for civil and one for criminal cases), and judicial superin-

---

*The three members of the railroad commission are elected for six-year overlapping terms. The voters in the congressional districts elect the members of the state board of education. Members of the board are elected for six-year overlapping terms.

tendency divided between the supreme court and legislature, the judicial system is neither integrated nor coordinated.

Rigid Restrictions on County and Municipal Government

Regardless of their size and population, or extent of assessed tax valuation, and whether urban or rural, all the counties have a common pattern of government that is frozen in the constitution. The defects of county government are more noticeable in the urban counties, where the twentieth century has outrun an eighteenth-century governmental system. The rigid constitutional and statutory restrictions on county and municipal government, especially in taxation and finance, have made the creation of water, navigation, conservation, drainage, and other special districts necessary, since these districts are authorized to levy and collect taxes. The expanding cost of local government is being met by use of the special district device, since maximum tax rates have been reached by many existing local units. The multiplicity of governmental units has only complicated the problem. These restrictions on local units of government have required the passage of hundreds of local and special laws for counties, cities, school districts, and special districts, thereby taking valuable legislative time that could be spent on legislation affecting the entire state.

Legislation Domination

Despite the limitations on the legislature, it remains the most powerful branch of government. This legislative power represents a reaction against the misrule and corruption of Governor E. J. Davis. The legislature refuses to delegate powers to the governor and administrative agencies; hence, much statutory detail is included in legislation. The creation of the legislative council, legislative budget board, and the attachment of legislative riders to appropriation bills have enhanced the powers of the legislature. There is no trend in this state toward the strong and responsible state executive.

Amending the Constitution

All constitutions in the United States have shown a similar pattern of growth; that is, all have grown by formal amending, the procedure for which is spelled out in the particular constitution, as well as by statutory elaboration, judicial interpretation, custom, practice, and usage. Yet the importance of these methods varies. In the states—especially in Texas—there has been considerable constitutional growth by formal amending.

Article XVII of the Texas constitution provides only one method of amending. "The Legislature," reads the constitution, "at any regular session, or at any special session when the matter is included within the purpose for which the session is convened, may propose amendments revising the Constitution." The proposed amendment or amendments must be approved, not by two-thirds of a quorum, but by a two-thirds vote of *all members elected to each house.* At least 100 house members and 21 senators would have to vote in favor of an amendment before it could be submitted to the people. Since amendments are not considered legislation, they may not be vetoed by the governor, although frequently the governor will sign house or senate joint resolutions proposing amendments. A brief explanatory statement of the nature of a proposed amendment, prepared by the secretary of state and approved by the attorney general, together with the date of the state-wide popular referendum and the wording of the proposition as it is to appear on the ballot, must be published twice in each newspaper in the state which meets requirements set by the legislature for the publication of official notices. Whether the amendment will be voted on at a special or regular election will depend upon the date specified in the proposed amendment. For an amendment to become a part of the state constitution, it must be ratified by a *majority of the voters voting on the amendment,* rather than a majority of those voting at the election, in the event the amendment was voted on at a general election. The several returning officers in each county make returns to the secretary of state of the number of legal votes cast for and against the amendment, and, if passed, the amendment becomes a part of the constitution upon proclamation by the governor.

Frequently a minority of the potential electorate determines changes in the fundamental law of Texas. There are several reasons for this.

1. Because of failure to register, a number of people may not qualify to vote.
2. A considerable number of qualified voters may not vote.
3. Sometimes less than one-half, and in some cases as few as 10 percent, of those voting for candidates will vote on amendments submitted at the same election. Voting on issues appears less popular than voting for people.
4. Seldom does a large percentage of the qualified voters vote on amendments at a special election.
5. The subject matter of the amendment may arouse little popular interest.
6. Inadequate publicity on proposed amendments is also a factor in the small vote on amendments. One may doubt if many people read and study the amendments. This inadequacy has been overcome in part by more newspaper analysis and comment upon pending amendments than in the past, as well as by pamphlets on amendments prepared and distributed by private groups such as the League of Women Voters, Tax Associations, and so on. Pamphlets containing a brief analysis of the proposals, with pro and con arguments of interested groups, could be prepared and distributed at state expense. Most voters simply lack adequate information to vote intelligently on one or several amendments.

Amending the Constitution Is Expensive

First, there is the legislative expense of considering the amendments in the house and senate. Second, there is the cost of publishing the required information about the amendments in the newspapers in the state. Third, there is the cost of holding an election on the amendments in each county. Since 1876, the state has spent millions of dollars on the amending process. A well-drafted constitution, which would make excessive amending unnecessary, would reduce the cost of constitutional upkeep.

Revision of the Constitution

The Texas constitution of 1876 contains no provision for its revision or complete rewriting. Yet this omission is not a serious obstacle to revision, certainly not in comparison to the obstacle of popular indifference.

Amendment to Provide for Revision

The constitution could be amended to provide for the constitutional convention and constitutional commission methods. A brief amendment might authorize the legislature to determine time and place of the convention, basis for representation in the convention, selection of delegates, provision of funds, and manner of submitting the work of the convention to the people. The details of the constitutional commission could be worked out by the legislature.

Asking the People

The legislature could submit the following question to the people: "Shall a constitutional convention be called to revise the Texas constitution?" If a majority of the people voting on the question voted favorably, the people could, at the same election, or at a later election, select delegates to attend the convention. The bill, concurrent, or joint resolution, submitting the question to the people, could include the time and place for holding the convention, manner of selecting delegates, per diem and mileage, provision for funds for the expenses of the convention, and provision for the submission of the work of the convention to the people. It would be advisable to introduce such a proposal in the legislature either in the form of a bill or concurrent resolution, since a joint resolution would require a two-thirds vote in each house before the matter could be submitted to popular vote. Since such a proposal initiated by the legislature would not be legislative in nature, the governor would have no power to veto such a bill or resolution submitting the question to the people. In 1923 the attorney general of Texas ruled that the legislature does not have the power to call a convention without first submitting the question to a popular vote,[5] but there are still those who hold a contrary view. In all likelihood, the legislature itself would, as a practical matter, consider it wise to hold a preconvention popular referendum on the question of calling a constitutional convention. If it had a part in initiating the revision, the public probably would be more receptive to the new constitution. The last time the question of calling a constitutional convention was submitted to the people by the legislature was in 1919, and it was defeated by a vote of 23,549 for the convention to 71,376 against.[6] In this referendum, less than 12 percent of the qualified voters expressed themselves on this important question. Other states have used this method to call a convention and in fact, the constitutional convention that drafted the present Texas constitution was called following a preconvention referendum on the issue.

If Texas should follow the same procedure in calling a constitutional convention as it did in 1875, an important question would confront the legislature before the issue is submitted to the people. The legislature would have to determine the basis of representation in the convention. If the legislature should decide that the people in senatorial or legislative districts would elect a number of delegates equal to their representatives in the house or senate, the urban areas would have considerable influence in the convention.

The Constitutional Commission

In the event the legislature desired to play a major role in constitutional revision, it could either establish a constitutional commission, set up a joint committee made up of members from both houses, or ask the legislative council to make the preliminary studies and recommendations.

In establishing a constitutional commission, the legislature determines size of the commission, manner of selecting members, powers, types of reports to be made, time within which the commission will make its study, and appropriation of funds for the work of the commission. The commission may be empowered to draft a new constitution and to submit the draft to the legislature, a convention, or directly to the people. If the new document goes directly to the people, the commission would take over a function usually reserved for a constitutional convention. On the other hand, the commission may be directed to study the existing constitution and make recommendations to the legislature.

The constitutional commission does have certain advantages over the constitutional convention method of revision. A commission should be able to operate more expeditiously because of its smaller size; being appointive, it is possible to secure able men. The constitutional commission is also the least expensive method of revising a constitution. A constitutional commission may play a major role in stimulating interest in constitutional revision, depending upon the extent of press releases and newspaper coverage.

A constitutional convention, once established, is independent of the legislature and reports directly to the people rather than to the legislature. The only real control the legislature has over a convention includes the limitations on the work of the convention, although such restrictions might be tested in the courts.

Preliminary studies by a constitutional commission or the legislative council might prepare the ground for a constitutional convention.

The constitutional commission method has its limitations. In some quarters the commission method is unpopular because it is a newer method of revision and a break with traditional practice. Some people consider the commission undemocratic because the members are not elected by the people and do not report directly to them. As a practical limitation, the legislature might provide inadequate time and funds for the work of the commission, or the legislature might refuse to act on the commission's recommendations. An awareness of possible disapproval in the legislature might lead the commission to make its draft or recommendations palatable to the legislature.

The Legislature as a Constitutional Convention

In Texas, as in other states where the legislature is not restricted as to the number or character of amendments that it may propose, the lawmaking body could sit as a constitutional convention. When the legislature completed the redraft, it could be submitted to the people as one amendment. From a political point of view, it might be advisable for the legislature to seek permission at the polls before assuming the role of a constitutional convention. Acting as a convention the legislature would not oppose a process over which it had complete control. On the other hand, one may doubt if the legislature would have adequate time to devote to revision. The normal legislative and executive functions are more than enough to keep the legislature well employed every two years. Furthermore, it might prove difficult for public opinion to concentrate on revision during a brief and crowded legislative session. A special session is limited to thirty days, which is a rather short time for a convention, but if the task were not completed during the first-call session, the governor could immediately call a second session.

A Plank for Both Parties

A plank favoring constitutional revision formed a part of the platform of the Democratic state convention meeting in September 1873, at Austin. Article XII of the platform declared, "We favor the calling of a constitutional convention by our next legislature." Although approved at the convention by almost unanimous vote, the plank had no legal effect because it was merely an expression of opinion by the party. Later the question of calling a constitutional convention was submitted to the people. Yet, the plank in the platform did help to crystallize public opinion on the need for constitutional revision.

The law in Texas requires that no party can include in its platform any demand for specific legislation on any subject,

> unless the demand for such specific legislation shall have been submitted to a direct vote of the people, and shall have been endorsed by a majority of all the votes cast in the primary election of such party; provided, that the State Executive Committee shall, on petition of ten percent of the voters of any party, as shown by the last primary election vote, submit any such question or questions to the voters at the general primary next preceding the State Convention.[7]

The plank in the party platform might be worded so that it does not constitute a demand for specific legislation and hence requires no party referendum. If enough party voters were interested they could, by the petition method just quoted, compel a vote on the issue at the primary preceding the September state convention. The vote would be merely an expression of opinion within the party. It still would take legislative action to set in motion the revision machinery. Nevertheless, such action might have some public-relations value.

Submission of the Constitution to the People

How to submit the new constitution to the people must be decided by the constitutional convention or the legislature. It could be submitted to the people in the form of a single amendment or several amendments. Supporters of the latter say the least controversial proposals could be submitted first, and, after they are approved, the more controversial articles could be presented. Those in favor of this technique believe that it would give the constitution a better chance of approval; however, there are those who believe a "yes" or "no" vote on the entire document is the wiser approach.

Important Role of the Legislature

Regardless of the method of constitutional revision, the legislature plays an important role in submitting a preconvention referendum to the people, calling a constitutional convention, establishing a constitutional commission or sitting as a constitutional convention, directing the legislative council or joint committee to make studies and submit recommendations, appropriating funds, and possibly deciding the manner of submitting the document to the people.

Cost of Constitutional Revision

If one considers the funds for research and drafting (by a constitutional convention, constitutional commission, or the Texas Legislative Council), the cost of legislative action before and possibly after the constitution is drafted, the cost of publication and distribution, as well as funds for a popular election, a new constitution for Texas would be expensive. It might nevertheless be cheaper than maintaining the present constitution by the amendment process.

Proposed Federal Constitutional Amendments

Article V of the U.S. Constitution provides, ''The Congress, whenever two-thirds of both Houses shall deem it necessary, shall propose Amendments to this Constitution, or, on the Application of the Legislatures of two-thirds of the several States, shall call a Convention for proposing amendments.'' Thus far, all federal amendments that have become a part of the U.S. Constitution were proposed in the same manner—by joint resolution of the two branches of Congress.

Federal amendments become a part of the national constitution ''when ratified by the Legislature of three-fourths of the several States, or by Conventions in three-fourths thereof, as the one or the other Mode of Ratification may be proposed by the Congress.'' All federal amendments thus far, except the Twenty-first, which repealed national prohibition, have been ratified in the same manner—by action of the state legislatures.

Federal amendments are proposed in Congress by way of a House or Senate joint resolution, and require a two-thirds vote in both Houses to be submitted to the states for ratification. For the Texas legislature to ratify a federal amendment requires only a majority vote (joint resolution) of the house and senate. If Congress specified ratification of an amendment by state conventions, one might assume that a majority vote in such a convention would be sufficient for ratification of the amendment by a state. However, by a resolution or law providing for a state ratification convention, the state legislature might require a majority or two-thirds vote in that convention.

Part Two

Organization, Powers, Procedures, and Politics

4 Suffrage and Elections

ON OCCASION THERE HAS been misunderstanding concerning the nature of suffrage and citizenship. The right to vote is often referred to as a "right" in the sense of the natural rights upon which so much emphasis was placed during the formative years of the American Republic. In this context, the suffrage is conceived erroneously as a right that belongs to a person by virtue of his status as a human being and as a citizen, a right that the government cannot justly deny. Suffrage, however, is not a right in this sense; it may be withheld from persons for a variety of reasons, among which are insufficient age, inadequate length of residence, failure to register, foreign nationality, mental incapacity, and conviction of a felony. Therefore, suffrage is a privilege, rather than a right, which a state may grant or withhold as long as the state's action is not in conflict with the Fourteenth, Fifteenth, Nineteenth, and Twenty-sixth amendments of the U.S. Constitution, as interpreted by the federal courts.

Suffrage and Citizenship

The terms *suffrage* and *citizenship* are frequently confused. A man is said to be "deprived of his citizenship" when convicted of a felony in Texas, but he has actually been deprived of his political privileges—the privilege of voting and holding office—and not of his citizenship. (Conviction of treason results in loss of U.S. citizenship.) Upon completion of the prison term or when pardoned or paroled by the governor of Texas (upon recommendations of the Board of Pardons and Paroles), a person may regain his political privileges. Such a person would have to register, be eighteen years of age, and not otherwise disqualified, in order to regain the voting privilege. The issues of citizenship and suffrage can be separated by observing that all voters must be citizens; yet because of age, residence, and other requirements for voting, all citizens may not be eligible to vote.

The Decision in 1787

There was considerable difference of opinion concerning the suffrage at the federal constitutional convention. The delegates decided to leave the matter of suffrage to the states. In providing for the selection of members of the lower House of

63

Congress, the framers did specify that "the Electors in each State shall have the Qualifications requisite for Electors of the most numerous Branch of the State Legislature" [Article I, Section 2 (1)]. Since in the original Constitution, U.S. senators were to be appointed by state legislatures, and the presidential electors of the states were to be appointed "in such Manner as the Legislature thereof may direct" [Article II, Section 1 (2)], the federal Constitution, as drafted by the convention, was indeed brief on the matter of suffrage.

Federal Constitutional Amendments

In the post-Civil War period the Fourteenth and Fifteenth amendments were added to the U.S. Constitution. Among other things, the Fourteenth Amendment declares that no state may "deny to any person within its jurisdiction the equal protection of laws." The Fifteenth Amendment provides, "The *right* of citizens of the United States to vote shall not be denied or abridged by the United States or by any State on account of race, color, or previous condition of servitude." In somewhat similar language, the Nineteenth Amendment, adopted in 1920, declares "The *right* of citizens of the United States to vote shall not be denied or abridged by the United States or by any State on account of sex." The Twenty-sixth Amendment permits eighteen-year-olds to vote in local, state, and federal elections if otherwise qualified. Within the limitations of the federal Constitution as interpreted by the federal courts, the states under their reserve powers have the right to determine the qualifications and disqualifications for voting.

Qualifications for Voting in Texas

To vote in local, state, and national elections in Texas (primaries and general elections), one must have attained the age of eighteen years, be a citizen of the United States, have resided in the district or county in Texas in which one plans to vote for thirty days preceding an election, and have registered as a voter.

Idiots, lunatics, paupers supported by the county, and persons convicted of a felony (subject to such exceptions as the legislature has made) are disqualified to vote in Texas. Qualified voters who are blind or otherwise handicapped, including illiterate persons, are assisted in voting.

The U.S. Department of Justice approved a law passed by the Texas legislature in 1983 that restored voting rights automatically to ex-felons five years after completion of their sentences. Unless challenged, eligible ex-felons may register without having to show documents proving when they completed their sentences. Justice Department approval was necessary under the 1965 Federal Voting Rights Act, which requires federal approval (preclearance) of state laws affecting elections and voter registration. However, under existing law, a convicted felon cannot hold public office in Texas. Prior to the 1983 law, a felon could not regain the right to vote unless one received a pardon from the governor. The 1983 law was supported by Citizens United for Rehabilitation of Errants (CURE) and other prison reform groups. Some members of the Texas legislature believe the five-year waiting period should be abolished either by law or by court action.

Expansion of the Suffrage in Texas

The rise of popular government in Texas is the story of the slow but steady increase in the number of people permitted to vote. Some of the expansion of the suffrage in Texas has resulted from voluntary action in the state. Yet federal amendments and federal court decisions have played a vital role in this process. Whether this suffrage expansion has resulted from state or federal effort or both, it evidences the broadening scope of democracy in this country.

Women's Suffrage

In 1915 the first vote was taken by the Texas legislature on a proposed constitutional amendment authorizing females to vote. The proposal failed by four votes of the necessary two-thirds required for the submission of amendments to the people. The main three arguments used by the opposition to defeat the proposed amendment were that it was contrary to the Bible, that it was "allied to socialism," and that such extension of the suffrage would "lower woman and rob her of those modest charms so dear to us southern men."[1]

In 1918 the legislature gave women who possessed the other qualifications of an elector the privilege to vote in the primary and in nominating conventions.* Under this limitation, women could not vote in the general election or on proposed constitutional amendments to the Texas constitution, nor could they vote for president and vice-president. Nevertheless, the law of 1918 was an important factor in the increase of voter participation in the Democratic primary in 1918.

In 1919, the legislature, without a dissenting vote in either house, submitted to the people a constitutional amendment providing for equal suffrage without regard to sex,[2] but this proposed amendment was defeated by the people (male voters).

The Texas legislature may have expected the defeat of the equal-suffrage amendment. The session that submitted this amendment also passed a concurrent resolution requesting the U.S. Senate to submit immediately to the legislatures of the several states for ratification an amendment to the U.S. Constitution abolishing sex as a qualification for voting. This concurrent resolution, memorializing the U.S. Senate to take such action, declared that:

> Whereas, In the Democratic Primary of July 27, 1918, the women of Texas spoke clearly and emphatically in behalf of civic righteousness and honor in its public servants, thus giving trustworthy proof of their eminent fitness for the ballot, without any limitations whatsoever, except such as may apply to all voters alike; Now, Therefore, Be it Resolved . . . that the United States Senate is hereby respectfully but urgently requested to act immediately and favorably upon the woman suffrage amendment which has already received proper recognition by the House of Representatives.[3]

In due season, Congress approved and submitted the Nineteenth Amendment to the state legislatures for ratification. The amendment was ratified in Texas at a special session of the legislature, which convened in June 1919.† This action by Texas placed it on record as the first state in the south and the ninth in the nation to

---

*Acts 1918. Thirty-fifth Legislature, Fourth Called Session, Chap. 34, pp. 61–64. Women were not required to pay the poll tax to vote in the primaries or to participate in nominating conventions in 1918. From and after January 1, 1919, women voters were required to pay the poll tax to vote. The fourth called session adjourned March 27, 1918, and the bill became law ninety days after adjournment.

†The Texas Legislature ratified the Nineteenth Amendment by House Joint Resolution No. 1, Thirty-sixth Legislature, Second Called Session, 1919.

vote for full enfranchisement of American women. By August 1920, the required three-fourths of the state legislatures had ratified it, and the Nineteenth Amendment became a part of the federal Constitution. Rather than giving women the *right* to vote, the amendment declares their *right* to vote shall not be denied or abridged because of sex. After the Nineteenth Amendment became effective, August 26, 1920, millions of women failed to qualify to vote because of age, residence, citizenship, and other qualifications.

Extension of the Suffrage to Military Personnel

Reflecting the distrust of military rule during Reconstruction, the Texas constitution of 1876 prohibited from voting all soldiers, marines, and seamen employed in the service of the U.S. Army or Navy. An amendment to the Texas constitution in 1954 provided that "Any member of the Armed Forces of the United States or component branches thereof, or in the military service of the United States, may vote only in the county in which he or she resided at the time of entering such service so long as he or she is a member of the Armed Forces.'"[4] If otherwise qualified, members of the armed forces of the United States from Texas could vote (in person or by absentee ballot) in the county of their residence at the time of entering the armed forces. This amendment prohibited voting by persons who had established residence in Texas solely through military service and was designed to prevent out-of-state military personnel from becoming voters and dominating local nominations and elections. The out-of-state military personnel in Texas could vote, if qualified, in their home state, if the state permitted absentee voting. This provision of the Texas constitution and state election code made no mention of the wives and dependents of servicemen. If qualified, they could vote in the state.

In 1965, the U.S. Supreme Court overruled the Texas supreme court[5] and declared the 1954 amendment to the Texas constitution and a similar provision of the state election code violated the equal-protection clause of the Fourteenth Amendment of the U.S. Constitution.[6] "By forbidding the soldier ever to controvert the presumption of nonresidence, the Texas statute," according to the U.S. Supreme Court, imposed "an invidious discrimination in violation of the [federal Constitution's] Fourteenth Amendment." Servicemen desiring to vote in Texas must show they have established or intend to establish a bona fide residence in the state.

The changes in the suffrage article of the Texas constitution above indicate that *voluntary* expansion of the suffrage through state action has been limited to two areas: granting women, otherwise qualified, the privilege of voting in primaries and nominating conventions (law of 1918), and extending the suffrage to military personnel (constitutional amendments of 1931, 1945, and 1954). A broadening of the suffrage to permit women to vote in general elections and Negroes to vote in primaries, as well as expansion of the military vote in 1965, resulted from the adoption of the Nineteenth Amendment of the U.S. Constitution and various federal court decisions. The federal government has applied a sort of spur on the flank to suffrage expansion in Texas as well as in other states. However, there was little opposition in the Texas legislature over the issue of ratifying the Nineteenth Amendment; on the other hand, there was considerable opposition to permitting Negroes to vote in the primaries.

Negro Suffrage

In the post-Civil War period some states continued to disfranchise the blacks, despite the addition of the Fourteenth and Fifteenth amendments to the U.S. Constitution. The techniques employed to disfranchise black voters in other states and the strategy in Texas involved a number of political and legal issues.

The Ku Klux Klan (KKK) and Literacy Tests

The work of the Ku Klux Klan and its program of threat and violence are well known. Some Southerners felt a more subtle form of depriving the black of his voting privilege should be put into operation. As a result, there evolved the literacy test, which in some instances was designed to curb the political inclinations of both the blacks and the Populists. In Mississippi, among other qualifications to vote, one had to be able either to read any section of the state constitution or give a reasonable interpretation of parts of the constitution when read by another person. Few blacks in Mississippi could read at the time the plan was instituted (1890), and still fewer could give a reasonable interpretation of selected passages from the state constitution. Even if an attempt at interpretation was made, it might be considered inadequate by the election officials. However, since many whites could not read or write, literacy tests disfranchised too many whites along with blacks. A remedy was found in the so-called grandfather clauses.

Grandfather Clauses

Louisiana, in 1898, established the ingenious "grandfather clause" that provided that one could not be registered as a voter unless he could read and write or unless he owned $300 worth of property. However, if one's father or grandfather had the privilege to vote on or before January 1, 1867, he was exempted from the above qualifications. This date was significant because it preceded by two months the first act of Congress, passed March 3, 1867, prohibiting the disfranchisement of freedmen. Grandfather clauses, of one form or another, were adopted as temporary constitutional amendments in seven states and were designed to permit the illiterate and propertyless whites to vote, while excluding blacks from the polls. In 1915, seventeen years after the establishment of the grandfather clause in Louisiana, the U.S. Supreme Court declared the grandfather clause amendment of the Oklahoma constitution violated the Fifteenth Amendment.[7] Nevertheless, the grandfather clauses did serve as temporary measures, since they did qualify white men to vote, after which other techniques could be developed and utilized to prevent blacks from voting.

The White Man's Primary

In the one-party states in the South, nomination in the party primary assured one of victory in the general election. Consequently, the place to limit the blacks' voting was in the primary. This is where Texas came into the national limelight with its all-out fight to save the white man's primary.

In May 1923, the Texas legislature enacted a statute providing "in no event shall a Negro be eligible to participate in a Democratic party primary election held in the State of Texas."[8] The Texas White Primary law was invalidated by the U.S. Supreme Court in 1927. The Court, speaking through Mr. Justice Holmes, declared, "We find it unnecessary to consider the Fifteenth Amendment, because it seems to us hard to imagine a more direct and obvious infringement of the Fourteenth." The U.S. Supreme Court held the Texas statute unconstitutional on the grounds that it violated the "equal protection of the laws" clause of the Fourteenth Amendment.[9] Promptly after the announcement of this decision the Texas legislature enacted a new statute that declared "every political party in this State through its State Executive Committee shall have the power to prescribe the qualifications of its own members and shall in its own way determine who shall be qualified to vote or otherwise participate in such political party."[10] The State Executive Committee of the Democratic party of Texas, acting under authority of the new statute, adopted a resolution "that all white Democrats who are qualified under the constitution and laws of Texas and who subscribe to the statutory pledge provided in Article 3110, Revised Civil Statutes of Texas, and none other, be allowed to participate in the primary election to be held July 28, and August 25, 1928." Nixon, a black and a citizen of the United States, and otherwise qualified to vote, was refused a primary ballot on July 28, 1928, by the election judges, on grounds that the petitioner was a black and that by force of the resolution of the executive committee only white Democrats were allowed to vote in the Democratic primary. The refusal was followed by an action for damages. When the case was heard by the U.S. Supreme Court, the Court declared that the petitioner had been denied a primary ballot for the sole reason that his color was not white. "The result for him is no different from what it was when his cause was here before." Again, the U.S. Supreme Court held that the Second White Primary law of Texas violated the "equal protection of the laws" clause of the Fourteenth Amendment.[11]

Shortly after the Second White Primary law was invalidated, the Democratic party leaders of Texas decided to take action through their party convention. As a result, the state Democratic convention adopted the following resolution on May 24, 1932: "Be it resolved, that all white citizens of the State of Texas who are qualified to vote under the Constitution and laws of the state shall be eligible to membership in the Democratic party and as such entitled to participate in its deliberations." By virtue of the above party resolution, Townsend, county clerk of Harris County, Texas, denied an absentee ballot to Grovey, a black resident of the county, who was otherwise qualified to vote in the county. This action had the effect of denying Grovey the right to participate in the Democratic primary on July 28, 1934. A suit for damages ($10) was filed in the justice court of the county. The U.S. Supreme Court granted certiorari because the justice of the peace court was the highest state court in which a decision in the case could be had. The U.S. Supreme Court held "that a proper view of the election laws of Texas, and their history, required the conclusion that the Democratic party in that state is a voluntary political association and, by its representatives assembled in convention, has the power to determine who shall be eligible for membership and, as such, eligible to participate in the party's primaries."[12] The Court said no "state action" was involved, as in the two earlier laws, and hence, no denial of rights guaranteed by the Fourteenth and Fifteenth amendments. In brief, political parties were not agents of the state, but possessed the inherent power of determining membership and participation in the party.

The principle laid down by the U.S. Supreme Court in 1935 remained the law of

the land for nine years until reversed in 1944 in the case of *Smith* v. *Allwright.**
This case came before the U.S. Supreme Court by writ of certiorari for review of a
claim for damages in the sum of $5,000 on the part of Smith, a black resident of
Houston, who was refused a ballot in the primary of 1940 and thus denied the right
to participate in the nomination of Democratic candidates for Congress and state
offices. In reversing the 1935 decision, Mr. Justice Reed, speaking for the Court,
said,

> We think that this statutory system for the selection of party nominees for inclusion on
> the general election ballot makes the party which is required to follow these legislative
> directions an agency of the state in so far as it determines the participants in a primary
> election. The party takes its character as a state agency from the duties imposed upon it
> by state statutes; the duties do not become matters of private law because they are per-
> formed by a political party. . . . This is state action within the meaning of the Fifteenth
> Amendment.

Attempts to Evade the Decision Reached in Smith v. Allwright

Action in South Carolina. The most determined effort to circumvent the Allwright decision was made in South Carolina. Within a few days after this decision
was handed down, a special session of the South Carolina general assembly was
called. This special session passed a law that provided that "each and every provision in the laws of this state authorizing, recognizing, or regulating the organization of political parties . . . and the primaries, elections, or nominations in primary elections for a federal, state, county, or municipal office, or for any office in
any other political division . . . is hereby repealed."[13] The same session initiated a
constitutional amendment, later ratified by the people, striking out the words in
the state constitution: "The General Assembly shall provide by law for the regulation of party primary elections and punishing fraud at the same."[14] Following the
repeal of the above statutes, party rules completely controlled nominations in the
state. Litigation to test the action taken by the general assembly was soon instituted
in the federal district court in South Carolina. Elmore, a Negro otherwise qualified to vote in the state, was—by party rules and because of race—deprived of the
privilege to vote in the Democratic primary. The federal district court in South
Carolina ruled in favor of Elmore in 1947,[15] the U.S. circuit court of appeals sustained the decision,[16] and certiorari was denied by the U.S. Supreme Court.[17]

The federal district court compared the situation in South Carolina before and
after the repeal of the primary statutes and concluded there was no "substantial"
difference. After the repeal, the state Democratic convention acted to embody all
the former statutory provisions in the party rules. Hence, the Democratic party
occupied the same determining position that it had under the primary statutes. The
party could not be treated as a private club, private business, or association because, as the court observed, these

> do not vote and elect a President of the United States, and the Senators and members of

---

*321 U.S. 649 (1944). In *United States* v. *Classic,* 313 U.S. 299 (1941), the U.S. Supreme Court
ruled that a *primary* in a one-party state (Louisiana) was an *election* within the meaning of the federal
Constitution. This decision paved the way for considering racial discrimination in primaries as contrary to the Fourteenth and Fifteenth amendments.

the House of Representatives of our national congress; and under the law of our land, all citizens are entitled to a voice in such selections. It is true that the General Assembly of the State of South Carolina repealed all laws relating to and governing primaries, and the Democratic Party in this State is not under the Statutory control, but to say that there is any material difference in the governance of the Democratic Party in this State prior, and subsequent, to 1944 is pure sophistry. The same membership was there before and after, the same method of organization of club meetings, of delegates to County Conventions, delegates to State Conventions, arranging for enrollment, preparation of ballots, and all the other details incident to a primary election. . . . It is time for South Carolina to rejoin the Union. It is time to fall in step with the other states and to adopt the American way of conducting elections.

The district court quoted the leader of the Democratic party, President Truman, in an address delivered on June 29, 1947:

> Our case for democracy should be as strong as we can make it. It should rest on practical evidence that we have been able to put our own house in order.
> For these compelling reasons, we can no longer afford the luxury of a leisurely attack upon prejudice and discrimination. There is much that state and local governments can do in providing positive safeguards for civil rights. But we cannot, any longer, await the growth of a will to action in the slowest state or the most backward community.
> Our National Government must show the way.

Action in Texas. Soon after the decision in *Smith* v. *Allwright* in 1944, the suggestion was made that Texas abandon the direct primary and go back to the convention system of nomination which had prevailed prior to 1907. In fact, the Texas legislature which met in 1945 considered a white primary bill based on the South Carolina pattern (repeal of the primary election laws). The bill was introduced in the senate and favorably reported by committee, but no further action was taken on the proposal. A similar bill was considered by the Texas lower house in 1947, but it was never acted upon by the committee. It would have been futile to attempt to revive the white primary in Texas after the decision in *Elmore* v. *Rice* in 1947. Furthermore, it appears that after the bitter struggle within the Democratic party in Texas over the 1944 electoral college vote, the liberal and conservative factions distrusted each other too much to risk removing all legal control over the conduct of primaries and vesting control solely in the party. For these reasons no serious effort was made in Texas to circumvent the U.S. Supreme Court decision in *Smith* v. *Allwright.*

The Jaybird Democratic Association in Fort Bend County, Texas

The Jaybird Democratic Association in Fort Bend County, Texas, was organized in 1889. Its membership was limited to white people, who were automatically members if their names appeared on the official list of county voters. The Jaybird party was one of two political factions in the county. The other, the Woodpeckers party, had long since passed into obscurity. The Jaybird Democratic Association conducted unofficial primaries for the nomination of county and precinct officers. Prior to 1953 the association plan was to hold a primary election and runoff primary a few weeks before the time set by state law for official primaries. In most cases, the nominees of the "Jaybird primaries" were then put on the ballots in the regular Democratic primaries, as well as on the general election ballot, without opposition. The Jaybirds contended that their racial exclusion did not violate the Fifteenth Amendment, since the latter applied only to elections or primaries held under state regulation. In short, they argued that their association was not regulated by the state at all, that it was not a political party but rather a self-governing voluntary club.

On May 4, 1953, the U.S. Supreme Court, on an appeal by a group of blacks protesting against primaries conducted by the Jaybird Association, held that the election plan illegally denied blacks an effective voice in nominating Democratic candidates in Fort Bend County.[18] The Court said:

> The use of the county-operated primary to ratify the result of the prohibited election merely compounds the offense. It violates the Fifteenth Amendment for a state, by such circumvention, to permit within its borders the use of any device that produces an equivalent of the prohibited election. . . . The only election that has counted in this Texas County for more than fifty years has been that held by the Jaybirds from which Negroes were excluded. The Democratic primary and the general election have become no more than the perfunctory ratifiers of the choice that has already been made in Jaybird elections from which Negroes have been excluded. It is immaterial that the state does not control that party of this elective process which it leaves for the Jaybirds to manage. The Jaybird primary has become an integral part, indeed, the only effective part, of the elective process that determines who shall rule and govern in the county. The effect of the whole procedure, Jaybird primary plus Democratic primary plus general election, is to do precisely that which the Fifteenth Amendment forbids.

The effectiveness of the Jaybird Democratic Association of Fort Bend County, Texas, was terminated by the 1953 U.S. Supreme Court decision. In 1959, the association disbanded.*

Impact of the Smith v. Allwright Decision in Texas

Prior to the *Smith* v. *Allwright* decision (1944), blacks were not excluded completely from voting in Texas. Those who paid their poll tax and who otherwise qualified to vote could vote in general, municipal, school board, special, and local option elections. However, their entrance into the primaries was a considerable step forward in the democratization of the electoral process in Texas.

Improved educational facilities for blacks, the appeal of candidates for the black vote, abolishment of the poll tax, the efforts of black leaders, and the popularity of civil rights issues have also stimulated increased black participation in local and state politics. An increasing number of blacks register and vote, attend precinct, county, state, and national party conventions; more blacks seek public office, contribute funds for political purposes, and participate in political campaigns.

The registrars of voters in the Texas counties make no official computation of qualified voters according to race. Even if they did, it would not indicate the number of blacks who actually vote. Therefore, the degree of increased black participation in politics is difficult to determine.

---

*The White Man's Union Association (WMUA) operated in Grimes County (Navasota near Bryan, Texas) from 1900 to 1961. The association, through the white man's union primary and runoff primary, selected nominees from various areas of the county for political offices in the Democratic primary.

One of the more popular clichés in the United States is that "you cannot change human nature by passing a law or by decision of the courts; you cannot legislate morality." *Human conduct,* in contrast to *human nature,* can be controlled or modified by law and judicial decisions. It may be impossible to overcome prejudice by law and judicial decision; yet the outward or visible manifestations of prejudice, such as denying the privilege to vote because of race, can be discouraged or even eliminated through proper governmental controls. In *Smith* v. *Allwright,* no deliberate attempt was made to change human nature; however, the decision did change ways of life, voting patterns, and social arrangements; and it *may have contributed to the changing of attitudes.* These changes were made, consciously or unconsciously, without reference to the more delicate question of human nature. In all likelihood the civil rights development in the future will follow a similar pattern; if so, we will move along in a positive way toward the democratic goal of becoming more human in mind and action.[19]

Abolishment of the Poll Tax as a Qualification ("Cover Charge") for Voting

The Texas constitution was amended in 1902 to provide a poll tax as one of the qualifications for voting. In some counties the poll tax was $1.75 and in others $1.50, depending upon whether the county assessed the optional $0.25 levy. One dollar of each poll tax was for the support of the public schools; $0.50 for the state's general revenue; and $0.25, if levied, for county funds. Persons over sixty years of age and otherwise qualified to vote were exempt from the poll tax, provided those who resided in a city of 10,000 or more obtained an exemption certificate from the county tax assessor-collector. The poll tax could be paid anytime between October 1 and January 31.

A primary purpose of requiring the poll tax as a precondition for the privilege of voting was the desire to disfranchise the black and the poor white supporters of the Populist party. The poll tax, which became a part of the Texas constitution twenty-six years after its adoption, did discourage voting in this state, especially among the lower-income voters.

The Twenty-fourth Amendment to the U.S. Constitution, which became effective in 1964, declared, "The right of citizens of the United States to vote in any primary or other election for President or Vice-President, for electors for President or Vice-President, or for Senator or Representative in Congress, shall not be denied or abridged by the United States or any State by reason of failure to pay any poll tax or other tax." As a result of this amendment, two types of ballots had to be prepared in Texas: (1) ballots that permitted persons to vote for local, state, and federal candidates; (2) ballots that were arranged to permit persons to vote only for federal candidates. Two separate lists of qualified voters were made available to the election judges. In November 1966, the voters of Texas approved a state constitutional amendment repealing the poll tax as a voting requirement and substituted annual registration of voters.

Prior to the repeal of the poll tax in Texas, the U.S. Supreme Court, on March 24, 1966, nullified a Virginia law requiring voters to pay a poll tax to vote in nonfederal elections. Thus, the poll tax as a qualification for voting was invalidated in

the remaining poll-tax states (Virginia, Mississippi, Alabama, and Texas). In the Virginia case, the U.S. Supreme Court said:

> We conclude that a State violates the Equal Protection Clause of the Fourteenth Amendment whenever it makes the affluence of the voter or payment of any fee an electoral standard. Voter qualifications have no relation to wealth nor to paying or not paying this or any other tax. . . .
> . . . the interest of the State, when it comes to voting, is limited to the power to fix qualifications. Wealth, like race, creed, or color, is not germane to one's ability to participate intelligently in the electoral process.[20]

The U.S. Supreme Court decision made the Twenty-fourth Amendment and the poll tax repeal provision of the Texas amendment unnecessary.

Voting in Bond Elections

Local governments in Texas frequently borrow money through the device of revenue bonds or general-obligation bonds. The principal and interest on revenue bonds are financed by charges or fees paid by individuals who receive a governmental service, for example, water or sewer bonds. General-obligation bonds are financed, for the most part, by property taxes.

Those who do not own taxable property pay property taxes in an indirect way. The rent one pays for a house or an apartment includes the property taxes paid by the owner.

The U.S. Supreme Court upheld a three-judge panel's finding, in a Phoenix, Arizona, case, that there was no significant difference between revenue bonds and general-obligation bonds. The court rejected contentions that property owners had a greater interest in general-obligation bond elections, since such bonds are secured primarily by property taxes. Prior to federal court decisions, the law in Texas and other states limited voting in bond elections to property owners, and a majority of the property owners who voted was necessary for approval of the bond program.

After the federal court decision in the Arizona case, Texas and other states adopted the "dual box" system of voting in bond elections. This permitted two separate vote tallies on bond issues, one for property owners and one for non-property owners. The question of one class approving a bond issue and the other class disapproving did not become a legal issue for some time in Texas. However, the problem did arise in Fort Worth where property owners defeated a library construction bond issue which won approval by a majority of all the voters. Three Fort Worth residents filed a lawsuit that was decided finally by the U.S. Supreme Court. The claimants contended that the dual box system deprived the majority of the voters of their rights since the bond issue could not be approved without approval of both boxes. The U.S. Supreme Court held that the dual system erected "a classification that impermissibly disenfranchises persons otherwise qualified to vote solely because they have not rendered some property for taxation." In addition to making it possible for more people to vote in bond elections, the decision made it easier and less expensive to hold such elections since there is no need to keep separate voting tallies.

As a result of federal court decisions, qualified voters who own taxable property and those who do not may vote in bond elections, and the votes are tabulated equally. The decisions of the federal courts invalidated franchise restrictions in fourteen states, including Texas, and represent a phase in the liberalization of the suffrage.

Extension of the Suffrage to Eighteen-Year-Olds

The Federal Voting Rights Act of 1965, as amended by Congress in 1970, lowered the voting age in local, state, and national primaries and elections in most states from twenty-one to eighteen years of age; abolished residency requirements of more than thirty days to vote in national elections; suspended literacy tests in all states for five years; and required all states to provide absentee ballots. In December 1970 the U.S. Supreme Court upheld all the voting-rights amendments of Congress, except lowering the voting age to eighteen in state and local elections for persons otherwise qualified to vote.

The Twenty-sixth Amendment to the federal Constitution, which became effective in 1971, extended the privilege of voting in state and local elections to qualified eighteen-year-olds.

Voter Registration

The Texas Election Code provides that a person is entitled to register as a voter in the voting precinct of legal residence if, on the date of applying for registration, the individual is a citizen of the United States and is subject to none of the disqualifications and, if within sixty days after applying for registration, the individual will be eighteen years of age or older. However, no person may vote at any election unless he or she fulfills all the qualifications of an elector for that election. One may register whenever the county tax assessor-collector's office (the registrar's office) is open for business. Registration is free and may be applied for in person or by mail. To vote, one must have been registered as a voter at least thirty days prior to the time of voting.

If a husband, wife, father, mother, son or daughter is a qualified voter, he or she may apply for voter registration as agent for the voter.

Persons, other than the county registrar and his deputies, who assist individuals in completing registration forms are subject to a fine. In the case of illiterate or aged individuals the county registrar or his deputy may offer assistance in securing a voter registration certificate. The county registrars may send deputies to hospitals, rest homes, convalescent homes, and similar institutions to register voters unable to register in person or by mail. The giving of false information to procure the registration of a voter is a misdemeanor.

The application for a voter registration certificate may include blank spaces for Social Security and telephone numbers. If an individual objects, this information need not be revealed. Although such information does not appear on the registration certificate itself, its inclusion on the application form is intended to aid in identifying voter registrants who have identical names.

Neither the application for a voter registration certificate, nor the certificate itself, specifies the race of the applicant or voter. Therefore, no separate lists of qualified voters are prepared according to race.

The registrar of each county reports to the state comptroller yearly the number of registered voters, and the state pays each county a fee for each voter registered to help finance this service. Also, the county registrar prepares lists of the qualified voters in each voting precinct in the county. These lists are distributed to the precinct election judges.

The voter registration certificate is valid only for the two-year voting period indicated on its face. The individual will receive a new certificate from the registrar of voters for each subsequent two-year period as long as the person resides in the county.

Registration of College and University Students

To be eligible to vote, students must register with the county registrar of voters either in their home county or in the county where they reside as students. A registrant must be a citizen and at least seventeen years of age. Proof of age of birth is required of seventeen-year-old registrants. Certain other information is required: name, address, Social Security number (if the student has one), sex, age, date of birth, date of arrival in Texas, county, and city. The student will receive by mail a small certificate indicating the date on which the holder may cast his vote; the voting certificate must be presented at the polling place. As is true of nonstudent voters, students in Texas colleges and universities must have resided in the state and county for thirty days prior to the election and must have made an application for a voter registration card at least thirty days prior to the election. Qualified students may register and vote (in person or by absentee ballot) in the county in which their school is located, in a county they consider their home county, or in the county where their parents reside.

The Voter Who Moves within the County and State

A registered voter who changes place of residence *within the election precinct* should notify the county registrar of voters of the change of address and obtain a corrected voter registration certificate. Also, those who move to another election precinct *within the county* should notify the county registrar of voters of their address change and have the change made on the voter registration certificate. Then the names of these individuals are added to the voter's list in their new voting precinct.

A registered voter who moves *from one county to another county within the state* should register in the county of his new residence in the same manner as an initial registrant. When the county registrar of voters receives an application for registration from a voter registered in another Texas county, the county registrar of voters of the former county is notified, and the voter registration in that county is cancelled. The name of the voter that moved to another county is added to the voter's list of the voting precinct of that particular county. Individuals are not qualified to vote for local and county candidates in their new county of residence until they have resided in that county for thirty days.

Declaration of Party Affiliation

When a person registers as a voter in Texas, should the individual be required to declare whether he or she is a Democrat, a Republican, or an independent, and should the information be included on the voter registration certificate? A law making this a condition or qualification for voting in the primary might raise a legal question. The qualifications for voting are prescribed in the Texas constitution and the imposition of an additional requirement or qualification might be held invalid. Such a requirement might be authorized by constitutional amendment.

Some favor the so-called closed primary. Only those registered as a Democrat or Republican could hold party office, participate in party conventions and primaries, seek the party nomination for local and state office, and vote in the primary of the respective party. Provisions could be made for a person to change or to declare his party affiliation within a given period before the election. Would such a change encourage the development of a two-party system in the state, as well as discourage party "jumping" and "raiding"? Tradition, and the unit system of casting the electoral vote of the state, among other considerations, have been factors in the dominance of the Democratic party in Texas.

The Texas election code provides:

> An applicant for party affiliation shall become a qualified member of a political party which is holding primary elections when he has voted within that party's primary or has taken part in a convention of that party prior to a primary. At the head of the signature roster for each primary election there shall be printed the following statement: ''I swear that I have not voted at a primary election or participated in a convention of any other political party during this voting year.''

At the time of voting in the primary, the code requires the voter registration certificate be stamped to indicate that the individual voted in the party's primary. Thus, the voter is prohibited from voting in the primary of another party held the same day, and an individual cannot legally vote in the first primary of one party and in the second primary of another party. A voter whose voter registration certificate has been stamped at a party primary may participate in the party conventions of that party held during the year.

Absentee Voting

If a qualified voter in Texas will not be in his or her voting precinct at the time of the general, special, or primary election, the individual may obtain an absentee ballot by making application for an official ballot in the county clerk's office and by voting in advance of the election before leaving the voting precinct. If out of the voting precinct, one may make written application to the county clerk for a ballot, the voter then marks and returns the ballot to the county clerk. In either case, the applicant for absentee ballot must exhibit, either in person or by mail, a voter registration certificate. Absentee ballots are tabulated with the ballots cast on the regular election date. The period for absentee voting begins on the twentieth day prior to the first primary and general election; on the tenth day prior to the second primary; and ends four days before the election. Only because of sickness, physical disability, religious beliefs, or confinement in the county jail may qualified voters receive absentee ballots by mail within the county of residence.

Special provisions for absentee voting are made for active members of the armed forces of the United States, their spouses and dependents (whether or not living with the husband, wife, or parent); members of the U.S. Merchant Marines, their spouses and dependents (as above); and citizens of the United States domiciled in Texas but temporarily living outside the United States. Such persons may cast absentee votes by mail upon making sworn applications for absentee ballots on official federal postcard application forms. If a person has not previously registered, his application for voter registration will be applied to all elections for which an absentee ballot has been requested.

Election Irregularities and Illegal Voting

Election irregularities and illegal voting have been rather common in Texas, especially in regard to absentee voting. Applications for absentee ballots have been issued to people who had no intention of voting. Some voters have voted absentee in order to haul voters to the polls on election day. Absentee ballot applications and ballots have been distributed by private individuals, business firms, and other unauthorized persons. Absentee ballots have been cast by persons who do not reside in the county. Some persons have voted both absentee and again on election day.

As the absentee law operates, it is subject to abuse in many localities. Behind such abuse may be a political boss or machine preying on the ignorant, the illiterate, the old, and the economically dependent, all of whom are subject to pressure and favors of various kinds. These favors, of course, are offered to those that vote absentee for the "right" candidates. It is usually difficult to pin down these and other abuses to the satisfaction of the courts. Thus there have been few prosecutions for election irregularities and illegal voting in the state.

The most extreme proposal to eliminate irregular and illegal absentee voting is to abolish absentee voting. Such an amendment to the code would not only decrease the number of potential voters, but would penalize hundreds of voters every two years who have valid reasons for voting absentee and who obey the law. There have also been irregularities concerning the registration of voters, despite the punishment provided in the Texas Election Code. Because of false statements about age and residence, some persons not eligible for a voter registration certificate have been issued them. Unauthorized persons have helped others secure voter registration certificates.

It is impossible for the election judges, especially in the urban areas, to recognize persons who vote more than once. Multiple voting is possible where an individual votes on his or her own voter registration certificate and secures such certificates for or from other persons (who do not plan to vote in person or absentee) and casts votes in their names. The names of dead people may have been signed on voter registration certificates and their ballots cast by someone else. Or an election judge might vote for some of the persons on the precinct voting list who did not vote. Poll watchers, who attempt to prevent illegal voting practices, may be appointed by the county chairman or members of the county executive committee, by the candidates, or by the voters.

The Master State Voter File

The secretary of state provides a service program to assist county registrars in maintaining accurate and current lists of registered voters. From information provided by the county registrars of voters, the secretary of state prepares a master state voter file on magnetic tape on March 1 and September 1 of each year. The tape includes each voter's county, voting precinct number, name, permanent residence and mailing address, sex, year of birth, and registration number, but does not include social security or telephone numbers. Any person may purchase a copy of the tape which may be used only for informing voters about candidates for public office or about public issues and may not be used to advertise or promote commercial products or services.

Ballots

In 1888 the Australian ballot was introduced in the United States and, with some innovations, was adopted by the states. Features of the Australian ballot include the following:

1. General election ballots are printed and distributed at public expense. Primary ballots may be printed and distributed at public expense, by party funds, and by private contributions.
2. The ballot includes the names of all candidates and is distributed only at the polling place.
3. The ballot is marked in secret by the voter. The original Australian ballot did not designate the parties of the candidates. Each group of candidates was listed under the office sought. In the interest of political parties, this feature of the Australian ballot has been modified in the United States.

Primary Election Ballots (Paper Ballots)

Any political party in Texas whose nominee for governor in the last general election received 20 percent or more of the total votes for governor must use the primary method of nominating candidates for precinct, county, district, and state office. If the party nominee for governor in the last general election received as much as 2 percent but not more than 20 percent of the total votes cast for governor, such party must nominate its candidates for the general election by party conventions. Party leaders may exercise a greater influence in conventions than in primaries, and the latter of course are more expensive.

With the paper ballot, the voter in the primary votes for the candidate of his choice in each race. If a candidate does not receive a majority of the votes cast for a particular office in the first primary, the two candidates with the most votes run against each other in the "run-off" or second primary. In states where nomination in the primary is tantamount to election, as in the one-party states, the dual primary insures the nomination and election of a majority winner.

At the bottom of the primary ballot there may be one or more referendum propositions that the voter may vote for or against—for example, the enactment by the Texas legislature of a law permitting horse racing with parimutuel wagering on a local option basis. Such referendum propositions are an expression of public opinion only and have no effect as law.

General Election Ballots (Paper Ballots)

In the general election, Texas uses the party-column ballot, since the nominees of the parties appear in separate columns. The voter may vote for the candidate of his or her choice in each race or vote a straight ticket (that is, vote for all candidates of a certain party).

One or more proposed Texas constitutional amendments may be included at the bottom of general election ballots. These must be voted on individually. The legislature may submit one or more proposed constitutional amendments to be voted on at a special election, the date of which would be specified in the proposed amendment.

Nonpartisan Candidates and Candidates of Third Parties

Nonpartisan and third-party candidates may be included on the general election ballot by petition approved by the secretary of state. As specified by law, the petition must be signed by the required number of qualified voters and submitted within a certain amount of time. Any person who has participated as a voter or as a candidate in either the first or second primary of a political party is ineligible to have his or her name printed on the ballot at the succeeding general or special election as an independent candidate or as the nominee of any other party for any office for which a nomination was made by such party.

Write-In Votes

In Texas's first primary there can be only write-in votes for precinct party chairman and county party chairman. These are elective party positions, rather than nominations, and individuals will be elected either in the first or second party primary. In the state's second party primary there can be no write-in votes.

In Texas, write-in votes are permissible in the general election. A space is left on the paper ballots and voting machine for write-in votes. In punchcard (electronic) voting, election officials provide a separate ballot and the voter must be sworn before voting.

A very small percentage of Texas voters are interested in write-in voting. Thus, persons whose names are written in have a slim chance of being elected to public office—although some voters enjoy writing in the names of movie, TV, and sport personalities, as well as girl and boy friends, and ex-husbands and wives.

Voting Machine

In some of the more populated areas of the state the voting machine is used in both primaries and general elections. Secrecy is assured in the voting booth by closing the curtain. Individual levers are pulled down for candidates and issues one wishes to vote for unless, in a general election, one chooses to pull down a single lever and vote a straight ticket. One advantage of the voting machine is that once the voting is over, the votes are tabulated mechanically on the machine, whereas hours are sometimes required to tabulate paper ballots. Also, there is considerable chance for error in tabulating paper ballots.

Electronic Voting

The Texas legislature has approved electronic voting, a system by which the vote is recorded by punching a ballot designed to be counted by data-processing machines. Some electronic voting systems use preperforated punch cards; the voters indicate their choice of candidates by punching holes in the card with a stylus. Another type of electronic vote counter scans paper ballots optically and records the votes, which are marked with a special ink.

The county commissioners' court of any county may adopt one or more electronic voting systems that have been certified by the Texas secretary of state as meeting the standards set out in the law for use in elections in part or all of the election precincts in the county. The commissioners' court must pay for the voting equipment and the automatic tabulating equipment. In counties that have their own data-processing equipment, the contracting for such service would not be necessary.

Voting machines are expensive to buy. In addition there is the expense of maintenance, storage, and transporting machines to and from the voting precincts. Electronic voting is considerably less expensive than voting by using voting machines. It may also reduce the waiting time at polling places and thus substantially increase voter turnout.

The State Election Board

The state election board (composed of the secretary of state, the governor, and one person appointed by the governor and senate for a two-year term) tabulates the returns, as reported by the county judges, for statewide offices and the votes cast for the presidential electors of the state in the general election. The state election board certifies the election of statewide officials, including presidential electors.

The Nomination of Presidential Electors and Casting the Electoral Vote

Party electors, equal to the number of representatives and senators Texas has in Congress, are nominated at state party conventions in June of the presidential election year. Thus, in the first phase of the presidential vice-presidential selection process, Texas and the other states, by action of the state political parties, must nominate their presidential electors.

The candidates for president and vice-president are *nominated* at national nominating conventions, which also endorse the platform for their respective nominees. This action is followed by a long and very expensive presidential campaign.

At one time Texas used the *presidential long ballot,* as the presidential electors of each party were included in the party columns below the names of the presidential and vice-presidential nominees of the parties. Some voters in Texas attempted to split their vote for president and vice-president by voting for some of the Republican and Democratic presidential electors—the so-called split-voting at the highest level. Such votes, of course, were invalidated by the canvassing election judges. At one time all counties in Texas used only paper ballots, which were party column ballots in the general election. The inclusion of the names of the presidential electors on the ballot, did, of course, increase the length and complexity of the ballot, as well as increasing the cost of printing the ballots.

Every fourth and even-numbered year the presidential short ballot is used in Texas, since the presidential electors of each party are not included as a part of the general election ballot; only the names of the presidential and vice-presidential candidates are included. A vote in November every fourth year for the presidential and vice-presidential nominees of a party is tabulated as a vote for the electors of the party, even though the names of the presidential electors do not appear on the ballot. A voter must cast his vote for both a presidential and vice-presidential candidate of the same party if his vote is to be counted for either position.

The Democratic or Republican slate of electors is elected by a *plurality vote* on the Tuesday following the first Monday in November every fourth year. On the first Monday after the second Wednesday in December following their election, the Texas presidential electors meet, as the Texas electoral college, at 2:00 P.M. in the Senate chamber in Austin and cast separate paper ballots for president and vice-president of the United States. These presidential electors are considered state officials, though elected for a very brief term, and to perform a state function that takes approximately thirty minutes. However, they qualify for state per diems and traveling expenses. The meeting of the Texas electoral college is open to the general public without charge. There is no nationwide meeting of the presidential electors to cast individual votes for president and vice-president. However, the presidential electors of the nation, or at least some of them, may meet in a body for a ceremonial purpose.

Thus far, neither the Democratic nor Republican electoral vote of Texas has been split among the presidential and vice-presidential candidates, which, on occasion, has occurred in some of the other states. On a few occasions, some of the Democratic presidential electors have resigned or declared they could not support all the planks in the party platform or party nominees for president and vice-president. They considered the nominees and some of the planks of the platform too liberal. The electors that found themselves in this position either resigned or were removed by the two-year Democratic September state convention which also appointed Democratic electors to fill the vacancies. (Both the Democratic and Republican parties in Texas hold state conventions every two years in September.) The right of the September state convention in Texas to withdraw presidential electors nominated at the Democratic and Republican June state conventions held every fourth and even-numbered year (presidential state conventions) and designate other electors in their place has been upheld by the Texas supreme court. According to the highest civil court in Texas, this was "a matter within the inherent power of the Party" and "a matter that [rests] entirely with the Party."[21]

The Electoral College—In Theory and Practice

The manner of selecting the president and vice-president of the United States was one of the most difficult matters considered by the American Constitutional Convention of 1787. "The subject has greatly divided this House," James Wilson observed on the floor of the convention. "It is in truth the most difficult of all on which we have to decide." In fact, more than thirty separate votes were taken on the matter. It was only near the very end of the convention that the decision was made to adopt the electoral system which was incorporated in Article II, Section 1, of the U.S. Constitution. The electoral system for selecting the president and vice-president was borrowed from the method for electing state senators in the Maryland constitution of 1776. Gouverneur Morris and James Wilson, delegates from Pennsylvania, were the only delegates to the convention that raised their voices clearly for election by the people. Nevertheless, serious questions have been raised regarding the manner of selecting the president and vice-president since the founding of the republic.

Article II, Section 1, of the U.S. Constitution, provides as follows:

> Each State shall appoint, *in such manner as the legislature thereof may direct*, a number of electors, equal to the whole number of Senators and Representatives to which the State may be entitled in the Congress; but no Senator or Representative, or person holding an office of trust or profit under the United States, shall be appointed an elector.

Thus, the state legislatures determine the manner in which presidential electors are selected. Presidential electors were not always chosen exclusively, or even mainly, by popular vote, as they are today. In the beginning, the state legislature itself elected in a majority of states and the people took no direct part at all. In time popular election of electors was substituted in one state after another; by the time of the Civil War, all states popularly elected their electors. However, in states in which the electors were first chosen by popular vote, it was not unusual for most of the electors to be chosen by congressional districts. In some states one elector was popularly elected from each of the state's congressional districts and two elected from the state at large, since each state has as many electoral votes as it has members of Congress. Under such a system, a state's electoral vote might be split among two or more presidential candidates. Nevertheless, such a system could be adopted by one or all of the state legislatures today. Michigan adopted the district plan in 1891, but only temporarily. Today, the voter casts his ballot for as many electors as the state is entitled to, and the winner, by a majority or plurality vote, captures the entire electoral vote of that state. Since party politicians preferred the general or statewide system, the latter gradually replaced the district arrangement.

The theory of the original U.S. Constitution, which became operational in 1787, was that the electors of a state would consider various persons for the high office of president and vice-president and vote their individual preferences. In the first two presidential elections, 1788 and 1792, every elector wrote the name of Washington on his ballot, and this remains to be equaled in American politics. The electoral vote for vice-president in the first two national elections was divided among a number of individuals, and this freedom of choice on the part of the electors was permitted by the Constitution as drafted. In the third presidential and vice-presidential election, in 1800, every elector, except one, wrote the names of either Jefferson and Burr or Adams and Pinckney. This significant change took place because two political parties—Federalist and Republican—had been organized to capture the American presidency. Each party agreed upon particular candidates for president and vice-president in advance of the elections in the states. Also, members of the two parties prepared lists of men who would, if chosen, cast their electoral ballots in all cases for the persons supported by the party to which they belonged. Such lists were made available to the voters and legislature for their decision.

As a result of the change in the method of selecting the president and vice-president, the door was opened for partisan, popular presidential campaigns, the "tumultuous" features of which the framers were fearful and would have deplored. Presidential electors became merely a rubber stamp, a "row of ciphers." Indirect election of the president and vice-president was replaced by direct election—indeed, a revolutionary change in the American constitutional system which was made possible without amending the U.S. Constitution, or passing a law by Congress, or by a decision of the U.S. Supreme Court.

The Types of Presidents—Vote-Wise

The national House of Representatives consists of 435 members representing the fifty states, and the U.S. Senate consists of 100 members, two senators from each state. According to the Twenty-third Amendment to the U.S. Constitution, the District of Columbia appoints, in such manner as the Congress may direct,

> a number of electors of President and Vice-President equal to the whole number of Senators and Representatives in Congress to which the District would be entitled if it were a State, but in no event more than the least populous State; they shall be in addition to those appointed by the States, but they shall be considered, for the purposes of the election of President and Vice-President, to be electors appointed by a State.

Therefore, there are 538 electoral votes in the nation (435 + 100 + 3), and to be elected by the electors the successful candidates for president and vice-president must receive a majority or more of the total electoral vote (a majority of 538 would be 270 electoral votes).

As a result of the combination of popular electoral votes, a candidate for president or vice-president might be a majority winner since he received a double majority, a majority or more of the electoral vote and a majority or more of the popular vote. This would be possible if there were no third-party presidential and vice-presidential candidates, or if such candidates received a rather limited popular vote.

Since those elected president and vice-president must have a majority or more of the electoral votes, the minority president is determined on the basis of the popular vote. The persons elected president and vice-president may have received only a plurality, or more popular votes than the nearest rival rather than a majority of the popular votes cast for the office. This can happen even if there are only two major tickets in the field. Also, the victorious candidates might not receive even a plurality of the popular vote, since the nearest rival received more popular votes or the winning candidates received less popular votes than the combined popular vote of the nearest rival and popular votes of other candidates. An opposing candidate may have swept the states which he carried by large pluralities and thus accumulated a large number of popular votes; but lacking the required number of electoral votes, the candidate, nevertheless, would be defeated.

Umpiring the Failure of the Electoral College to Elect a President and Vice-President

The Twelfth Amendment of the U.S. Constitution, effective in 1804, which superseded part of Article II of the original Constitution, provides for the meeting of the presidential electors in their respective states and the manner of voting for president and vice-president. Also, provision is made for the selection of these two high officials in the event the Electoral College failed in its allotted task.

The Twelfth Amendment provides that in the event no candidate for president receives a majority of the electoral vote, the election is thrown into the House of Representatives, where each state has one vote as determined by the majority of the state delegation. The amendment provides for selection among "the persons having the highest numbers not exceeding three. . . . A quorum for this purpose shall consist of a member or members from two-thirds of the states, and a majority of all the states shall be necessary to a choice.'' Hence, it would, under such a situation, take a minimum of twenty-six votes in the U.S. House of Representatives to elect a president. The one state-one vote was a victory for the small states in the federal convention of 1787, along with the provision that each state would have two U.S. senators.

If the members of the house of representatives of a particular state could not agree on how the one vote should be cast, the vote of the state would be forfeited. There could be bickering or party conflict within the delegation that might make agreement difficult, if not impossible.

In the event the candidate for vice-president does not receive a majority of the whole number of electors, ''then from the two highest numbers on the list, the Senate shall choose the Vice President; a quorum for the purpose shall consist of two-thirds of the whole number of Senators, and a majority of the whole number shall be necessary to a choice.'' Thus, it would take a minimum of fifty-one votes in the U.S. Senate to elect a vice-president.

To Change the Method of Electing the President and Vice-President

From the time of the constitutional convention of 1787 until today, there has been considerable concern about how the two top executives of the nation should be elected. Over the years there have been any number of proposals, several in the form of proposed constitutional amendments. Since there appears little chance for any significant change to be made, only a few of the proposals will be noted.

1. Elect the president and vice-president by plurality or majority vote of the people. The country would be thrown into a single grand constituency. (By constitutional amendment.)
2. Abolish the electoral college and the electors, but retain the unit electoral vote of each state. The chief election officer of the state (secretary of state in Texas) would, on the basis of the popular plurality vote, cast the entire electoral vote for the candidates who received the most popular votes in the state. (By constitutional amendment.)
3. Discard electors; permit the people to vote directly for president and vice-president; translate popular votes into electoral votes, and allot state's electoral quota among the candidates in proportion to the statewide popular votes polled. (By constitutional amendment.)

The various proposed constitutional amendments in Congress to alter the method of electing the president and vice-president have raised a number of political issues. For example, would direct election of the president and vice-president, by plurality or majority vote, or the translation of the percent of the popular vote into a percent of the electoral vote of each candidate (proportional sharing of the total electoral vote of the state) promote or hinder the interest of the Democratic party? The Republican party? Minor parties? Large states? Or small states? These and other political questions, in addition to the long tradition of the electoral college, make alteration of the system difficult indeed.

The Regulation of Political Activity in Texas

The Texas election code, as amended, provides for the regulation of voting, nominations, elections, campaigns, and convention activity. As interpreted by the courts and the party leaders, these regulations, plus party customs, constitute the rules under which the game of politics is played in Texas. Although lengthy, the code contains three major features: the regulation of political campaigns, the prevention of election fraud, and provisions for the conduct of party politics.

The Regulation of Political Campaigns

At one time in Texas, the campaign cost for governor and U.S. senator in the primary was limited to $10,000 each, and there were limitations on campaign expenses for other offices. The practice of specifying by law the maximum that could be spent by candidates in their campaigns was common in Texas and many other states. The $10,000 figure was written into the Texas law in 1919, and in actual practice it was not realistic. Few, if any, campaigns for governor or U.S. senator were won by the expenditure of a mere $10,000. The purchase of radio and television time by friends of the candidates, paid political advertisements by loyal supporters, as well as the purchase of newspaper space and the hiring of powerful public relations firms by friends and supporters made a mockery of the limitations on campaign expenses. Local, district, and state committees could organize, solicit, and spend funds on various candidates. As long as this was done in an individual or group capacity, no state or public accounting and reporting was required. By these and other devices candidates and their supporters might spend several hundred thousand dollars—or even more than a million dollars—in their particular campaigns. Yet the candidate, in making his official report on expenditures, would stay within the statutory maximum.

The Texas election code eliminates the ceiling on campaign expenses. A candidate may spend as much as he gets his hands on, as long as he or his contributors report the expenditures and contributions. If money flows too freely, however, the mass of the voters might think that the rich candidate and his friends were attempting to purchase the office. Votewise, such action might have serious repercussions. Hence, there is considerable expenditure of funds by individuals and groups rather than by the candidate.

In lieu of the maximum on campaign expenditures, the Texas election code provides for a stricter accounting of real expenditures both by the candidate and by his friends. Each candidate must file sworn itemized financial statements of campaign receipts and expenditures. Each sworn statement must include the names and addresses of all persons from whom money or any other item of value has been received or borrowed by the candidate, his campaign manager or assistant campaign managers, as well as the date and amount of such gifts or loans.

In the event any candidate should fail to file the above sworn statements, or swear falsely in regard to same, such person, upon conviction, is subject to a fine, or may be imprisoned. Such a person forfeits his right to have his name placed upon the ballot at that particular primary or election, or on any subsequent ballot. However, if the qualifications of the office the candidate is seeking are prescribed by the state constitution, the candidate's name cannot be kept off the general election ballot. Only those financial transactions made under the authority of the candidate must be reported. Therefore, the reporting requirement does not guarantee a true picture of campaign finance. Nevertheless, the rather severe penalties prescribed by the election code have encouraged candidates to file more accurate reports of campaign expenses than they did under the old law.

Candidates are required to make financial reports to the secretary of state and county clerk (for county office), within a certain number of days before and after each primary and general election. Candidates frequently declare minimum expenses in the first report and report complete costs only in the final declaration. As a result, publicity about spending is misleading before elections and publicity concerning complete spending comes too late to affect voting. And it is not uncommon for candidates to file the reports after the deadline or fail to file altogether.

Any person making one or more contributions or loans aggregating more than $100 to any candidate for the purpose of furthering his candidacy must ascertain whether the candidate properly reported the contributions or loans. If not reported, it is the duty of the contributor to report the contributions or loans under oath to the proper official. This provision of the law frequently is ignored, and the amount of money spent by friends and supporters of a candidate may never be made public.

The election code provides the purposes for which campaign money may be lawfully spent, and provides a civil penalty in case of violation. Also, the code provides a criminal penalty for an unlawful campaign expenditure by any candidate, campaign manager, or other person.

Corporations and labor unions may not give, lend, or pay any money or other thing of value, directly or indirectly, for the purpose of aiding or defeating the election of any candidate. Any candidate or campaign manager who knowingly receives such a gift or loan, as well as every officer or director of the corporation or labor union, is criminally liable. A labor union or a corporation may conduct political fund-raising drives through special committees for this purpose. Since these funds do not come from the union or corporate treasury, there is no violation of state law.

The legislature established an eleven-member state ethics advisory commission to inform officials what conduct is right and wrong. Those who seek office are prohibited from spending campaign contributions for certain personal purposes.

5   Political Parties

POLITICAL PARTIES, WHETHER AT the state or national level, have both a temporary and permanent party organization. The temporary party organization includes the caucus or conference of party leaders and workers, as well as the party conventions. These caucuses, conferences, and conventions may last a few minutes or several days (if a national convention). The permanent party organization consists of elective or appointive party officers and committees that serve for a definite period—two or four years— and administer party affairs. The temporary party organization in Texas revolves around the two- and four-year convention system and includes all the preconvention and convention party activities at the precinct, county, and state levels.

Temporary Party Organization

State Party Convention Series (Even-Numbered Years)

The county commissioners' court—the administrative and legislative body of the county—divides each county into a number of voting precincts according to population. Each even-numbered year on the first Saturday in May (the first-primary date), the Democratic and Republican voters hold separate precinct conventions. The convention passes resolutions and selects delegates to attend the county or senatorial district convention. These conventions are held the third Saturday in May of each even-numbered year. After the conventions are organized, resolutions are approved and delegates and alternates are selected to attend the state convention.

Each county and senatorial district convention selects delegates for all state conventions held throughout the remainder of the year. This means that delegates and alternates selected at county and senatorial district conventions every fourth and even-numbered year attend both the June state convention (presidential state convention) and the September state convention (regular two-year state convention).

The state convention, which meets in September of each even-numbered year, is called the "Governor's Convention" because it is held after the party's gubernatorial candidate has been nominated in either the first or second primary and the top nominee of the party usually dominates the work of the convention.

The two-year September state convention performs three important functions:
1. It drafts a platform for the gubernatorial and other statewide nominees for the general election in November every fourth year.
2. It must select the state executive committee that is made up of the state chair, vice-chair, secretary, and one man and one woman from each of the thirty-one senatorial districts into which the state is divided. This group constitutes the permanent state party organization for two years. The selection of the chair and the members of the state committee is the most important thing done at the September state convention. The major conflict between liberal and conservative Democrats in Texas centers around the contest to control the state chair and the state executive committee. This group determines how party funds will be spent and recommends the seating of delegates at the state convention. For one faction to control the permanent party organization, its candidate for governor must win the Democratic nomination in the primary.
3. It may change the list of presidential electors nominated at the state June convention every four years. The right of the September state convention to withdraw presidential electors nominated at the June convention and designate others in their place has been upheld by the Texas supreme court as "a matter within the inherent power of the Party" and "a matter that [rests] entirely with the Party."[1]

The precinct, county, senatorial district, and state conventions held during May and September of the even-numbered years have nothing to do with the national party organizations. These conventions are concerned solely with the organization and operation of the state party machinery and for this reason are referred to locally as the state party convention series.

State Presidential Conventions Held Every Fourth and Even-Numbered Year

The Republican and Democratic presidential state conventions are held in June, every four years. These conventions have four important functions:

1. They must nominate the party's presidential electors. Each state is entitled to as many electoral votes as it has congressmen and U.S. senators.
2. The Republican state convention nominates men and women to serve on the Republican National Committee. Later, as a matter of formality, these nominations will be approved at the national convention on what is frequently the last roll call vote in the national party meeting. Texas Democrats also select their national committee members at the June state convention.
3. The June state conventions approve party resolutions with the hope that they may influence the formulation of the national party platform.
4. The Republican and Democratic state conventions in June may select delegates and alternates to the national convention. As a result of party regulations or state law, some or all of the party delegates and alternates may be selected in presidential primaries held in either congressional districts or state senatorial districts. The number of delegates the state party may send to the national convention depends upon the delegate formula for all the states and territories worked out by the national committees of the respective par-

ties. Of course, the national parties can, and do, alter the allocation of delegates and alternates from time to time.

The delegate formulas of the parties have been criticized because they are not based on a "one Democrat (or one Republican), one vote formula." One delegate's vote in the convention may outweigh the vote of other delegates.

The Republican and Democratic parties in Texas could, within limits set by their respective national committees, select more delegates to the national convention than they are entitled to and give each delegate a fractional vote. This would augment the noise-making power of the delegation. However, because of lack of seating space, the national committees are compelled to limit the number of delegates and alternates to the national convention.

The June presidential conventions in Texas every four years are tied in with the national conventions and the national party machinery. These conventions have nothing to do with establishing the permanent party organization in the state, an important function of the regular two-year conventions. Yet there is a relationship between the two series of conventions. The national committeemen and women work with the party organization in the state, and usually the state chairs and state executive committees work with the national committees during a presidential campaign. Nevertheless, there may be friction between the state and national party organization.

Convention Activities

According to the delegate formula law in Texas, each voting precinct is allocated one delegate to the county convention for each 25 votes, or major fraction thereof, cast for the party's candidate for governor in the last general election. Each county is allotted one delegate to the state convention for each 300 votes, or major fraction thereof, cast for the party's candidate for governor in the last general election.

At one time the "unit rule," or the practice of instructing delegates to the next higher convention, was a vital part of the Democratic party in Texas. Under this rule, for example, the delegates selected at a precinct convention by the majority faction could, by party resolution of the convention, be required to cast a single block vote on any action in the county convention. Thus, the minority in the precinct convention had little or no influence in either the precinct or county convention. The unit rule was very undemocratic.

The unit rule encouraged factionalism or infighting, especially in the Democratic party. As a result, individuals and issues were designated frequently either as liberal or conservative, and nothing or little in between, which has continued to some extent to the present time.

The preconvention caucus played an important role. For example, each faction might hold a caucus at a designated time and place in which it would be agreed what person would be nominated chair of the precinct convention, secretary of the convention, and what resolutions would be supported in the precinct convention; a list of delegates to the county convention would be agreed upon as well.

The caucus might agree that the "test vote" of strength in the precinct convention would be made on the selection of a temporary or permanent chair of the convention, or on the selection of the convention secretary. Once the test vote was determined in the convention, the convention could move with speed to complete its work by the appointment of a committee on delegates to the county convention; the appointment of a committee on resolutions; and the report of the committees. Since the majority faction was in complete control, the convention might complete its work within a few minutes, since everything had been agreed upon in the caucus of the majority that had complete convention control. This was known as "railroading the convention."

The minority faction could suffer through the precinct convention or stage a "walkout" and hold their own "rump precinct convention." Whether the delegates and alternates selected at such a gathering would be seated at the county convention would depend upon whether the liberal or conservative faction controlled the county executive committee and the credentials committee of the county convention.

The liberal and conservative Democrats could hold a caucus prior to the county and state conventions, and the infighting, or strategy to control the county or state convention, would be similar to that in the precinct conventions. The delegates of the majority faction in control selected the delegates and alternates to the county and state conventions, and such delegates were "instructed" and placed under the "unit rule"; that is, the allotted votes of the precinct in the county convention—as well as the allotted votes of the county in the state convention—would be cast as "block votes" under the so-called unit rule of the Democratic party in Texas. The minority faction had no representation, other than a token representation, in the next higher convention.

Under national Democratic party rules as they exist today, men, women, young people, and minorities must be represented, under certain conditions, in the group of delegates to the next higher convention. Thus, a departure from the "instructed" delegation and unit rule, so long a vital part of the Democratic party in Texas and the national party rules.

The changes in the national democratic rules, which are binding in the states and territories, are certainly more democratic, but have created considerable confusion; the process may be time consuming in the various party conventions, and has necessitated the use of computers at the conventions, and presented the problems of fractional votes on issues and numbers of delegates. These are difficult matters in the party conventions, where only small number of delegates are allotted to a precinct or county.

Of course, conservative and liberal democrats in Texas are anxious to have as large a representation in the various conventions as possible in order to be entitled to a large delegation to the next higher convention. Therefore, what persons will be elected to chair the convention, or what person will function as secretary is no longer of great importance. Hence, the actual organizing of the convention is less important than under the previous rules. The leaders of groups with similar views will attempt to encourage as many of their supporters as possible to attend conventions.

In the Republican party in Texas there is evidence of some factionalism, but not approaching that in the state's Democratic party. However, the Republican party of the state continues to expand its power and influence in local and national affairs.

Senatorial District Conventions

In addition to the Republican and Democratic precinct and county conventions, some areas in Texas have senatorial district conventions. The law in Texas regulating party activity provides that "whenever the territory of a county forms all or part of more than one state senatorial district, in lieu of the county convention in such county there shall be held a . . . senatorial district convention in each part of the county constituting all or part of each of such senatorial districts," with certain exceptions. Since some of the senatorial districts in the urban counties are liberal and conservative, the county may send split delegations to the state convention.

Permanent Party Organization

Precinct Chair

The precinct chair is elected in either the May or June primary by the party voters of the precinct. Candidates for this office may have their names included on the official primary ballot by filing with the county chairman of their counties.* If no one files for the office of precinct chair, a blank space is left on the ballot for the voter to write in the name of his or her choice. A lot of voters will not take the time or trouble to write in the name of their choice; hence, a write-in candidate might be elected by a small vote. If more than two candidates filed for the office and no one received a majority of the votes cast, the highest two in the first primary would run against each other in the second or run-off primary in June. The successful candidate, elected for a term of two years, assumes the duties of the office one week after the county executive committee declares the results of the run-off primary. The precinct chair receives no compensation.

The precinct chair is the chief party official in the precinct and serves on the county executive committee. For this reason he or she is referred to as both precinct chair and executive committee member. As precinct chair he calls to order the precinct convention (held the first Saturday in May every two years) and presides over it until organized. It may be that those attending the precinct convention will designate the precinct chair as permanent chair of the precinct convention. In such event he would preside throughout the meeting. At the conclusion of the precinct convention, the chair of the precinct convention, with the assistance of the secretary of the convention, must make a written report of all proceedings to the county clerk. The report includes the list of all delegates and alternates elected to the county or senatorial-district convention and copies of all resolutions passed at the convention.

As a member of the county or senatorial-district executive committee, the precinct chair may attend all meetings of the committee, has one vote on each matter before the committee, has the privilege of debate, and making of motions, and may consider and act upon all of the matters that ordinarily come before the county or senatorial-district executive committee.

---

*Party primaries in Texas are financed by reasonable (modest) fees paid by candidates, state funds, and by voluntary contributions. By petition signed by a certain number of voters, a candidate is not required to pay a fee.

County and Senatorial-District Chairs

In counties where there are two or more senatorial districts, there is a senatorial-district party organization. The precinct chairs within a senatorial district elect one of their number as senatorial-district chair. The latter is the temporary chair of the senatorial-district convention.

The county chair is the presiding officer of the county executive committee, elected by the qualified party voters of the entire county in either the May primary, if a candidate receives a majority of the votes cast in the first primary, or in the June run-off. Like the precinct chair, the county chair assumes office one week after the county executive committee has declared the result of the run-off primary election. If the office of county chair becomes vacant, it is filled by a majority vote of the county executive committee. The combined compensation of the secretary (appointed by the county executive committee) and the county chair may not exceed five percent of the amount actually spent for necessary expenses in holding the primary election, exclusive of the compensation of the chair and secretary. The term of office of the county chair is two years.

The county chair is head of the party in the county. He or she presides over all meetings of the county executive committee, calls the county convention to order, and presides over the latter until the convention is organized and a temporary chair of the convention is selected. Under instructions of the county executive committee, he or she posts notices in the voting precincts informing the voters of the time and place of holding the precinct conventions. It is also his or her duty to provide for the holding of the elections in the several voting precincts in the county, to appoint the primary-election judges with the approval of a majority of the county executive committee, and furnish instructions, in writing, to each precinct primary-election judge as to the manner of conducting the primaries. The county chair receives the requests of candidates for county and precinct offices in the county for a place on the primary ballot, and these names are presented to the county executive committee for its approval. Requests to be included on the primary ballot in the county for statewide offices are transmitted to the county chair by the state chair.

Subject to the approval of the county executive committee, the county chair appoints a subcommittee, known as the primary committee, composed of members of the county executive committee. They prepare the official ballot for the primary and fix the order of names thereon. Later the county executive committee, through the county chair, will contract with some firm for the printing of the primary ballots. The county chair receives the returns of the first and second primaries from each precinct primary-election judge and transmits these returns to the county executive committee for canvassing. The primary returns of statewide races are transmitted to the state chair and state executive committee. By such canvassing of the primary returns, candidates for precinct, county, district, and state offices may be certified as winners of the nominations in the first primary. If not, the top two candidates for particular offices will be certified to run against each other in the second primary. Likewise, a similar canvass and certification by the party machinery at the county and state level following the second primary determine the nominees who will represent the party in the November general election.

If more than one group claims to be the regular delegation from the precinct to the county convention, the county chair appoints from the county executive committee a credentials committee to hear the claims of the contesting delegations. After a hearing and finding thereon, the credentials committee makes a report to the county executive committee, which decides the matter.

County and Senatorial Executive Committee

In addition to the county chair and county executive committee in counties with two or more senatorial districts, there is a chair and executive committee for each of the senatorial districts. The precinct chairs within the district compose the district executive committee and also serve on the county executive committee.

The county executive committee is composed of all the precinct chairs in the county. All vacancies in the county executive committee are filled by the latter. The county executive committee receives the reports from the county clerk of the proceedings of the precinct conventions, and from these reports prepares the temporary roll of delegates to the county convention. The committee also approves candidates for the May and June primaries and draws names for places on the ballot and designates the hour and place of holding the precinct conventions. The county executive committee is charged with the duty of distributing the election supplies to the primary-election judges not later than twenty-four hours before the polls open on primary-election day.

As mentioned earlier, the county executive committee canvasses the returns of the first primary for precinct and county office and certifies the names of those who are to participate in the run-off primary. Returns for statewide offices in the first primary are transmitted to the state chair and state executive committee who will canvass and certify the names of those candidates who will participate in the second primary.

Following the second primary, the county executive committee canvasses the returns of the run-off primary for precinct and county office and declares the nominees for these offices as the party's candidates in the following November general election. The returns for state offices in the second primary are transmitted by the county chair and county executive committees to the state chair and state executive committee who certify the party nominees for these offices to the September state convention.

The county executive committee—through its primary committee—prepares and arranges for the printing of the primary ballot in the county. The committee also designates the time and place of the county convention.

The secretary of the county executive committee is chosen by a majority vote of the committee itself. He or she keeps a record of all the proceedings of the committee, is the custodian of its records, signs its minutes along with the chair, and sits as secretary of the county convention until a temporary secretary is chosen.

From what has been said one could conclude that the county chair and county executive committees in the various counties are active and powerful bodies in the party organization. Their supervising of the primary elections in the county and arranging for the county conventions keep the party organization active at the county level. This multitude of functions offers considerable opportunity for controversy if there is a split between conservative and liberal Democrats in the county.

The District Executive Committee

It is common for senatorial, legislative, congressional, judicial, and other districts to include more than one county. For such districts the Texas election code provides for district executive committees, each of which is composed of all the county chair in the district. Persons seeking the Democratic nomination of a district office comprising two or more counties would file with the district executive committee. The latter would canvass the returns and certify the run-off candidates or nominees following the first and second primaries. There are few, if any, district executive committees in operation, and, in practice, a person seeking the nomination of a district office that includes two or more counties would file with the county chair of his party in each county. Each county executive committee would then canvass the returns of the votes for the office cast in the county after the first and second primaries.

State Chair

The chair of the state executive committee is the titular head of the party in the state. He or she is selected for a two-year term at the September convention meeting during the even-numbered years. Hence, the chair is the personal choice of the gubernatorial nominee and, at least in the Democratic party, is the leader of the governor's faction.

The state chair presides over all meetings of the state executive committee, calls the state conventions to order, and remains in authority until the convention is organized and a temporary chair chosen. He or she receives the requests of candidates for state offices to have their names placed on the official primary ballot and, at the direction of the state executive committee, certifies the names of such candidates to the respective county chairs. He or she certifies also the names of the run-off candidates for state office to all county chairs. Upon approval by the state executive committee, he or she certifies the nominees for state office to the state convention that meets in September every two years.

State Executive Committee

This committee is chosen by the September state convention. It consists of a chair, vice-chair, and one man and one woman from each of the thirty-one senatorial districts into which the state is divided. The committeemen and committeewomen are recommended by the delegates at the convention representing the counties composing the respective senatorial districts. These nominations may or not be accepted by the state convention, although the acceptance of these nominations has been the customary practice. The acceptance or nonacceptance of these nominations is a major point of controversy between conservative and liberal Democrats. Members of the committee hold office for two years or until a successor is elected and has qualified. In the event of death, resignation, removal from the district, or other disqualification that vacates the office of any member, a successor is chosen by the state executive committee. In such event this committee must fill the vacancy with a person of the same sex as the vacating member and from the same senatorial district. The secretary of the state executive committee is chosen by the state convention. If the latter fails to act, the state committee itself selects the secretary.

The state executive committee determines the place where the state convention will meet and makes up the temporary roll or list of delegates entitled to participate in state conventions as certified by the various county and senatorial-district chairs. The committee also directs the state chair to certify to the respective county chairs the names of candidates for state offices. The committee places initiatory and proposed constitutional amendments on the ballot when petitions requesting such are presented by the statutory number of names (10 percent of the votes cast at the last primary).

Suggestions for Improving Party Activity in the State

Those who have participated in the Democratic party in Texas have had ample opportunity to observe the tumultuous gatherings of the factions, the conducting of party conventions under police protection, the rump conventions, the shouting, heckling, name-calling, clapping, foot stomping, threatened fist fights, and the snatching and grabbing of microphones. For those that enjoy rough-and-tumble politics, Texas offers unlimited opportunities. It is a truism of politics within the state that all too frequently nothing is more undemocratic than a Democratic convention in Texas.

Party Loyalty

Some Democrats in Texas—both party leaders and individual voters—have supported the nominees of the party for local and state offices in the general election but refused to support the party's nominees for president and vice-president. Thus they placed themselves in a dual role of being state Democrats and national Republicans. Liberal leaders contend one cannot or should not be half-Democrat; rather, support the local, state, and national party ticket. This is the national concept of the party as opposed to the federal or states' rights position.

If the two-party system is to remain responsible, *party leaders* are obligated to support and work through the party; otherwise, they should remove themselves from the party. Honesty and principle could demand nothing less.

Selection of the State Executive Committee

Both conservative and liberal Democrats compose the Democratic state executive committee. Some conservative Democratic gubernatorial nominees have, on occasion, rejected some liberal Democrats who were nominated to serve on the state executive committee. Those rejected were replaced by persons who supported the gubernatorial nominee and his program. As a result, the matter of nominating and selecting the members of the Democratic state executive committee has caused some controversy between conservative and liberal Democrats.

Liberal Democrats contend there is no room for screening within the language of the statute and there is no authority conferred upon the convention, its committees, or subcommittees to alter the recommendations of the senatorial-district caucuses.

The conservative leaders argue that the gubernatorial nominee is the leader of the Democratic party; that he or she should dominate the September convention and should have the authority to handpick the members of the state committee so that the latter support the governor and his program, as well as represent the governor's faction of the party. Liberal leaders counter with the view that such domination of the September state convention by the gubernatorial nominee and his aides is in conflict both with the Texas election code and the theory of representative government within the party.

The faction that controls the state party offices has its foot in the door for controlling the four-year state convention, which selects delegates and alternates to attend the national convention. The fight between liberal and conservative Democrats over control of the state executive committee is usually a preliminary skirmish for control of the four-year state convention.

It has been suggested that the party voters in each senatorial district elect their committeeman and committeewoman in the primary election, but the legislature has not shown much interest in such a proposal. There is some question whether or not judicial action could be invoked to force compliance with the election code provision. Effective judicial action might require legislation in Austin.

Abolish the Precinct Convention

Some of the leaders of the conservative faction of the Democratic party have recommended the abolishment of the precinct convention. The main features of the plan may be summarized as follows:

1. Abolish the "outmoded" precinct convention. The voters in each voting precinct should have the right to popularly elect their delegate to the county convention as precinct chairs are now chosen. Such a delegate would cast the proportionate vote due his precinct at the county or senatorial-district convention.
2. As an alternate plan, the precinct chair could be designated by law as precinct delegate with authority to cast the proportionate vote in the county or senatorial-district convention.
3. Any party voter could attend the county or senatorial-district convention and present resolutions for consideration by the elected delegates.

The proposal to abolish precinct conventions has found little support among liberal Democrats in the state, since precinct conventions are considered "an important vehicle for political expression." Some members of the liberal faction believe the proposal would "do away with the people's forum" in Texas party politics and "take the democracy out of the Texas Democratic party."

A dangerous factor for the liberals is that large numbers of Republicans do vote in the Democratic primaries and many of these Republican voters would join with the conservative Democrats to elect their delegates to the various county or senatorial-district conventions. This, the liberals believe, would perpetuate the control of the party by the conservative faction. The liberals contend that the adoption of a code of ethics for Democratic party procedures would guarantee fair play and honest conventions. In such conventions the liberals feel they can control the party, and, since this is true, the conservatives would rather abolish the precinct-convention system and try to keep control of the party under their own recommended changes. Right or wrong, the liberals argue that with the adoption of either "fair-play rules" or a system of party registration they would become the controlling power in the party. Be this as it may, the internal struggle for power in the Democratic party dominates politics in Texas.

One State Convention in Presidential-Election Years

It does not appear necessary to hold two state conventions in presidential-election years. Every four years the state convention held in June could perform all those party functions currently handled by the June and September state conventions in presidential years.

Formally Recognize Two Democratic Parties in Texas

In actual practice there are two Democratic parties in Texas: the Democratic party and the Liberal Democrats of Texas. Leaders of the conservative faction refer to the Liberal Democrats of Texas as a "splinter group" or "minority faction." They accuse the liberal faction of attempting to "steal" the name and symbol of the party. Accordingly, the conservatives have challenged the liberal Democrats to officially declare the Liberal Democrats of Texas a third party in the state, hold their own conventions, and through separate primaries nominate their own candidates to run in the general election. Since the conservatives have not been very successful with this approach, the state executive committee of the Democratic party has been interested in devising ways and means of preventing the liberals from using the word "Democrats" in their party designation. In this regard the Texas election code provides, "No new political party shall assume the name of any preexisting party; and the party name printed on the official ballot shall not consist of more than three (3) words." Does the name "Liberal Democrats of Texas" amount to an assumption of the name of the preexisting Democratic party in the state? This question could possibly be resolved by court action, whereupon the conservative faction might seek an injunction to prevent the further use of the name "Liberal Democrats."

A solution might be to formally recognize by statute the two factions, for example, the Liberal Democratic party of Texas and the Conservative Democratic party of Texas. Separate conventions and primaries could be held and separate columns, along with the Republican column, could be included on the general election ballot. To recognize formally the two groups would require an amendment to the Texas election code.

Conflict between Conservative and Liberal Factions of the Democratic Party

The conservative faction's support comes from the crude oil, natural gas, and sulphur interests, Texas Manufacturers' Association (TMA), Sons and Daughters of the American Revolution, some of the large daily newspapers, Texas Medical Association, American Legion and Veterans of Foreign Wars, some of the larger public relations firms in the state, and various other groups. Both reactionaries and more moderate conservatives are to be found in this group, and there is little doubt that the conservative faction has greater financial resources than the rival liberal faction.

The conservative program includes the following: it supports constitutional government; integrity in government; states' rights; reduction of federal taxes;

balancing of the budget; general government reform; restoration of Jeffersonian principles; restoration of the two-thirds nominating rule in the Democratic national convention. It opposes organized labor and civil rights legislation; federal aid and control of education; and it is unalterably against federal control over oil, gas, water, and other resources. The program's opposition to the "left-wing elements in the northern Democratic party" is unyielding.

The liberal faction draws its support from organized labor (Texas AFL-CIO); local chapters of NAACP; Negro and Latin-American groups (GI Forum), the Political Association of Spanish-Speaking Organizations (PASO), and the League of United Latin-American Citizens (LULAC); the Democratic Coalition (composed of leaders of Negro, Latin-American, labor and independent liberal groups); some of the newspapers; some intellectuals; supporters of Roosevelt, Truman, Stevenson, Kennedy, and Johnson; and from certain other groups.

Liberal Democrats in Texas have supported the nominees of the national party organization; the Roosevelt, Truman, Kennedy, and Johnson administrations; the right of the U.S. Supreme Court to interpret the federal Constitution and recognition of such decisions as part of the "supreme law of the the land"; federal civil rights legislation; the passage of a party registration law; water conservation; farm-to-market roads; expanded public-health services; just labor-management legislation; and the presidential primary.

Conclusion

An effective democratic system, whether it be the legislative, judicial, or party process, requires general agreement upon fundamental principles of procedure or rules of the game. Without such agreement on fundamentals there is immaturity and lack of stability in the governmental processes. In Texas there is need, as previously observed, for a legal and political framework within which the competitive game of factional politics can be conducted with wisdom and fair play.

The more one involves himself in Texas politics, the more one is led to believe that "Texas remains essentially a one-party state, a 'no-party' state, or if one chooses, a multi-party state."[2]

6   The Legislature

ALEXANDER HAMILTON, IN THE *Federalist* No. 70, pointed out the "almost irre-sistible" tendency in republican governments for the legislative authority to ab-sorb every other: "The representatives of the people are sometimes inclined to fancy that they are the people themselves and to assert an imperious control over the other departments. As they commonly have the people on their side, they al-ways act with such momentum as to make it very difficult for the other members of the government to maintain the balance of the constitution." Whether one believes Texas legislators "fancy that they are the people" and act in the latter's behalf, thus expanding their powers, the trend of which Hamilton spoke can be observed in Texas.

Of the several organs through which the will of the state is expressed in Texas, the legislature unquestionably is paramount, for it exercises tremendous powers by its control over public funds, the constitution, and activities of other state or-gans, and through its power to create public offices and to establish new services or expand old ones. Thus the legislature—whether national or state—is both a law-making body and a regulator of the administrative machinery. In a sense, the law-making power is, and of necessity must be, superior to the executive and judicial branches. This is true because the will of the state must be formulated and ex-pressed before it can be interpreted and enforced.

The Texas constitution, as adopted in 1876, placed numerous restrictions on the legislature and on the executive and judicial branches. Hence, the state legislature was not placed in a disadvantageous power position in the constitution. Through constitutional amendments, the legislature has assumed more and more power. The trend has resulted in the legislature's establishing subsidiary organs (legisla-tive council and legislative budget board) to perform functions that the legislature, either because of its size or its lack of continuity, otherwise could not perform effectively.

The increase of legislative power may be justified in the light of the inadequacy of the Texas constitution and the absence of executive leadership; nevertheless, it represents a radical departure from the original conception of the fundamental law as drafted. The dominant role assumed by the legislature—as opposed to the executive branch—has tended to destroy the equilibrium that is an essential condition in the successful operation of a separation-of-powers system. In a sense, Texas has moved from a system of *separated* to one of *integrated* powers resulting from the ascendancy of the legislature and the decline in the power and prestige of the governor.

The buildup of power in the legislature should encourage voters to consider more seriously candidates for the house and senate. Furthermore, tremendous responsibilities are placed on each member of the legislature not to abuse the power of the office. Of course, the greater the legislative power, the more pressure is applied to the legislative process by vested-interest groups, which in turn make necessary the strengthening of lobby regulations.

Legislative and Nonlegislative Powers of the Legislature

Legislative Powers

In a general sense, the legislative power is synonymous with lawmaking and is exercised by the legislative department when it frames, considers, and enacts bills and resolutions. The drafting of these bills, reference to committees, committee consideration, action on the floor of the two houses, working out a compromise in the event the houses are in disagreement, submission of the work of the legislature to the governor, and reconsideration by the legislature in case the governor should veto represent phases of the legislative power.

Simple Resolution

A simple resolution is an expression of opinion by one house relating to the organization and procedure of the chamber or it may relate to some other subject. These resolutions are not sent to the governor and they may or may not be referred to a committee. Examples of simple resolutions include requests for the return of bills from the governor, house, or senate for further consideration or correction; assignment of desks for members; fixing salaries of officers of the house or senate; adoption of temporary rules; requesting an opinion of the attorney general on a particular subject; extension of the privilege of the floor to persons not members of the house or senate; fixing the order of business.

Concurrent Resolutions

Concurrent resolutions require action by both houses and, with few exceptions, these resolutions are sent to the governor for his signature. Termination of the legislative session or final adjournment (*sine die*) is by concurrent resolution and is not submitted to the governor.

Other illustrations of concurrent resolutions are: to recess for three or four days; to suspend the joint rules to consider a certain house or senate bill; to memorialize congress; to instruct the enrolling clerk of the house or senate to make certain corrections in a bill; to permit suing the state (may take the form of a bill); to recall a bill from the governor's office for correction (may take the form of a simple house or senate resolution); to provide for an investigation by a committee composed of members from both houses.

· *Joint Resolutions*

Constitutional amendments take the form of a joint resolution and require a two-thirds vote of all the members elected to each house. Also, the joint-resolution form may be used to ratify a proposed amendment to the U.S. Constitution in the event Congress, in the amendment, specified ratification by state legislatures. The legislative product in Austin may take one of several forms.

BILLS:	H. B. No.___	RESOLUTIONS:	H. S. R.	No.___
	S. B. No.___		S. R.	No.___
			H. C. R.	No.___
			S. C. R.	No.___
			H. J. R.	No.___
			S. J. R.	No.___

Nonlegislative Powers

State legislatures concern themselves with numerous functions that do not come within the strict classification of legislative powers. In Texas, the nonlegislative powers of the state legislature may, for the sake of convenience, be classified as constituent, electoral, executive, directory and supervisory, investigative, and judicial.

Constituent Powers

A "constituent" is a person who has given authority to another to act for him. The constituents of a legislator are those whom he represents—sometimes referred to as the electors of his district. Consequently, it could be said that all powers of the legislature, both legislative and nonlegislative, are constituent powers, since the legislature acts as agent of the people. However, to distinguish between regular lawmaking powers and the power to alter the constitution of the state, by amendment or complete revision, the term "constituent power" of the legislature has come into use.

Unlike some states, Texas does not have the constitutional initiative whereby 10 percent or so of the people who voted in the last general election may sign a petition, file it with the proper state official, and have a proposed constitutional amendment submitted to the people with or without prior consideration in the legislature. The only way a constitutional amendment may be proposed is by the legislature and, if it is approved by the legislature, by submission to the people at a general or special election. Therefore, in Texas, as regards the amending process, we have optional legislative initiation and obligatory constitutional referendum.

On the other hand, bills may be introduced in regular and special sessions (the constitution requires that the subject matter be within the topics included in the governor's call for a special session), passed by a simple majority vote, and not submitted to the people. To establish a constitutional commission or authorize the legislative council to make a study of the constitution and possibly submit a redraft, as well as to submit the question of calling a constitutional convention, would require action in the legislature.

Electoral Powers

According to the Texas constitution, and unless otherwise provided by law, the returns of the election (in November) for governor, lieutenant governor, comptroller of public accounts, treasurer, commissioner of the general land office, and attorney general are transmitted by the returning officers to the secretary of state, who delivers the returns to the speaker of the house as soon as the latter is chosen in January every odd year. It then becomes the duty of the speaker, in the presence of both houses, to open and publish the returns, declaring those executive officers with the highest number of votes (plurality) for each office to be elected. In contested elections, or if two or more candidates have the highest and equal number of votes, one of them would be chosen by joint vote of both houses. This joint session, which sits as a canvassing board and umpires in case of ties and contested elections, is of little significance. There would seldom, if ever, be a tie or a contest of the election. Consequently, the electoral power of the legislature is a mere formality.

Executive Powers

The Texas senate confirms by a two-thirds vote or rejects gubernatorial appointees. The selection of the speaker of the house and the president pro tempore of the senate, the designation of chairmen and members of committees, and the selection of sergeant at arms, pages, and other house and senate employees constitute part of the executive powers of each house.

Directory and Supervisory Powers

The legislature has considerable control over the administrative machinery. It establishes boards and commissions, determines their functions, provides them with funds, subjects the agencies to periodic investigation and review, receives annual reports from some of the agencies, and exercises general directory and supervisory control over the administrative organization. Some review of the departments, boards, and commissions occurs when representatives of these agencies appear before legislative committees to defend budgetary requests for each biennium. The legislative budget board, composed of members of both houses, selects the budget director, who prepares the state budget covering the expenditures of all agencies of the state for the next two years. The legislature also appoints the state auditor, who is responsible to the legislature. Irregularities and inefficiency in accounting, as well as any misapplication of public funds, might be uncovered either by the state auditor or the budget director. Officers of the executive branch could be impeached by the house and tried and convicted in the senate.

Investigative Powers

Legislative investigations may be conducted by the house and senate as a body or, more commonly, by standing or special committees composed of members of one or both houses. The resolution directing a committee to make an investigation normally would indicate the agency, topic, or activity to be probed, the reasons for the inquiry, and possibly the nature of the charges. The committees may subpoena witnesses, administer oaths, and compel the presentation of books and papers. For refusal to appear or to answer pertinent questions, or for failure to produce books and papers, a witness might be held in contempt of the legislature. Of course those appearing before legislative committees in Texas may refuse to answer on grounds of self-incrimination. The bill of rights of the Texas constitution (Art. I, Sec. 10) provides that in all *criminal prosecutions* the accused shall not be compelled to give evidence against himself. This protection against self-incrimination has been interpreted to apply not only to an accused person on trial before a jury, but to proceedings before a grand jury, a legislative committee of inquiry, or in fact to any legal proceeding. When the investigation is completed, the committee findings and recommendations, if any, are reported to the legislature, which may or may not pass remedial legislation.

Judicial Powers

Under its judicial action the legislature can decide, pronounce judgment, and carry into effect its investigative findings. Whatever is uncovered by an investigating committee is turned over to the legislature, grand jury, or prosecutors for further action. Such action involves, at least in part, judicial procedures. In the exercise of the judicial function each house is the judge of the qualifications and election of its own members (contested elections are determined as provided by law) and may "punish members for disorderly conduct, and, with the consent of two-thirds, expel a member, but not a second time for the same offense." Each house may "compel the attendance of absent members, in such manner and under such penalties as each House may provide." Furthermore, each house "may punish, by imprisonment, during its sessions, any person not a member, for disrespectful or disorderly conduct in its presence, or for obstructing any of its proceedings; provided, such imprisonment shall not, at any one time, exceed forty-eight hours." The governor, lieutenant governor, attorney general, treasurer, commissioner of the general land office, comptroller, and the judges of the supreme court, court of appeals and district courts may be impeached in the house and tried in the senate. In impeachment proceedings, the house sits as a grand jury to hear the charges and decide whether an indictment should be brought against the officeholder. If the indictment were presented to the senate, the latter would resolve itself into a "high court of impeachment" to try the party impeached on the charges. Conviction requires the concurrence of two-thirds of the senators present. Judgment in cases of impeachment extends only to removal from office and disqualification from holding any office of honor, trust, or profit under the state. Any further action against an officeholder so removed and disqualified would have to be taken in the regular state courts.

Organization and Structure

Size, Term, Vacancies

The Texas constitution is specific on the maximum size of both houses. "The Senate shall consist of 31 members, and shall never be increased above this number" and "the number of Representatives shall never exceed 150." Since Texas has reached the maximum of 181 house and senate members, any enlargement of either house would require a constitutional amendment. One may doubt the wisdom of freezing in the constitution such a limitation since the legislature should have more freedom in determining the size of each house. The legislature must reapportion legislative seats within the above limitation.

House and senate members are elected for two- and four-year terms, respectively. Half of the senators are elected every two years. After redistricting every ten years, Texas state senators draw slips of paper, numbered one through thirty-one, from a box. The sixteen senators drawing odd numbers get four-year terms, the others two. When vacancies occur in either house, the governor issues writs of election to fill them. If the governor should fail to order an election within twenty days after the vacancy occurred, the returning officer of the particular district is authorized to order an election for the purpose.

The Texas constitution requires state legislators to develop and deliver to the secretary of state a list of potential successors to assume the reins of government should lawmakers become "unavailable" because of a nuclear war or enemy attack. The governor is authorized to convene the legislature in secret when there exists "the immediate threat of an enemy attack." The constitution and enabling legislation do not define "immediate threat"; this decision rests with the governor with no provision for legislative review. The latter might not be practicable in time of grave emergency. If a legislator does not designate successors, the lieutenant governor and speaker of the house will designate successors. In event of an attack, the secretary of state notifies the highest (on the lists) surviving designees of their assumption of the duties of a legislator. Each legislator is required to designate at least three, but not more than seven, names.

Qualifications

A member of the Texas house of representatives must be (1) at least twenty-one years of age, (2) a citizen of the United States, (3) a qualified elector of the state, and (4) a resident of the state for two years preceding the election—the last year thereof a resident of the district from which elected.

The requirements for membership in the senate are somewhat higher than those of house members. A senator must be (1) at least twenty-six years of age, (2) a citizen of the United States, (3) a qualified elector of the state, and (4) a resident of the state for five years preceding the election—a resident of the district during the last year.

Compensation and Social Security

The Texas constitution provides that members of the legislature shall receive a salary of $7,200 a year and a per diem for each day during regular and special legislative sessions. Also, the members of each house are entitled to mileage at the rate prescribed by law for state employees. Legislators are provided funds out of the legislative contingent fund for secretarial assistance, telephone service, postage, and stationery. The speaker of the house and the lieutenant governor, as presiding officers of the two houses, receive the same pay as house and senate members; additionally, an apartment is made available for each in the capitol building.

Each house, by resolution, may provide its members a monthly expense allowance for the interim period between regular sessions. The purpose of the additional funds may or may not be specified in the house or senate resolution. A portion of these funds may be used by legislators to pay for the operation of a permanent office in Austin, as well as one or more offices in the legislative or senatorial district. Personnel in these offices take care of the mail flow, write and make speeches, draft letters, meet with constituents, perform research on and draft bills, attend meetings, coordinate the house or senate member's schedule, operate a word processor, and take care of many other matters for the legislators. If the legislator serves as chairman or member of one or more interim committees, state funds are available for research and staff work for such committees.

House and senate members are covered by Social Security, at no cost to the legislators—since the state, as employer, contributes to the federal Social Security fund and has assumed the payments that otherwise would be made monthly by its employees (state legislators). Also, members of the legislature belong to the state employee-retirement system.

Other Benefits

Nepotism, favoritism shown to relatives, especially in appointment to desirable positions, is prohibited by law in Texas. State officials are forbidden to hire their relatives. However, Texas legislators, as well as heads of state administrative agencies, have employed each other's relatives as a means of attempting to circumvent this statute, which provides that no legislator "shall appoint, or vote for, or confirm the appointment of" certain close relatives or persons closely related to other members of the legislature. Violation of the law is a criminal offense punishable by fine.

Legislators may be retained by individuals and interest groups as legal or business consultant (40 to 50 percent of the legislators are lawyers). These retainers (fees) are legal in Texas, although they may constitute a conflict of interest. The legislators have shown little or no interest in legally prohibiting or restricting these retainers. Even if such legislation were enacted, the matter of conflict of interest would remain, since favors could be bestowed in various ways, e.g., advice on investments, purchase of company stock, purchases at below cost, employment of relatives, and donations of campaign funds. Conflict of interest is a perennial problem in democratic government.

The many personal contacts members of the legislature have with individuals and interest groups in their legislative districts promote their own economic interest—and possibly more clients for the lawyer-legislators. Members of the legislature, as with all public officials, must be concerned constantly with the promotion of favorable public relations.

State law in Texas permits legislators who are attorneys to request postponements (or legislative continuances) of any civil or criminal court proceedings that may conflict with their state duties while the legislature is in session. Legislative continuances filed by attorney-lawmakers tend to "delay justice." In criminal cases, delay may undermine the state's case since witnesses' memories tend to fade with time. However, criminal defense lawyers contend they need the continuance privilege to effectively prepare their clients' defense and serve in the legislature. On the other hand, these postponements could be left to the discretion of state judges, as is the practice in federal court, where automatic legislative continuances are not granted.

By law, state legislators who are attorneys may delay court action on cases during a regular or special legislative session, as well as thirty days before and after a session. The trial judge has the option of denying a postponement in a case where an attorney-legislator was employed within ten days before a case was set for trial. However, the Texas supreme court has made an exception to the law by declaring a judge could deny a continuance if the party opposing it would suffer irreparable harm from delay. Legislative continuances provide an additional source of income for attorney-lawmakers in Texas.

Each house, by resolution, may provide its members a monthly expense allowance for the interim until the next regular session. The purpose of the additional salary may or may not be specified in the resolution.

Privileges

Except in cases of treason, felony, or breach of the peace, legislators are privileged from arrest during the session of the legislature, and in going to and returning from the latter. This immunity would appear to prohibit only arrests in *civil suits* at a time that would interfere with the performance of legislative business. Members may not be questioned in any other place for words spoken in debate in either house, and this immunity applies to statements made before committees. Each house may discipline members for excesses by calling a member to order or censure; by two-thirds vote, a member may be expelled.

Legislative Sessions

The constitution states that "The Legislature shall meet every two years at such time as may be provided by law and at other times when convened by the Governor." As provided by law, the regular session convenes the second Tuesday in January at noon in odd-numbered years. A regular session may not exceed 140 days and a special session called by the governor may not exceed 30 days.

A legislature covers a two-year period. If the legislature meets only in regular session, there is only one session during the two-year period. However, the governor may call one or more special sessions of a particular legislature. The political repercussions resulting from a special session and the expense involved limit the calling of such sessions.

Redistricting

Prior to the U.S. Supreme Court decisions in the 1960s, the Texas constitution provided no county could have more than seven representatives unless the population of the county exceeded 700,000 people, in which event the county was entitled to one additional representative for each 100,000 persons in excess of 700,000. Also, the Texas constitution provided no county was entitled to more than one senator. These provisions were included in the fundamental law at the time Texas government was rural controlled. As a result, legislative "misrepresentation," or the overrepresentation of the rural areas and underrepresentation of the urban areas in the state legislature, was recognized in the state constitution. With the increase in population, a person in a rural legislative district with fewer people might cast a vote for house or senate members that might outweigh the vote of a person in a populated urban district 500 to 1.

According to Article III, Section 28, of the Texas constitution, "The Legislature *shall*, at its first regular session after the publication of each United States decennial census, apportion the state into senatorial and representative districts." The Texas legislature redistricted in 1921, but failed to redistrict following the 1930 and 1940 federal censuses, despite the constitutional mandate. The failure of the legislature to redistrict was a "silent gerrymander"* and, along with the constitutional provisions concerning apportionment and redistricting, created a "rotten borough" system.†

Colegrove *v.* Green[1]

Although involving congressional districts, the U.S. Supreme Court, in *Colegrove* v. *Green* (1946), held that the issue was political in nature and that the remedy lay with the Illinois legislature and not with the courts. "The remedy," so said the Court majority, "of unfairness in districting is to secure state legislatures that will apportion properly, or to invoke the ample powers of Congress." Notwithstanding strong dissent, the principle announced in *Colegrove* v. *Green,* by a four-to-three decision, remained the law of the land until 1962.

The majority opinion in *Colegrove* v. *Green* was not very realistic. In many states the legislature was controlled by rural legislators who had no desire to pass a redistricting act or propose an amendment to the state constitution that would increase urban representation and decrease rural representation. Neither would the voters in the rural districts elect legislators who favored such action. There was no chance that "the ample powers of Congress be invoked" in the matter of congressional districts because of the power and influence of the rural areas in Congress, especially in the House of Representatives. Few steps were taken to provide fair and equitable representation in the state legislative and congressional districts from 1946 to 1962.

Under rural control, rural legislators in Texas had considerable influence in selecting the speaker of the house, passing legislation, approving proposed constitutional amendments, enacting the governor's legislative program, confirming the governor's appointments, and determining where and how the state's money would be appropriated. Many rural legislators held key assignments as chairmen and vice-chairmen of important committees. The rural legislators showed little interest in the problems of urban areas, and they believed organized labor should be restricted.

---

*The terms "gerrymander" and "gerrymandering" were coined around 1800 when Elbridge Gerry of Massachusetts carved out a legislative district in the shape of a salamander that was referred to as a "gerrymander." The terms came to mean any attempt by a party or faction in the legislature to establish legislative districts in such a way as to scatter opposition votes in many districts or concentrate them in as few districts as possible. A successful gerrymander prevented the opposition from electing any representatives or only a limited number. Unfair and inequitable representation was the consequence of such action.

†In England prior to the Reform Act of 1832, many boroughs contained but few voters, yet retained the privilege of sending a member to Parliament.

From Rural to Urban Control of the Texas Legislature

The Legislative Redistricting Board: An Attempted Solution in Texas

The increase in population in south and west Texas, as well as in the urban areas, necessitated legislative action if representative government was not to become a farce. Representatives and senators of the underrepresented areas joined in support of a constitutional amendment that created the legislative redistricting board of Texas to redistrict the state after each decennial census if the legislature failed to act. The amendment was adopted November 2, 1948, and became effective January 1, 1951.

The legislative redistricting board is composed of the lieutenant governor, the speaker of the house, the attorney general, the comptroller of public accounts, and the commissioner of the general land office. If the legislature should fail to apportion the state into senatorial and representative districts at the first regular session following the publication of the decennial census, the apportionment will be done by the redistricting board. The board must assemble within ninety days after the final adjournment of such regular session; and within sixty days after assembling, it is directed to submit the apportionment plan to the secretary of state. If signed by three or more board members, the plan has the force of law after submission to the secretary of state. Under the amendment the supreme court of Texas can compel the commission to perform its duties.

Since the legislature did redistrict in 1951 and 1961 (giving control of both houses to the urban areas), the board may have provided a "spur on the flank" to the legislature. The house of representatives was redistricted in 1971, but the legislature could not agree on senatorial redistricting and the governor requested that the board take action.

Baker *v*. Carr[2]

In 1962 the U.S. Supreme Court ruled lower federal courts may determine whether city voters are unconstitutionally discriminated against in the apportionment of legislative seats. "We have no cause at this stage," said the Court, "to doubt the district court will be able to fashion relief if violations of constitutional rights are found." The decision did not provide any guidelines or advise the lower court *how* to proceed.

If a state legislature failed to redistrict, or passed a redistricting act that was held invalid because it did not provide fair and equitable representation, the federal district court could draw up a redistricting plan. If the state legislature should refuse to adopt the plan, the federal district court might order an at-large election in which all legislative candidates must be voted on statewide, instead of by districts. The urban areas would control the election of legislators elected at-large.

State legislators do not want the federal district courts to draw up a redistricting plan or order at-large elections.

Reynolds *v*. Sims[3]

In 1964, in a historic six-to-three decision, the U.S. Supreme Court held that both houses of a bicameral state legislature must be apportioned on a population basis.

Chief Justice Warren declared

As long as ours is a representative form of government, and our legislatures are those instruments of government elected directly by and directly representative of the people, the right to elect legislators in a free and unimpaired fashion is a bedrock of our political system.

We hold that, as a basic constitutional standard, the Equal Protection Clause [of the U.S. Constitution] requires that the seats in both houses of a bicameral state legislature must be apportioned on a population basis.

But was not the issue "political" in nature? To this the Court replied:

We are cautioned about the dangers of entering into political thickets and mathematical quagmires. Our answer is this: a denial of constitutionally protected rights demands judicial protection; our oath and our office require no less of us.

Since the U.S. Senate is not based on population, may a state's senate be apportioned on a basis other than population? According to the Court,

The original constitutions of 36 of our States provided that representation in both houses of the state legislatures would be based completely, or predominantly, on population. And the Founding Fathers clearly had no intention of establishing a pattern or model for the apportionment of seats in state legislatures when the system of representation in the Federal Congress was adopted.

Furthermore,

Political subdivisions of States—counties, cities, or whatever—never were and never have been considered as sovereign entities. Rather, they have been traditionally regarded as subordinate governmental instrumentalities created by the State to assist in the carrying out of state governmental functions.

The Supreme Court said it realized

that it is a practical impossibility to arrange legislative districts so that each one has an identical number of residents, or citizens, or voters. Mathematical exactness or precision is hardly a workable constitutional requirement . . . the Equal Protection Clause [of the Constitution] requires that a State make an honest and good faith effort to construct districts, in both houses of its legislature, as nearly of equal population as is practicable.

The Court suggested redistricting every ten years. The Court did not say that each state had to redistrict every year because of the population changes. Such continuous redistricting would be impractical.

The U.S. Supreme Court and the 1964 decision have been subjected to severe criticism. Some said the issues were "political" rather than "judicial" in nature; that the Court "legislated" and "amended" the U.S. Constitution; that the decision interfered with a fundamental right of the states.

It has been suggested that the national Constitution be amended to overrule all or part of the U.S. Supreme Court decision. One proposal would amend the Constitution to permit representation in the state senate on some basis other than (or in addition to) population.

Some who agreed with the decision said the failure of the states to protect constitutionally guaranteed rights, or operate within the framework of the U.S. Constitution, created a void that made it necessary for the federal courts to intervene. Furthermore, it was said the states could have prevented federal intervention by recognizing rights guaranteed to the people by the Fourteenth Amendment: that the initial decision rested with the states. It has been said that to recognize equality of voting and to protect constitutional rights will *strengthen* the states and thereby strengthen the American democratic system.

Whether the Court did legislate or amend the Constitution depends on what one means by "legislating" and "amending." It is the contention of some that all courts, whether federal or state, legislate when they interpret constitutions and laws, and their decisions may, on occasion, be construed as amending the Constitution; that the judiciary could not operate otherwise. If this be true, the U.S. Supreme Court has been legislating and amending the Constitution ever since it decided the first case, and it will continue to do so.

Kirkpatrick v. Preisler[4]

The constitutional standard of equal representation for equal numbers of people "as nearly as practicable" was established in an earlier case. In 1969 the Court found it necessary to elucidate the "as nearly as practicable" standard.

> We reject Missouri's argument that there is a fixed numerical or percentage population variance small enough to be considered *de minimis* and to satisfy without question the "as nearly as practicable" standard. The whole thrust of the "as nearly as practicable" approach is inconsistent with adoption of fixed numerical standards which excuse population variances without regard to the circumstances of each particular case. The extent to which equality may practicably be achieved may differ from State to State and from district to district . . . the "as nearly as practicable" standard requires that the State make a good-faith effort to achieve precise mathematical equality. . . . Unless population variances among congressional districts are shown to have resulted despite such effort, the State must justify each variance, no matter how small.

The Court could see no nonarbitrary way to determine a cut-off point at which population variances became *de minimis*. "Moreover, to consider a certain range of variances *de minimis* would encourage legislators to strive for that range rather than for equality as nearly as practicable."

The Constitution, in the view of the U.S. Supreme Court, "permits only the limited population variances which are unavoidable despite a good-faith effort to achieve absolute equality, or for which justification is shown." The Court felt the population variances among the Missouri congressional districts were not unavoidable; rather, they resulted from an expedient political compromise.

As the population of the urban counties increased, the counties gained additional house and senate members. The members of the house of representatives from the urban counties were nominated and elected county-wide for position or place (1,2,3,4 etc.), rather than from single-member districts within the counties. The county at-large election of Texas legislators was to the disadvantage of the Spanish-speaking and black people, as well as of Republicans. In time the federal courts voided the county-at-large nomination and election of legislators and required the urban counties to be divided into the appropriate number of single-member districts of approximate equal numbers of persons.

Political Impact of the Redistricting Decisions in Texas

Upon retiring in 1969, after sixteen years as presiding judge, Chief Justice Earl Warren said the redistricting decisions of the "Warren Court" would have the greatest long-term impact upon the American democratic system. Assuming the decisions will not be overruled by the U.S. Supreme Court or by an amendment to the U.S. Constitution, what will be their political consequences in Texas in five, ten, or fifty years?

The one man-one vote, and equal representation for equal numbers of people "as nearly as practicable," is applicable to state legislative and congressional districts, county commissioners' precincts,[5] local school boards, and other governmental bodies that exercise general governmental powers.

Within the limitations of the 1969 U.S. Supreme Court decision, the politics of redistricting will continue; the conflict will, however, be within and among urban areas rather than between rural and urban areas. To redraw the boundaries of legislative districts has a direct effect on legislators seeking reelection. Other than this practical consideration, the conflict between labor and management, liberals and conservatives, as well as the concern of lobbyists, make equitable redistricting by the legislature difficult.

Will redistricting encourage the growth of the two-party system in Texas? Both Republican and Democratic strength is concentrated in the big cities and the suburbs, and the urban areas dominate the permanent state party organization. Although some Republican state legislators and congressmen have been elected in Texas, a vigorous two-party system appears to be far from a reality. However, Republican presidential and vice-presidential candidates may carry the state in some elections. Redistricting might be stimulus to the two-party system in Texas. Both liberals and conservatives will continue to increase their strength in Texas in the urban areas; which will increase more is a matter of speculation.

The requirement of single-member districts within the urban counties, rather than the election of legislators county-wide, has been a factor in the election of more black, Spanish-speaking, and Republican representatives to the Texas legislature.

Labor, management, and other pressure groups and lobbyists, as well as the rural-urban conflict, were important factors in the legislative process when the legislature was controlled by the rural counties. But since direct conflicts between the rural and urban counties as such were rare, there has not been as much change with the increase in urban representation as some persons anticipated.

There are now fewer legislators to support what urbanites consider rural prejudices. Legislation has been passed favorable to the urban areas; for example, the optional municipal sales tax. Farm-to-market roads have become less popular subjects of legislation. State highway programs, once shaped by a rural legislative majority, have become more urban oriented. With the increase of political power of organized labor in the urban areas, the Texas legislature enacted a minimum-wage law. Thus more equitable representation has influenced the substantive aspect of legislation in Texas.

Despite these developments, persons from rural areas may be selected speaker of the house and rural legislators may hold key committee assignments. Thus rural legislators and the lobbyists who influence them may have considerable power in any legislative session.

Occupations of Texas Legislators

Texas legislators have various occupations other than their part-time one of law-making. Lawyers probably constitute a majority in both houses in most sessions of the legislature. The other legislators may be involved in farming, ranching, public relations, insurance, newspaper work, radio-television, the oil industry, education, and many may be university students.

To a degree the predominance of lawyers in both houses lends a conservative tone to legislative policy. Yet there are both liberal and conservative lawyers, and many practicing attorneys formed some views on politics before finishing law school. Of course if a lawyer-legislator receives a substantial retainer as a legal adviser for some firm his interest would of necessity be associated rather closely with that of the firm he represents. The association could be so intimate on occasion as to raise the issue of "conflict of interest" or the conflict between public trust and private interest. In such event the legal adviser of a corporation who sits in the legislature would likely support the legislative program of his employer. The continuation of his retainer is dependent upon his support of the economic interest he represents.

The number of house and senate members retained is not recorded. It takes a scandal and an investigation to make public much information on the retainership system.

Legislative Assistance (Public)

An important development in the state legislative process generally has been to make more research and technical facilities available to state legislators. Unlike some states, Texas does not have a bill-drafting agency, although legislators may call upon certain agencies and individuals for assistance.

The Attorney General's Staff

A committee or individual legislator in Texas may secure some help in drafting a bill from the staff of the attorney general. If in doubt about the constitutionality of a proposed bill, the legislature may seek an advisory opinion from the attorney general.

The Legislative Reference Library

The legislative reference library is an invaluable aid to the legislature, other public officials, and the general public. The library keeps records of the legislative history of all bills and resolutions introduced in the legislature, showing which ones were introduced in the preceding sessions, by whom, and the outcome. It also provides information to the legislators on what legislative action has been taken in the other states on a particular topic. Needless to say, the library is a busy place during legislative sessions.

The Legislative Council

The president of the senate and speaker of the house are ex-officio members of the council and serve as chair- and vice-chairpersons, respectively. Other members of the council include four senators appointed by the president of the senate; nine representatives appointed by the speaker of the house; and the chair persons of the senate and house administration committees. The council is a study committee with broad powers to make investigations for the legislature, as well as prepare draft legislation based on its recommendations.

The council staff consists of an executive director and a varying number of other employees. The executive director and his staff conduct most of the research carried on by the council.

Legislative research and bill drafting by the council staff are supposed to be objective; however, final decisions must be made by members of the council. Since all or some of its members are on the speaker's or president of the senate's team, political considerations are an important factor in the appointment of members and in the work of the council.

Between legislative sessions, the council staff is generally assigned to research projects under the direction of the council members. When the legislature is in session the council's staff receives requests from individual legislators and chairmen for bill and resolution drafts, information on legislation, bill analysis, and bill or resolution amendments. About half of the house and senate members call on the council staff for assistance during each regular session. A number of bills and amendments drafted by the staff of the council have been enacted into law. Statutes are better drawn when based upon research by a capable staff experienced in state government.

Members of the legislature who serve on the council gain considerable insight into the operation of state government. This educative function has its place in the legislative process.

As the work of the legislative council continues to expand, it tends to decrease the power of the governor. A program drafted by a council of legislators and citizens appears to have a better chance than recommendations made by the governor.

The Legislative Budget Board

Texas has a rather unusual budget procedure. The legislative budget board is composed of the speaker of the house and the four members of the house appointed by the speaker (including the chairman of the appropriations committee and the chairman of the revenue and taxation committee). The lieutenant governor, who is a member of the board, appoints four members of the senate (including the chairman of the finance committee and the chairman of the state-affairs committee) to the board. A director of the budget, who serves for a period of one year from September 1 of each year, unless sooner discharged, is appointed by the board. According to the law creating the agency: "The Director of the Budget shall, within five days after the convening of any Regular Session of the Legislature, transmit to all members of the Legislature and to the Governor copies of the budget of estimated appropriations prepared by him." The director of the budget prepares the general appropriation bills for introduction at each regular session of the legislature.

The work of the director of the budget and his staff, which operate under the supervision of the legislative budget board, duplicates the work of the director of the budget in the executive office of the governor. As a result, each department, institution, and agency of the state must submit budget estimates and reports to both agencies and participate in budget hearings conducted by both agencies. The state ends up with two budgets; but the legislature tends to follow the budget prepared by its own agency. This duplication is wasteful and contrary to sound budgetary procedure. This development in Texas illustrates the trend in the legislature to further undermine executive functions in the state.

Comptroller of Public Accounts

The comptroller of public accounts, in advance of each regular session of the legislature, prepares and submits to the governor and legislature (upon its convening) a statement under oath showing the financial condition of the state treasury at the close of the last fiscal period and an estimate of the probable receipts and disbursements for the current fiscal year. The report of the comptroller is an aid to the legislature in considering the budget and taxation.

7 Legislative Procedure and the Politics of Legislation

BILLS AND RESOLUTIONS MAY be drafted by individual legislators with the aid of the legislative council or the staff of the attorney general, by someone in the executive branch, by local officials, or by lawyers employed by various interest groups. Bills may take one of several forms.

Types of Bills

1. *Remedial Bills.* Remedial bills are designed to make improvements in existing law. The old law may be either amended or replaced.
2. *General Bills.* General bills apply to the whole state or apply uniformly to all persons or things within a class.
3. *Local, Special, and Private Bills.* Local bills affect one or more specific cities, towns, counties, school districts, judicial districts, precincts, drainage or flood-control districts. Special bills provide exceptions to general laws. Private bills grant benefit or privilege to an individual, class, or corporation.
4. *Civil and Criminal Statutes.* Civil statutes provide for the enforcement or protection of private rights, or the prevention or redress of private wrongs. Domestic relations, contracts, and all manner of suits for damage are covered by civil statutes, as are such matters as public education, local government, and charities. Criminal or penal statutes establish certain actions as offenses against the public and impose punishment if the statutes are violated. Punishment for robbery, rape, theft, murder, and manslaughter, among other criminal violations, are covered by the statutes, and the state will prosecute persons who violate them.

The Mechanics of a Bill

A bill, of whatever type, has all or some of the following features:

1. *Caption.* The title of a bill is referred to as the caption. It contains a brief summary of the contents of the bill, which provides a ready reference as to the nature of the bill. A bill placed on the desk of the speaker of the house or the president of the senate would be read by caption and then referred to committee. Such action would constitute the first reading.

2. *Enacting Clause.* The Texas constitution stipulates that the enacting clause of all laws shall be: "Be it enacted by the Legislature of the State of Texas." The enacting clause indicates official action in the state legislature. When a city council passes a city ordinance the enacting clause reads "Be it ordained by the City of—."

3. *Short Title.* "This Act shall be known as the Representation before the Legislature Act," illustrates the short-title provision of a proposed bill.

4. *Definitions.* "As used in this Act, unless the context otherwise requires," the words, terms, and phrases, as used in this bill, are understood to mean—(then follows a list of words, terms, and phrases). Such definitions are intended as an aid to interpretation and application of the law.

5. *Preamble.* The preamble is considered a policy-expressing device. Historically it preceded the enacting clause and for this reason was not considered part of the act itself. Today, the preamble may or may not precede the enacting clause and the courts may or may not consider it a part of the law. A well-drafted preamble may aid in interpreting and applying the statute, as well as encourage popular support of the statute. *Bills* introduced in the Texas legislature seldom contain a preamble.

   In some resolutions, especially concurrent resolutions, most of the space may be devoted to the preamble in which each succeeding "whereas" statement indicates the justification, motive, or intent of the legislative action. The meat of such resolutions may be very brief.

6. *Purview.* The purview refers to those sections that contain the body of the enactment. It may constitute almost the only part of an act: in the case of an amendment to an existing law, the purview may contain several sections, or only a few lines where a single specific change in the old law is to be made.

7. *Savings Clause.* The exclusion of a class from the general operation of an act is included in the savings clause.

8. Penalties or Sanctions. The bill might provide "any person who willfully and knowingly violates any of the provisions of this Act shall be guilty of a misdemeanor and, upon conviction thereof, shall be punished by a fine of not more than Five Thousand Dollars ($5,000.00) or imprisonment in the county jail for not more than two (2) years, or by both such fine and imprisonment." Sections like these provide the "starch" or enforcement machinery.

9. *Repealing Clause.* The new law or part of it may be in conflict with existing law and the legislature may decide this conflict should not be left to judicial resolution. Hence, the repealing clause will state that the specific conflicting sections of the old law are repealed.

10. *Statute of Limitations.* Such a provision in a statute limits the right of action on certain described causes of action. It might provide that no suit or other type of action could be maintained on such causes of action unless brought within a specified period after the right accrued. Thus, the legislature might permit certain types of claims to be brought against the state if filed within eighteen months after the passage of the law. In criminal cases a statute of limitation is an act of grace or a surrender by the state of its right to prosecute after a specified time.

11. *Severability Clause.* The severability clause may read as follows: "If any sec-

tion, subsection, sentence, clause, or phrase of this Act is for any reason held to be unconstitutional, such decision shall not affect the validity of the remaining portions of this Act.'' If part of the law was declared unconstitutional, that part would be severed from the act and the remaining sections would continue effective.

12. *Emergency Clause.* In cases of imperative public necessity—emergency—(stated in the preamble or body of the bill), and by a four-fifths vote in the house in which the bill may be pending, the constitutional rule requiring three readings in each house may be suspended.

13. *Schedule.* The schedule indicates when the bill will go into effect. According to the constitution, no law, except the general-appropriation act, shall take effect until ninety days after the adjournment of the session at which it was enacted, unless in case of an emergency (expressed in the preamble or body of the act), the legislature shall, by a vote of two-thirds of the members elected to each house, otherwise direct. Hence, a bill (emergency legislation passed by two-thirds vote of the entire membership of each house) may become effective when signed by the governor or filed without a veto with the secretary of state; or it may become effective at the end of ninety days after the adjournment of the session, or at some later date specified in the act. When such a date is given, the act might simply state ''This Act shall take effect on January 1, 19—, and it is so enacted.''

From Bill to Law

Constitutional Provisions

The Texas constitution places numerous limitations on the legislature. One procedural limitation is the division of the regular sessions of the legislature into three specific periods.

1. *First thirty days*—''devoted to the introduction of bills and resolutions, acting upon emergency appropriations, passing upon the confirmation of the recess appointees of the Governor and such emergency matters as may be submitted by the Governor in special messages to the Legislature.''

2. *Next thirty days*—''the various committees of each House shall hold hearings to consider all bills and resolutions and other matters then pending; and such emergency matters as may be submitted by the Governor.''

3. *Next sixty days*—''the Legislature shall act upon such bills and resolutions as may be then pending and upon such emergency matters as may be submitted by the Governor.''

A regular session may not exceed 140 days. If the above constitutional schedule were followed, it would not cover the last 20 days of a 140-day session.

The constitution also provides that either house may otherwise determine its order of business by an affirmative vote of four-fifths of its membership. At the beginning of each regular session a simple or concurrent resolution is passed by a four-fifths vote in each house altering the thirty-thirty-sixty day periods set up in the constitution. Under the rules under which both houses agree to operate, unrestricted introduction of bills is permitted during the first sixty days. Thereafter, introduction of bills is by unanimous consent, suspension of the rules by a four-fifths vote, and the submission of emergency matters by the governor. As a result of this alteration of the legislative schedule, it is not too difficult—especially in regard to noncontroversial legislation—for house and senate members to secure permission to introduce bills rather late in the session. Both the original constitutional provision and the practice of the legislature were designed to prevent the end-of-the-session rush, although neither has accomplished this objective, for the Texas legislature still has a very serious end-of-the-session rush every two years.

"All bills for raising revenue," reads the Texas constitution, "shall originate in the House of Representatives, but the Senate may amend or reject them as other bills." From the days of the first constitutions in this country, it has been an accepted practice that revenue or tax legislation should originate in the lower house, whose members are closer to the people. In practice, this is not very serious limitation upon the upper house, for it may amend or reject revenue bills as other bills. In fact, the Texas senate could completely rewrite a tax bill from the enacting clause, although it could not change the title of the bill. Yet the senate cannot act *first* on a revenue measure. However, all other types of bills and resolutions may be introduced in either chamber or concurrently in both houses.

Introduction of Bills

To introduce a bill, a house or senate member can simply introduce it from the floor if the house is in session; otherwise he could file it with the clerk of the house or secretary of the senate. The bill is numbered by the clerk of the house or secretary of the senate, and the reading clerk of the respective house reads the caption of the bill, which constitutes "first reading." Some bills are prefiled before the Legislature meets.

Committee Stage

Bills are referred to committee by the speaker of the house and president of the senate (or president pro tem). The presiding officers of both houses may be able to determine the fate of a bill in committee by referring it to a sympathetic or unsympathetic committee. (In Congress bills are referred to the appropriate committee by the parliamentarian in accordance with the rules.) Some committee hearings are held at the discretion of the committee chairman. Many bills never get a hearing. Nevertheless, some of the most important work of the legislature is done through committees and subcommittees.

The chairman of a house or senate committee may designate members to serve on subcommittees. Subcommittees may consider only certain sections of a proposed bill, and they report to the full committee. A considerable amount of committee work is done through small, specialized subcommittees.

A committee may approve, disapprove, amend, rewrite, or pigeonhole (take no action) a bill referred to it for consideration. The committee might make a favorable or unfavorable report, or both a majority and minority report might be made to the house or senate. Under certain limitations a committee may be required to report (discharge from further consideration) by a vote of the house or senate.

Committee of the Whole

As a means of giving further consideration to a bill on second reading or to enable *all* members to hear testimony on a given subject, either house, by majority vote, may sit as the Committee of the Whole, a temporary committee. The speaker of the house or lieutenant governor (or president pro tem) designates some other member to act as chairman of the committee of the whole. While in such committee, members operate more informally; they enjoy more freedom from the parliamentary restrictions that apply in the house and senate. In time the committee of the whole will resolve itself back into the house or senate and receive and act upon the report presented by the chairman of the committee of the whole.

Action on the House and Senate Floor

A bill reported out of committee may not be debated immediately because there is a serious "calendar problem" in each house. The house's solution is the suspension calendar, which is controlled entirely by the speaker. Since committees are scheduled to meet on certain days, delay in getting to a bill on a given day may delay floor consideration of the bill for at least a week.

If the committee reports favorably on the bill, the committee chairman and other members of the committee might carry the major portion of the advocacy of the bill on the floor, whereas the minority members of the committee, if any, along with other members, might oppose it. The order of speakers, time limits on speeches, and other matters could be worked out in consultation with the presiding officers.

Limitation on Debate in the House of Representatives and Senate

Debate in the house of representatives is more limited than in the senate because of the larger membership. Speeches in the house are limited to ten minutes unless the house by a majority vote extends the time of any member, but such extension may not be for more than ten minutes. The mover of any original proposition before the house, or the member reporting any measure from a committee, has the right of opening and closing debate on the proposition, and for this purpose may speak each time not exceeding twenty minutes. A house member may be given permission to take the floor on personal privilege and thereby have more time to present his views.

In an effort to delay a vote, a house member may offer motions and amendments that are not germane. The house substitute for a filibuster is sometimes referred to as "chubbing." If the speaker wishes to delay consideration of a matter, or delay a vote, he may encourage "chubbing." The speaker and the house members on the "speaker's team" have the power to control debate if they so desire.

With some exceptions, a Texas senator may keep the floor so long as he has the stamina to keep talking. The senate may be put on a twenty-four-hour-a-day schedule during a filibuster to wear down the speaker. The rules of the Texas senate provide, "While a Member has the floor, no Member shall interrupt him or otherwise interrupt the business of the Senate, except for the purpose of making a point of order, calling him to order, *moving* the previous question, demanding that a point of order under discussion or consideration be immediately decided, or making a motion to adjourn or recess." The latter has been applied in various ways by the presiding officers and parliamentarian of the senate. A senator may be required by the senate to discontinue his address or the chair may warn the senator to confine his remarks to the pending question. If a senator moves the previous question and it is approved, the chair may rule that the member who has the floor may continue until he has concluded his remarks. The chair's interpretation of the rules in each house is seldom, if ever, overruled on a point of order.

Cloture in the senate, as in the house, may be brought about by the adoption of a motion calling for the previous question, special orders brought in by the rules committee limiting debate, and informal agreements by the leaders in the house and senate.

Engrossment

Once a bill has been considered on the floor in one house and the amendments, if any, considered and disposed of, a vote must be taken on passage to engrossment. Each house has an engrossing-enrolling clerk, and the house of representatives has a standing committee on enrolled and engrossed bills. When a bill passes on second reading in one house it is passed to engrossment, after which all amendments are added and corrections made as the bill is put in its final form. The engrossed copy of the bill shows it as amended and corrected on second reading. A rule of the house permits the house engrossing and enrolling clerk to write into a bill any amendments that are tacked on in final passage. At one time such amendments were forwarded to the senate as "engrossed riders," separate from the measure. Also a house rule permits the engrossing and enrolling clerk to amend the captions of all house bills and joint resolutions ordered engrossed and finally passed if approved in writing by the author.

If the bill carries the emergency clause, the house or senate may, by a four-fifths vote, suspend the rules and take up the bill on third reading and final passage immediately after it has been passed to engrossment. Third reading is usually by caption only, after which a simple majority vote constitutes final passage in the particular house. A bill may be discussed following third reading; nevertheless, it takes two-thirds vote to amend the proposal at this stage.

Action by Both Houses

A bill passed in one house may be defeated or passed in the other chamber with or without amendments. If passed without amendments, it would be enrolled, signed by the speaker of the house and president of the senate, and transmitted to the governor. If passed with amendments in the second house, it would be returned to the chamber of origin "with accompanying house or senate amendments." In the event the house of origin accepts the amendments, the bill is enrolled, signed, and sent to the governor's office. If the house of origin is unwilling to accept the amendments, it probably would request a conference committee. The chamber that amended the bill might insist that the chamber of origin accept its amendments and refuse the request for a conference committee. Such a deadlock could kill the bill.

The Conference Committee

The chamber that passed a bill but was unable to accept the amendments of the other house may request a conference committee by a simple majority vote. If the second chamber accepts the request for a conference committee, the speaker of the house appoints five house members, and the president of the senate appoints five senators to serve on the committee. Either house may instruct its members to follow a certain course of action so long as the instructions are not in violation of the rules of the house or senate concerning conference committees. Furthermore, members of the committee usually are restricted to adjusting the *differences* between the two houses on a particular bill and are prohibited from tinkering with those sections that have been accepted in the house and senate, and from adding new material. Yet conference committees, like other official bodies, do not always hew to the line, and they may insert new provisions and alter things not in disagreement.

There are two votes in a conference committee, one house and one senate vote. The members from each house must decide how their one vote will be cast. Three house or three senate members could prevent the conference committee from reaching an agreement. This voting arrangement has considerable advantage for the lobbyists who may attempt to influence members of the committee. The report of the conference committee must be accepted or rejected "as is" by both houses, since the report is not subject to amendment. This offers opportunities for "riders" to be attached to the conference committee report, especially "legislative riders" on appropriation bills. If a compromise on appropriations has not been worked out until late in the session, and a house or senate member can get a legislative rider attached to the appropriation bill in the conference committee, the two houses would have to accept or reject a rider with the bill. This practice undermines the voting rights of other members of both houses and also undercuts the item veto power of the governor, which only extends to items in appropriation bills and not to attached legislative riders. It is too late in the session to veto appropriations for the next two years. Politically, the legislature and the governor are in no position to take responsibility for not providing the necessary state funds.

Enrollment

After a bill has passed in the house and senate it is enrolled. An enrolled bill is the final copy, with all amendments and corrections, as passed by both houses. Enrolled bills are signed by the speaker of the house and the lieutenant governor and are transmitted to the governor's office.

Action or Inaction by the Governor

Once a bill is on the governor's desk, either house by a simple resolution or both houses by concurrent resolution may ask the governor to return the bill for correction. The governor may sign the bill, or permit the bill to become law without his signature. If the legislature is still in session, and the governor takes no action within ten days, the bill automatically becomes law. If the legislature has adjourned after submission of the bill to the governor, he has twenty days to consider the legislation before the bill becomes law.

The governor of Texas, like the president, has the right to veto or the "qualified negative" as it was referred to by the writers of the *Federalist*. In the event the governor vetoes the bill, it may be repassed over his veto by a two-thirds vote in both houses. In this negative sense, at least on occasion, the governor can exert an influence in legislation equivalent to more than one-third of the legislature. Vetoes by the chief executives of the states and nation are referred to as the "qualified" or "suspensive veto" if the legislature is in session. Rather than being an absolute veto it may be overridden by the legislature, and final judgment is suspended until the legislature decides whether to override the veto. Of course, if the legislature has adjourned, a postadjournment veto by the governor within the twenty-day period would constitute an absolute veto. A vetoed bill could be passed at the next legislative session and resubmitted to the governor.

On appropriation bills, the governor can veto—but not reduce—individual items. These item vetoes may be overriden, just like any other veto, by two-thirds vote in both houses.

When Do Laws Become Effective?

As noted earlier, no law, except the general-appropriation act, shall take effect until ninety days after the adjournment of the session at which it was enacted, unless in case of an emergency (expressed in the preamble or body of the act) the legislature shall otherwise direct by a vote of two-thirds of all the members elected to each house. Thus an appropriation bill, or any bill that receives the two-thirds vote as an emergency matter, may become effective immediately following consideration by the legislature and the governor. These bills are transformed into law at the time they become effective. Other bills are "laws in waiting" until the expiration of the ninety-day period or until the date specified in the bill.

Where May the Laws Be Found?

Bills and resolutions approved by the legislature and signed or unsigned by the governor, or passed over the governor's veto, are sent to the secretary of state, who has them published as the *General and Special Laws of Texas* for the particular legislative session. Also the laws may be found in Vernon's *Civil and Criminal Statutes* published by Vernon's Law Book Company. Most people find it more convenient to use Vernon's *Statutes* because it is a compilation of the law as amended and is kept up-to-date by a pocket supplement.

The Politics of Legislation

The Texas legislature offers a good laboratory for the study of practical politics in action. No other branch of state government is subjected to such pressure and counter pressure within the same time period. What powers—both legal and extralegal—are available to the governor, presiding officers, individual legislators, and interest groups in the accomplishment of desired legislative objectives?

The Governor

The governor campaigns for nomination and election on the basis of a proposed legislative program. It is to the political advantage of the governor to get a large part of this legislative program enacted into law, especially if he intends to go before the people for reelection at the end of four years. At the beginning of each regular session the governor will recommend to the legislature certain areas in which legislation is needed. Further legislative recommendations by the governor may be made to the legislature throughout the session. If the governor calls a special session, he can specify the topics for consideration. The governor has the general veto power and item veto on appropriation bills, which he may exercise at both regular and special sessions.

The governor has many extralegal powers, which he may use to influence legislation. How much he uses them depends upon the personality, prestige, and ingenuity of the governor. Among his extralegal legislative powers are the threat of veto and threat of a special session. The governor may inform legislators individually, or by press release or in speeches, that he will veto a certain bill then before the legislature. He may want it defeated in the legislature or encourage certain changes in it. The threat of veto, if indicated early enough, may discourage the introduction of the proposal in the legislature. Gubernatorial vetoes are difficult to override, and individual legislators may think it politically unwise at a particular moment to bring themselves into conflict with the chief executive.

If the governor does not get the legislation he wants in a regular session, he may threaten to call a special session. Frequently legislators show little interest in holding a special session; most of them are usually anxious to return to their own professions and businesses. The fact that the legislature might be called into special session by the governor may encourage the legislators to pass the legislation supported by the governor.

The governor cannot afford to antagonize the legislature too much if he wants his legislative program enacted. It would be better for him politically, at least in his relations with the legislature, if he found no need to resort to the threat of veto or special session. In some quarters these techniques are interpreted as failure on the part of the governor in his executive-legislative relationship.

A thirty-day special session of the Texas legislature is expensive. The governor and members of the legislature may jockey for public approval or disapproval of a special session. Members of the legislature may, by public statement or press release, play up the cost of such a session in the hope public opinion will not be in sympathy with a called session.

During a special session the governor may submit matters for legislative consideration that were not included in his proclamation calling the session. Members of the legislature may wish to consider various proposals not included in the governor's proclamation. In order to gain support for legislation he is interested in, the governor may agree to submit additional topics during the special session. If the governor includes only one or two topics in his proclamation, he might increase his bargaining power by being able to open the session to more topics.

The number of proposals that should be submitted to a special session by the governor would depend upon the legislation passed during the regular session, public need, nature of the proposals, previous consideration of the proposals by the legislature, the political power of the governor, interest of the legislators, and public opinion. There is a limit to what the legislature can do in a thirty-day special session.

During a legislative session it is common for the governor to have breakfast or lunch with house and senate members. At these and other informal meetings with members of both houses the governor might secure support for his legislative proposals. To gain the support of those meeting with him, he may find it necessary to offer his support for the proposals the legislators are interested in passing. Such an informal conference attended by one, several, or a group of legislators can turn into a good "horse-trading meeting." Also, as a result of such informal meetings, the governor might agree to appoint to a board or commission a person who was recommended by a house or senate member, providing that the legislator will support legislation favored by the governor. The governor makes the appointment (subject to senatorial confirmation) and gains support for legislation, while the legislator has built or mended some political fences by getting the right person appointed to a state job. Hence, informal contacts, compromise, bargaining, pressure, and threats are techniques that permeate the entire legislative process.

The governor can appeal to the people over the heads of the legislature if there is a conflict over legislation between him and the lawmakers. Such an appeal could be made to the people by way of press releases or through speeches made on the banquet circuit. The governor of Texas, unlike the president, seldom makes use of radio, or television, to build up popular support for legislation while the lawmakers are in session. Such an appeal to the people could backfire; and it would, in all likelihood, antagonize the legislature, thereby making compromise more difficult. If a conflict between the governor and the legislature is not resolved during a particular legislative session, it might become the main issue in the next gubernatorial and legislative elections. In that case the governor could go so far as to recommend or oppose the election of certain legislators. Again, the governor would be in a predicament if such action backfired. Because of the weak position of the governor in Texas, he seldom makes such direct appeals to the people and must rely upon informal contacts and other techniques to influence legislation.

The governor frequently has his own lobbyists in the legislature. Under the rules, only the governor may lobby within the brass rails, yet it is common for the lobbyists of the governor to work hard for his legislative program. The director of the budget in the executive office of the governor, the executive assistant to the governor, the campaign manager, the public-relations people, among others, comprise the lobbying staff of the chief executive. Sometimes they go on the floor and sit at the press table to watch the progress of a bill or talk to members, risking a challenge at the microphone. Often they work the reception rooms or show up at committee meetings.

The governor may meet, discuss, and bargain with lobbyists representing business firms and corporations. For example, it was reported by the press that former Governor Shivers held a secret conference with major industry lobbyists at the governor's mansion. The subject was the governor's tax program that bypassed any new taxes on natural resources but increased the tax on gasoline two cents per gallon and raised the tax on cigarettes one cent per pack. Naturally, the governor's tax program had the support of the lobbyists representing the natural-resources industries. It may be that the governor used his tax program as a bargaining device to secure support for other legislation favorable to the governor.

Speaker of the House and Lieutenant Governor

The governor, individual legislators, and interest groups are vitally concerned with the election of the lieutenant governor and the selection of the speaker by the house. These presiding officers assign house and senate members to committees, refer bills to committee, recognize speakers, and apply the rules of the two houses. If the presiding officers are friends of the governor or in sympathy with his legislative program, they can go a long way in supporting the governor's program in the legislature. As a matter of practical politics, the speaker of the house and the lieutenant governor are much more influential in legislation than the governor. Little wonder that considerable money is poured into the campaigns for these positions.

Service in the legislature, as presiding officer, house or senate member, often leads to employment as a lobbyist, once legislative work is terminated. The contest for the speakership begins during the regular session. After the adjournment of the regular session but prior to the convening of the next legislature, candidates for the speakership may contact all the house members who were elected or reelected in the first and second primaries in an attempt to line up at least 76 (out of a total of 150) votes or pledges necessary to election as presiding officer in the house. Candidates for the speakership may issue conflicting statements concerning the number of pledges for the speakership each has secured. These announcements are made for political purposes in an attempt to discourage the opposition candidate or secure the votes of unpledged house members. Few Texans realize the importance of the contest for the speakership that is waged vigorously, both openly and behind the scenes. On the road to the speakership, promises are made in regard to committee assignments and support of legislation. The personal contacts, bargaining, pressure, and maneuvering are the environment in which politics must operate. For politics, as some would say, is the "art of the possible."

The bargaining that candidates for the speakership must engage in does enhance the power of the one elected. At times it also limits the power of the speaker because he is compelled to designate certain members as chairmen or members of committees who were not his preference for the position. If any good committee assignments are open when the legislature meets, independent house members should be able to secure these positions in return for support of one of the candidates. If the desired position is not open for the uncommitted house member, the candidate for the speakership might attempt to shift some of the chairmanships and committee assignments. This is a delicate maneuver and could make enemies.

The presiding officers of both houses exercise control over their calendars, and they may expedite passage of a proposed bill by placing it at the top of the calendar or they may make a show of wanting certain legislation passed but delay "pressuring" the committee chairman to report the bill out of committee until it is too late for consideration on the floor.

Any time a senator can secure a two-thirds majority (twenty-one votes), his bill may be debated. However, the senator must convince the lieutenant governor in advance that he has twenty-one votes. If he wishes, the presiding officer may be even more arbitrary by refusing to recognize a member for a motion to take up a bill. Private polling may indicate enough house or senate votes to pass a bill; under such conditions the bill probably would come up for debate.

> This means, of course, that the Speaker can put his lieutenants to work vigorously to line up votes for those bills he wants considered, or can have them work hard to align members against bills he considers too hot to handle.
> There is a cliché that the presiding officers of the Senate and House cannot maintain one-man control without the implied consent of a majority.
> But there are many ways in which members can be convinced discretion is the better part of valor when it comes to challenging the presiding officer's authority.

And some members, unhappy with the way a lieutenant governor or a Speaker of the House operates, may be too busy on other matters to join in any "reform" movement.

The cliché ignores the fact that a lieutenant governor is elected by the voters of the state, not by members of the Senate, and therefore may feel no particular obligation to majority Senate opinion.

This power of the lieutenant governor and the Speaker to control the progress of bills is delegated to some extent to committee chairmen.

The Committees

Under a rule of the house of representatives all bills automatically go to a sub-committee for further study after a hearing.

The reason given for this rule is that it allows more time to analyze bills, but many suspect the real purpose is to protect members from having to vote on measures while a crowd of witnesses is present to see, and remember, the way they voted.

The subcommittee rule can be waived by a two-thirds vote of the committee, but a great majority of bills go to a subcommittee of three or five members, appointed by the committee chairman. The subcommittees work in secret; even the author does not usually know what they are doing to his bill, or why. Moreover, a bill in subcommittee is at the mercy of the committee chairman, who may or may not allow the subcommittee to report on it, depending on his own inclination. He can, therefore, effectively kill a bill by stowing it away in an unfriendly subcommittee, and only rarely can the sponsor, through appeals to the House as a whole, break it free or have it referred to a more amenable committee.[2]

Individual Legislators

House and senate members may seek adjournment and reconvene fifteen minutes later for the start of another legislative day to expedite final passage of legislation. This does not affect the duration of legislative sessions, which are based on *calendar* days.

It is shrewd legislative politics for legislators to introduce any number of bills regulating labor unions, the professions, and businesses. The sponsors of such legislation may have little interest in actually regulating a particular interest. However, once the "bills to regulate" are introduced, their sponsors have bargaining power because the lobbyists or representatives of the interest to be regulated will want them killed in committee. In exchange for an agreement not to push such legislation the lobbyists representing the particular interest may agree to swing their support behind other legislation. Sometimes a proposal to regulate some profession or interest group may result in the offer of a bribe to withdraw the legislation.

For bargaining power the house and senate members must operate in such a way that individuals or groups will come to them for favors. Firemen in a particular city may want more vacation time and better pay and appeal to the home-district legislator for a local law as a means of bypassing or overruling the city council. The legislator is the man holding the key that may unlock the special favor. Once a lawmaker attracts people, he in turn gains fence-mending and horse-trading power.

Sometimes a senator or senators operating as a relay team will engage in a filibuster. By this practical strategy they attempt to obstruct legislative action by speaking merely to comsume time, to prevent a vote on a measure. The threat of a filibuster may discourage the introducing of certain legislation or cause it to be modified. As the end of the session approaches, the filibuster gains in potency. Wishing to defeat the legislation, those filibustering might agree to stop talking if the bill is withdrawn. They might discontinue their filibuster if a substitute or amended bill is agreed upon. Or those conducting the filibuster may realize they have little chance for success but want to dramatize the legislation. There is always the possibility that the delay may help to mobilize public opinion against the measure.

Lobbyists—The "Third" House

Many lobbyists are active the entire year; others only when the lawmakers assemble in Austin. When the legislature is in session, lobbyists may contact legislators in person on the house or senate floor, call members from the floor by messenger, or contact them by telephone. Contacts also may be made at hotels and clubs. Of course, the *modus operandi* (way of doing) varies considerably among lobbyists.

What Makes a Lobbyist Effective?

To be effective, a lobbyist should have a thorough understanding of the legislative and political system. Some individuals who at one time served in the house or senate, or both, and are familiar with the intricacies of the legislative process, and who know members of the legislature, may be among the most effective lobbyists. Also, effective lobbyists must understand their clients and their needs; know what will promote or damage the interests of those they represent; be able to quickly grasp the impact of a proposed bill or amendment on their clients; help secure both campaign contributions and workers; provide information on their client's position; make personal contacts with the legislators at an appropriate time and place; and be adept in letter writing and phone calls. There are professional—and something less than professional—lobbyists.

Lobbyists provide legislators with considerable information. To be most effective, this information should be presented in a logical manner that indicates the client's interest; it is more effective if both sides of the issues involved are mentioned. A lobbyist may quickly lose his or her effectiveness by lying (possibly on a single occasion). Many legislators are skeptical of "single shot" lobbyists—those who are concerned with only one issue or problem.

The recognized professional lobbyists—those who are quite effective and who are active session after session in Austin—strive to build and maintain a respectable level of credibility. This is essential in order to be effective and retain the respect of the legislators. And not surprisingly, a pleasant personality is a vital element of the successful lobbyist's total package.

Probably the single most effective action a lobbyist can take is to generate public opinion in the legislative district. The more successful lobbyists maintain local contacts in cities and towns throughout the state and are thus able to generate stacks of mail and phone messages easily.

These, and other so-called tools of the lobbyist trade, will, of course, vary somewhat from legislator to legislator, and from session to session. However, lobbyists (and lobbying) is as old as democratic government itself, and no doubt has a lively future.

Lobbyists as Technicians

Aid in Nominating Candidates. Pressure groups, through their public relations staff, influence the nomination of the governor, the lieutenant governor, and members of the house and senate in the primaries. Both labor (AFL-CIO) and the Texas Manufacturers' Association (TMA), among other interest groups, make substantial contributions to campaign funds. Big-city Texas businessmen, through the Public Interest Political Education Fund (PIPE), finance legislative campaigns. A map of the state may indicate the legislative districts whose legislators oppose the conservative position in the legislature. TMA supports a legislative program that provides a favorable climate for business; for example, the organization supports the general sales tax and opposes the personal and corporate income tax. Prospective legislators must meet these and other tests to be eligible for financial aid in their campaigns. Since the big-city areas are well organized, and since rural campaigns are less expensive, TMA may devote more attention to the rural districts. The AFL-CIO, through its committee on political education (COPE), supports candidates and a legislative program favorable to labor.

Because of its small membership, longer terms, and power of the presiding officer, the lobbyists are extremely interested in the senate races and in the nomination of the lieutenant governor. Not only are the pressure groups concerned with the legislative influence of the governor and senators, but they are vitally aware of the appointive power shared by the governor and the senate. After all, it is important that the right people be appointed by the governor and confirmed by the senate for membership on the various state boards and commissions. The administration of a law, as far as the interest groups are concerned, may be as important as the passage or defeat of a law itself. Legislative and administrative pressure make lobbying almost a year-round activity.

Interest groups take an active part in the contest for the speaker of the house, for he appoints members to serve on committees, designates committee chairmen, and has considerable power over the direction and flow of legislation in the lower house.

Favors. There are innumerable ways in which the "third" house can provide favors to individual legislators as a means of obligating the lawmakers. Retainers' fees, open-end accounts paid by the lobbyist or his employer, job openings for relatives and close friends of legislators, opportunities to buy at wholesale, advice on business opportunities and investments, and helpful hints on purchasing, selling, or leasing property are among the many ways available to make legislative friends, influence people, and promote one's own interests.

Free transportation for business or recreation is frequently made available to legislators. A private plane, sometimes a chartered commercial plane, will fly legislators to the Kentucky Derby or to some area for fishing or hunting. During sessions of the legislature some lobbyists maintain open house for free meals and liquor for all legislators who wish to drop by their hotel suites. Whatever is needed for an escape from the pressures of legislative business, be it a party or some other form of entertainment, it can be arranged by the lobbyists and their retinue.

Speech Writing. Lobbyists are available for writing speeches. The legislator may not have the time to prepare a scheduled speech. Such background material as topic, general approach, type of audience, and desired length is turned over to the lobbyist and in due season the speech is written and returned to the lawmaker, ready for delivery.

Research and Bill Drafting. Since the state does not maintain a bill drafting agency, the lobbyist can be of service in bill drafting. Needless to say, some lobbyists have become rather competent draftsmen.

The Texas legislature follows the practice of "farming out" research to the Texas Research League, a private organization financed by the business community. This saves the state money, but the "research findings" may be influenced too much by the chambers of commerce and the Texas Manufacturers' Association. The Texas Research League recommended the sales tax and prepared a draft of the bill, and members of the league supported the legislation in committee. After the legislature passed the sales tax, the staff of the league offered their services in interpreting the law.

Letters and Telegrams. Pressure groups encourage people to send letters and telegrams to house and senate members and to attend committee hearings. A large volume of mail may leave the impression with the legislators that there is widespread public interest in proposed legislation. As a matter of practical politics, a large number of letters and telegrams might make it politically unwise to ignore the predominant view expressed.

Committee Hearings. The same situation might exist where large numbers of persons attend committee meetings during a public hearing on proposed legislation. Is the committee in a position, politically speaking, to oppose or ignore the predominant view evidenced by those who attended the hearing? It is important that interest groups have many of their supporters appear before the committee when a public hearing is held. Throughout the session, the lobbyist may keep in contact with the members of a particular committee. Once a bill is in conference committee, lobbyists have considerable influence because of the smaller group and the voting arrangement in the committee.

"Climate of Opinion." Pressure groups are active throughout the year. Some of the best-organized and financed groups in Texas believe that it is necessary to create a "climate of opinion" favorable to the election of sympathetic legislators and other state officials. Their public relations staffs prepare "educational aids," pamphlets, brochures, filmstrips, and releases for press, radio, and television. They provide speakers for schools, church functions, civic groups, and veterans' organizations.

The National Association of Manufacturers (NAM) has made "educational aids" and pamphlets available to schools. Some pamphlets distributed by the NAM have supported state "right-to-work" laws or laws prohibiting the requirement of membership in a labor organization as a condition of employment. One pamphlet indicated increased discussion of these laws is "significant of mounting public concern over unrestricted and monopolistic powers exercised by union bosses . . ." and the public interest is "aroused to fever pitch by disclosures of the senate rackets' committee, investigating racketeering, violence, coercion, and a wide variety of abuses by union bosses against the public interest." The NAM pointed out "what compulsory unionism means to the individual, the union, the company, the nation, and why it should be rooted out of the American system." Some pamphlets contained "a broad background of impressive quotations showing (1) the power complex and irresponsibility of union leaders, (2) expressions by public figures in government, industry, education and the press, [and] (3) a variety of direct quotes from talks made by NAM speakers." The immediate objective of such "educational aids" is to influence young minds in matters relating to labor-management relations, and the long-range objective is to encourage a "climate of opinion" favorable to more statutory restrictions on organized labor. By molding public opinion, the NAM hopes the right people will be elected to the legislature in Texas and in other states.

The above-mentioned technique is similar to the filmstrip that may purport to show how an interest group operates, and to associate a candidate with the interest. The immediate objective is to win an election whereas the long-range view is to promote a favorable "climate of opinion."

The General Welfare. As a means of securing broad popular support for their program, pressure groups attempt to identify their own interest with the general welfare. A pamphlet circulated by organized labor in Texas claims:

> In line with the general policy of favoring legislation good for the general welfare and of opposing legislation inimical to the general welfare, organized labor's representatives in Austin took an active interest in legislative issues other than those directly concerned with union rights. We have recorded the votes of senators and house members on such issues as taxes, education, social security, working conditions for state employees, appropriations for hospitals and water conservation. We believe that what is good for Texas is good for the members of organized labor and base our position on these issues in that light.

The Score Card. Organized labor and other pressure groups keep a "score card" on how each member of the legislature voted on key issues. This information is circulated among the supporters of the organization. This vote record can be used by voters. The score cards are in effect a post adjournment analysis of legislative votes for the benefit of the particular interest.

Some of the pressure groups or lobbyists active in past sessions of the Texas legislature may be listed:

The Texas Independent Producers' and Royalty Owners' Assn. (TIPRO)
   (Oil and gas producers)
Brown and Root, Inc. (Houston-based construction firm)
Texas Midcontinent Oil and Gas
Tennessee Gas
Texas Good Roads Assn. (Main contributors are oil and gas companies
   and contractors)
Texas Truckers' Assn.
Texas Manufacturers' Assn. (TMA) and Texas AFL-CIO
The Texas Railroad Assn.
Texas Motor Bus Assn.
Small Loans Assn.
Texas Medical Assn.
Texas Brewers' Institute

The Farm Bureau
Texas State Teachers' Assn. (TSTA)
The Texas Municipal League
Texas Gulf Sulphur Co.
Phillips Chemical Co.; Phillips Petroleum Co.; and Phillips Pipe Line Co.
Humble Oil & Refining Co.; Humble Gas Transmission Co.; and
    Humble Pipe Line Co.
Lone Star Gas Co.; and Lone Star Producing Co.

Favorable Aspects of Lobbying

Enhances the Influence of the Individual in Government

Lobbying determines whether or not the influence of the individual in lawmaking is continuous or sporadic. A voter who does not belong to an organization that employs a lobbyist in Austin may exert an influence on legislation only through elections. Also he may exercise some influence through an occasional contact with the house and senate members elected from his district. On the other hand, an individual who belongs to a labor union, professional organization, or some other interest group that maintains a lobby at the capitol has a continuous influence upon the formulation of legislative policy. The extent of this influence depends upon the number of members and financial resources of the lobbyist, and whether he is employed only during the session or year-round.

Keeps the Public Informed

Lobbyists make every effort to keep the members of the organization they represent informed on how house and senate members vote. These tally sheets are given wide distribution to members and nonmembers of the organization alike. About the only information many people have on voting in the house and senate is received through this medium, since few people have ready access to the house and senate journals and the newspapers throughout the state comment only on the vote of the lawmakers from the local district. The press of the state carries no vote tabulation on key issues by all members of the legislature during an entire session. Thus the lobby does provide an important informational service.

Provides Services for the Legislators

Lobbyists are also an aid to the legislators. They provide valuable information to house and senate members in the form of bill analysis and the effect of proposed legislation, if enacted, upon the interest concerned. The research staffs of some of the larger organizations have established a reputation for their accuracy and this information is important in legislative decision making in Texas.

Permits Functional or Economic Representation

As far as the public is concerned, representation in the state legislature is geographical. This raises a question whether it is possible for a single legislator to represent adequately all the different interests in the district. The bonds of common interest that draw people together today are probably more economic than geographic. Therefore, pressure groups fill the need for functional representation in actual practice, a compromise that contains the elements of both geographical and functional representation.

Provides a Balance Between Competing Interests

The third house also provides a balance between competing interests. Before the committees and subcommittees, as well as in contacts with individual legislators, one interest group may find itself opposed by another, since all are maneuvering to protect and promote their own interest. Competition within the third house is severe, and legislative policy, though difficult and complex, must somehow be hammered out. This economic check-and-balance system may prevent a particular pressure group from pushing its own interest to the detriment of other pressure groups and the general public. The check-and-balance system may be as important as the traditional check between the legislative, executive, and judicial branches.

There is considerable cohesion within the "corporation" lobby and individuals may be employed to coordinate the business lobbyists. When the objectives of the top business groups are coordinated, the check-and-balance of competing interests is thereby limited. However, conflicts between interest groups do occur and play an important role in legislation.

There is an unfavorable consequence of the balance between competing interests in the legislature. The conflict of interests between the Texas and out-of-state loan companies, as well as between the large and small loan companies for example, has prevented the enactment of suitable regulations.

8 Legislative Reform

MARK TWAIN OBSERVED THAT "Once, when [the] Wisconsin legislature had the affixing of a penalty for the crime of arson under consideration, a member got up and seriously suggested that when a man committed the damning crime of arson they ought either to hang him or make him marry the girl!" The Texas legislature has produced its hilarious moments. For example, the house of representatives on one occasion considered a resolution which, if passed, would have had the effect of putting the lower house on record as "opposed to sin." On another occasion the Texas legislature had under consideration a bill requiring that all menus at hotels, restaurants, and cafés be printed in English, and omit all foreign words and phrases, so that members of the legislature would know what they were eating during their stay in Austin. And who can forget the famous yo-yo epidemic that hit the house of representatives at the peak of the fad? It was quite a scene to look down from the house gallery and observe one hundred fifty members standing and yo-yoing with gadgets given to the members. Of course anything can happen during the going-away parties when the legislature adjourns. Nevertheless, the American public has become accustomed to a considerable amount of fun and frolic in its legislative bodies, along with the more serious business.

Another side of the legislative personality, as it is publicly conceived, is reflected in cartoons, newspaper stories, and movies that have created a symbol of the "claghorn." Many legislators appear to enjoy playing the part of the legislative character. The black cigars, Texas-size hats, and of course the vigorous handshake and hardy backslap are all associated with house and senate members.

Yet despite the human interest of legislative business, there has developed a lack of public confidence in lawmaking bodies in general. This lack of confidence can be explained, at least in part, by the caliber of members elected to serve in the legislature, lack of strong lobby-control laws, the retainership system, and legislative scandals that have shocked the public. Certainly this loss of public confidence has pointed up the need for legislative reform.

Changes in the Texas Legislative System

Prefiling of Proposed Bills

Members of the legislature may prefile proposed bills after the November general election and thereby receive a low filing number. This may provide more publicity for at least some of the prefiled bills during November and December prior to the meeting of the regular session in January of the odd year. Also, prefiling is helpful for the staff of the legislature in printing and processing the proposed bills.

When the legislature is in session there is a drawing for priority numbers to use for one proposed bill, or the priority number may be transferred to another member as a favor, or a member may not have legislative proposals at the moment which he or she is anxious to introduce.

Lobby Control

The lobby control act includes two major features—registration and activities reports. Persons required to register with the secretary of state include the following:

> a person who makes a total expenditure in excess of $200 in a calendar quarter, not including his own travel, food, or lodging expenses, or his own membership dues, for communicating directly with one or more members of the legislative or executive branch to influence legislation or administrative action; and
>
> a person who receives compensation or reimbursement in excess of $200 in a calendar quarter from another to communicate directly with a member of the legislative or executive branch to influence legislation or administrative action. This subsection requires the registration of a person, other than a member of the judicial, legislative, or executive branch, who, as a part of his regular employment, has communicated directly with a member of the legislative or executive branch to influence legislation on behalf of the person by whom he is compensated or reimbursed, whether or not any compensation in addition to the salary for that regular employment is received for the communication.[1]

Those who own or are employed by a newspaper, radio station, television station, wire service, or other news media are not required to register, provided they represent no other persons in connection with influencing legislation. Also, persons appearing before a legislative committee at the invitation of the committee, who receive no compensation for their appearance other than reimbursement from the state, and engage in no other activities to influence legislation are not required to register.

Persons who file a registration form with the secretary of state must provide certain information, including the name, address, business and business address of the registrant; name and address of each person who made a contribution in excess of $500 during the preceding twelve-month period to the registrant or to the group or person by whom the registrant is retained or employed; a specific description of the matters on which the registrant expects to communicate directly with a member of the legislative or executive branch to influence legislation, including, if known, the bill numbers and whether the registrant supports or opposes each bill listed.

The reports must be filed each month immediately following a month in which the legislature is in session and must cover the activities during the previous month. Reports must be filed each month immediately following the last month in a calendar quarter and must cover the activities during the previous quarter. These reports must include the total expenditures made by the registrant for directly communicating with a member of the legislative or executive branch to influence legislation and must be itemized to show expenditures for postage, publication and advertising, travel and fees, entertainment, gifts, loans, political contributions, and other miscellaneous items. All reports filed under the act are a matter of public record and thus available for public inspection.

Contingent fees are prohibited; that is, "no person may retain or employ another person to influence legislation for compensation contingent in whole or in part on the passage or defeat of any legislation, or the approval or veto of any legislation by the governor." No person may accept any employment or render any service for compensation contingent on the same action. A violation of this provision of the law constitutes a felony, whereas violation of any other part of the law is a misdemeanor.

Persons registered, or required to be registered, may not go on the floor of the house or senate while either is in session except by invitation.

House and Senate Rules of Procedure

Rules of legislative bodies are somewhat vague in actual operation. Each house may approve a new rule (or rules), as well as suspend, amend, or repeal existing rules at any time, and either house may ignore the existing rules. The same is true with regard to joint rules that apply to both houses. Furthermore, custom plays an important role in legislative rules of procedure, and the rules are, on occasion, subject to strange interpretations by the speaker of the house and the presiding officer of the senate (the lieutenant governor or president pro tem). Also, some of the legislative rules of procedure may be included in the state constitution.

In many states, legislative rules are outdated and in need of modernization; in fact, some rules are unworkable.

The Speaker of the House of Representatives

Candidates for the house speakership must file sworn statements with the office of the secretary of state, on the dates specified in the law, of personal funds received and expended in their campaign for speaker. These records are in addition to those required by the Texas election code for those who campaign for election to the house, senate, and other public office.

In the campaign for the speakership, the successful candidate, by promises of committee chairmanships and committee appointments, as well as by other devices, must secure the backing of at least a majority of the house members (seventy-six votes). House employees are prohibited from campaigning for any candidate for speaker. Supporters of the speaker, since they are in the majority, can prevent any serious revolt against him if they so desire. The speaker of Texas is not anxious to antagonize any individual or faction in the house; this and other practical considerations somewhat limit his arbitrary use of power. Nonetheless, there are complaints about the extensive powers of the presiding officer.

There is no limit on the term of office for the speaker, although there has been some support for limiting the speakership to two consecutive regular terms, or four years. To change the rules of the house in this manner is difficult because of the power position of the speaker.

Although still possessing considerable power, the speaker has been somewhat limited by the rules of the house, which, of course, may be changed at any time by the lower chamber. At one time, the speaker appointed the chairmen and vice-chairmen, all other members of the house standing and special committees, as well as the five house members to serve on various conference committees with five senators appointed by the lieutenant governor to represent the senate on conference committees.

As a result of changes in the house rules in 1983, the speaker appointed the entire membership (including the chairpersons and vice-chairpersons) of each standing procedural committee (committee on calendars, committee on local and consent calendars, committee on rules and resolutions, general investigating committee, and committee on house administration). Also, the speaker appointed the chairperson and vice-chairperson of each standing substantive committee and a minimum of one-half of the remaining membership of such committees, and could remove all committee chairpersons and vice-chairpersons. The speaker appointed all the members of the appropriations committee. For each substantive committee to which portions of the general appropriations was assigned, the speaker designated a member of that committee to serve as the chairman for budget and oversight and these individuals also served as members of the appropriations committee.

Also, the rules of the house, approved in 1983, provided that membership on each standing committee would be determined by seniority to the extent of no more than one-half of the membership of such committee, exclusive of the chairperson and vice-chairperson. Each member of the house, in order of seniority, could designate three committees on which he or she wished to serve, listed in order of preference. Membership was granted on the committee of his or her highest preference on which there remained a vacant seniority position. If members of equal seniority requested the same committee, the speaker was authorized to select one of them for the particular committee appointment. Seniority was based upon years of cumulative service as a member of the house of representatives. Seniority did not apply to the committee on appropriations or to the standing procedural committees, since all members of these committees were appointed by the speaker.

Also, the speaker's power has been reduced by transferring authority and numerous duties to the house administration committee. His power to change record votes on the request of the members has been removed; only the house may permit such changes.

The President of the Senate

The president of the senate, like his counterpart, the speaker of the house, at one time appointed the chairperson, vice-chairperson, and other members of the standing committees. As a practical matter, both presiding officers did consider seniority of legislators, and there were other political considerations that limited both in determining committee assignments. However, the rules of the house and senate have further limited the power of the presiding officers to make committee appointments. The president of the senate, however, does have considerable power in the upper house.

The rules of the senate in 1983 authorized the president of the senate to appoint all the members of the standing committees in the Senate, including the chairperson and vice-chairperson of each committee and subcommittee. For each committee with more than ten members, the president of the senate was required to appoint at least four senators who served on that committee during the previous legislative session. Also, with the consent of two-thirds of the senate members, the president of the senate could appoint special and subcommittees in addition to the committees listed.

Thus, the Texas legislature employs a limited, rather than full, seniority system in making committee appointments. Determining all assignments by seniority would remove some of the taint of spoilsmanship from the race for speaker. Using the principle of seniority in making committee assignments also would prevent squabbling and bargaining for committee posts, discourage shifting from one committee to another, and reward members for long service. It would be to the advantage of a member, if he wished to become chairman, to work with certain committees in order to become the senior member. By remaining on the same committees for a long time, one would become a specialist in a given area; thus, the system would promote legislative specialization.

Notwithstanding the arguments in its favor, the seniority rule in designating committee chairmen and appointing members to committees is subject to criticism. It offers no assurance that the most capable people would head committees or be appointed to the most important committees. The system would tend to hold back young and able legislators. The seniority system tends to perpetuate legislators in office, the not so able as well as the able ones. Furthermore, one area of the state might supply most of the chairmen and members of influential committees.

The Committee System Other Than Appointments to Committees

The house and senate have reduced the number of standing committees in order that legislators may devote more time to the work of fewer committees. At one time a number of committees in both houses had little to do and seldom met, although it was impressive for legislators to include an extensive list of committees of which they were either chair, vice-chair, or committee members in their correspondence. Although the number of committees might be reduced, the actual workload and committee assignments might be increased with the creation of more subcommittees. Also, there is the chance that either house, at any time, may increase the number of standing committees and subcommittees.

In past sessions the legislature has limited membership on the more important committees and restricted the action of committee chairmen. For example, the house changed its rules to provide that no member could serve concurrently on more than a certain number of standing committees, and could serve concurrently on more than one of certain other committees (appropriation, revenue and taxation, and state affairs). The chairman of the house appropriations committee could not serve concurrently on any other standing committee. Indeed the house appropriations committee must hold many hearings on the budget requests of the various state agencies, and thus the work of the committee is time consuming. Also, in past legislative sessions, the chairmen of other house standing committees could serve concurrently on only one other standing house committee. Again, the rules of the house, including those concerning the number of standing committees, their chairmen, and members, can be changed by the house at any time.

In past legislative sessions, the Texas senate has limited the number of standing committees on which a senator may serve, and has prohibited a senator from holding more than one chairmanship of a committee. Also, no member could serve on more than two of certain key committees (finance, state affairs, and jurisprudence).

The senate and house rules, as changed from time to time, have attempted to better distribute the work of committees among the members of both houses. An effort has also been made to prevent the chairmanship and membership on certain important committees being monopolized by a limited number of house and senate members.

Another significant change in the rules of the house provided for the creation of the committee on house administration. This committee has jurisdiction over the administrative operation of the house and its employees, i.e., the contingent expense fund of the house, with control over all expenditures from the fund; all property, equipment, and supplies for the use of house members; all office space for members of the house; all admissions to the floor during sessions; and all witnesses appearing before the house or any house committee. The house administrator, under the direction of the committee on the house administration, supervises all officers and employees of the house and organizes all its administrative and clerical operations. Thus, the house administrator coordinates the housekeeping functions of the lower chamber. The result has been a major improvement in the operations of the house of representatives.

The house rules require electronic tape recording of testimony before committees and subcommittees except where suspended by a two-thirds vote of the committee. Transcript of testimony must be furnished any house member upon request; the expense is charged to the requesting member's contingent expense account. The rules require that complete records of all committee proceedings in the house are kept, including records of attendance on reconvening from adjournment or recess, and records of votes on all bills. Such records are required to be available for public inspection.

Local, Special, and Private Laws

Article III, Section 56, of the Texas constitution provides that the legislature shall not, except as otherwise provided in the constitution, pass any local or special law in regard to twenty-nine topics listed in the section. Placing this type of restriction on state legislatures became common after 1850. It was a natural reaction against the abuse of legislative power. State legislatures had passed a mass of bills for special-interest groups, including special favors or privileges for utilities, cities, counties, corporations, and private individuals. In some instances local, special, and private laws made up 80 percent or more of the total legislative output during a particular session. As a result, there was a general feeling that this abuse of power could be curtailed by amending the state constitutions so as to prohibit the passage of local, special, and private laws on specified topics. These efforts proved ineffectual, since the lawmakers devised some ingenious schemes of classification to circumvent the constitutional restrictions. When constitution makers or reformers attempt to limit legislative bodies in great detail, they invite schemes and devices to evade the restrictions.

Population-Bracket Laws in Texas

Except as otherwise provided in the constitution, the Texas legislature is prohibited from passing any local or special law "regulating the affairs of counties, cities, towns, wards, or school districts." This is one of the twenty-nine topics listed in Article III, Section 56, of the Texas constitution that cannot be covered by local or special law. To write the name of the county, city, or school district in the local or special law would be the most obvious violation, in most cases, of the constitutional prohibition. The Texas legislature resorted to classification by population figures or population brackets as a means of limiting the application of a law to one or a few local areas. To illustrate: "Be it Enacted by the Legislature of the State of Texas, that in all counties having a population of not less than 50,000, or more than 50,100, according to the last Federal Census, the county commissioner's court shall have authority to create the office of . . . or spend county funds for the purpose of . . .," etc.

Frequently bills to amend existing population-bracket laws were introduced and passed because the population of the county, city, or school district had increased or decreased and the population bracket no longer fit the population of the local area. Over the years literally hundreds of population-bracket laws were passed.

On occasion, several house or senate members included population brackets in a single bill in order that the same legislation would apply to their district or county. For this reason a bill might be single or multibracket in form.

Much of the population-bracket legislation found in the statutes is in conflict with Article III, Section 56, of the Texas constitution, and would be declared invalid if tested in the courts. In fact, the courts have declared some of the laws unconstitutional, and the attorney general, by way of advisory opinions, has advised legislators and local officials on numerous occasions that a particular local law or proposed bill was invalid.

Not all classification by population is invalid. Such terms as "real," "substantial," "arbitrary," "artificial," "natural," and "unnatural" enable the attorney general, by way of advisory opinions (which are not legally binding), and the courts to declare a population-bracket law or proposed bill unconstitutional. The courts may cite advisory opinions of the attorney general.

Population may be made the basis of classification, provided the law applies uniformly to all persons or things in a particular class. The attorney general and the courts have not declared specifically how broad the population span must be. Instead, the practical effect and operation of the law must be determined in individual cases. However, the classification must have some relation to the objectives to be obtained by the legislation. Furthermore, the courts have held there must be a substantial or reasonable justification for the classification. And the law must also establish a flexible classification, that is, it must not be so absolute, exclusive, or perpetual as to prevent local governments from growing into or out of a particular class.

There has been a decrease in the number of population-bracket laws passed by the Texas legislature, due in large measure to the rules of the house and senate. House rules prohibit the introduction and passage of bracket bills; the joint rules of the house and senate provide that "each house shall hereafter refuse to accept, and shall not file, . . . any bill which attempts to limit its application to a single county or part thereof by means of population brackets or other device, in lieu of identifying the county by name. This section does not preclude the filing and consideration of *bills amending existing law which change the substance but not the application of the existing law"* (italics added). However, the joint rules permit a considerable amount of bracket-bill legislation to be passed and do not affect bracket laws passed prior to the adoption of the legislative rule. Much, of course, depends on whether the legislature will follow its own rule of procedure or amend or repeal this particular provision. Nevertheless, there has been a considerable decrease in population legislation passed in Austin, and this is a welcomed change.

In Texas, local governments are very limited by the Texas constitution and state law. Consequently, local officials and their representatives must seek the necessary authorization from the legislature prior to taking action. This imposes a burden on the legislature and local officials, as well as creates a spirit of localism in the legislature which should be concerned with statewide matters. The state should grant broader powers, by way of general laws, to the local governments.

Local Game and Fish Laws

The constitutional prohibition against the passage of local and special laws does not apply to local game laws, since Article III, Section 56, of the Texas constitution provides that "nothing herein contained shall be construed to prohibit the legislature from passing special laws for the preservation of the game and fish of this State in certain localities." At one time the game and fish laws (and regulations) applied to one or more counties, a precinct, a river, a senatorial district, or a particular game zone or preserve. Because of the above constitutional exception, the name of the local area could be designated in the law or regulation to establish open and closed seasons, bag and possession limits, and other regulations that applied to the game birds, game animals, furbearing animals, and fish. Local laws of this character were passed each session of the Texas legislature. As a result, some counties had local control or veto authority over game and fish regulations, while other counties had regulations set by the legislature. Frequently, game and fish regulations were the product of local politics rather than scientific management.

Although some legislators gained local support from sportsmen in voting for or against a local game or fish bill, on occasion a legislator would be confronted by groups that supported and groups that opposed a certain type of regulation. In such a situation, the legislator would attempt to secure an acceptable compromise, but this was not always possible. In time the necessary legislation was enacted transferring this regulatory function to a state agency, although the legislation was opposed by the commercial fishing industry and some large landowners in deer-hunting areas.

Today, the local areas of the state are under the regulatory authority of the Texas parks and wildlife department, which determine seasons, bag limits, and other conservation measures. Information concerning these regulations may be obtained from the department. To zone the state for local game and fish regulations was not a proper function of the Texas legislature, and it was a welcomed change to transfer this administrative function to a state department.

State biologists conduct surveys throughout the state to determine the extent of game and fish in the local areas. For example, there may be an excessive number of deer in one local area and a limited number in another area. As a result of the surveys, the Texas parks and wildlife department determines such matters as the date of open and closed seasons, bag limits, and other game and fish regulations that apply in local areas.

The "politics of wildlife" continues, since interested individuals and organizations must support or oppose the regulations of the Texas department of parks and wildlife.

Permission to Sue the State

The English concept, "the king can do no wrong," provided the legal basis for the theory, "the state can do no wrong." Therefore, the state could not be sued without its consent. This was rather a strange doctrine in America where the monarchical system of government was never popular. Fortunately, the concept has been modified in England and the United States, as well as in other democratic countries.

The concept of state immunity from suit was severely criticized, since the delay and expense involved in bringing suit against the state often amounted to a denial of justice. In order to bring suit against the state, three separate types of actions were involved: (1) permission to sue the state, authorized by either a bill or concurrent resolution passed by the legislature, (2) suit for damages filed in the state district court, with possible appeal to the courts of appeals and to the Texas supreme court, and (3) an appropriation by the legislature, which might not be in session, to pay such judgment rendered against the state. This procedure discouraged valid claims against the state. Many persons suffered losses rather than subjecting themselves to the delay and expense; thus, serious miscarriages of justice resulted. Further, as governments expanded, and more persons were employed, as well as the operation of all types of machines and equipment, there was greater danger that individuals would be killed or injured, as well as property destroyed or damaged by government action.

Some claims paid by Texas involve merely an appropriation by the legislature and may be enumerated in a miscellaneous-claims bill: for example, reimbursement of state taxes and fees paid in error; funds for unpaid salary or expenses incurred by state employees; and money to pay claims in which payment is prohibited by the statute of limitations. Some appropriations made by the legislature to pay claims against the state, not involving action in the courts, may be provided for in individual appropriation acts, rather than included in a miscellaneous or omnibus claims bill.

The Texas constitution provides that the legislature may grant aid and compensation to any person who has paid a fine or served a prison sentence for an offense he or she did not commit under such regulations and limitations as the legislature may deem expedient.

A tort is a wrong done to another person; a civil (as opposed to criminal) wrong that does not involve a contract. Examples of torts are negligence (failure to exercise reasonable care that results in harm to someone or something), battery (an unprovoked, harmful contact by one person with another individual), and libel (false and malicious written statements that injure a person's reputation.

The Texas Tort Claims Act provides that each unit of government in the state is liable for money damages, not to exceed a certain amount, for property damage or personal injuries or death when proximately caused by the negligence of any officer or employee acting within the scope of his or her employment arising from the operation of a motor-driven vehicle and motor-driven equipment. Liability does not extend to punitive (exemplary) damages—damages beyond the actual loss, imposed as a punishment. To the extent of such liability, the state waives its immunity to suit and grants claimants permission to institute suit directly against the state of Texas and all other units of government covered by the law in the state courts.

All units of government are authorized to purchase insurance providing protection for such governments and their employees against claims that may be brought against them. The insurance company has the right to investigate, defend, compromise, and settle such claims. The state or a political subdivision may not require any employee to purchase liability insurance as a condition of employment where the government unit is insured.

A settlement of a claim under the law is a bar to any action by the claimant, by reason of the same subject matter, against any governmental employee whose act or omission gave rise to the claim.

Other than claims arising out of motor-driven vehicles and motor-driven equipment, claims against the state follow the traditional procedure: the legislature must grant permission to sue; action in the courts; and appropriation of funds by the legislature if the suit is successful.

Since the state and local governments have secured liability insurance, the Texas Tort Claims Act has reduced the workload of the legislature, is less expensive, and has reduced the delay in settling claims. The act should be amended to include property damages, as well as damages for personal injuries or death, other than those arising from the operation of a motor-driven vehicle and motor-driven equipment, even though the cost of government would be increased by the purchase of additional liability insurance.

Reimbursement for property damage or personal injuries or death resulting from action or inaction of the state and local governments, their officials, and their employees should be considered part of the cost of government. For this reason the damages to be paid should be the responsibility of all the people and hence financed through the process of taxation. No single individual or group should have to suffer the burden of injury alone. Injustice results if the claims machinery, because of the time and expense involved, discourages the recovery of damages.

As a result of the limited Texas Tort Claims law, the legislature continues to approve many resolutions permitting suits against the state. In one regular session, ninety-six "sue the state" resolutions were introduced, and sixty-four were approved.

Revision of the Civil and Criminal Laws

Vernon's Annotated Revised Civil and Criminal Statutes of the State of Texas, published and kept up to date privately by Vernon's Law Book Company, is a compilation of the law under appropriate titles, chapters, and sections. Vernon's Statutes practically have official status, since they are quoted so frequently by judges and other government officials, as well as by lawyers who represent both the public and private individuals. Annotated statutes are law books that include the laws and commentary (history, explanations, and judicial decisions interpreting the laws).

The state of Texas publishes *The General and Special Laws* (referred to as the session laws) following the termination of each legislative session. Copies of the session laws may be purchased from the Texas secretary of state and are available in public libraries.

In contrast to a compilation of the law, a revision involves changing words and phrases, as well as rewriting and deleting passages. Also, a revision of the law must be approved by the legislature. The Texas civil and criminal laws were revised in 1925, and in 1965 the legislature adopted a code of criminal procedure by revising and rearranging the statutes that pertain to criminal trials.

The Texas family code, education code, agriculture code, tax code, and property code are a part of the state's continuing statutory revision program instituted by the Texas legislative council in 1963, as directed by the legislature. The legislature indicated the purpose of the tax code, approved in 1981, was "to make the general and permanent state tax laws more accessible and understandable by: (1) rearranging the statutes into a more logical order; (2) employing a format and numbering system designed to facilitate citation of the law and to accommodate future expansion of the law; (3) eliminating repealed, duplicative, unconstitutional, expired, executed, and other ineffective provisions; and (4) restating the law in modern American English to the greatest extent possible."

The continuing statutory revision program contemplates a topic by topic revision of the state's general and permanent statute law *without substantive change*.

Suggestions for Improving the Legislative Process

Constitutional Revision

The basic obstacle to governmental reform in Texas is the outdated Texas constitution of 1876. The inadequacy of the state constitution is especially reflected in Article III, which places many procedural and substantive limitations on the legislature. Some of the matter concerned with the introduction, consideration, and passage of bills and resolutions should be transferred to the legislative rules of the house and senate. The fundamental law of the state should, as is true of the federal Constitution, be limited to the general framework of government.

Other material in Article III should be embodied in statutes. Because of this statutory material in Article III, as in other parts of the constitution, Texas has a legislative code rather than a state constitution. Matters relating to teacher retirement, rural fire-prevention districts, veterans' land board, state medical education board, and so on, included in the existing article on the legislature, are statutory in nature.

If a new constitution for the state should be drafted, those responsible for framing the new document should recognize the differences between fundamental (constitutional) law, statutory law, and legislative rules of procedure. In short, the architects of the constitution should distinguish between the general framework of government (its structure, powers, limitations, and method of amending) and the operational details.

Annual Sessions

Annual legislative sessions might be included in a revised state constitution or authorized by constitutional amendment. Annual sessions would make the legislative process more continuous and give the lawmakers more time to consider legislative proposals. Also, the state budget and appropriations could be on an annual basis instead of requiring the legislature and the comptroller to estimate finances two years in advance. Lobbying would be more continuous and expensive with annual sessions.

House and Senate Rules

The rules of both houses should be revised and simplified, and some of the provisions should be deleted. On occasion the presiding officers of the Texas house and senate and members of the legislature have ignored or misused the rules for political purposes, and one or two examples illustrate the point.

The Consent or Uncontested Calendar

The speaker of the house appoints the chairperson, vice-chairperson, and the other members of the house calendar committee. This committee is a part of the power apparatus of the speaker.

Unlike the regular legislative calendars, consent calendars in the legislature are supposed to contain only local or noncontroversial measures. This usually insures passage of items on consent calendars with little or no debate. As the end of the session nears, the legislature may rely on the consent calendars to get action on bills that might otherwise be buried by the end-of-the-session rush. The use of consent calendars makes possible the nearest thing to instant lawmaking in Austin. A hundred or more pieces of legislation may pass in the house and senate in a matter of hours on consent calendars, with the legislators having little or no knowledge of the contents of the items of legislation. Thus, some undesirable legislation may be passed in this manner—legislation that should never have been placed on the consent calendar in the first place.

In the house bills eligible for the consent calendar are limited to those recommended by a standing committee and are subject to review and decision as to placement by the calendar committee. Bills placed on the consent calendar are withdrawn automatically if debate exceeds ten minutes. A bill can be removed from the consent calendar by the protest of five members. The removal of a bill from the local and consent calendar virtually assures its death unless the sponsor is able to secure a two-thirds vote to suspend the rules and secure recognition by the speaker. House rules require that a bill must be on a calendar, and, if the end of the session is approaching, no further calendars may be planned or are possible.

There have been occasions in which "revenge time" was observable in the house or senate. For example, the required five house members removed certain senate-passed bills from a calendar of uncontested measures because the house members were displeased with the efforts of a senator to delay or prevent passage of a certain proposal in the senate.

In the senate, one senator can block the uncontested status of a bill in committee; if a measure reaches the floor on a consent calendar, objections from three senators can remove it.

Despite these stringent rules, legislation that does not belong there continues to appear on the uncontested calendar. Therefore, the house and senate rules are no stronger than what the legislative leadership is willing to enforce.

It is important to remember that each house and senate member has one or more constituencies, for example, the people of the legislative district and various interest groups. As a result, legislators desire that certain proposals be included on the consent or uncontested calendar. In order to protect their own interests, they do not wish to vote against other legislators who have proposals which they want placed on the consent or uncontested calendar.

To "Tag a Bill" in the Senate

A tag is a legislative maneuver where a senator may demand—and must get—forty-eight hours advance written notice that a given bill will be heard in committee. If the notice is not received or if the bill is not publicly posted seventy-two hours in advance of the hearing, then a senator may "tag" it by objecting to the hearing without the notice, and the hearing must be delayed.

The "tagging tactic" usually does not surface until the last ten days of a session and has been used successfully to kill bills which a senator does not otherwise have the support to defeat or amend.

An outbreak of "tagging" in the senate may force a delay in a number of public hearings, leaving scores of witnesses unable to speak on measures they may have come hundreds of miles to address. Other witnesses on other proposed bills may find themselves victims of "counter tagging" of bills in another committee. And, believe it or not, there may be even a tag on one or more measures not scheduled to be heard!

There has been considerable abuse of the tagging and countertagging technique (the spate or flood of bill-tagging) in the Texas senate. It may be merely a form of personal and petty politics, in which case it undermines the very foundation of representative government, which should have as its purpose the promotion and protection of the welfare of all the people. In some cases tagging is a special device to protect or promote some special interest, and makes a mockery of representative government in a democracy. The rules of the senate should restrict or prohibit tagging.

"Button-Pushing" in the House of Representatives

At the front of the house chamber there is a large board with the names of the house members and lights that indicate how each member voted on a particular issue—"aye" (yes), "nay" (no), and "not voting." Also, the speaker can press a button requesting a member to come to his desk or contact another member of the house. The voting results are tabulated by the machine immediately. A member can press the appropriate button on his or her desk and the vote will be recorded on the board. The speaker may lock the machine immediately following the vote in order to prevent or limit multivoting by individuals. Sometimes a member of the house, by request or handsignals, will authorize another member to vote on his or her desk.

The rules of the house provide that a member must be on the house floor or in an adjacent room or hallway on the same floor of the capitol in order to vote. According to the rules of the house:

> During each calendar day in which the house is in session, it shall be the duty of the reading clerk to lock the voting machine of each member who is excused or who is otherwise known to be absent. Each such machine shall remain locked until the member in person contacts the journal clerk and personally requests the unlocking of the machine. Unless otherwise directed by the speaker, the reading clerk shall not unlock any machine except at the personal request of the member to whom the machine is assigned. Any violation, or any attempt by a member or employee to circumvent the letter or spirit of this section, shall be reported immediately to the speaker for such disciplinary action by the speaker, or by the house, as may be warranted under the circumstances.

The rule of the house has been violated without house members being disciplined. Some who have been caught at multivoting have been merely reprimanded, and nothing more. Members of the press have reported the names of legislators who voted more than once on the voting machine—and such votes resulted in the swing vote on certain important legislation. A member of the house may request a verification of the vote on the machine, and if the speaker of the house grants the request, there will be a verification roll call which could result in an alteration in the voting results. However, the verification roll call is seldom employed in the house.

Again, the rules of the house are no stronger than the willingness of the legislature leadership to enforce them. The legislature should establish a tradition of observing its own rules, and hopefully help to establish greater popular respect for legislative bodies—whether the national Congress or the legislative bodies of the states.

The Speaker of the House of Representatives

The speaker of the house of representatives in Texas is a powerful person in state government. In fact, one may seriously doubt if the presiding officer of any other state legislature has greater power and influence. For this reason, various proposals have been made to limit the speaker's power in Texas. Some of the major proposals to limit the speaker include the following: A secret ballot for the election of the speaker to avoid possible reprisals against members who vote on the losing side—since members should have the same right of privacy on that vote that the public has in the voting booth; and a one- or two-term limit on the speakership, both through a house rules change and by constitutional amendment.

Also, it has been suggested that chairpersons of standing committees, which conduct hearings on bills, should not serve on procedural committees, such as calendars, rules, and house administration because it concentrates much of the decision making power in the house in the hands of very few members. The calendar committee members are viewed by some as "power brokers," holding members' bills hostage unless they play ball with the speaker.

Since the speaker appoints the chairperson and vice-chairperson, and all other members of the calendar committee, it has been proposed that the latter should be limited to scheduling bills on appropriate calendar days and prohibited from refusing to set a bill on any calendar.

To limit the power of the speaker, it has been suggested that the rules of the house should be altered to provide for the election of the chairpersons and vice-chairpersons by the committee members, rather than by appointment of the speaker. Since the speaker is elected every two years by a majority or more of the house members, it would be difficult to restrict his or her powers. Without the speaker's support, it would be equally difficult to change house rules.

The speakership was originally viewed largely as honorary in that it gave a member the opportunity to serve as presiding officer of the house. Today it is a *truly powerful* position in state government.

The Committee System

The powers of standing committees should be enlarged to conduct investigations. This would tend to reduce the need for special committees. Furthermore, there should be equivalent committees in each house as far as possible. Parallel committees in each house would encourage the use of joint hearings and the same research material.

The joint-committee system has been established in some states, although most states, including Texas, continue to use the bicameral-committee system.* In those states with the joint-committee scheme, members from both houses make up the committees on local government, public welfare, education, the judiciary, agriculture, and other matters. The joint-committee system eliminates the duplication of committee hearings and saves time and money.

There is need in Texas to regularize committee activity. A definite schedule as to time and place of committee meetings should be announced early in the session. No action should be taken by a committee unless there is a quorum of the committee members present. The more important committees should keep an adequate record of all committee action. It is meaningless to have testimony before legislative committees under oath if that testimony is not recorded. A record of testimony should improve its quality. Each committee should report its actions promptly to the house concerned. Also it is important that the subjects to be dealt with by each committee be carefully outlined to prevent jurisdictional conflicts between committees. The house and senate rules need to be strengthened in this area of legislative procedure.

Adequate Research and Technical Services

Legislation has become complex and time consuming; therefore, legislators need adequate technical assistance.

There is no agency of the legislature in Texas that devotes full time to the drafting of bills. Many bills have been drafted by the legislative council and submitted to the lawmakers as a part of its research and recommendations on assigned topics. The creation of the legislative council was a step in the right direction for providing the legislature with more research and technical services. Nevertheless the council has been hampered by inadequate budget and staff in making the numerous studies required by the legislature. In the future the legislature must enlarge the budget and staff of the council, or else limit the number of research projects sub-

---

*A joint legislative committee on state finance and a joint legislative committee on administration were created by the Texas legislature in 1972.

mitted to it. The legislature could establish a bill-drafting service as a separate agency.

The legislature should establish a review agency or committee to check bills for errors before they are finally approved. Some such service is needed to correct mistakes or omissions in the caption and other faults of draftsmanship that often invalidate bills or distort their meaning. Lawyers could be assigned from the attorney general's staff or employed for each session of the legislature. Permanent legal assistants could be assigned to the committees in each house to check bills for errors before they are finally approved.

The review committee or agency could also establish some uniformity in regard to the stylistics of legislation. For example, in some bills the entire enacting clause is capitalized, in others only the first letter of each word. There is no standard form followed concerning the numbering of sections and subsections. The same is true of the schedule, savings clause, and repealing clause, among other stylistic features of bills and resolutions. The attorney general's department has prepared a manual for the assistance of members of the Texas legislature. This manual contains valuable information on the correct style in drafting bills and resolutions, but legislators and the third house frequently disregard the form or style laid out in the sample drafts.

To bring about better coordination and to prevent duplication, it might be advisable for the legislature to create the office of research and technical services. The functions of the legislative council, legislative reference library, and house and senate committees on engrossed and enrolled bills could be transferred to appropriate units of the central legislative office. Also, a bill-drafting agency could be established as a part of the office, and the office could employ, assign, and supervise research assistants for committees.

End the Practice of Including Legislative Riders on Appropriation Bills

Consideration of appropriations should be separated from other legislative decisions in order that members of the legislature and the governor may act upon them independently. There has been a growing tendency in Texas toward "government by rider." The riders include both appropriating and nonappropriating (legislative) riders. In practice, the use of riders gives the ten members of a conference committee almost unlimited power. If unrelated legislative provisions or nonappropriating riders are written into an appropriation bill by the conference committee, the bill comes back to the house and senate as a conference-committee report, which must be accepted "as is" or returned to the committee for further consideration. Generally speaking, appropriation bills are enacted in the closing days of a session. Whether the majority of the legislators approve of the riders, or are aware of them, the bill as a whole is usually accepted. The same thing holds true for the governor. He has power to veto items and appropriating riders attached to appropriation bills, and if enough time remains in the session these vetoes may be overridden by the legislature. However, the governor's item veto does not extend to legislative riders attached to appropriation bills, notwithstanding the fact that such riders are in conflict with the Texas constitution. If the governor questions the provisions of a legislative rider, he faces this choice: (1) veto the whole appropriation bill and possibly leave the state without money, or (2) accept the legislative riders in order that the bill as a whole may become law.

The Texas constitution leaves little doubt about the unconstitutionality of legislative riders attached to appropriation bills. "No bill, (except general appropriation bills, which may embrace the various subjects and accounts, for and on account of which moneys are appropriated) shall contain more than one subject, which shall be expressed in its title" (Art. III, Sec. 35, Texas constitution). Nevertheless, the Texas legislature does pass "omnibus" or "multisubject legislation" by attaching diverse and unrelated legislative matters to appropriation bills. Frequently these riders could not be passed individually on their own merits. As a result, undesirable riders may be attached to a money bill, which must be passed to keep the government operating.

The attorney general of Texas has stated the general rule:

> In addition to appropriating money and stipulating the amount, manner, and purpose of the various items of expenditure, a general appropriation bill may contain any provisions or riders which detail, limit or restrict the use of the funds or otherwise insure that the money is spent for the required activity for which it is therein appropriated, if the provisions or riders are necessarily connected with and incidental to the appropriation and use of the funds, and provided they do not conflict with general legislation.[2]

Valid and invalid riders may be illustrated by quoting from a general-appropriation bill.

> . . . No motor-propelled passenger-carrying vehicle may be purchased with any of the funds appropriated in this Article, . . .

The above is a constitutional rider because it limits and restricts the use of the funds appropriated.

> All State-owned motor-propelled passenger-carrying vehicles under the control of any department, commission, board, or other State agency are hereby declared to be no longer needed. Such motor-propelled passenger-carrying vehicles shall be sold in compliance with and as provided for in Article 666, Revised Civil Statutes of Texas, as amended, or otherwise as provided by law, not later than . . .

The foregoing rider is not incidental to the appropriation of money or a limitation or restriction of the use of money appropriated. It relates to an entirely different subject and is general legislation prohibited by the Texas constitution (Art. III, Sec. 35).

Local Judicial Bills

Local judicial bills apply to a particular judicial district or some court in a local area. Since they relate to the judicial system of the state, they are in a sense general bills. The name of the county, judicial district, and court are included in legislation of this type.

Local judicial bills may provide for the reorganization of a judicial district by adding or removing a county from a particular judicial district; increasing or decreasing the jurisdiction of some court; changing the term of court; or increasing the salary of judicial officials. They may also create additional county and district courts or establish special courts (domestic relations courts and juvenile courts). A local judicial bill may create a new judicial district, or authorize additional attorneys or assistant attorneys for local courts, or provide for the employment of court reporters, stenographers, and other court personnel.

Local judicial bills are administrative in nature and should not be the responsibility of the legislature. The civil judicial council or an administrative unit within the state supreme court and the state court of criminal appeals should be delegated the power to formulate rules and regulations concerning the organization and structure of the courts in the state, as well as approve the creation of new courts and judicial districts. The reorganization of judicial districts, creation of judicial positions, determination of salaries, and the like, should be handled administratively, rather than by the legislature.

The Conference Committee

According to house and senate rules, the conference committee is limited to resolving differences between the two houses and may not, by its own action, introduce new material at the conference stage. Nevertheless, the conference committee does originate a considerable amount of legislation and will continue to do so until the legislature follows its own rules of procedure.

Legislative Retainers

A member of the house or senate may be employed by one or more interest groups or individuals as a legal or business consultant, or in some other capacity which, of course, provides that legislator added income. The person or interest group paying the retainer often wants protection in the legislature—possibly the defeat or passage of certain legislation. Thus, acceptance of the retainer could involve the legislator in a conflict of interest. For any legislative session no one knows how many legislators are on retainer. Since they are not required to register or to report a retainer, it is not a matter of public record. For obvious reasons, the legislature has little or no interest in prohibiting legislative retainers by law or even in requiring legislators receiving retainers to register information relative to the matter with the secretary of state, chief clerk of the house, or secretary of the senate. Even if a law was passed prohibiting the legislative retainer, no doubt it could be evaded by interested parties or groups providing various financial benefits or privileges to the lawmakers in lieu of retainers. How much inadequate regulatory legislation in the state has been the result of legislative retainers? Unfortunately, no one knows for certain, and this in itself is a serious weakness of the governmental system.

9 The Governor

"THE MOST DISTINGUISHED STATESMEN," said Judge Story, "have uniformly maintained the doctrine that there ought to be a single executive and a numerous legislature. They have considered energy as the most necessary qualification of the executive power, and this is best attained by reposing it in a single hand."[1] In the organization of the executive branch, plurality tends to conceal faults and destroy responsibility. "Where a number are responsible, the responsibility is easily shifted from one shoulder to another, and hence both the incentive in the executive and the advantages of the restraint of public opinion are lost."[2]

The present Texas constitution vests the executive power in the entire magistracy composing the executive branch, with the powers of each separately defined.[3] "The Executive Department of the State," so declares Article IV, Section 1, of the Texas constitution, "shall consist of a Governor, who shall be the Chief Executive Officer of the State; a Lieutenant Governor; Secretary of State; Comptroller of Public Accounts; Treasurer; Commissioner of the General Land Office; and Attorney General." The office of the commissioner of agriculture was established by statute in 1907. All of these officers, except the secretary of state, are popularly elected. Rather than being the "chief executive officer of the state," the governor is one among several elective administrators. For Texas, as well as for other states, the observation of de Tocqueville remains valid: "The executive power of the state is *represented* by the governor . . . the governor *represents* this power, although he enjoys but a portion of its rights." The division of executive authority in Texas represents a popular reaction against the E. J. Davis administration, carpetbag rule, and Reconstruction following the Civil War.

The governor is the political and ceremonial head of the state and, at least in the eyes of the people, the chief administrative official. Regardless of his actual authority, the governor alone, in most cases, is praised or censured for the successful and unsuccessful operations of the government, even though other state administrators are almost a law unto themselves.

Qualifications

The governor must be at least thirty years of age, a citizen of the United States, and must have resided in the state at least five years immediately preceding his election. One need not be a qualified voter to serve in the highest office of the state; hence, failure to register as a voter would not constitute a disqualification. There is no specific religious qualification. However, the bill of rights provides that "no religious test shall ever be required as a qualification to any office, or public trust, in this State; nor shall anyone be excluded from holding office on account of his religious sentiments, provided he acknowledge the existence of a Supreme Being" (Art. I, Sec. 4). Under this provision of the bill of rights it would appear that an atheist would be disqualified from holding any office or public trust in the state; however, the U.S. Supreme Court has held the states may not bar from public office persons who refuse to take an oath that they believe in God. But it is doubtful if an avowed atheist could get elected to any office in Texas.

During the term for which elected, the governor may not hold any other office (civil, military, or corporate), "nor shall he practice any profession, and receive compensation, reward, fee, or the promise thereof for the same; nor receive any salary, reward, or compensation, or the promise thereof from any person or corporation, for any service rendered or performed during the time he is Governor, or to be thereafter rendered or performed."

Nomination and Election

According to the Texas election code, any party whose nominee for governor in the last preceding general election received 20 percent or more of the total votes for governor must use the primary method of nominating candidates for precinct, county, district, and state office. If the party nominee for governor in the last general election received as much as 2 percent, but not more than 20 percent, of the total votes cast for governor, that party must nominate its candidates for the general election by party conventions.

Candidates seeking the nomination for governor in the primary file with the state executive committee of the party. The names of the candidates who file are transmitted to the county executive committees who, by lot, determine the order of names on the ballot and arrange for printing the primary ballot. Following the first primary, the county chairmen transmit the returns for statewide races to the state chairman, whereupon a canvass is made by the state executive committee. In the event there is a runoff for the gubernatorial nomination, the state chairman transmits the names of the two candidates receiving the most popular votes to the county chairmen, who include their names on the second primary ballot. Again, the state executive committee canvasses the returns for statewide races after the second primary. The result of this canvass is reported to the September state convention (even year) which must certify the statewide party nominees in order for the names to be included on the November general ballot. Certification by the state convention is a mere formality.

Whether nominated by the primary or convention method, the gubernatorial nominees of the respective parties run against each other in the general election, held in November every four years. It sometimes happens that a candidate failing to get the nomination at the state convention or in the primary will receive a few write-in votes in the general election. Write-in votes for other independent candidates may be cast in the November election. In any event, the independents make only token campaigns.

The general election returns for governor (and other statewide offices) are reported to the state election board by the county judges. The secretary of state transmits the returns to the speaker of the house as soon as the speaker is chosen by the incoming regular session of the legislature that meets in January, following the general election. The speaker of the house appoints a joint committee of both houses to canvass the returns. The two houses act as an umpire in case of an equal number of popular votes or contested election, through the Texas legislature has never performed this function, and there is little likelihood that it ever will.

Term of Office and Salary

The governor assumes office the first Tuesday after the organization of the legislature, or as soon thereafter as practicable, and holds office for four years, or until his successor shall be installed. There is no limitation, as in the federal system, on the number of terms the "first citizen" of the state may serve. Other than health, the only obstacle to long tenure is the ability to secure renomination and reelection.

The Texas constitution was amended to authorize the legislature to determine the salary of the governor. In addition to salary, the legislature supplies funds for the running of the governor's mansion, and an airplane is available for the governor's convenience.

Succession

The office of governor might become vacant because of death, resignation, removal from office, inability to serve, or if the governor is out of state. In such cases the lieutenant governor, who presides over the senate and is elected by the voters every four years, would exercise the powers of governor. The qualifications for lieutenant governor are the same as those for governor; and while acting as chief executive he receives the same compensation as the governor. If the office of lieutenant governor becomes vacant, the president pro tem of the senate is next in line of succession, followed by the speaker of the house, the attorney general, and the chief justice of each of the courts of appeals in the numerical order of the districts.

An amendment to the constitution provides that if the governor-elect should die before taking office, "then the person having the highest number of votes for the office of Lieutenant Governor shall act as Governor until after the next general election." It also provides "that in the event the person with the highest number of votes for the office of Governor . . . shall become disabled, or fail to qualify, then the Lieutenant Governor shall act as Governor until a person has qualified for the office of Governor or until after the next general election. Any succession to the Governorship not otherwise provided for in this Constitution, may be provided for by law." The legislature passed a law that declares that if both the governor and the lieutenant governor-elect should die or become permanently disabled before assuming office, the speaker of the house and president pro tem of the senate must call a joint session of the legislature to elect a governor and lieutenant governor to hold office until the next general election, at which time the unexpired two-year remainder of the term shall be filled by election.

Removal from Office

Chief executives of the states may be removed from office before their term of office expires by impeachment and popular recall. Popular recall may or may not involve specific charges; none of the judicial procedures of impeachment are brought into play, and the people make the final decision. Few chief executives have been removed by popular recall or impeachment.* The only method of removing the governor from office in Texas before his term expires is by impeachment.

The Ferguson Affair

The Ferguson affair in 1917 represents the only instance of the impeachment and conviction of a governor in Texas. James E. Ferguson was removed from office during his second term as governor of Texas (January 19, 1915, to August 25, 1917). Miriam A. Ferguson, his wife, was twice elected governor of Texas, serving from 1925 to 1927 and from 1933 to 1935.

As a result of the conflict between Governor James E. Ferguson and the University of Texas, charges were brought against the governor for the misapplication of public funds. These charges served as a basis for most of the articles of impeachment approved by the Texas house of representatives. It is possible that, had there been no conflict with the University of Texas, the governor might have escaped an investigation of his handling of public funds.

The conflict with the University of Texas had its beginning with the appropriations by the legislature for the university. The caption of the university section of the appropriations bill declared that the appropriations were made "with such changes and substitutions within the total of the following items for the University as the Regents may find necessary." The governor thought the appropriations law vested too much power in the university board of regents. This was the beginning of the conflict: the governor of Texas versus the University of Texas board of regents.

The university board of regents appointed a president of the university. To some of the regents the governor expressed the opinion that he should have been consulted in the matter, notwithstanding the fact the Texas constitution vests in the board of regents the power to superintend the university. The governor named six members of the university faculty and said they must be discharged, although no reasons were given by the governor why such action should be taken. The governor charged the faculty members with political activity, speculation, fraud, and outright theft. He demanded the dismissal of these faculty members without a hearing. The board of regents refused to act in such an arbitrary manner, and after an investigation, acquitted the professors and refused to terminate their services with the University.

In time, the governor centered his attention on the university board of regents. He wrote to one member of the board saying, "unless I may be assured of your full and complete cooperation, I will much appreciate your sending to me at once your

---

*In 1921 Governor Frazier of North Dakota was removed from office. This is the only instance of a governor being removed by the recall method.

resignation as a member of the Board of Regents under my appointment." The governor asked the cooperation of other regents meaning that they vote as he desired. Finally, the governor asked the president of the university and certain regents to resign, but they refused to do so. The failure of the board of regents to follow the advice of the governor and the attempt of the latter to stack the board with his own appointees were important factors in the conflict between the governor and the university. A climax was reached in the struggle when the governor vetoed the university appropriation in 1917.

The governor took his appeal to the people and vilified the "university crowd" in a number of speeches. Some of the epithets which he applied to the university faculty included "butterfly chasers," "daydreamers," "educated fools,"* etc. The governor made it appear that the university was autocratic and unfriendly to the common schools; he maintained that higher education was undemocratic and was seeking more rights than were guaranteed the average citizen. The governor declared "I call on you my friends that this is a fight of the state university on a governor of Texas because he is not a college graduate and refuses to bow to their will, and the question is whether I am going to be sustained for fighting for the people or whether they are going to be sustained for robbing the people."

Action in the House of Representatives

The house of representatives, sitting as a grand jury, indicted Ferguson on twenty-one counts, of which ten were sustained by the senate. The house passed a resolution to investigate the conduct of the governor. He appeared before the house investigating committee and also before the committee of the whole house. These hearings indicated there was sufficient evidence of wrongdoing to justify bringing impeachment charges against the governor. As a result, the house appointed a board of managers, which drew up the articles of impeachment and served as prosecutors for the house during the trial in the senate. The articles of impeachment were approved by a vote of seventy-four to forty-five in the house.

The articles of impeachment, as approved by the house, included the following charges.

1. Governor Ferguson deposited state funds in the Temple State Bank, a bank in which he owned more than one-fourth of the stock. The bank and the governor used the state funds and received the profit and benefit.
2. State funds deposited with the Temple State Bank were used to pay a note of $5,000, together with $600 interest, due by James E. Ferguson to the First National Bank at Temple, Texas. That said amount was never refunded to the state.
3. The governor deposited other state funds in banks in which he was interested as a stockholder, and in the American National Bank in Austin, to which he shortly afterwards became indebted.
4. The governor used, misapplied, and diverted state funds for his own benefit and profit.
5. When investigated by the committee of the whole house of representatives, the governor testified that during the regular session of the thirty-fifth Legislature, and shortly thereafter, he received from parties certain currency in varying

amounts, the total of which was about $156,500. When questioned as to who loaned him the money, the governor declined to answer, although the officer of the committee of the whole appointed to pass on the admissibility of testimony ruled that he should answer, and the committee sustained the ruling. Hence, the governor was in contempt of the house and its committee. The receipt of this money, and the failure to account for it, constituted official misconduct in office.

6. The board of regents of the University of Texas, established by the constitution of Texas, is given the management of the university. After the faculty members were exonerated by the board of regents, the governor sought to have them expelled from the university. Thus, he sought to set aside the constitution and law and to assert his own autocratic will.

7. The governor sought to remove members of the board of regents of the university without "good and sufficient cause," as provided by law. He attempted to remove them or force their resignation because he could not dictate to them as to how they should cast their votes in matters arising before them. Such conduct was a violation of the law and would have made inoperative the provision of the Texas constitution, which provides for six-year terms of office for members of the university board of regents.

The state depository board did not exist at the time James E. Ferguson was governor of Texas. Today, the board is composed of the state treasurer (as secretary), a citizen of the state appointed by the governor and senate for a two year term, and the banking commissioner. The board designates the state depositories and determines the amount of state funds to be deposited in state and national banks in the state, as well as contracts with the depositories concerning the payment of interest on state deposits.

Approval of each of the twenty-one articles of impeachment required only a majority vote in the house of representatives. The impeachment article of the Texas constitution (Art. XV) provides that "no person shall be convicted without the concurrence of two thirds of the Senators present." Also, the article provides that "judgment in cases of impeachment shall extend only to removal from office and disqualification from holding any office of honor, trust or profit under this State. A party convicted on impeachment shall also be subject to indictment, trial and punishment, according to law."

The Law of Impeachment[5]

The law of impeachment, as it has thus far evolved in Texas, is based upon the proceedings of the Ferguson trial, the opinions of the attorney general, and the case of *Ferguson* v. *Maddox* (263 S.W. 888), decided by the supreme court of Texas in 1924. In the Maddox case, suit was brought by the appellee, John F. Maddox, a resident and qualified Democratic voter of Harris County, against James E. Ferguson and the members of the Democratic state executive committee, to enjoin the placing of the name of the defendant Ferguson, as a candidate for governor, on the official ballot of the Democratic primary, held in July 1924. Some interesting legal issues were presented in this case and in the advisory opinions of the attorney general.

Impeachment at a Special Session

The Texas constitution provides, "When the Legislature shall be convened in special session, there shall be *no legislation upon* subjects other than those designated in the proclamation of the Governor calling such session, or presented to them by the Governor; and no such session shall be of longer duration than thirty days" (Art. III, Sec. 40 italics added).

The speaker of the house, on his own motion, issued a call for the house to meet in special session on August 1, 1917, to consider the impeachment of the governor. Because of the above constitutional provision, Governor Ferguson thought he could limit the action of a called session. Hence, before the house members could assemble in Austin, the governor issued a call for a special session of the legislature to meet at the same time as that set by the Speaker's call. In his proclamation calling the special session, the governor declared the legislature was meeting "for the purpose of considering and making additional appropriation for the support and maintenance of the State University for the two fiscal years beginning September 1, 1919." Notwithstanding the governor's proclamation calling the special session, the house proceeded with the investigation and impeached the governor, which resulted in his suspension from office. Was the legislature's action in conflict with Article III, Section 40, of the Texas constitution?

The Texas supreme court held that

> . . . the sole function of the House and Senate is not to compose "the Legislature," and to act together in the making of laws. Each, in the plainest language, is given separate plenary power and jurisdiction in relation to matters of impeachment. . . . These powers are essentially judicial in their nature. Their proper exercise does not, in the remotest degree, involve any legislative function.

The court was able to conclude that Article III, Section 40, of the constitution imposes no limitation, *save as to legislation.* Therefore, the court held that the house had authority to impeach Governor Ferguson, and the senate to enter upon trial of the charges at the special session, though the matter of his impeachment was not mentioned in the governor's proclamation convening it.

It would have raised an interesting legal issue had Governor Ferguson not called the special session and the legislature instead assembled on the call of the speaker of the house. In short, may the house and senate meet for impeachment purposes at any time, regardless of the governor, and independently of regular or special sessions? There is no precedent for such a self-convened special session for impeachment purposes. Although the question was not involved in the Ferguson impeachment, the court did say in the Maddox case that:

> The powers of the House and Senate in relation to impeachment exist at all times. They may exercise these powers during a regular session. . . . Without doubt, they may exercise them during a special session, unless the Constitution itself forbids . . . the broad power conferred by article 15 [impeachment] stands without limit or qualification as to the time of its exercise.

This seems to imply that if the legislature had convened without the call of the governor, it would have been upheld. To eliminate any possibility that the legislature could not meet for impeachment purposes except by call of the governor (except in regular session), the third called session of the 35th Legislature, 1917, passed a law whereby each house may convene itself for this purpose.

Resignation of the Governor

On September 24, 1917, Governor Ferguson filed in the office of the secretary of state his resignation—"same to take effect immediately." This was one day prior to the judgment of impeachment, which was rendered on September 25, 1917.

> On no admissable theory could this resignation impair the jurisdiction or power of the court to render judgement. The subject matter was within its jurisdiction. It had jurisdiction of the person of the Governor; it had heard the evidence and declared him guilty. Its power to conclude the proceedings and enter judgement was not dependent upon the will or act of the Governor. Otherwise, a solemn trial before a high tribunal would be turned into a farce. If the Senate only had the power to remove from office, it might be said, with some show of reason, that it should not have proceeded further when the Governor, by anticipation performed, as it were, its impending judgement. But under the Constitution the Senate may not only remove the offending official; it may disqualify him from holding further office, and with relation to this latter matter his resignation is wholly immaterial. . . . The purpose of the constitutional provision may not be thwarted by an eleventh hour resignation.

Impeachable Offenses

Ferguson's lawyers contended in the Maddox case that the impeachment judgment was invalid, since neither the constitution nor statutes of the state defined or designated the specific acts and conduct for which an individual could be removed from office and disqualified thereafter from holding any office of honor, trust, or profit under the state. The court did not think this argument was well taken:

> While impeachable offenses are not defined in the Constitution, they are very clearly designated or pointed out by the term "impeachment," which at once connotes the offenses to be considered and the procedure for the trial thereof. . . . There is no warrant for the contention that there is no such thing as impeachment in Texas because of the absence of a statutory definition of impeachable offenses.

Status of the House and Senate in Impeachment Proceedings

The supreme court of Texas, in 1924, presented a clear statement on the status of the house and senate in impeachment proceedings:

> In the matter of impeachment the House acts somewhat in the capacity of a grand jury. It investigates, hears witnesses, and determines whether or not there is sufficient ground to justify the presentment of charges, and, if so, it adopts appropriate articles and prefers them before the Senate. . . .
> . . . During the trial the Senate sits "as a court of impeachment," and at its conclusion renders a "judgment." . . . The Senate sitting in an impeachment trial is just as truly a court as is this court. Its jurisdiction is very limited, but such as it has is of the highest. It is original, exclusive, and final. Within the scope of its constitutional authority, no one may gainsay its judgment.

Penalty on Conviction for Impeachment

The Texas constitution stipulates that "judgment in cases of impeachment shall extend only to removal from office, and disqualification from holding any office of honor, trust or profit under this State. A Party convicted on impeachment shall alsc be subject to indictment trial and punishment according to law'' (Art. XV, Sec. 4). This provision leaves little doubt that the penalty that may be inflicted upon conviction in the senate may not extend beyond the person removed from office. However, when the court ruled, in June, 1924, that Mr. Ferguson was ineligible to seek public office, his wife filed for the nomination for governor in the Democratic primary. Her filing fee was accepted by the state executive committee, her name included on the primary ballot, and in the ensuing campaign she won the nomination. A suit was filed to prevent the inclusion of her name on the general-election ballot. The suit was based in part on the fact she was the wife of an impeached and convicted former governor. Part of the argument by counsel for the appellant was based upon the theory of legal identity of husband and wife. That is, since the emoluments of the office of governor were community property, Mr. Ferguson could not receive his community half of Mrs. Ferguson's salary without violating the impeachment judgment. The supreme court of Texas repudiated this argument and held that if Mrs. Ferguson were elected in the general election, her husband would not receive any emolument or ''profit'' *derived from any office held by himself.* Hence, the penalties on conviction of impeachment do not extend to members of the family of an official removed from office by impeachment.

Notwithstanding the unsuccessful attempt to convene the house of representatives in the fall of 1925 to investigate certain alleged irregularities in the administration of Governor Miriam A. Ferguson, the latter was twice elected governor and served two full terms.

The Clemency Power in Impeachment

In 1925 the Texas legislature passed a law that was designed to restore to Mr. Ferguson the political right to hold public office in the state. (He was not ineligible for an elective or appointive federal office or position.) The law granted to *any person* convicted on impeachment ''a full and unconditional release of any and all acts and offences of which he was so convicted,'' and provided that all the penalties imposed by the impeachment court should be ''fully cancelled, remitted, released, and discharged.'' The house of representatives requested an advisory opinion from the attorney general and on February 12, 1925, the chief law officer of the state advised the legislature that the amnesty legislation was unconstitutional. The following legislature, meeting in 1927, repealed the act. The amnesty power, whether exercised by the legislative or executive branch of government, does not extend to those removed from office by impeachment.

10 The Role of the Governor

IN THE PERFORMANCE OF his various executive, legislative, and political functions, the governor is assisted by the individuals that make up the executive office of governor.

The Executive Office of the Governor

The newly elected governor has the important task of staffing the executive office. The selection, appointment, and retention of capable assistants and secretaries will in no small measure determine the success or failure of the governor.

The number of persons and units in the executive office of the governor, and its organization, depends upon the governor's personality and manner of operation, as well as the amount of funds appropriated for the office by the legislature.

The governor might have on his staff an executive assistant and chief coordinator who would take care of many of the official, but lesser, functions of the governor and handle most of the governor's personal correspondence and telephone calls. At any press conference of the governor, the executive assistant may be standing "off" or "on" stage to offer his assistance to the governor on various major issues during the question-and-answer period of the press conference.

An administrative assistant may handle matters concerning city planning and development. Another administrative assistant may keep track of the governor's bills—see that they are introduced, and so on. Another administrative assistant may handle the governor's itinerary. One administrative assistant may serve as the governor's budget assistant. The governor's press secretary is a key man on the governor's staff.

Powers of the Governor

As a matter of convenience, the powers of the governor may be classified as executive, legislative, and political. The chief executive's legislative and political powers, his most important powers, have been discussed previously. This chapter is devoted primarily to his executive functions.

Executive Powers

Law Enforcement

The Texas constitution declares the governor "shall cause the laws to be faithfully executed," yet the chief executive has little direct influence on law enforcement. In criminal actions the prosecutors, attorney general, district and county attorneys, as well as city attorneys, who prosecute in the name of the state or local unit, are popularly elected or locally appointed (city attorneys), and thus, are not directly responsible to the governor. The same is true of the locally elected county sheriffs and locally appointed municipal law-enforcing officials. In fact, the governor has no power to remove a state or local prosecutor or police officer for failure to prosecute or enforce the law. Law enforcing and prosecuting are very much decentralized in Texas, which in part accounts for the high crime rate. As far as wrongdoing by state employees is concerned, say the misapplication, misuse, or diversion of public funds, the state auditor would discover the illegal practice in his postaudit of state accounts. This information would be turned over to the grand jury and legislature for appropriate action. It might lead to prosecution in the regular courts, impeachment proceedings, or both, depending upon the official or employee involved.

The Texas highway patrol and the Texas Rangers operate under the director of public safety, who is appointed by the public safety commission. Many of the agencies in the state, such as the departments of banking and health, state board of insurance, alcoholic beverage commission, among others, have their own attorneys and investigators. In case of law violation they turn over the evidence to the attorney general or to the local district or county attorneys for grand-jury action and prosecution.

Despite the lack of direct control over law enforcement, the governor, as first citizen of the state, can use his official position to focus public attention on such matters as loan sharks, juvenile delinquency, and so on. The governor may also make recommendations to the legislature for strengthening the law and law-enforcement machinery. One of the big problems in Texas is lack of adequate staff and budget for prosecutors, attorneys, investigators, and law-enforcing agencies at both the state and local level. This represents poor management and false economy.

Military Power

According to the state constitution, the governor is "Commander-in-Chief of the military forces of the State, except when they are called into actual service of the United States. He shall have the power to call forth the militia to execute the laws of the State, to suppress insurrections, repel invasions, and protect the frontier from hostile incursions by Indians or other predatory bands" (Art. IV, Sec. 7). The last sentence in the section above indicates how out-of-date is the fundamental law of the state. If the civil authorities are unable to maintain law and order in a certain area, the governor may declare martial law and dispatch units of the state militia to the trouble spot. The occasion for most declarations of martial law and calling out the state militia in the past have been times of disaster, riot, and during the oil-boom days.

The adjutant general, who is appointed by the governor and subject to his orders, represents the governor in the actual administration of the military forces of the state. The Texas state guard is not subject to mobilization by the federal government. It was created by state law at the beginning of World War II and remained on active-duty status until the National Guard returned to state service after the war, at which time it was continued by law as the reserve corps. It was changed from an infantry-trained unit to one of internal security and military police and was made an internal-security adjunct of the Texas National Guard. The Texas state guard takes over as the state militia when the National Guard is called to active duty. Members of the Texas state guard receive no regular pay; however, they do receive pay if called into active duty by the governor and for mobilization drills once a year.

The Texas National Guard is composed of the Texas Army National Guard and the Texas Air National Guard. The governor of the state commissions all the National Guard officers, but if an officer does not meet federally prescribed standards, although his National Guard commission cannot be withdrawn, federal pay will terminate and the state will be required to provide an officer who can meet national standards. Each acceptable National Guard officer also receives a commission as a reserve officer issued by the president. A person could hold a commission as a Texas Guard officer while being denied one as a National Guard officer.

The National Guard Association of Texas and the Texas State Guard Association strive to promote the interest of the National Guard and the Texas State Guard. These associations are in fact pressure groups. The National Guard Association of Texas is a part of a national organization with comparable objectives and with a fairly effective lobby both inside the defense establishment and in Congress.

A state may find itself unable to cope with a local disturbance, such as insurrection, riots, and other forms of domestic violence, in which case the state may request assistance from the national authorities. The state request may be made by the legislature or governor, and the president will comply unless he believes the state can handle the situation alone. If a federal function is interfered with in the state, the president has the power to dispatch federal marshals or troops to the area without a formal request from the state and, if necessary, over the protest of the state. If there is conflict between the national and state authorities over carrying out a federal function in the state, the president may eliminate some of the friction by federalizing the National Guard in the local area. Furthermore, a federal court may enjoin a state governor from using troops to obstruct carrying out a federal function.

On October 13, 1931, owners of Texas oil and gas interests brought suit, in the federal district court, against members of the Texas railroad commission, the attorney general of the state, and others, to restrain the enforcement of orders of the commission limiting the production of oil. The federal district court issued a temporary restraining order, and Governor Sterling, on learning that the railroad commission orders could no longer be enforced, ordered the use of state troops to carry out the railroad commission's orders. In *Sterling* v. *Constantin* (53 S.Ct. 190, 1932), the U.S. Supreme Court unanimously affirmed the federal district court order enjoining Governor Sterling from using martial law and state troops in an effort to override a federal court decision. A strongly worded opinion by Chief Justice Charles Evans Hughes concluded:

> If it be assumed that the Governor was entitled to declare a state of insurrection and to bring military force to the aid of civil authority, the proper use of that power in this instance was to maintain the federal court in the exercise of its jurisdiction, and not to attempt to override it; to aid in making its process effective and not to nullify it, to remove, and not to create, obstructions to the exercise by the complainants of their rights as judicially declared.

Chief Justice Hughes admitted that a governor has wide discretion in ordering the use of troops to meet an emergency. Yet, it does not follow:

> from the fact that the executive has this range of discretion, deemed to be a necessary incident of his power to suppress disorder, that every sort of action the Governor may take, no matter how unjustified by the exigency or subversive of private right and the jurisdiction of the courts, otherwise available, is conclusively supported by mere executive fiat. The contrary is well established. *What are the allowable limits of military discretion, and whether or not they have been overstepped in a particular case, are judicial questions.* [Italics added]

Appellants asserted "that the court was powerless thus to intervene, and that the Governor's order had the quality of a supreme and unchallengeable edict, overriding all conflicting rights of property and unreviewable through the judicial power of the federal government." In reply to this contention Hughes said:

> If this extreme position could be deemed to be well taken, it is manifest that the fiat of a state Governor, and not the Constitution of the United States, would be the supreme law of the land; that the restrictions of the Federal Constitution upon the exercise of state power would be but impotent phrases, the futility of which the state may at any time disclose by the simple process of transferring powers of legislation to the Governor to be exercised by him, beyond control, upon his assertion of necessity. Under our system of government, such a conclusion is obviously untenable. There is no such avenue of escape from the paramount authority of the Federal Constitution.

The federal district court made the following finding:

> It was conceded that at no time has there been any actual uprising in the territory. At no time has any military force been exerted to put riots or mobs down. At no time, except in the refusal of the defendant Wolters [brigadier general of the Texas National Guard] to observe the injunction in this case, have the civil authorities or courts been interfered with or their processes made impotent. . . . We find, therefore, that, not only was there never any actual riot, tumult, or insurrection, which would create a state of war existing in the field, but that, if all of the conditions had come to pass, they would have resulted merely in breaches of the peace, to be suppressed by the militia as a civil force, and not at all in a condition constituting, or even remotely resembling, a state of war.

To maintain law and order—and to keep the peace—are noble objectives in Democratic government. However, as "desirable as this is, and important as is the preservation of the public peace, this aim cannot be accomplished by laws or ordinances which deny rights created or protected by the federal Constitution."[1]

Clemency Power

The constitution of Texas provides,

> The Legislature shall by law establish a Board of Pardons and Paroles and shall require it to keep record of its actions and the reasons for its actions. The Legislature shall have authority to enact parole laws.

> In all criminal cases, except treason and impeachment, the Governor shall have power, after conviction, on the written signed recommendation and advice of the Board of Pardons and Paroles, or a majority thereof, to grant reprieves and commutations of punishment and pardons; and under such rules as the Legislature may prescribe, and upon the written recommendation and advice of a majority of the Board of Pardons and Paroles, he shall have the power to remit fines and forfeitures. The Governor shall have the power to grant one reprieve in any capital case for a period not to exceed thirty (30) days: and he shall have power to revoke conditional pardons. With the advice and consent of the Legislature, he may grant reprieves, commutations of punishment and pardons in cases of treason.

The legislature provided the board of pardons and paroles be composed of six persons appointed by the governor with consent of two-thirds of the senate. The members are appointed for terms of six years.

Clemency—or the act of leniency or mercy—may be granted only to those persons who have been convicted of violating some law of the state. Furthermore, the governor's clemency power does not extend to persons convicted of impeachment charges in the senate. Also, the governor is limited by the board of pardons and paroles and the legislature (in cases of treason), and the board has the power to revoke paroles. The limitations on the governor by the amendment represent a distrust of the chief executive that grew out of previous executive misuse of the power.

At his own discretion, the governor may grant one thirty-day reprieve in any capital case. Other acts of clemency by the governor may be granted upon the recommendation of the board of pardons and paroles. If clemency is recommended by the board, the governor may use his own judgment in determining whether it should be granted. In most cases the governor does follow the recommendation of the board of pardons and paroles. The governor might ask the board to investigate a particular case, but he could not take any official action in the matter of clemency until a recommendation had been made by the board. The court of criminal appeals has held the governor may grant *less,* but not *more,* clemency than that recommended by the board of pardons and paroles.[2] The types of executive clemency are listed below.

Reprieve. A reprieve temporarily suspends execution of the penalty imposed. There are several types of reprieves. (1) *Reprieve and stay of execution of death sentence.* The governor may grant each prisoner sentenced to death one thirty-day reprieve and stay of execution without the board's recommendation. Additional reprieves may be granted only upon recommendation of the board. (2) *Trial reprieve.* Trial reprieve is a type of clemency used in cases in which the convicted person is assessed a jail sentence that temporarily suspends the execution of the penalty imposed. In almost all instances this would mean a misdemeanor conviction. However, there are a few felony convictions that are also punishable with a jail sentence. This type of sentence is not covered under the probation and parole law, and the procedure of trial reprieve is the only type of clemency that can be used.

Trial reprieve "does not release the subject from his sentence, nor does time out on reprieve count on his sentence. It merely releases the subject from jail for the period of time covered by the reprieve; and unless it is extended or the penalty remitted by clemency, [the individual] must return to jail at the expiration thereof or be subject to immediate arrest." (3) *Emergency reprieve.* An emergency reprieve may be recommended only in cases of critical illness or death in the immediate family of the inmate. (4) *Emergency medical reprieve.* If a prisoner needs medical or surgical services not available in the Texas prison system, an emergency medical reprieve may be granted. (5) *Emergency reprieve to attend civil court proceedings.* The civil suit must involve a vested interest of the inmate.

Commutation of Sentence. A commutation of sentence is the means by which a death penalty or a period of confinement or fine (or both imprisonment and fine) may be reduced. The board can recommend the "equalization" of penalties downward but not upward.

Full Pardon and Restoration of Civil Rights. A full pardon is forgiveness for the offense, and in felony cases, full civil rights are restored. It is the board's policy not to consider an applicant for full pardon until one year after release from parole or discharge from the Texas department of corrections.

Parole. Parole is an outgrowth of trial reprieves, trial paroles, and commutation of sentence. An offender may be paroled, after he has served a part of his sentence, under the continued custody of the state and under conditions that permit his reincarceration in the event of his misbehavior. The purpose of parole is to bridge the gap between the closely ordered life in prison and the freedom of normal community living. In some cases, the board may be of the opinion that a parolee is not yet deserving of a full pardon, but is eligible for some consideration. In such cases, the board may release the individual from reporting to his parole supervisor.

A parole has no connection with forgiveness, nor is it a reduction of sentence. In fact, the term to be served is lengthened, since the parolee is credited only with calendar time after parole. In the event of revocation of parole, no time served on parole is credited against the remaining sentence. Any person confined in a penal institution of the state, except a person under sentence of death, is eligible for parole consideration after having obtained credit for one-third of the maximum sentence, provided that in any case one may be paroled after serving twenty calendar years. Time served is total calendar time served with all credits allowed under existing law.

If a prisoner has served a total of two years of a three-year term and is released on parole, he will have one calendar year on parole. In other words, the duration of parole is determined by the amount of time (in calendar days) left to serve on the original sentence. In the case of a life sentence it is possible for a person to remain on parole and under supervision for the remainder of his life. The law does not allow either the board of pardons and paroles or the governor to terminate a sentence because of good behavior, except by full pardon. However, it is possible for a parolee to be released from reporting and to serve the remainder of his parole period without supervision. An individual who has a life sentence may be placed on an annual reporting status after he has been on parole for a minimum of three years.

Parole differs from pardon and probation. A pardon is granted by the governor upon recommendation of the board of pardons and paroles, whereas parole is granted by the board. Parole may be granted only after imprisonment; a pardon may occur both before and after imprisonment. Unlike a pardon, which forgives a prisoner and may restore civil rights, parole does not devote forgiveness or restore civil rights.

Probation is a suspension of sentence during good behavior. If one successfully serves the probated term, a probationer does not serve any time in prison. Parole presupposes service of part of the sentence in prison.

Since Texas is a member of the interstate parole compact, out-of-state parolees in Texas are supervised by Texas parole officials; Texas parolees, when outside the state, are supervised by the parole officers of the particular state.

Shock Probation. Shock probation gives a first offender sentenced to ten years or less a brief taste of prison life in order to deter the individual from committing future crimes. Only the original sentencing judge may grant shock probation, and the law allows judges 180 days to decide whether to grant it. Crimes for which the defendant is ineligible for shock probation include homicide, rape, robbery, kidnapping, and bribery.

State law permits judges to set conditions for probation that can require offenders to repay crime victims for property damage or medical expenses. Restitution also can be made to the community in the form of work for nonprofit social agencies or programs. Community service is often ordered by courts when a defendant is financially unable to make monetary restitution, or in those cases where a fine would have little significance to the offender as punishment.

Interstate Rendition. Interstate rendition is somewhat similar to extradition, a recognized practice between nations. In the domain of international relations, extradition may be accorded as a matter of comity (courtesy or good will) or may result from treaties entered into between two or more nations. However, the basis for interstate rendition is the U.S. Constitution rather than interstate compacts. According to the federal Constitution, "A person charged in any State with treason, felony, or other crime, who shall flee from justice, and be found in another State shall, on demand of the executive authority of the State from which he fled, be delivered up, to be removed to the State having jurisdiction of the crime." (Art. IV, Sec. 2). Hence, interstate rendition and extradition differ both with regard to the governmental authorities involved (states or nations) and the basis for the practice (an extradition treaty, comity, or the U.S. Constitution).

The rendition clause of the federal Constitution appears to be mandatory. Normally, rendition is handled as a purely routine matter between the governors and law-enforcement officers of the states concerned because it is to the mutual advantage of the states to honor rendition requests.* In fact, states have not hesitated to give up even their own citizens on proper demand. Yet governors have not always

---

*There appears to be no rule against trying a fugitive for some offense other than that for which his return was demanded.

elected to honor rendition requests. The reasons for the occasional refusals are usually based upon the fact that the individual has become a law-abiding citizen of his new state, unnecessary delay in making the request, fear of an unfair trial in the requesting state, and insufficiency of evidence. There is the classic case of Robert E. Burns, who escaped from a chain gang in Georgia, settled in New Jersey, and wrote the popular book *I Am a Fugitive from a Georgia Chain Gang*. Georgia officials, who were very unhappy about the unfavorable publicity given the state and its penal methods as a result of this literary effort, requested the governor of New Jersey to extradite the author. Since the chief executive of New Jersey was sympathetic with Burns and his cause, the rendition request was refused. As a result, Burns lived safely in New Jersey for many years. In time Burns was granted a full pardon by Governor Ellis Arnall of Georgia.

Despite the mandatory nature of the rendition clause of the federal Constitution, and the occasional denial of rendition requests, there is no way—by writ of mandamus or otherwise—to force a governor to render up an out-of-state fugitive from justice. Because of this fact the federal government has taken action to strengthen the position of the states in regard to the flight of persons committing crimes. In 1934 Congress passed the Fugitive Felon Act that makes it a federal offense for a person to flee from a state to avoid prosecution or testifying in a criminal case. Nevertheless, the only force impelling a governor to render up a fugitive is his own judgment and conscience. It should be pointed out that the U.S. Supreme Court, in 1952, upheld the conviction of a person kidnapped from Illinois by Michigan officers and returned forcibly to Michigan to stand trial.[3]

The governors of Texas, as well as the chief executives of other states, have experienced little difficulty in the matter of rendition. The governor of Texas merely signs the rendition papers and transmits them to the appropriate law-enforcing officials, who travel to the other state to pick up and return the fugitive.

Financial Powers—A Different Executive Power

As regards the executive budget, prepared by the budget officer and his staff in the governor's office, the chief executive may recommend to the legislature less funds than have been requested by one or more agencies. The governor may ask one or all state agencies to reconsider their budgetary requests.

Despite the joint budget hearings held by the staffs of the legislative budget board and the executive budget officer in the governor's office, as well as the comparative budget analysis of both agencies made available to the executive and legislative branches, one may doubt that the dual budget in Texas has justified its continuation. The governor has little control over state finance, and this is due in no small measure to the dual budget system. In a sense, Texas has a headless budgetary system.

If one or more state agencies run out of money before the end of the two-year budget period, or if confronted with an emergency, the governor may approve deficiency warrants; however, they may not exceed $200,000 for all purposes for the biennium. These deficiency warrants permit the agencies to operate in the red until the legislature, at a special or the next regular session, enacts a deficiency appropriation bill. Such an appropriation bill is always a possibility as long as Texas operates under the biennial budget plan. It is rather difficult for the budget officials and the legislature to estimate the funds the various agencies of the state will need for a two-year period.

The chief executive may request financial reports from the departments, boards, commissions, and institutions, but he has no means of enforcing his requests.

Channel of Communication

Much of the official and unofficial communications between the state of Texas and the national and state governments are channeled through the governor's office. Besides the formal written communications, the governor meets his fellow governors at the governor's conference and other meetings. Attending conferences of national or state officials—or joint meetings between state and national officials—the governor is informed of what cooperative action is planned or in operation. These meetings permit the governor to present the position of Texas, and, if the occasion demands, he may attempt to line up out-of-state support for the Texas program. Communicating with those beyond the borders and attending conferences with national and state officials from other states with all the personal contacts involved constitutes an important phase in the life of the governor. With adequate public relations, the governor can use the communications, especially the conference and personal contacts, to promote himself politically. Favorable press releases and local news coverage would do the governor no harm in his campaign for reelection or efforts to secure some federal position (appointive or elective).

The Appointive Power

Because of the large number of boards and commissions in Texas, the governor's appointive power is extensive. All vacancies in state or district offices, except members of the legislature, and unless otherwise provided by law, are filled by the chief executive. However, appointments to vacancies in offices elective by the people only continue until the first general election thereafter. If a vacancy occurs in the Texas house or senate, a special election is called by the governor to fill the vacancy. He also fills any temporary vacancy in the U.S. Senate until an election can be held to elect a junior senator from Texas. Other appointments of the governor include some local officials (as public weighers, branch pilots, and pilot boards) and members of his office and military staff.

The politics of gubernatorial appointments compel the governor's staff to consider a number of matters in screening prospective appointees, for example, interest and availability of the individual, qualifications and reputation; whether the appointment would give satisfactory geographic representation on the board; whether the person under consideration is a strong political supporter of the governor; and whether the appointment would antagonize any interest group on which the governor relies for support. Other limitations on the governor's appointive power are summarized below.

The Long Ballot. Popular election of the attorney general, comptroller of public accounts, treasurer, commissioner of the general land office, commissioner of agriculture, members of the railroad commission, and members of the state board of education as well as the election of judges not only lengthens the ballot, but also decreases the number of persons who might be appointed by the governor. In contrast, the heads of departments and judges in the federal system are appointed by the president and the Senate. The long ballot in Texas contributes its part in establishing disintegration and irresponsibility in the executive or administrative branch. It has weakened the governor's control over administration and made it difficult, if not impossible, to establish a direct and responsible line of control for action and inaction in government. In short, it has established something approaching the plural executive system in Texas.

Action in the Senate. The constitution of Texas requires a two-thirds vote of the senators present to confirm appointments made by the governor. Such a limitation on the appointive power of the governor appears unnecessary.

The senate has, on occasion, changed its rules on executive sessions (closed-door meetings in which senators privately discuss various persons a governor has nominated to a state agency). Senators may move to close such a session, and the motion requires only a majority vote. At one time the senate rules provided that such sessions be closed automatically unless the senate voted to keep them open. The rules of the upper house permit individual senators to divulge how they voted in closed session. Committee hearings on the governor's appointments are open to the public unless a majority of the nominations committee votes in favor of closed committee hearings.

The matter of recess appointments has its political aspects and sometimes involves controversy. May the senate of Texas lawfully convene, of its own motion, to consider recess appointments made by the governor? The Texas supreme court, when answering this question in the negative, admitted there was nothing in Article IV, Section 12, of the Texas constitution that declares that the senate may or may not convene on its own motion. However, the majority was mindful of the fact that the constitution confers on the governor the power to call special sessions. Hence, the senate could not enlarge, restrict, or destroy the powers of the governor except as the power to do so was expressly given by the constitution.[4]

The court emphasized the fact that the governor must submit the names of his recess appointments to the senate *during the first ten days of its session,* and it gave considerable weight to the fact that forty-eight legislatures had met prior to the controversy and none had ever asserted this power, even though there had been much conflict between the governor and the senate in the past. In other words, had the power existed, it would have been exercised.

By way of summary the opinion of the court was based upon the following: (1) The constitution authorizes the governor to call special sessions; (2) the constitution does not authorize the senate to call itself into special session; (3) the salary of legislators at the time was based upon time spent in regular and called sessions by the governor; (4) if the senate could call itself into special session to act upon recess appointments, the governor would have been required to submit his nomination to the senate immediately rather than anytime within ten days; and (5) the alleged power of the senate to convene itself for this purpose had never been exercised before.

The decision by the Texas supreme court was a five to four opinion. In a strong dissenting opinion, Chief Justice Alexander considered the confirmation of appointments by the senate a nonlegislative function; therefore, like impeachment proceedings, the meetings of the senate are not limited by the constitutional provision. The chief justice reasoned that the state constitution confers upon the senate the authority to pass upon appointments made by the governor. It contains no limitation as to when the senate may exercise this authority.

Under the majority opinion, at least in the opinion of the chief justice, the governor could defeat the power conferred upon the senate by the basic law, which in a sense defeats the will of the people. The fact that the senate had not previously asserted the power did not indicate that the power did not exist.

The dissenting opinion pointed out the strict construction given the constitution by the majority opinion. Rather than a tendency toward rigid or strict construction, it was argued that state constitutions should be more liberally construed.

Senatorial Courtesy. Another limitation on the appointive power of the governor is the matter of senatorial courtesy. Normally if there is a vacancy to be filled in one of the thirty-one senatorial districts, the governor will consult with the senator from the district before making the appointment. If the governor did not appoint a person recommended by the home district senator, the latter would state in the senate that the appointee was objectionable to the senator, in which he might or might not give his reasons, and the other senators would vote against confirmation. Even if the legislature is not in session, the governor will consult with the home district senator before making a recess appointment. This is a practical maneuver on the part of the senators to exercise some control over patronage in the senatorial districts. Actually, it forces the governor to consult with the senators before making a nomination. It is a good example of political pragmatism, which permeates government at all levels in the United States.

Since a number of state agencies are located in Austin and Travis County, the state senator that represents this area is in a favorable patronage position. However, a senator may nominate a resident of the district for a state position that is not within the senatorial district. The governor might feel less inclined to appoint such a person to fill the vacancy.

Technical, Economic, and Geographical Considerations. If the appointment calls for technical qualifications, the representation of different economic or professional groups, or if the members must be from certain geographical areas of the state, the governor's appointive power would obviously be limited by these considerations.

Submission of Names by Governmental Agencies and Private Organizations. The governor is limited in the exercise of the appointive power by the requirement that certain appointments be made from a list of persons submitted to him by various governmental agencies or private organizations.

The Appointive Power of Boards and Commissions. The governor and senate appoint members to serve on various boards and commissions. In many instances the members of these boards appoint and remove the real heads of the particular agencies and the governor has no voice in the exercise of this power. The boards and commissions and the executive heads they appoint include the following: state purchasing and general services commission (executive director; state's purchasing agent and has charge of state buildings), public safety commission (director of the department of public safety), finance commission (state banking commissioner; heads the banking department of Texas), alcoholic beverage commission (administrator; administers Liquor-Control Act), parks and wildlife commission (executive director; the parks and wildlife department is under the policy direction of the parks and wildlife commission; the executive director is the chief executive officer of the department), state board of human resources (commissioner of the state department of human resources), state board of health resources (director, department of health resources; heads the Texas department of health resources), and the elective state board of education (commissioner of education).

The Removal Power

The constitution and statutes of Texas provide three methods of removal: (1) by impeachment, (2) by the governor (in some cases) on address or request of two-thirds of the legislature, and (3) by quo warranto proceedings. The right of any person to hold public office may be tested in the courts by a writ of quo warranto.

The Texas constitution provides that the legislature shall provide "for the trial and removal of all officers of this state, the modes for which have not been provided in this constitution" (Art. XV, Sec. 7). This article of the state constitution was amended as follows: "In addition to the other procedures provided by law for removal of public officers, the governor who appoints an officer may remove the officer with the advice and consent of two-thirds of the members of the senate present. If the legislature is not in session when the governor desires to remove an officer, the governor shall call a special session of the senate for consideration of the proposed removal. The session may not exceed two days in duration."

There is no expressed or implied theory in Texas that the governor's power to appoint purely administrative officials involves the power to remove them. Until the governor is given adequate appointive and removal power, the governor can never be the real chief executive of the state.

Legislative Powers

Messages

Article IV, Section 9, of the Texas constitution provides, "The Governor shall, at the commencement of each session of the Legislature, and at the close of his term of office, give to the Legislature information, by message, of the condition of the State; and he shall recommend to the Legislature such measures as he may deem expedient." During the session the chief executive will send specific proposals to the legislature. At the close of his term of office, the governor's message to the legislature reviews the accomplishments of his administration and the condition of the state in general.

Prior to the convening of the regular session, the governor will consult with members of the house and senate, party leaders, members of the executive branch, and representatives of various interest groups in order to get their views on legislative proposals; he includes these views in his address to the legislature. In matters of finance, the governor will confer with the comptroller, director of the budget, and with the staff and members of the legislative budget board.

The amount of legislative leadership the governor can provide depends, in no small measure, upon the relationship of the governor with the speaker and the leaders of both the house and senate. The legislature tends to rely more and more upon such individuals and agencies as the speaker, lieutenant governor, legislative council, legislative budget board, and interim study committees. This weakens the legislative position of the governor. As a consequence, legislative leadership, involving the formulation and coordination of legislative policy, is decentralized in Texas. For legislative action or inaction, who can be held responsible?

The Governor's Session

Before deciding to call a special session, the governor may contact some of the legislators regarding the need for a special session and their position on proposed legislation. If the legislators, by conversation or letter, gave their support for calling a special session for consideration of specific legislative proposals, the governor and the public might expect the lawmakers to pass the necessary legislation. In other words, it might be considered a presession commitment. For this and other reasons the legislators might not favor a special session unless there was considerable pressure by the people in their districts. The governor might ask the people to inform the legislators of a need for a special session and this way attempt to build up popular support for a called session. A few of the practical considerations involved are the type of legislation or taxes to be considered, the time of meeting, and the question whether a special session would be advantageous to the governor, lieutenant governor, the speaker of the house, and other members of the legislature.

At the end of the first called session the governor could convene a second called session for thirty days. Sometimes the threat of a special session will spur the legislature into great effort during the regular session. Because of the need to look after their own private interests, legislators do not look with favor upon one or more called sessions. The expense involved, public reaction, and extent or nature of legislation passed in the regular session are factors that influence the governor's decision on a special session.

It would be a rather simple matter for the courts to examine the proclamation and messages of the governor, as well as the house and senate journals, to determine if the constitutional requirements had been met. The courts, though, will not make such an investigation. Consequently, it is not uncommon for some local and special legislation to be passed at a special session, although the subject matter was not within the governor's call or submitted by him. The constitutional limitation on the legislature pertains merely to legislative activity, since it does not prohibit the legislature from performing other functions, such as acting upon gubernatorial appointments and considering impeachment charges.

By limiting the major topic or topics to be considered by the legislature in special session, the governor can limit legislative action and focus public attention upon the immediate issue or issues before the house and senate. The governor may limit the special session to one or two major matters and submit other topics to the legislature once it is in session. Since house and senate members may want certain legislation passed during a special session, the governor may bargain with legislators. He may include additional topics in the proclamation calling the special session or suggest additional topics once the legislature is in session to include legislation favored by some legislators in return for their support of the governor's legislative program.

Rather than introduce legislation at a special session, the governor indicates the topic for consideration. In actual practice a friend or spokesman for the governor in the house or senate could introduce legislation drafted by the advisors of the chief executive.

The Veto

Bills vetoed by the governor while the legislature is in session may be overridden by a two-thirds vote of each house. If vetoed after adjournment, it is an absolute veto. At the next called or regular session a postadjournment vetoed bill could be reintroduced and resubmitted to the governor. On appropriation bills the governor may veto—but not reduce—separate items. These item vetoes can be overridden like any other veto by a two-thirds vote in each house. Sometimes the appropriation bills are passed late in the regular session and the legislature may or may not have time to reconsider and repass items of an appropriation bill vetoed by the governor. If the appropriation bills are passed late in the session, such an item veto could amount to an absolute veto.*

Sometimes the governor may threaten to veto a bill if introduced or submitted to his office. Such a threat could discourage the introduction of a bill, or the author might amend or rewrite the bill prior to introduction. If introduced, the threat of veto might prevent its passage in the legislature. The governor will try to avoid such action because he has no desire to involve himself in a conflict with the legislators. He is too dependent upon the legislature as it is.

The governor of Texas has a strong veto power in a constitutionally "weak" office.[5] "The governor has been sustained by the Legislature approximately 95 percent of the time, which indicates the importance of the veto power in Texas."[6]

Political Powers

The governor is one among several individuals in the state who possess important political powers. The speaker of the house, the lieutenant governor, and some of the lobbyists are also important political figures. Usually the governor and his faction of the party dominate the two-year September state convention. In the past the Democratic nominee for governor has vetoed some of the nominees of the senatorial districts at the convention in regard to membership on the state executive committee. By controlling the September convention, the nominee for governor will secure a state executive committee and platform favorable to his views.

---

*Legislative riders on appropriation bills, as a limitation on the item veto power of the governor, have been discussed in a previous chapter.

11 The Administrative System

In THE BROAD SENSE of the term, the administration of government means the management and direction of the functions or activities of government. It includes the operations of the executive, legislative, and judicial branches. One may speak of the administration of justice or judicial administration when referring to the operation of the judicial system. On the other hand, a considerable amount of administrative machinery is involved in the formulation of policy by legislative bodies, for example the work of clerks, secretaries, researchers, and the committee machinery. However, most people conceive of the administrative system as revolving around the chief executive (president, governor, or mayor) and the multiplicity of departments, boards, and commissions that make up the executive branch. Though analyses of administrative systems, as well as suggestions for improvement through administrative reorganization, may take into consideration all three branches, the greatest emphasis is upon the executive branch.

Administration and State Government

The characteristic activity of the executive branch is administration. State administration is the attempt to realize in practice the policies established by the state legislature and governor. It is an oversimplification to say that public policies are determined by the elected representatives of the people and are carried out by the executive branch. The line that separates policy execution is neither precise nor stable, and therefore difficult to draw. Many legislative enactments and executive orders leave considerable discretion to the administrators, and frequently the latter exert a tremendous influence upon the formulation of both laws and orders.

The governor faces both ways—in collaboration with the state legislature he is a policy determiner, and in collaboration with the executive agencies he is a policy executer. The state legislature, and this is especially true in Texas, does not limit itself to policy alone; it is constantly involved in the administrative process. Policy determination and the execution of policy cannot be neatly isolated, separated, or compartmentalized. The total operations of government influence, and are influenced by, the web of administration.

The Importance of Administration

With the rising cost of government, deficit financing, increase in taxes, budgets, and appropriations, coupled with the demand in some quarters for more governmental services, the importance of administration is being more and more thrust upon the American people. The problem of efficient and responsible administration has become serious indeed in Texas. If it arouses no more than a slight interest in improved administration then, without doubt, the people of the state are dedicated to the perpetuation of state inefficiency or state wrongs. If the crusading or reforming zeal is out of fashion, Texans, nevertheless, should take a long, hard look at state administration. As a bearded oldster said on the courthouse bench in east Texas: "Man, if this won't arouse us, we are beyond redemption—or dead in the law!"

Passing wise laws, as difficult as it is, is much easier than having them administered economically and effectively. Certainly no laws are better than their administration. What is more, there are many problems that cannot be solved by laws. The only method available for government to deal with them is through some type of administrative procedure. Throughout the nineteenth century, administration was dominated by partisan politics—"to the victor belong the spoils of the enemy." Under such a concept administration was considered the legitimate war booty of the political party struggles. It was commonly held that almost any adult with average mentality could administer government programs formulated by those who determined policy. It could not be otherwise, so it was held, since governmental operations were simple and direct. Thanks to the early efforts of Woodrow Wilson, a pioneer in public administration, since about 1920 administration at all governmental levels has been subjected to extensive research, writing, experimentation, and reorganization. In recent years numerous studies have been made of the administrative systems of the states. At the national level we have had the reports of the Hoover Commission. A considerable improvement in the administration of government, through administrative reorganization, has resulted from these studies, task force reports, and recommendations.

The administrative reform movement has not kept pace with the problem. With the increase in government services, public administration continues to grow into a swelling cloud of money and employees. Without doubt, none of the changes in government in the United States at all levels through the years have been as startling or as consequential as the rapid growth of administration. No matter how you look at it, in terms of cost, types and number of activities, and numbers of people employed, big government, which is a household word these days, is in reality big administration.

Types of State Administrative Systems[1]

Generally speaking, the existing administrative systems of the several states can be divided into four types, each of which is discussed briefly below.

The Completely Integrated Type. This is the ideal or model form that vests control of administration in the governor through a limited number of departments, the heads being appointed and removed by the chief executive. Thus it uses the short ballot and envisages a strong and responsible executive at the apex of the administrative pyramid. Popular control is exercised by periodic election of the governor, power of the legislature to remove the chief executive from office, right of the legislature to levy taxes and make appropriations, and the authority of the legislature to exact accountability from the governor and heads of administrative agencies through the mechanism of legislative audit and review. No state is operating under a completely integrated administrative system; however, some states, like New York, do have something approaching the integrated form.

The Partially Integrated Type. The administrative system of the state is said to be partially integrated if only part of the administrative functions are centralized under the direction of the governor. This type retains all or most of the constitutional limitations on the administration, including the elective administrative officials who compete with the governor for authority and power in their particular areas of operation.

The Fiscal-Control Type. This type seeks to give the governor authority to manage the affairs of the state, not through administrative integration, but through financial control and supervision. The essential fiscal procedures, namely, budgeting, accounting, expenditure control, centralized purchasing, and personnel supervision are made tools of top management by being placed in the stream of management. This plan, which strengthens the governor's powers of financial control and supervision, could be accomplished in one of two ways.

A department of finance and administrative services might be created, the internal organization of which might include the bureau of the budget, bureau of accounts, bureau of audit and control, bureau of purchases and property control, and bureau of personnel. There would be a direct line of control, since the heads of bureaus would be accountable to the head of the department, and the latter to the governor, since he would be appointed and serve at the pleasure of the chief executive. To complete the chain of responsibility, the governor would be responsible to the legislature and the people. By integrating the fiscal and personnel procedures in such a department, the governor's powers of financial control and supervision would be increased by authority to appoint and remove the head of the Department of Finance and Administrative Services.

Another way in which the objectives of the fiscal-control type of administration might be accomplished would be to transfer all or part of the fiscal and personnel procedures to the executive office of the governor. In other words, the office of finance and administrative services, with the above-mentioned internal organization, could be established as a part of the executive office of the governor.

The fiscal-control type, which in a sense is the partially integrated form of administration, has become popular in recent years as a number of states have moved in this direction. Where this development has taken place—completely or in part—the disintegrated fiscal and personnel procedures, which at one time were scattered among a number of agencies, have been centralized in one or a few agencies and brought more directly into the stream of management. Since the fiscal and personnel procedures are important tools of management, a strengthened and responsible chief executive should be placed in a better position to exercise greater control and supervision over them. The fiscal-control trend inevitably leads to greater efficiency and specialization in top management. More states are becoming aware of the success of business with the integration or centralization of fiscal-control activities.

The Commission or Plural-Executive Type. Under this plan the governor is only one among several executives. Various elective officials, who head departments, boards, and commissions, share with the governor in administration. It resembles the commission form of city government with the governor as a sort of honorary or ceremonial head of the state machinery. However, unlike the commission form of municipal government, the governor and heads of departments do not constitute the legislative body. To this extent there remains separation, rather than combination, of executive and legislative functions. It resembles the commission form as regards the plural executives, each of whom is responsible to the people rather than to the governor or mayor. Plurality in top management, long ballot, lack of a single line of responsibility, disintegration, absence of coordination, and a weak executive usually characterize this form of state administration.

State Administration in Texas

Texas has a commission or plural-executive type of government. Identifying the chief administrator of Texas is not an easy task. Article IV, Section 1, of the Texas constitution declares that the governor is the chief executive. Yet the executive department of this state is one of divided leadership, with six elected members and one appointed member. Although the constitution names the governor as chief executive, it denies him the authority to carry out his responsibilities. State administration should be an executive responsibility, but in Texas state administration is scattered far and wide in numerous agencies that are administered in a great variety of ways, with no central authority to coordinate their activities, functions, or finances. This is in opposition to every principle of modern management. The most effective way to make the governor accountable is to give him authority equal to his responsibility. Only in this way, to quote the council of state governments, 1950, can "the twin goals of administrative effectiveness and political responsibility . . . be achieved."

Frankly speaking, state administration is organized disorganization in Texas, and it is not an overstatement to say that in some parts of the state government there exists—as in the old Chinese army—one general to approximately three privates! Certainly the plural and weak executive form of administration, divided responsibility, disintegration, lack of coordination, and the confusion and overlapping functions must provide almost ideal conditions for pressure groups. Is it possible that so much waste and confusion are so profitable for so many as to make reform impossible?

Fiscal Administration in Texas

Fiscal management is a very important function, in government as in business. In state government, it includes all activities that are designed to make funds available to public officials and to ensure their lawful and efficient use.[2] Budgeting, accounting (preauditing and fiscal control), purchasing, property control, postauditing, assessment of property for taxation, and collecting, safeguarding, and disbursing funds are considered the principal fiscal functions of the state. Since in Texas these functions are handled by various agencies, the state has a disintegrated type of fiscal administration.

The Comptroller of Public Accounts

The comptroller of public accounts is elected for a four-year term in Texas and his department is, under the state constitution, a part of the executive branch of government. Employees of the department—many of whom work in field offices or travel—include accountants, investigators, administrators, and district supervisors. The staff administers a variety of functions, some of which are required by the constitution and others by statute.

Although the assessing and collecting of taxes usually is not associated with the accounting, preaudit, fiscal-control, and claims functions, approximately 85 percent of the personnel of the comptroller's office are devoted to tax administration. Various taxes are assessed and collected directly by this office, for example, severance taxes (crude oil, natural gas, and sulphur), gross-receipts taxes, chain-store taxes, admissions taxes, and motor-fuel taxes. As a part of assessing and collecting these taxes, the comptroller must devise forms and procedures, as well as process the reports from individuals and firms. Employees of the comptroller's office must make frequent checks to prevent tax evasion. The producer and purchaser of crude oil must file separate reports with the comptroller. If one does not pay the tax, the other is liable for it. Before oil is trucked, the capacity of the vehicle is checked. The same is true of gasoline. Spot-checks are made of trucks on the roads.

Some state taxes and fees, including the automobile sales and use taxes, are collected for the state by the county tax assessors. The comptroller supervises the assessing and collection of these taxes and fees, specifies forms, receives reports, audits, keeps records, and distributes the funds to various state-fund accounts as provided by law.

The comptroller's office keeps records of all state property. An effort is made to provide a central property record for the state.

The annual report of the comptroller provides information as to revenue, expenditures, and unexpended balances held in the state treasury for the credit of each fund. A considerable amount of miscellaneous information also is included in the annual report. Monthly comparative statements show current expenditures in each major disbursement area. The comptroller furnishes the departments each month with statements on each of their appropriation accounts, which are similar to bank statements.

In advance of each regular session of the legislature the comptroller must submit to the governor, and to the legislature upon its convening, a statement showing the financial condition of the state treasury at the close of the last fiscal period and an estimate of the probable receipts and disbursements for the current fiscal year. The statement also includes an itemized estimate of the anticipated revenue, based on the laws in effect, that will be received during the succeeding biennium, and such other information as may be required by law. Supplemental statements as may be necessary to show probable changes may be submitted at any time. In performing this constitutional duty the comptroller provides the governor and legislature with information in their consideration of budgetary requests by the departments and agencies for the ensuing biennium. The financial outlook of the state is an important factor in what the governor recommends to the legislature. Also, the financial statement of the comptroller is an aid to the legislature in the matter of appropriations and taxation.

Except in cases of emergency and with a four-fifths vote of the total membership of each house, no appropriation in excess of the cash and anticipated revenue of the funds from which such appropriation is to be made shall be valid. No bill containing an appropriation may be considered as passed or be sent to the governor unless the comptroller certifies that the amount appropriated is within the amount estimated to be available in the affected funds. If the comptroller finds that an appropriation bill exceeds the estimated revenue, the legislature must bring the appropriation within the revenue, either by providing additional revenue or reducing the appropriation. This constitutional provision is an attempt to keep the state on a cash or pay-as-you-go basis. However, neither the constitutional provision nor the report of the comptroller may prevent deficit financing. Certain revenue collections may be less than the estimates of the comptroller. For example, an unforeseen decrease in crude-oil production could result in millions of dollars less tax revenue from this source. Also, expenditures may exceed those anticipated in official predictions. Thus far the legislature has not, by four-fifths vote of each house, appropriated money in excess of the cash and anticipated revenue of the funds from which the expenditure was made.

The comptroller of public accounts is the principal accounting and fiscal control officer of the state. One of the important accounting functions of the comptroller's department is serving as watchdog over the various state funds. State revenue collected from a specified source must be deposited in a certain fund, for example, the general-revenue fund, the state-highway fund, or the available school fund. The money so deposited must be spent for a particular purpose. As a consequence, the state may be poor in one fund and rich in another. Without legislative authorization, money in one fund may not be transferred to or consolidated with another fund.

The general-revenue fund is the general operating fund of the state. Most of the state income that is not earmarked for special purposes is deposited in the general-revenue fund. In a sense, the general-revenue fund is the superpurse of the state, but from a practical standpoint, it forms a relatively small portion of the total financial picture of the state. The legislature may appropriate money from the general-revenue fund at its own discretion, subject only to general constitutional limitations.

The state receives funds and pays obligations through the use of deposit and expenditure warrants. Deposit warrants must be approved by the comptroller and treasurer. Keeping an accurate account of the money going in and out of state funds involves a considerable amount of bookkeeping.

Money cannot be spent unless there is a prior existing law. The purposes for which it may be spent are in the appropriation bills. The comptroller sets up an appropriation account that indicates the amount appropriated and the authority to spend the money. Frequently, in addition to analyzing the appropriation bill, the comptroller will request an opinion from the attorney general. Authority to spend money must be specific; it cannot be implied. As expenditure warrants (checks) are issued against an appropriation, the comptroller charges them against the appropriation and the amounts available.

The comptroller must audit and approve in advance of payment all expenditures to be made from state funds for which appropriations have been made by the legislature for salaries, travel expenses, operational expenses, capital outlays, pensions, investments, and refunds of trust accounts. All claims for payment must be examined as to legality of form and purpose. If no legal question is involved, the comptroller will issue warrants on authority of the claims filed and they must be countersigned by the treasurer. The voucher is the bill or expenditure request filed with the comptroller on which the warrants are issued.

The preaudit on purchases consists of determining if the requested purchase is necessary to the business of the state, and if there is a preexisting law authorizing the purchase. The comptroller has no cognizance of a claim until it is presented for payment, at which time a check is made to determine if an appropriation exists authorizing the purchase. Since the comptroller makes no examination in regard to the propriety of the obligation before it is incurred, he is somewhat limited in the performance of preaudit or fiscal control. It should be an important function of the comptroller to disallow extravagant and unnecessary purchases during the preaudit process.

The State Treasurer

The state treasurer is elected for a four-year term and is a part of the executive branch.

The work of the treasury department differs from that of most state departments in that each day is a separate entity and a definite result must be attained before the work is complete. The department is like a bank in that each day's work must "balance" and the employees cannot leave until the "balance" is obtained. Occasionally on peak days, usually after holidays, the employees are required to work several hours overtime. As in a bank, the department has employees doing the work of cashiers, tellers, auditors, and bookkeepers.

By law the state treasurer is the custodian of state funds. He receives state money and disburses it on proper authority and keeps on deposit with Texas banks all unspent balances. During any ordinary working day, these balances change hourly. Unlike a private bank, the department cannot make loans or hold private funds on deposit.

The state treasurer, as secretary, together with one citizen of the state appointed by the governor and senate for a term of two years, and the banking commissioner constitute the state depository board. The board designates the state depositories and determines the amount of state funds to be deposited in state and national banks throughout the state. The board contracts with the depositories in regard to the payment of interest on deposits. The treasurer requires each bank so designated as a state depository to pledge certain types of securities or deposit a depository bond signed by some surety company authorized to do business in Texas. No depositories may keep on deposit state funds in an amount in excess of their paid-up capital stock and permanent surplus.

State excise-tax stamps affixed to cigarettes, wine, and liquor are sold, packaged, and shipped by the treasury department. Only about 10 percent of the workload of the department is devoted to the tax function, since the deposit and banking board activities constitute the major work of the state treasurer and his staff.

Monthly and annual reports are prepared by the treasury department. These statements show transactions in the state funds for the period covered. Also, the state treasurer serves ex officio as a member of various state boards.

State Purchasing and General Services Commission

The commission is composed of three members appointed by the governor and senate for overlapping six-year terms. Members of the commission serve part time. A full-time executive director, employed by the commission, acts as chief administrator.

Purchase requisitions of the departments and agencies are channeled through the commission and, in most cases, the commission receives bids from individuals and firms. The commission is the centralized purchasing agency for the state, and through its executive director and staff, receives requisitions from the state agencies, advertises for competitive bids, checks and verifies invoices, and recommends payment of purchases.

Local governments may enter into agreements for cooperative purchase of goods and services. They may also negotiate cooperative agreements with the state purchasing and general services commission.

The Executive Budget Office and the Legislative Budget Board

Preparation of the state budget, its submission to the legislature, and execution of the budget are considered, at least in most states, to be a function of the governor. However, in Texas two biennial budgets are prepared for legislative consideration. One budget is prepared by the executive budget office in the governor's office. Another budget, along with the general appropriation bill, is submitted to the legislature by the legislative budget board.* Although the legislature may use both budgets for comparative purposes, the legislators take their own document as a basis for budgetary consideration.

The fiscal year in Texas covers the period from September 1 to August 31. Two fiscal years are included in the budgetary period. Preparation of the biennial budget begins in May or June of each odd-numbered year, or shortly after adjournment of each regular session of the legislature. Both budget agencies, in order to avoid duplication and confusion, have worked out similar forms and instructions that are sent to each state agency. Each operating agency must submit its budget request to the budget agencies on forms provided them. Examiners from the budget agencies consult with the personnel in the operating agencies and assist them in the preparation of their budget requests. In order to save time and prevent duplication, joint hearings are held by examiners from the two budget agencies with all the departments and boards.

Once the budget estimates of each administrative unit have been completed, they are submitted to the executive office of the budget in the governor's office and the legislative budget board, where they are analyzed by the respective staffs of each agency. After the hearings and analyses are completed, each budget agency

*The legislative budget board is composed of ten members of the legislature: four senators appointed by the lieutenant governor, four house members appointed by the speaker, and the presiding officers of the senate and house serving as chairman and vice-chairman respectively. A budget director is named by the board as its executive officer.

prepares a separate budget document that includes estimates of expenditures and revenues. Both budgets are later transmitted to the regular session of the legislature for consideration by the committees and each house. In due season, the legislature will pass the general appropriation bill for the next two years. New tax revenue may or may not be necessary, depending upon the financial condition of the state at the time. In any event, the general appropriation bill and, possibly, a new tax program are among the more important decisions the legislature must make.

The State Auditor

The legislative audit committee appoints the state auditor with approval of two-thirds of the senate.[3] He may be removed from office by the legislative audit committee. Certified public accountants, senior and junior accountants, and auditors are employed by the state auditor.

Since the legislature appropriates money, it is obligated to determine if financial transactions are made in accordance with law. To perform the function of postauditing, the legislature, through the legislative audit committee, appoints an independent or legislative auditor. This is a more desirable system than an internal audit or a check on financial transactions by someone within the executive branch. As an agent of the legislature, the state auditor and his staff audit all financial records and transactions of the state agencies after the transactions have occurred. This postaudit of transactions would reveal any misapplication of public funds. Such information would be reported to the grand jury and legislature for any action they deemed necessary, for example, as a basis for prosecuting the parties involved or passage of corrective legislation. As an aid to establishing a more uniform system of accounts, the state auditor may require any department or agency to change its system of keeping accounts.

Prior to the convening of the regular session of the legislature, the state auditor submits a biennial report to the governor. This report contains a balance sheet for the last fiscal year and an estimate of revenue available for appropriation during the ensuing biennium. In addition to the biennial report, the state auditor makes annual and departmental reports.

Personnel Administration in State Government

All persons employed by government are a part of the civil service, but many such employees are not a part of the merit system whereby individuals are recruited, employed, and promoted on the basis of merit objectively determined. The state government of Texas does not have a statewide civil service commission and merit system. However, many cities in Texas have civil service commissions and the merit system as provided in their city charters and municipal ordinances passed by the city councils.

A number of agencies in Texas receive federal funds and are required to select and promote agency personnel on the basis of merit objectively determined; otherwise the agencies could not qualify for federal funds. In Texas, the merit system council serves the employment commission, the department of health resources and affiliated local units, the department of human resources, the department of mental health and mental retardation, the governor's committee on aging, the air control board, and various other state agencies, all of which are equal opportunity employers.*

To provide state employees with equal pay for equal work, the Texas legislature passed a law establishing a position-classification plan for certain departments, institutions, and agencies of the state. The job classification plan represents another step toward establishing an adequate system of personnel administration in Texas.

Suggestions for Strengthening the Administrative System in Texas

There has never been a real administrative reorganization movement in Texas. However, a number of suggestions have been made for strengthening the administrative system.

1. Institute a short ballot. It has been suggested that only the governor, lieutenant governor, and attorney general, among the major executive officials, be elected by the people. To make the short ballot effective would require constitutional change, since under the existing constitution the members of the executive department (governor, lieutenant governor, comptroller of public accounts, treasurer, commissioner of the general land office, and attorney general), excepting the secretary of state, are popularly elected. Since the office of the commissioner of agriculture was established by statute in 1907, the law could be amended to provide for the appointment of this official.

2. Increase the powers of the governor. The other major officials in the executive department should be appointed by the governor without fixed terms of office, and the governor should be given the power to remove all officials subject to appointment by him, for good cause, under appropriate restrictions.

3. Limit the number of departments. The executive branch should be organized into not more than twelve departments in lieu of the numerous departments and agencies.

4. Establish a department of finance and administrative services. The auxiliary or housekeeping functions should be coordinated and brought together in a single department. Such a projected department might include all of these bureaus: treasury, budget, accounting, preauditing and fiscal control, purchases and property control, financial reporting, legal advice, and personnel.

The functions of the treasury department, the two budget agencies, comptroller of public accounts (accounting functions), and the state purchasing and general services commission would be transferred to the new department, and these agencies, as now constituted, would be abolished. The attorney general's department would be retained but limited to prosecuting and defending in the name of the state. If and when the merit system of personnel administration is adopted on a statewide basis, the function could be taken over by the bureau of personnel in the projected department.

The budget function might be located either in the department of finance and administrative service or in the executive office of the governor. Likewise, per-

---

*The merit system council is composed of six members appointed by the governor and senate for six-year terms.

sonnel administration might be located in the executive office of the governor, the department of finance and administrative services, or in an independent civil-service board or commission. There has been considerable discussion of the proper location of the budget and the personnel functions.

The director of the department of finance and administrative services would be appointed by, and responsible to, the governor. The bureau chiefs would be appointed by the director on the basis of merit. Other employees of the department would be selected and promoted on the basis of merit objectively determined.

Creation of the department of finance and administrative services along lines indicated above would require constitutional change. For example, the constitution directs the attorney general to "give legal advice in writing to the governor and other executive officers, when requested by them." This function could not be transferred without a change in the constitution. The comptroller of public accounts and state treasurer are constitutional elective offices and a constitutional amendment would be necessary to abolish or make these positions appointive. Part of the recommended program could be put into operation by the passage of legislation.

5. Establish a department of taxation. The tax function in Texas is divided among a number of individuals and agencies, although the comptroller of public accounts is the chief tax official of the state. Disintegration within the tax field has resulted in the failure to assess and collect taxes owed the state by some individuals and firms. A single state agency should be responsible for the assessment and collection of state taxes.

The director of the department of taxation, bureau chiefs, and other employees would be selected in the same manner as their counterparts in the department of finance and administrative services.

The tax department would be divided into a number of bureaus, including those of franchise taxes, gross-receipts taxes, production taxes, tax research, and a bureau for other state taxes.

The bureau of tax research would subject the tax structure to continuous examination to uncover tax inequities and new sources of revenue, as well as make recommendations to the governor and legislature. Tax research by a public body on a continuing basis is badly needed in Texas.

The tax functions of the comptroller of public accounts, state treasurer, and other agencies would be transferred to the tax department in order to centralize the assessment and collection of taxes. This would enable the comptroller and state treasurer and their staffs to devote full time respectively to fiscal or current audit control, and to custody of state funds—which, after all, should be their major functions.

In order to do the job efficiently, the tax department, as is true of other departments, would need an adequate budget and competent personnel.

6. Establish a statewide merit system. All state employees, other than those elected by the people, a limited number of political appointees, and manual laborers, should be selected and promoted on the basis of merit objectively determined. The experience of the federal government, many states, and municipalities has shown the merit system to be superior to the spoils of office whereby a person secures public employment by supporting a successful candidate, or by being a

friend or ally of the appointing authority, or through the influence of a member of the legislature. The spoils system has had a long history in Texas.

7. Establish a statewide compensation plan. As a part of a modern personnel program, all provisions in the state constitution fixing salaries should be removed in order that a consistent statewide compensation plan might be established. The compensation plan should be based upon classification of positions and equal pay for jobs requiring similar qualifications.

8. Prepare one state budget instead of two. The preparation of the executive budget should be the responsibility of the budget officer and his staff in the executive office of the governor. Since the governor's budget officer and his staff should prepare the state budget and the general appropriation bill, the legislative budget board should be abolished. The staff of the legislative budget board could serve as an aid to the appropriations and revenue and taxation committees of the house and the finance and state affairs committees in the senate. Instead of preparing a separate budget and general appropriation bill, the professional staff of the legislative committees should concern itself with budgetary research and investigation.

9. Prepare an annual instead of biennial budget. Since the Texas constitution provides for biennial legislative regular sessions that meet in the odd-numbered years, the state constitution would have to be amended to provide for annual regular sessions, which could approve the state budget and general appropriation bill each year.

Requiring spending agencies to live within their budgets is a major problem in execution of the budget. Unforeseen emergencies or an increased workload may make it difficult for an agency to stay within its budget. If one or more agencies spend more money than appropriated, the legislature at the next session may find it necessary to pass a deficiency or supplementary appropriation bill to cover the deficit. Such appropriations indicate the inadequacy of budgetary planning. Annual legislative sessions and the annual budget would make budget estimates and budget planning, as well as the execution of the budget, less difficult.

10. Adopt the accrual system of accounting. Unlike the practice followed by many business concerns, the accounts of the state are set up on a cash instead of an accrual basis. This means that the state, under its system of bookkeeping, enters the receipts (state revenue) when actually received in the form of cash, rather than at the time they are earned. Likewise, expenditures are accounted for or entered when the money is paid rather than when the obligation is incurred. Keeping the various accounts on a cash basis permits obligations to be incurred in one fiscal year and carried over to the next year, at which time they may be paid. The legislature might also face a larger deficit than is actually the case, because state revenue or receipts are taken into account at the time received rather than at the time earned. In other words, under the cash system, some state revenue may not have been received at the beginning of the legislative session. Consequently, in view of the time when receipts and expenditures are entered, the cash system of keeping accounts does not reflect the current financial picture and complicates the task of the lawmakers.

Under the accrual system of accounting, receipts are taken into account at the time the money is earned, expenditures at the time debts are incurred. This system gives a more current view of state finances.

11. Establish a uniform system of accounting. Since agencies differ in organization and function, a rigid, uniform accounting system throughout state government would be impossible. Some steps have been taken toward establishing such a system. For instance, accounting in the institutions of higher education has been uniform for a number of years. Likewise, some uniformity has been established in the matter of claims and purchasing. The more uniform the accounting procedures, the less difficult the task of the state auditor and his staff in making the postaudit. Further progress toward uniformity in accounting is a desirable objective.

12. Consolidate special funds. The state of Texas has developed the practice of earmarking revenue and expenditures; that is, revenue from a certain tax or other source frequently must be deposited in a special fund and the money may be spent only for a designated purpose. Because of the numerous special funds, the state may be rich in one fund and poor in another, and this makes it difficult to determine the true financial condition of the state at any one time. The special funds increase the work of the accounting and auditing officials.

The legislature has taken steps to consolidate some of the special funds and the money has been transferred to the general-revenue fund. Other special funds should be consolidated and the earmarking of revenues and expenditures should be discontinued.

11. Carry out an effective preaudit of expenditures. An effective preaudit of the expenditures of all agencies should be established in the department of finance and administrative services. It is important that the preaudit be integrated with the purchasing procedure in order that purchases can be refused before the incurrence of an obligation. This would provide an additional check against extravagant and wasteful purchases. Under existing practice, the state purchasing and general services commission cannot disapprove a purchase order or requisition if the ordering agency has funds available to pay the obligation.

Obstacles to Administrative Reorganization

There are many obstacles to administrative reorganization in the states. Many oppose increasing the powers of the governor for fear he would build up a personal machine. This fear does not appear justified in view of the various checks on the chief executive that would be built into the reorganized administrative system. Besides, some effective machines have been created by governors in states with disintegrated systems where it is difficult to enforce accountability and locate responsibility. Nevertheless, unwillingness to increase the governor's power, for whatever reason, is a substantial obstacle that tends to discourage administrative reform.

Those within the administration do not look with favor upon the abolition of their agency or consolidation with some other department, board, or commission. As a matter of self-interest the agencies frequently seek more funds and personnel as evidence of their importance and expanded programs. Centers of power from within are built and expanded. The creation of more departments, boards, and commissions means the legislature will be subjected to more administrative pressure, making reform all the more difficult. In fact, the longer administrative reorganization is delayed, the greater the obstacle to achieving it. The self-interest of the administrators, which is a sort of bread-and-butter affair, offsets the interest of those concerned with reform. This is not to say all agencies and administrators oppose reform; yet there are many agencies that profit from an irresponsible and disintegrated system, for some would be abolished or consolidated with other units if reorganization became a reality.

The more administrative units, the greater the opportunity for legislators to place friends in state jobs. Hence, the legislature may show little or no interest in reform. This legislative inertia often results in the failure to provide funds for preliminary studies of the administrative machinery. The fact that it is common for legislators to represent interested parties before boards and commissions has weakened administration in Texas. After all, the legislators must vote the funds for the agencies, and the administrators, in the process of hearing controversies, are certainly aware of this fact.

Interest groups that retain legislators may not be interested in making administration more responsible. For example, the multiplicity of departments and boards, with overlapping functions and inadequate budgets and staff (prosecutors, investigators, accountants, and so on), could be advantageous for some interest groups, since continuous and effective regulation of the interests concerned might be difficult if not impossible. The vigor with which interest groups support states' rights frequently is in proportion to the degree of ineffectiveness of state administration. Conversely, the opposition to federal control and regulation is due, in a large measure, to the greater effectiveness of federal administration. The disintegrated system has the support of numerous interest groups.

Mismanagement and corruption, although a headline story at times, may have little constructive impact on public opinion. This may become an accepted fact in local politics or else the public develops an immunity to misrule. A vigilant opposition party should encourage a more effective government.

Extensive reorganization in most states would require constitutional change. Revising, or even amending the state constitution, is a slow process. Constitutional change would have to be followed by statutory implementation. Such extensive legislative action is almost too much to expect from an unwilling legislature.

Unless administration interferes with one's financial interest, it is too far removed and impersonal to attract widespread attention. For most citizens and taxpayers there is no sustained interest in the overall problems of government and administrative reorganization. This public apathy may result from lack of understanding, other interests, or inadequate time to seriously consider the problem. Whatever the cause, unless there is a ground swell from the grass roots, we may expect little or no action in the state legislature.

Efficient state government, above all, demands strong local leadership, which is lacking in most states. Unless there is a will for governmental efficiency and positive local leadership, further disintegration of state administrative systems, with mediocrity, inefficiency, and lack of responsibility, will continue. Under such conditions the perpetuation of state inefficiency remains respectable as a cloak for state rights.

Administrative Reorganization—Economy and Efficiency

It is difficult to determine when a state is operating economically, since profit and loss cannot be as easily tabulated in government as in business. Governments provide a number of services for which there are no profits other than the protection of life and property. In short, governmental operations involve more than buying and selling commodities for profit or loss. For this reason it is unfair to compare government and business in the matter of operational efficiency and economy. In any event, since both business concerns and governments are operated by human beings, not all are operated efficiently or economically. However, there is no reason why the proven business practices, as regards organization of departments, budgeting, accounting, and auditing, cannot, among other methods, be adapted to government.

In the event Texas carries out a full-scale reorganization of state administration, the operating cost of government could possibly be cut by $3 million, $4 million, $10 million, or more annually. Additional funds for public schools, higher education, welfare. highways, prisons, and other services will result in a steady increase in governmental cost. However, any savings accrued by more economical operations could be applied to the additional cost.

Reorganization should not be viewed merely as an economy measure, as desirable as this may be. Even if no financial savings would result, reorganization should be carried out because it would increase the government's efficiency and make it more responsible. True, an integrated system would not eliminate interest groups and their influence, but it should strengthen the role of government so that administrative decisions could be made more objectively.

Despite the lack of a reorganization movement in Texas, some reforms have been carried out, such as the establishment of the independent auditor, centralizing the educational function in the Texas Education Agency, job classification, retirement system for state employees, and the merit system of personnel administration for certain agencies that receive federal grants. Although there have been some accomplishments, the need for reorganization continues.

The Texas Sunset Law

A law passed by the Texas legislature in 1977 requires that 178 of the state's agencies, boards, and commissions be reviewed over a twelve-year period by the legislature, which will decide whether to abolish an agency, recreate it unchanged, or modify its operations. The agencies up for review every two years must be recreated by the legislature or they will go out of existence; in other words, the sun will set on them.

The sunset review process puts under the microscope agencies that have operated virtually unnoticed for years. It offers a means of cutting the cost and increasing the efficiency of government. And it gives the legislature a way to assure that agencies are serving the public.

The sunset advisory commission is composed of four members of the senate, one public member appointed by the lieutenant governor, four members of the house, and one public member appointed by the speaker of the house. Each appointing authority may designate himself as one of the legislative appointees. The legislative members appointed by the presiding officers of the two houses serve four-year terms. The advisory commission and its staff compiles detailed information on the agencies under review, questioning agency personnel and developing and voting on proposed legislation. Self-evaluation forms in which the agencies describe their functions and evaluate their own operations are returned to the advisory commission staff. Also, the staff mails out a series of questionnaires to those licensed by agencies under review, those who have filed complaints, board members, and trade and professional associations that deal with the agencies. After considering staff reports and hearing testimony, the sunset advisory commission decides whether to recommend to the legislature that agencies continue operation or be disbanded.

This commission has documented a number of instances where the agencies work hand in hand, rather than at arm's length, with the businesses and professions they are supposed to be regulating. This was in the nature of self-regulation by the particular interest, rather than regulation to protect the public interest. Also, sunset staff investigators found that the legal counsel for some boards and agencies was also the registered lobbyist for the interest group regulated. Thus, the "sunsetters" were confronted with the need to find ways to place more distance between those who regulate and those who are regulated. In fact the review of state agencies revealed that many boards and agencies appeared to be controlled by the interest to be regulated. The interest groups contended they needed representation on the boards and agencies in order to protect their interests, and that their representatives were familiar with the general and technical considerations involved in regulating particular economic interests. But how may balance be secured in membership on boards and agencies to secure both the protection of the general public and various economic interests? Persons appointed to boards and agencies with a concern for protecting the public interest might, in time, accept the position of the particular interest to be regulated. Hence, the age-old problem in Democratic government: How can both the protection of the general public and various economic interest groups be assured by the regulators?

Sunset reviewers also found that investigators for certain boards and agencies were assigned to inspect businesses where they once were employed, or where they or family members had financial interests. A further discovery was that some boards issuing licenses to operate certain businesses employed the lobbyists for those businesses in order to make their legislative wishes known. State agencies in Texas had recommended legislation requested by the group or association they regulated thereby ensuring that narrow interests were served. Many bills supported by various state agencies found their genesis in the offices of the special interest groups subject to state regulation.

The changes mandated by the Texas legislature include public membership on regulatory and licensing boards, conflict of interest guidelines, automatic expulsion of board members on failure to attend half the regular meetings, specific inclusion under the Open Meetings Act, and a requirement that funds be kept in the state treasury and subject to the appropriations process. Under previous practice, agencies could secure higher interest on funds deposited outside the state treasury.

With the exception of the state bar of Texas, the legislature went along with most of the sunset advisory commission's recommendations aimed at opening up agencies to public scrutiny. The state bar was protected by the fact that about one-third of the state's 181 legislators are lawyers. However, the bar's spending and budget must be approved by the Texas supreme court, which exercises the oversight function, and a public hearing on the budget is required. Also, six non-lawyers are appointed by the Texas supreme court to serve on the bar's board of directors. The law also requires that one-third of the members of the bar's forty-seven grievance committees, which hear complaints against attorneys, be non-lawyers. However, the state bar continues to keep its funds outside the state treasury and beyond legislative control. Spending by the bar, however, will be checked by the state auditor. Therefore, the state bar remains the "neither fish nor fowl" agency that it always has been.

The Texas state board of medical examiners was continued and recreated. The board consists of fifteen members, of which nine must be MDs, three doctors of osteopathic medicine (DOs), and three public representatives who are not licensed to practice medicine, who are not financially involved in any organization subject to the regulation of the board, and who are not providers of health care. The annual registration fees of the MDs and DOs are deposited in the state treasury.

At one time the state board of morticians was composed entirely of funeral directors (undertakers). As a result of the sunset review process, non-undertakers must be appointed to the board and mandatory itemized pricing of various funeral merchandise and services, instead of quoting a set price for the entire funeral, is required. This somewhat limits the practice of "grief therapy,"—encouraging the bereaved to pay out the maximum amount to assuage or lessen guilt feelings.

As a result of the Sunset Law, some inactive commissions and agencies have been abolished, some transferred to retained agencies, and a number of agencies opened to the public. Notwithstanding the antibureaucratic fervor that has swept state and federal politics, many of the changes appear minimal and cosmetic. They amount to tokenism, but they nevertheless represent some improvement.

12 Financing State Government

WHAT WILL GOVERNMENT SERVICE cost and who will foot the bill are important questions in any governmental system. At the heart of these questions is the tax problem. Tax experts tell us a sound tax structure should be based upon the ability to pay. Under this doctrine the wealthy should pay more taxes than those in the lower-and-middle-income brackets.

Types of Taxes

Taxes, at whatever level of government, are of two types, (1) "progressive" or "regressive" and (2) "broadly" or "narrowly" based. A graduated tax on personal income is said to be progressive because it falls "progressively" on those people with higher incomes. In other words, those who have greater wealth have the ability to pay more taxes. Excises or taxes on consumer goods, for example, general sales taxes, are classified as a regressive revenue measure. Those in the low- and middle-income brackets spend a larger proportion of their net income on such items than do the wealthy, so that consequently any tax that imposes a proportional burden on consumption would absorb a larger proportion of their income. Conversely, such a tax would absorb a smaller proportion of the income of wealthy persons. A tax on tobacco, gasoline, or sugar would be felt more by a family with a $1,000 income than by one with a $50,000 income. If food, clothing, and medical items are exempted under a general sales tax, the latter loses much of its regressive effect.

Personal and corporation income taxes account for about two-thirds of the federal revenue. The personal income tax levied by the federal government is progressive and tends to redistribute income between rich and poor. The remainder of federal revenue comes from the so-called regressive taxes on payrolls and from excises. Like the federal government, the states and localities have both progressive and regressive taxes. The popularity of the selective and general sales taxes in the states illustrates the regressive tax trend; personal and corporation income taxes are progressive in nature. The tax structure of most states is not as progressive as that of the federal government.

Whether a tax is "broadly" or "narrowly" based depends upon the number of persons directly subject to the tax. These taxes may be either progressive or regressive and might or might not be based upon the ability to pay. Selective and general sales taxes, excises, payroll taxes, and personal income taxes are broadly based taxes, whereas franchise, occupation, and corporate income taxes, among others, are narrowly based.

Types of Taxes in Texas

Tax on Natural Resources (Production or Severance Taxes)

There is considerable variation among the states in regard to natural resource taxation. Three approaches currently are in use: (1) property taxes only to tax natural resources, (2) severance taxes (taxes levied when the resource is "severed" from its environment) in lieu of property taxes, and (3) severance taxes in addition to property taxes.

Crude Oil. There are two severance taxes in Texas on crude oil. The so-called oil-production tax is levied at 4.6 cents per barrel if market value of oil is $1 per barrel or less. If the market value exceeds $1 per barrel, the tax is 4.6 percent of market value. For many years the market value of crude oil has greatly exceeded $1 per barrel. Therefore, the current severance tax on crude oil is 4.6 percent of market value. In addition, there is a severance tax imposed primarily to pay for the cost of regulation and conservation. The local ad valorem tax on crude-oil reserves varies, depending upon the locality.

> The Texas severance tax rate [on crude oil] is generally low as compared to states which impose the tax in lieu of property taxes. . . .
> On the other hand, the Texas rate is high compared to other states which impose the tax in addition to property taxes. . . .[1]

There is no way to ascertain the ad valorem or property taxes paid on oil production in Texas. For this reason much stress is laid on this phase of the tax question by the oil interest. Most of the local taxing units, such as school districts and towns, do not report their tax collections to the comptroller, and even if they did the figures are not broken down so as to represent the different phases of the industry such as production, pipelines, refining, and marketing. The practice frequently resorted to, of charging all property taxes paid by all phases of the industry, including pipelines, refineries, and distribution, to production alone, violates all principles of cost accounting. It gives an erroneous view of the tax burden paid by the producing end of the industry, since only about sixty percent of the oil industry in Texas is engaged in production.

The amount of tax revenue from crude oil depends upon the production allowable set by the Texas railroad commission and the price charged for crude oil by the major oil companies. The amount of oil production in the state, as well as the price of crude oil, is influenced by the importation of foreign oil. Because the state is so dependent upon natural resources for financing state government, excessive foreign imports and crude-oil price cuts can slash state revenues and thereby cause a tax crisis.

The comptroller of public accounts receives the production-tax payments on crude oil concurrently with the reports required of producers and purchasers.

The Texas legislature could enact a graduated severance tax on producers of crude oil, for example

Number of barrels per month:	*Severance tax:*
Less than 75,000	4.0 percent
75,000 to 700,000	4.6 percent
700,000 to 1,000,000	5.6 percent
1,000,000 to 1,300,000	6.6 percent
over 1,300,000	7.6 percent

Such a tax would provide tax relief for Texas oil producers who produce less than 75,000 barrels a month. These producers have been hurt by the oil-importing policies of the major companies. The severance tax on these producers would be decreased from 4.6 percent to 4 percent. For the "major independents" who produce from 75,000 to 700,000 barrels per month, the tax would remain unchanged (4.6 percent). For the major companies who produce over half the oil in Texas, the severance tax would be increased.

Natural Gas. The severance tax on natural gas is 7.5 percent of wellhead value. In addition, gas reserves are taxable as part of the local property-tax base. As in the case of crude oil, the comptroller is designated as the state agency responsible for administration of the severance tax on natural gas.

Sulfur. Texas and Louisiana produce almost all domestic U.S. sulfur. Both states tax sulfur production. The severance tax on sulfur in Texas is $1.03 per long ton. Sulfur reserves are also subject to the ad valorem taxes levied by local governments.

The administration of the sulfur tax is handled by the comptroller. Quarterly tax payments and production reports are submitted upon forms prescribed by him. Like other production taxes in Texas, the sulfur tax is self-assessed by the producer.

In addition to the severance taxes on crude oil, natural gas, and sulfur, Texas could levy the tax on such minerals as stone, sand, gravel, salt, lime, clays, and gypsum.

Opposition to Additional Taxes on Natural Resources. Any effort to increase taxes on natural resources is opposed by the lobbyists representing the natural-resources interest. They offer impressive figures showing the increased costs of production, transportation, wages, as well as the vast sums spent on technology and research. The oil people say that an increased tax on crude oil, plus the increase in consumer prices, will make it impossible for the domestic producer to compete with the importation of foreign crude oil.

The natural-resources interests argue that increased taxes on natural resources are passed on to the consumer, which means Texans would pay more for gasoline and other commodities refined or manufactured from natural resources. With millions of consumers living in other states and foreign countries, 60 percent or more of the natural resources are consumed beyond the borders of Texas. Even if Texas consumers did assume part of the increase in taxes by the purchase of the refined or finished products, the increase in local consumer prices would be offset by the increase in revenue collected from out-of-state consumers.

The state taxes of New York, Michigan, Illinois, Pennsylvania, and other states are added to the cost of hundreds of articles produced in these states and sold in

Texas. The producers or manufacturers are the tax collection agencies in these states, and they pass the local state tax to consumers who live in Texas and elsewhere.

Taxes on Business (Other Than Production or Severance Taxes)

In Texas, the nearest approach to a universal or statewide business tax is the franchise tax paid, with certain exceptions, by both foreign and Texas-chartered (domestic) corporations and levied on the privilege of conducting business in the state. The tax, administered by the state comptroller, is imposed upon the invested capital, surplus, and long-term debt of each firm to the extent that it does business in Texas. This tax is paid by these corporations in addition to local property taxes.

Although a part of the Texas tax structure since 1907, only in recent years has the franchise tax rate been increased so as to make the tax more than a minor revenue source.

Selective Business Taxes

Insurance-Premiums Tax. Texas imposes a tax on insurance companies measured by gross premiums collected within the state in addition to local ad valorem taxes on their real and personal property.

> A unique and important feature of insurance taxation is the use by most states, including Texas, of retaliatory taxes that are imposed on foreign insurance companies. Essentially, each state with a retaliatory law says to every other state: "We will tax your companies at least as severely as you tax ours." Thus, if state A has a 2 percent tax and state B has a 3 percent tax, then state A will tax companies incorporated in state B at the rate of 3 percent. Any increase in Texas insurance taxes, therefore, will have a chain reaction by increasing the taxes paid to other states by Texas companies operating in such other states. This is true regardless of whether the increase takes the form of raising the rate or modifying the exemptions allowed.[2]

The tax rate varies somewhat with the type of insurance, amount collected from premiums, investments in Texas securities, and whether a company is domestic or foreign. Hence, the tax on insurance premiums is of a dual nature: to provide tax revenue for the state and to encourage investments in Texas securities.

Nonprofit group hospital-service plans, fraternal organizations, local mutual-aid societies, burial associations, and farm mutual fire companies are exempt from payment of the insurance premiums tax in Texas. Administration of the tax on insurance premiums is handled by the State Board of Insurance.

Gross-Receipts Taxes. A number of companies in Texas pay taxes on the basis of gross receipts. Included in this category are express companies, telegraph and telephone companies, motor carriers, collection agencies, car-line companies, textbook publishers, pullman companies, producers of cement, public utilities, and a 10 percent gross receipt tax on sales and service of liquor-by-the-drink paid by private clubs and public bars. The tax rate is based upon a certain percentage of gross receipts and varies among the concerns subject to the tax. As is true of most other state taxes, various exemptions are provided in the law. The tax is administered by the comptroller's office.

Cement Tax. Sometimes the cement tax is grouped with the severance and production taxes on natural resources; yet, it is a tax on a manufactured product. The tax is assessed at the rate of 2.75 cents per 100 pounds of cement produced, distributed, or used in the state. The tax is administered by the comptroller's office.

Cement is prepared in several combinations and marketed in many forms. However, Texas does not tax allied products of cement such as cement plaster, gypsum, or gypsum products.

Miscellaneous Business Taxes and Fees. There are a number of miscellaneous business taxes and fees that yield a small amount of revenue to the state. These include corporation charter fees, cigarette-tax permits (for dealers), real-estate fees (from brokers and salesmen), motor-carrier fees, licenses and fees from the brewers of alcoholic beverages, fees from dealers in alcoholic beverages, insurance agents, and vending-machine operators. Occupation taxes, other licenses and permits are included in this category also.

Taxes Paid by Individuals

The state collects its revenue from two categories of taxpayers: individuals and businesses.

> There is no strict delineation in Texas between the two types. Some taxes are so levied that only businesses pay them—although they may eventually be passed on to those who buy from the business taxpayer. Other taxes are paid predominantly by individuals. . . . In many instances—as in the case of the property tax or motor-fuels tax—both business and individuals pay the same tax. . . .
>
> It is pertinent to remember that Texas is somewhat unique among the states in that it levies neither a general tax upon individuals nor a general tax upon business. Traditionally, the Texas pattern has been selective in attaching levies to certain activities or, in the case of individuals, to certain tastes or purchases.[3]

Since it is common for the states and federal government to have selective sales taxes on the same commodities, the states are vitally concerned with any proposal in Congress to increase the federal rate on one or more items. As the search for additional state and federal tax sources continues, governors and state legislators complain about certain tax fields being preempted by the federal government. Certainly the tax policy of the federal government has a considerable impact upon the tax structure of the states.

Selective Sales Taxes in Texas

Motor-Fuels Tax. The state tax on gasoline and diesel fuel per gallon is 5 and 6.5 cents respectively. Of the state taxes collected in Texas, the tax on motor fuel is one of the most productive.

Three-fourths of the tax on motor fuel is dedicated to roads and highways and one-fourth is deposited in the available school fund for distribution among the local school districts of the state. The comptroller of public accounts has primary responsibility for the administration of the tax.

Among the major revenue sources in Texas, the motor-fuel tax stands alone as a "benefit" tax. The theory is that the recipients of special benefits (use of highways) should pay for them. It is probably true that those paying the tax on motor fuel can see a more direct relationship between the tax paid and the service received than is true with other taxes. Since the tax is paid on a per gallon basis, it is paid somewhat in proportion to the use made of the highways by the purchaser.

Under the benefit principle, the Texas motor-fuels tax is imposed only on motor fuel consumed on public highways. Those who purchase motor fuels for non-highway use are eligible for a tax refund. Hence, taxes paid on gasoline used in aircraft, both interstate and intrastate, are refundable. Those who operate motor-boats on the rivers and lakes in Texas and the ocean waters adjacent to the state are entitled to refunds. Refunds are also authorized for those who use gasoline for industrial and agricultural purposes and contractors and oil operators are eligible for tax refunds.

The increased mechanization of Texas agriculture, industrial expansion, and greater use of gasoline by those who operate airplanes and boats, both for commercial and private purposes, have resulted in the state refunding millions of dollars a year to nonusers of highways. Undoubtedly, a large amount of such gasoline is used in automobiles. Gasoline purchased for nonhighway use may be resold tax free or used in one's own automobile. Although illegal, such tax diversion is difficult to establish, which hinders the enforcement of the law.

Some states provide no tax refund for the nonhighway use of motor fuels, other states provide only partial refunds to certain groups. Texas could improve its financial position by eliminating all tax refunds on gasoline, or by refunding only one half of the present tax on motor fuels. All individuals and business firms, either directly or indirectly, profit from the highway system. Therefore, the concept of the tax on motor fuels as a "benefit" tax is unrealistic.

Tobacco Tax. The tax on cigarettes, established as a depression finance measure in 1935, is 18.5 cents per package in Texas, of which 1 cent goes to the state parks fund. Chewing and pipe tobacco are taxed at 25 percent of the manufacturer's price. There is no tobacco tax on snuff, although it is subject to the sales tax.

Increase in population, urbanization, and the spread of the tobacco habit to new groups are significant factors in the increased consumption of tobacco products. Tax administration and enforcement are divided between the comptroller and state treasurer. Tax collection, through the sale of tax stamps, is a function of the state treasurer. Licenses or permits, which distributors, wholesalers, and retail dealers are required to have, are issued by the comptroller. The permits are issued annually, and those who hold permits are required to keep a record of sales and receipts and submit monthly reports to the comptroller. For violations of the law or regulations issued by the comptroller, the latter may revoke or suspend the permits.

In Texas, as in other states, there are certain exemptions to the tax. Those entering Texas from out-of-state may bring two packs of cigarettes with them without being liable for the "use tax." Most states, including Texas, exempt cigarettes sold in post exchanges to men and women of the armed forces, although the federal government grants no such exemption. In Texas this is important because of the large number of domestic-based service personnel stationed in the state. Over the years the exemption has meant the loss of millions of dollars in state tax revenue.

Alcoholic Beverage Taxes. Since the repeal of prohibition, Texas selective sales taxes on alcoholic beverages have produced a considerable amount of revenue. State license and permit fees provide an additional source of revenue.

As is true of cigarettes, beer sold on military bases in Texas is exempt from the selective sales tax, although the federal tax does apply at these installations. Texans have never looked with favor upon increasing the taxes affecting military personnel.

The administration of the selective sales taxes on alcoholic beverages, besides the handling of licenses and permits, is divided among the alcoholic beverage commission, the state treasurer, and the county tax collectors (who collect the fees for the beer licenses annually).

Motor-Vehicle Excise Tax. When a resident of Texas purchases a new or used car in the state, he or she must pay the motor-vehicle excise tax which is levied at 4 percent of the purchase price less any federal taxes or carrying charges that might be included. If a used vehicle is traded for a new one, the tax applies to the difference between the total purchase price of the new vehicle and the trade-in value of the exchanged vehicle. Motor vehicles purchased at retail outside Texas and brought into the state for use by a resident, firm, or corporation (domiciled or doing business in Texas) are subject to a compensatory use tax computed on the same basis as the excise or sales tax. If a person moves to Texas he does not pay the sales or use tax; however, he must pay a flat $15 tax regardless of the type or value of the vehicle involved. In the event one person makes a free gift of an automobile to another, there is no sales tax, but the person receiving the gift is liable for a $10 tax regardless of the type or value. The sales tax does not apply to individuals who exchange vehicles of equal value, although each party must pay a $5 fee.

Those who purchase motor vehicles exclusively for resale, as automobile dealers, are not subject to the excise or sales tax. This exemption does not include dealers' demonstrator vehicles, since they are not purchased exclusively for resale and for this reason are not considered as stock-in-trade. Trailers and semitrailers are taxable; however, farm tractors and road-building machinery are exempted.

The 4 percent motor vehicle excise tax also is levied on automobiles rented or leased for less than thirty-one days.

The motor-vehicle sales tax is collected locally by the county tax collector in the county where the motor vehicle is first registered by the tax payer, and is administered at the state level by the comptroller. The purchaser is required to file the necessary papers with the county tax collector and the latter must not accept any vehicle for registration or transfer until the sales tax has been paid.

As is true of any tax, there are ways in which the motor-vehicle sales tax may be evaded. For example, one could state falsely in the affidavit that the transaction was a gift, an exchange or trade of equal value, or involved a resale. A large number of these evasions involve transactions between individuals rather than dealers. One could admit a taxable purchase but understate the total consideration. A dealer might, for his own benefit or that of the customer, collect the full amount of the tax and remit a smaller sum to the county tax collector. Because of these and other methods, many feel that evasion of the tax is rather widespread in Texas.

Admissions and Award Taxes. Admissions to various types of amusements in Texas are subject to taxation: motion pictures, plays, nightclubs, skating rinks, and various types of racing. If the amusements are conducted exclusively for the benefit of state, educational, religious, or charitable institutions they are exempted from the tax. The comptroller's office is responsible for the administration of these taxes.

Motor Vehicle Registration Fees

The counties receive a fee for collecting the license receipts and sending them to the state. The amount each county receives is based on the number of miles of county-maintained roads and other factors.

Some local tax jurisdictions assess and collect property taxes on automobiles and others do not. If a local jurisdiction does not levy the property tax on automobiles, or has a lower tax rate, it may encourage persons from the counties that levy the tax to seek registration in the nontaxing counties. The law requires registration of vehicles in the county where the owner resides.

Inheritance Tax

Sometimes an estate tax is confused with an inheritance tax. An estate tax is paid on the property of a deceased person. It is paid on the property as a whole before it is divided. An inheritance tax is based on the property each individual inherits and is paid by each heir separately.

Since Texas is a community property state, all of the deceased person's separate property and one-half of the community estate is subject to the inheritance tax. The law in Texas allows all persons to receive from an estate a portion which is exempt from the inheritance tax. The exemption is greater for beneficiaries closely related to the deceased person and less for distant relatives and unrelated persons. Property left by a deceased person for the use of charitable, educational, or religious organizations is exempt from the Texas inheritance tax. The Texas law provides other exemptions, for example, Class A—spouse, direct lineal descendant/ascendant (ancestor)—$200,000 to be divided among all Class A beneficiaries.

The inheritance tax paid by the estate to the state can be deducted from the taxes to be paid the federal government—the so-called federal credit for the state death tax.

Sales Tax

For many years selective sales taxes had been included in Texas's omnibus-tax statutes.* The sales tax levies a 4 percent state sales tax on most purchases of 10 cents or more. Cities—with the approval of the voters of the city—may levy an additional 1 percent sales tax (optional municipal sales tax).†

The retailer adds all tax charges to the regular bill for merchandise and in this way the use of mills or tokens, which the law prohibits, is eliminated. It is unlawful for any retailer to assume the tax or to advertise that the tax or any part of it will be assumed by him, whether by not adding the tax to the selling price or, if the tax is added, by refunding all or part of it. In other words, the retailer must pass the tax on to the consumer.

The state and cities that have local sales taxes collect a sales tax on beer and liquor sold in package stores, grocery stores, and taverns. The 4 percent sales tax does not apply to private clubs.

---

*An omnibus law refers to a law that includes many things or classes.
†The 5 percent sales tax is levied on taxable items that cost 12 cents or more.

A number of articles are exempted from the sales tax. It does not cover most of the items that were under state sales taxes prior to 1961, such as motor vehicles, cigarettes, cigars and other tobacco products, and motor and special fuels. The law repealed some of the existing sales taxes and the items they covered were made subject to the sales tax.

Food products for human consumption are exempted. Meals served in restaurants are taxed. Drugs and medicines are exempted when prescribed for humans or animals by a licensed practitioner of the healing arts or by a veterinarian. Other exemptions include animal feeds, seeds, fertilizers, annual plants, farm machinery or equipment employed in agricultural pursuits, and books consisting wholly of writings sacred to any religious faith. Religious periodicals published or distributed by any religious faith are also exempted. No tax is levied on water, telephone, and telegraph services.

The sales tax applies to the sale of personal property, but not to real property. Materials incorporated into the performance of services are taxable in those instances where separate amounts are charged for labor and materials.

The state sales tax includes a 4 percent use tax. For example, taxable items purchased out-of-state but used in Texas are taxable.

State Surtax on Criminal Violations

The state courts collect a $2.50 state surtax on all traffic violations except parking tickets, a $5 levy on all other misdemeanor convictions, and $10 for each felony conviction. The funds are assigned to the Texas Criminal Justice Council, a division of the governor's office which promotes police training, and regional and local law enforcement improvement programs.

Federal Revenue Sharing

States and local governments in the United States receive billions of dollars from federal revenue sharing each year, administered in Washington by the office of revenue sharing, Department of the Treasury. Of the funds received by a state, one-third are made available to the state government and two-thirds to cities and counties. There are few federal controls on state and local expenditure of the funds, and the latter have been expended for a variety of purposes, including public safety, education, transportation, general government, health, environment/ conservation, recreation/culture, social services, and capital projects.

The method of computing federal revenue sharing is based on a complex mathematical formula including the population of states and local governments, a general tax effort factor, and a relative income factor. Two Texas cities of approximately the same population may be used to illustrate the concept in a general way. The general tax effort factor favored City B because of the lower average income per year and high tax rate.

	Population	Average income per year	Tax rate	Amount of federal revenue sharing
City A	18,500	$19,000	Low tax rate	Less than city B
City B	18,750	$ 9,000	High tax rate	More than city A

Other Revenue Sources

Texas receives millions of dollars annually from the federal government for public welfare, highways, and public health.

Texas also receives revenue from oil and gas royalties, mineral lease rentals and bonuses, land sales, sand, shell and gravel sales, and grazing-lease rentals. Some revenue is also derived from sale of other properties. The major revenue sources in Texas are federal grants, federal revenue sharing, gross-receipts and production tax, sales tax, motor-fuel tax, cigarette and tobacco tax and licenses, and motor vehicle licenses, registrations, and fees.

The cost of state government in Texas will continue to expand. Growth in population and an expansion of the economy will increase the state's revenue under the existing tax structure. This gain in state revenue will not offset the rising cost of government; therefore, additional revenue will be necessary.

State Expenditures

The major state expenditures in Texas include the following: educational, highway maintenance and construction, public welfare, eleemosynary and correctional, state-cost teacher retirement, and payment of public debt. The growth in population, increase in public school, university, and college attendance, increase in crime and prison inmates, and expansion of welfare activities will increase state expenditures.

13 The Judicial System

MANY PEOPLE LOOK UPON the judicial systems of the states as subordinate and inferior to that of the national government. This impression is due to a number of factors: (1) the existence of a dual system of courts in this country; (2) the fact that many cases may be instituted in either a state or a national court; (3) the right of appeal and removal of cases from state to federal courts; (4) the increased reliance on the federal courts to protect civil rights; (5) the more businesslike manner of operation, greater respect, and prestige of the federal judiciary; and (6) the delays, miscarriage of justice, and disintegrated court structure that characterize the judicial system in many states.

If the judicial systems of the states are subordinate and inferior to the national judiciary, much of the responsibility rests with the states. The federal and state courts have their own field of jurisdiction and, for the most part, operate independently within their assigned areas. The great majority of cases heard by state courts do not involve federal questions; state courts are concerned with the adjudication of rights claimed under the state constitution, state statutes, or the common law. Nearly all judicial actions instituted in state courts are terminated there. Probably nine-tenths of the judicial business in the United States is transacted in state courts; and it is here, rather than in the national courts, that most people have their contacts (if any) with the judicial process (as plaintiffs, defendants, jurors, or witnesses). For this reason the proper functioning of state courts is of paramount importance in providing substantial justice.

The Language of the Law

Mr. Justice Holmes once observed that, "A word is not crystal, transparent and unchanged, *it is the skin of a living thought* and may vary greatly in color and content according to the circumstances and the time in which it is used."[1] The adaptability of language alone would make law and the judicial process both intriguing and confusing for the general public. A long legal tradition, with an abundance of words and phrases from the common and Roman law, adds to the complexity of the law and courts. Since many legal terms frequently occur in newspapers and conversation, it might be helpful to consider their legal aspects.

Stare Decisis

The expression *stare decisis* is Latin and means to stand by decided cases or uphold precedents. Lawyers will argue that the principle of the case at hand was established in an earlier case (or cases) and should not be overruled; in short, "let the (prior) decision stand."

The principle of *stare decisis* lends an element of stability and continuity to the growth of law, since it provides a fixed, definite, and known law by which men are governed. To adhere to precedents can, and frequently does, result in the promotion of legal conservatism. Moreover, the principle is in the nature of a judicial restraint upon so-called "judge" or "court-made" law. It may mean that the injustices and inequities of an earlier period are projected into the present. Law, of necessity, in a democratic society must be progressive; its principles are expanded and liberalized by the spirit of the age. Legal principles must be brought to the test of enlightened reason and liberal principles. Nevertheless, settled principles of law, in most cases, are not lightly overturned.

Res Judicata

Sometimes in reading a court opinion or listening to legal discussions one comes in contact with the expression *res judicata*, which means a matter judicially acted upon or decided. The court will not reconsider the issue or question. It permits the courts, if need be, to compress the legal boundaries within which the immediate case must be decided.

Writ of Habeas Corpus

From the Latin, "you have the body," *habeas corpus* includes a variety of writs for the purpose of bringing a party before a court or judge. It dates back to the English Habeas Corpus Act of 1679, prior to which the English king could muzzle his opponents by holding them without trial or explanation. Similar statutes have been enacted in all the states of the Union. Federal and state constitutions place limitations upon the suspension of the writ.* These limitations, plus the legislative enactments, are designed to put an end to arbitrary imprisonment by providing a remedy for deliverance from illegal confinement. Certainly this "writ of liberty" is one of the great constitutional landmarks for the protection of personal liberty.

A person has the right to be brought before a magistrate within a reasonable time and informed of the charge against him. The person might be discharged or released on bail or bond, although in certain cases bail may be refused.† This process enables the person to know the nature of the charges and secure legal counsel. Many a person has been released temporarily (until tried) or permanently by the writ.

---

*The Texas constitution provides, "The writ of Habeas Corpus is a writ of right, and shall never be suspended. The Legislature shall enact laws to render the remedy speedy and effectual" (Art. I, Sec. 12, Bill of Rights).

†The Texas constitution provides, "All prisoners shall be bailable by sufficient sureties, unless for capital offenses, when the proof is evident; but this provision shall not be so construed as to prevent bail after indictment found upon examination of the evidence, in such manner as may be prescribed by law" (Art. I, Sec. II, Bill of Rights).

Writ of Injunction

A writ of injunction, if granted by the court, requires a party to do or forbear to do certain acts. In the latter sense, it is used as a preventive process. For example, a city may seek an injunction to prevent a private concern from increasing the rates for services it provides for the general public, or a company may seek injunctive action to prevent a strike before the workers walk off the job. In fact, there are a variety of ways in which the writ may be used to prevent damage to person or property before the action is taken by the party concerned.

In equity practice a restraining order may be issued upon the filing of an application for an injunction forbidding the defendant from taking action until a hearing on the application can be held. The restraining order forbids the defendant from taking action until the propriety of granting an injunction, either temporary or permanent, can be determined. For this reason the terms "injunction" and "restraining order" are not synonymous.

Writ of Mandamus (We command)

When a court issues a writ of mandamus it may direct a private or municipal corporation, or any of its officers, an executive, administrative, or judicial officer, or inferior court to perform a particular act belonging to his or their public, official, or ministerial duty. The writ may direct the restoration of rights or privileges of which one has been illegally deprived. A writ of mandamus may be used to compel a public official to perform some duty, which is required by law, not involving his discretion. Consequently, it can be employed to prevent public officials from arbitrarily refusing to perform ministerial duties required by law and as a result, it provides a legal check on governmental officials.

Writ of Quo Warranto

The writ of quo warranto may be employed for trying the title to a corporate or other franchise, or to a public or corporate office.

Writ of Certiorari

The writ of certiorari is an order issued by a higher court instructing the lower court to "certify" or turn over the record in a given case. A litigant may petition the Supreme Court in Washington to take such action; however, certiorari may or may not be granted, since it is a discretionary power of the high court.

Judicial Procedure

Civil Action

Through civil action in the courts one may secure enforcement or protection of private rights or the prevention or redress of private wrongs. A suit for divorce, a suit for damages for breach of contract, a suit for damages for libel or slander, and various types of injunctive actions to prevent injury to persons or property, among other types of legal action, come within the field of civil action. Some types of action may involve one in both a civil and criminal case. The state could prosecute one for libel or slander while the injured party might bring a civil action in a suit for damages.

In most civil cases private individuals or corporations appear as plaintiff and defendant. In such cases the state is interested that justice be done. As an interested party—rather than a direct participant—the state provides the legal forum (state courts) in which the parties may have their day in court. On occasion the state may appear in court as plaintiff or defendant in a civil action. For example, the state may bring a civil action against a private individual or the legislature may authorize an individual to bring suit against the state.

Only a few observations will be made here concerning civil procedure in Texas. In civil cases in Texas trial by jury may be waived if both parties agree. In a complex civil case the jury is confronted with a difficult problem. Because of the complexity of the case, as well as to prevent delay and reduce the cost of litigation, the parties may agree that the judge sit as both judge and jury. More and more civil cases are being decided without a jury.

In civil and criminal cases there is what is known as the "instructed verdict" where the judge may instruct the jury to decide in favor of one of the parties involved if he is of the opinion that the law, as applied to the facts in the case, is in favor of either the plaintiff or the defendant. If the judge instructs the jury to decide in favor of one of the parties and the jury returns a verdict for the other party, it is the duty of the court to render judgment notwithstanding the verdict of the jury, upon motion and notice. The court may disregard the findings of the jury on special issues that have no support in the evidence.

Criminal Action

Criminal or penal statutes establish certain actions as offenses against the public and impose punishment in case the statutes are violated. Punishment for robbery, rape, theft, murder, and manslaughter, among other criminal violations, are covered by these statutes. In case of violation of such a statute, the state will prosecute (*State of Texas* v. *John Doe*).

There has been a revival of interest in criminal law and criminal procedure among the general public, lawyers, judges, law schools, and legislators. This revival has been due in part to the increased crime rate and decisions of the federal courts that have guaranteed greater rights for the accused. As regards the rights of the accused, steps have been taken to establish national minimum standards and, as a result, a uniform penal code for the nation has evolved in this field of criminal procedure.

In 1965 the Texas legislature adopted a one-hundred-fifty-page code of criminal procedure by revising and rearranging statutes that pertain to the trial of criminal cases. Numerous changes, omissions, and additions to the criminal code were made by the legislature. The code in existence prior to 1965 had not been revised for forty years. There was need for revision, since the old code encouraged delay, excessive appeals, and numerous retrials. Also, certain provisions of the old code concerning the rights of the accused, and certain criminal law practices that had evolved in the state, were in conflict with federal court decisions.

The revised code of criminal procedure increased the power and responsibilities of the county and district judges and moved criminal procedure in Texas closer to the procedures followed in the federal courts. The code was designed to provide fair and just trial procedure for the state and accused alike.

Crime News

The Texas code of criminal procedure declares,

> It is the duty of the trial court, the attorney representing the accused, the attorney representing the state, and all peace officers to so conduct themselves as to insure a fair trial for both the state and the defendant, not impair the presumption of innocence, and at the same time afford the public the benefits of a free press.[2]

This provision of the criminal code is merely declaratory, since no punishment is provided for violation of it.

Pretrial statements by attorneys and law enforcement officers about the crime and the accused may be carried as headline and front-page news in the local press. Such statements and news coverage make it difficult to secure qualified jurors and the "trial by newspaper" may prejudice the rights of the accused to a fair trial. The issue confronts the individual's right of fair trial with the public's right to a free press.

It has been suggested that officers, attorneys, and judges be held in contempt of court for public statements following the arrest of a suspect concerning the existence or contents of a confession, any statements attributable to the accused, references to physical evidence, laboratory tests, prior police records, statements by witnesses, and any personal statements or observations about the case or the character of the accused. Also it has been recommended that reporters be barred from pretrial hearings and that press interviews not be allowed until the accused consults a lawyer.

The Right of Counsel

The Texas code of criminal procedure provides,

> In each case enumerated in this Code, the person making the arrest shall without unnecessary delay take the person arrested or have him taken before some magistrate of the county where the accused was arrested. The magistrate shall inform in clear language the person arrested of the accusation against him and of any affidavit filed therewith, of his right to retain counsel, of his right to remain silent, of his right to have an attorney present during any interview with peace officers or attorneys representing the state, of his right to terminate the interview at any time, of his right to request the appointment of counsel if he is indigent and cannot afford counsel, and of his right to have an examining trial. He shall also inform the person arrested that he is not required to make a statement and that any statement made by him may be used against him. The magistrate shall allow the person arrested reasonable time and opportunity to consult counsel and shall admit the person arrested to bail if allowed by law. [Art. 15.17]

The code does not authorize the questioning of a person between the time of arrest and arraignment. The accused must be informed of his legal rights by a magistrate—usually a justice of the peace—rather than by the arresting officer as permitted by the U.S. Supreme Court.

Under the existing code the defendant has the right of counsel at every stage of the criminal proceedings, including the immediate appearance before a magistrate after arrest, the examining trial, arraignment, or at any other time in both misdemeanors and felonies.

Written and Oral Confessions

A written confession must show that prior to its taking the defendant was brought before a magistrate and informed of his right to remain silent, his right to counsel, and the fact that his confession might be used against him. The confession must reflect the date, place, and name of the magistrate who administered the warning—otherwise it is inadmissible as evidence.

The code of criminal procedure provides: "No *oral or sign language statement* of an accused made as a result of custodial interrogation shall be admissible against the accused in a criminal proceeding unless an electronic recording, which may include motion picture, videotape, or other visual recording, is made of the statement" (italics added). Prior to the statement, but during the recording, the accused must be given the statutory warning and knowingly, intelligently, and voluntarily waive any rights set out in the warning. The protections provided in the code do not apply to any statement found to be true and which conduce to establish the guilt of the accused, such as the finding of secreted or stolen property or the instrument with which (one) states the offense was committed (physical evidence, "fruits of the crime"). If the accused is a deaf person, a qualified interpreter must be provided in order that the individual be guaranteed the above protections.

Voluntary oral confessions, made under proper safeguards, are admissible in the federal courts.

Wiretap Evidence

Texas law permits the use of electronic surveillance only for the investigation of felony drug offenses, except marijuana possession. The presiding judge of the court of criminal appeals is authorized to designate one district judge in each of the state's administrative judicial districts the authority to allow the Texas department of public safety to eavesdrop on suspected drug offenders. "A judge may issue an order authorizing interception of wire or oral communications only if the prosecutor applying for the order *shows probable cause* to believe that the interception will provide evidence of the commission of a felony" (italics added). As regards the investigation of felony drug offenders, wiretapping is considered a "search" and must meet the requirements of the Fourth Amendment of the U.S. Constitution. The latter provides "the right of the people to be secure in their persons, houses, papers, and effects, against unreasonable searches and seizures, shall not be violated, and no warrants shall issue, *but upon probable cause,* supported by oath or affirmation, and particularly describing the place to be *searched,* and the persons or things to be seized" (italics added).

Thus, wiretap evidence is admissible in Texas courts only when involving the investigation of felony drug offenses, except marijuana possession, and under the limitations specified in the state law. Federal law permits acquisition and introduction of wiretap evidence under certain conditions; a wiretap may be installed when suspected organized crime is involved and only with the specific permission of a judge.

The Polygraph Test

The polygraph is an instrument that simultaneously records changes in a person's blood pressure, respiration, and pulse rate while that individual is responding to a series of questions presented by the operator. The polygraph test is used by some employers for employee recruitment and to test the veracity of company workers. Generally, during the examination, no one is permitted in the examining room other than the polygraph operator and the individual being tested.

The results of a polygraph test are not admissible in court unless the prosecution, the defense, and the presiding judge agree on the matter. If, despite his or her objection, a person is compelled to take the test, this constitutes self-incrimination and thereby violates that person's constitutional rights. If an individual *agrees* to a polygraph test, he or she automatically agrees to have that information communicated to at least his or her attorney.

If, while on the witness stand, an accused *volunteered* the statement that he or she had passed a polygraph test, the prosecution, in order to test the credibility of the accused, could request that the polygraph operator take the witness stand. If the operator stated the accused did not pass the polygraph test, the jury could consider this fact in reaching its verdict.

Breathalyzer Test-Intoxilizer*

The law in Texas does not prohibit drinking while driving, the so-called open-container privilege.

Under the statutory standard in Texas a defendant is legally considered intoxicated if the blood-alcohol level is .10 percent or more. A previous law provided only a "presumption of intoxication" at this level and authorized a judge or jury to determine if a defendant were intoxicated. The state must, of course, prove beyond a reasonable doubt to the judge or jury that the .10 percent reading was a correct one.

The law further provides that a person arrested for driving while intoxicated (DWI) *must submit* to an alcohol level test or provide a blood or urine sample, or face automatic suspension of his or her driver's license for ninety days. Refusal to submit to such a test is admissible in court testimony.

Other provisions of the law include the following: maximum punishment of two years in jail and a $2,000 fine for first-time DWI offenders; probation for a first-time offender by participating in an alcohol or drug dependency evaluation program; suspension of the driver's license of a first-time offender from three months to a year; and increased penalties for DWI violations involving death or injury.

In a 7-2 decision (1983), the U.S. Supreme Court overturned a South Dakota supreme court decision requiring the evidence of the driver's refusal to take the test to be suppressed during his trial. The Supreme Court said, in an opinion written by Justice Sandra Day O'Connor, that introduction of such evidence did not violate the defendant's Fifth Amendment rights. "The simple blood test is so safe, painless, and commonplace, that respondent concedes, as he must, that the state

---

*Texas uses intoxilizer machines to test the percentage of alcohol in a suspect's breath. From that, the machine determines the blood alcohol level, after which it blows the breath sample into the air. The U.S. Supreme Court may decide whether the U.S. Constitution requires the police to save a portion of the breath so the accused drunken driver can later has his or her own chemist test it. The Texas Department of Public Safety certifies all intoxilizer machines and their operators.

could legitimately compel the subject, against his will, to accede to the test." To quote further from the decision of the U.S. Supreme Court, "We recognize, of course, that the choice to submit or refuse to take a blood alcohol test will not be an easy or pleasant one for a suspect to make. But the criminal process often requires suspects and defendants to make difficult choices. We hold, therefore, that a refusal to take a blood alcohol test after a police officer has lawfully requested it, is not an act coerced by the officer, and thus is not protected by the privilege against self-incrimination (see *U.S. Supreme Court Reports,* in press)."

The breathalyzer test should determine the alcohol contents of the air circulating through the lungs. However, even the smallest amount of alcohol present in the mouth at the time of testing may contaminate the air expelled, and the results obtained may in no way represent the true alcohol level of the blood. "It is well known that the oxidizing reagents used in the 'Breathalyzer' (potassium dichromate and sulphuric acid) will react with many substances, and the reaction is by no means confined to ethyl alcohol alone. . . . As a result, concern is often expressed that a falsely high reading may be obtained from a person who has consumed little or no alcohol."[3]

Videotapes

A law passed by the Texas legislature requires police in counties of more than 25,000 population to take videotapes of suspected drunk drivers. The tapes should protect the innocent as well as aid prosecutors in obtaining more DWI convictions. Also, it should reduce the number of DWI trials. A videotape might provide convincing evidence to a dubious jury hearing a DWI case. However, the videotape may be evidence of innocence as well as guilt. In the past many DWI suspects did not believe they were too intoxicated to drive and did not plead guilty. When they see themselves on TV slurring their speech, the individuals on trial and the juries should have little doubt about the matter. Individuals may be more inclined to plead guilty after seeing themselves on tape. Such tests as having suspected drunken drivers walk a straight line, touch their noses, and answer questions may be videotaped.

Plea Bargaining

Plea bargaining in a criminal violation may occur when an individual pleads guilty to a lesser change rather than being prosecuted and tried for a more serious offense. For example, an individual might refuse to plead guilty to a check forgery charge that carries a five-year jail sentence and be indicted instead, and possibly convicted, under a Habitual Criminal Offender Act, which carries a life sentence. The prosecutor may accept the plea bargain because it will save time and money, because the prosecutor can never be certain that a jury will convict, and because the courts are so overcrowded with pending criminal cases. Defendants are inclined to accept plea bargains because, if convicted of a more serious crime, they spend more time in jail and because they are never certain how the jury will vote.

The actors in the plea bargaining process include the presiding judge, the prosecutor, the defense attorney, and the accused. Of the criminal cases tried each year in American courts, it is estimated about 90 percent are disposed of by plea bargains.

The U.S. Supreme Court has recognized that the plea bargaining power can be abused by prosecutors. As a result, the Court has attempted to establish certain standards or guidelines and prohibit judicial "vindictiveness" for the accused. For example, the process must be explained and clearly understood by the accused. The court has prevented a prosecutor from indicting a convicted person on a second charge because the individual decided to *appeal* the first conviction. And the High Court has ruled that if a junior prosecutor accepts a plea bargain without authority from his superior, the state must keep its part of the plea bargain anyway. The fair "give and take" at the negotiating table is one thing—and "prosecutorial vindictiveness" is something else.

Indictment

In Texas a person might be indicted either by information (misdemeanors) or by grand jury (felonies).

By Information. If the offence committed is not punishable by confinement in the penitentiary, the complainant may file a sworn statement with the county attorney. In this complaint the individual indicates that he believes a certain party has committed an offense. On the basis of this complaint the county attorney makes an investigation, after which he may or may not formally charge the party with the offense. If the county attorney believes the party should be brought to trial, a document known as "Information" is filed with the county court. As a result of the complaint, investigation, and information (indictment), the defendant is brought to trial.

As one can see there are practical limitations upon indictment by information. (1) The individual must make the statement under oath, and a false statement made under such conditions is a serious offense. (2) The county attorney makes an investigation on the basis of the sworn statement, and since he is an elective official he will proceed cautiously.

By Grand Jury. The Texas constitution contains two important statements on the grand jury. "No person shall be held to answer for a criminal offense, unless on an indictment of a grand jury, except in cases in which the punishment is by fine or imprisonment, otherwise than in the penitentiary, in cases of impeachment, and in cases arising in the army or navy, or in the militia, when in actual service in time of war or public danger."[4]

Waiver of indictment for noncapital felonies is authorized by state law. On waiver by the accused (in open court or by written instrument), he shall be charged by information.* "Grand juries impaneled in the district courts shall enquire into misdemeanors, and all indictments therefor returned into the district courts shall forthwith be certified to the county courts, or other inferior courts having jurisdiction to try them, for trial."[5] As an arm of the state district courts the grand jury performs important functions.

The jury commission, composed of not less than three nor more than five persons designated by the district judge, selects not less than fifteen nor more than twenty persons (as directed by the district judge) from the citizens of different por-

---

*A capital offense is one for which the death penalty may, but need not, be imposed.

tions of the county to be summoned as grand jurors. From this list twelve are selected to compose the grand jury. When the grand jury is completed, the district judge appoints one of the number foreman. A vote of nine is necessary to indict a person. If, after investigation, the grand jury feels there is sufficient evidence of wrong-doing, a true bill, signed by the foreman, is presented to the court. On the basis of this charge or indictment, the defendant will be tried. The true bills and no bills, as reported by the grand jury, provide news items for the local press.

Persons selected for the grand jury serve for the term of the court, usually three or six months. An urban county may have three or more grand juries in service at the same time.

Prior to revision of the code of criminal procedure in 1965, there were frequent reversals of criminal convictions by the court of criminal appeals on grounds the indictments were defective. When the court of criminal appeals found an indictment defective, it reversed the conviction and the matter was again presented to the grand jury, after which a proper indictment was returned, and the accused was again tried. Such delay weakened the state's case, since it was more difficult to secure the evidence.

Under the present criminal code of procedure "An indictment shall not be held insufficient, nor shall the trial, judgment or other proceedings thereon be affected, by reason of any defect of form which does not prejudice the substantial rights of the defendant" (Art. 21.19).

Pretrial Hearings

Because of extensive news coverage in the locale, the defense might believe a fair and impartial jury could not be selected in the county or district where the crime was committed. Under such conditions the defense might request a change of venue. On the basis of the testimony introduced by the defense, which will be challenged by the state, the presiding judge, at a pretrial hearing, must decide whether or not the trial is to be held in the originating county. If the motion for change of venue is granted, the case is transferred to another county or district.

Also at pretrial hearings the judge may rule on preliminary motions for continuance, suppression of evidence, special pleas, and the like.

Selecting the Trial Jury

On a plea of innocent or guilty, a defendant may, in writing, waive a jury trial and ask for a trial by the judge. However, in felony cases the state can demand a jury. This provision makes it possible for the judge, in collaboration with the prosecutors, to escape from trying a ticklish case himself. If the defendant does not have an attorney, the judge must appoint one to represent him when he waives the jury trial.

The trial or petit jury in the justice of the peace and county courts consists of six persons, while district court trial juries consist of twelve individuals. No jury is used in the appellate courts (courts of appeals, court of criminal appeals, and the supreme court).

District judges may direct that not more than four jurors, in addition to the regular jury, be called and impaneled to sit as alternate jurors. County judges may direct that not more than two jurors, in addition to the regular jury, be called and impaneled to sit as alternate jurors. Alternate jurors in the order in which they are called replace the jurors who, prior to the time the jury retires to consider its verdict, are unable or disqualified to perform their duties. Alternate jurors are selected in the same manner, have the same qualifications, and are subject to the same examination and challenges as the regular jurors. An alternate juror that does not replace a regular juror must be discharged after the jury retires to consider its verdict.

Qualifications and Exemptions for Jury Service. Any person, in order to qualify as a competent juror must:

1. be a citizen of this state and county and qualified to vote;
2. be of sound mind and good moral character;
3. be able to read and write the English language;
4. not have served as a juror for as long as six days during the preceding six months in the district courts or the preceding three months in the county courts;
5. not have been convicted of theft or any felony (includes felony probation);
6. not be under indictment or other legal accusation of theft or of any felony; and
7. be at least eighteen years of age.

The following are exempt from jury service provided they claim exemption:

1. persons over sixty-five years of age;
2. persons who have legal custody of a child or children under the age of ten years, if jury service would leave children without adequate supervision;
3. students of public or private high schools;
4. persons enrolled and in actual attendance in an institution of higher education.[6] (It should be noted that business reasons are not lawful excuses.)

Selection of Veniremen. Veniremen* are members of a panel of jurors from whom jury selection will be made for individual cases. In other words, a venireman is a person summoned for jury service. He may or may not serve on a jury.

A special venire may be drawn for capital trials, such as murder, criminal assault, and robbery by firearms. This group of citizens, four or five hundred persons, are summoned for a particular trial and from them twelve jurors will be selected. Once the jury reaches a decision or cannot reach a verdict, their job is finished. Others who are summoned by regular venire, and qualify for jury service, may serve on one or more juries during the term of court. This is possible through the use of the central jury room.

Veniremen are selected through the use of jury wheel or by computer. The jury roll is made up only of registered voters who are eighteen years of age or older. The constable and city marshal may select the jurors for the justice and municipal courts.

Jury Examination in a Criminal Case.[7] Some of the veniremen reporting to the county courthouse will be assigned to civil jury duty, whereas others will hold cards informing them they have been selected for criminal jury duty. In either case the citizen is paid for his time.

The same day that the trial is set, the veniremen, in the urban counties, report to the central jury room after which examination of the jury for the case begins. Con-

---

*Venire is Latin and means "to come or to appear."

siderable care is used in the selection and rejection of jurors, since the case may be won or lost at this stage. In the hands of skilled lawyers, the examination of the jury is a work of art.

A venireman may be rejected for jury service because of his predetermined opinion concerning the defendant's guilt or innocence. Newspaper, radio, or television coverage of the crime may have prompted the prospective juror to form an opinion, which would prevent any objective evaluation of the evidence and pleas of prosecution and defense.

Knowledge of the case, however, does not necessarily excuse one from jury service. Further questioning will determine whether the opinion is of such weight that it cannot be removed by competent evidence. The test is whether a juror can set aside anything he has heard, or opinion he has formed, and return a verdict based on court testimony. In reaching a verdict the jurors must rely solely on competent and credible sworn testimony from the witness stand.

A defendant may or may not testify in his own behalf. By law he is not required to do so in order to prove he is innocent of the offense charged. Veniremen, at the beginning of jury examination, are informed that failure of the defendant to testify must not be construed as proof of guilt. If a venireman believes the defendant should testify to prove himself innocent, the venireman would be excused. Furthermore, a venireman, if he is to be selected as a juror, must believe in the presumption of innocence of the defendant, and that the indictment, rather than being proof of guilt, is merely the legal instrument or process that brings the defendant into court.

The criminal law provides certain defenses for murder (self-defense, insanity, accident, and alibi). Also the law provides only two years as the minimum penalty for murder. The prospective juror need not agree with the law, but if one has prejudices concerning the rights or defenses of the accused as stipulated in the law, he must be excused from jury service.

If an eighteen- or nineteen-year-old person is charged with murder, the defense lawyers are interested in securing jurors who are sympathetic to youthful defendants. On the other hand, the state's prosecutors want jurors who will not consider the defendant's age in arriving at a verdict. So the familiar question is asked: "Would the defendant's relative youth—and this fact alone—influence you in arriving at a verdict?" Such a question, like all others that may be asked veniremen, must be clothed in the proper legal dress or phraseology.

In capital cases, the state and defense can excuse as many veniremen as may be legally excused for cause, as one who has an unshakeable opinion. But only fifteen peremptory challenges are allowed each side, although the court sometimes authorizes additional challenges. In noncapital felonies and misdemeanors the state and defense each are entitled to ten and five peremptory challenges whereby a prospective juror's name is stricken for other than legal reasons. Lawyers strive to conserve their peremptory challenges and disqualify persons for cause if possible.

The Trial

After a jury is impaneled, the indictment or information is read to the jury by the prosecuting attorney. The state's attorney informs the jury as to the nature of the accusation and the facts that are expected to be proven by the state, after which the testimony on the part of the state is offered. Witnesses called by the state are sworn and directly examined by the state's prosecutors and cross-examined by counsel for defense. The state may enter various exhibits in the record, for example, the murder weapon, pieces of clothing, blood analysis, and ballistic information.

The nature of the defenses relied upon and the facts expected to be proven in their support are stated by the defendant's counsel after which the testimony on the part of the defense is offered. Witnesses for the defense are directly examined by counsel for defense and cross-examined by the prosecutors for the state. Some witnesses for both the state and defense may be recalled to the stand for redirect and recross-examination.

Before the argument begins, the judge delivers to the jury a written charge setting forth the law applicable to the case. The judge may express no opinion as to the weight of the evidence, sum up the testimony, discuss the facts, or use any argument calculated to arouse the sympathy or excite the passions of the jury. Before the charge is read to the jury, the defendant must have a reasonable time to examine the charge and present his objections in writing.

The order of argument may be regulated by the presiding judge but the court may never restrict the argument in felony cases to a number of addresses less than two on each side. The prosecutors for the state and counsel for defense present their case and summation to the jury. Counsel for the state has the right to make the concluding address to the jury.

If during the trial of any felony case one of the original twelve jurors dies or becomes disabled from sitting at any time before the charge of the court is read to the jury, the remaining eleven jurors may hear the case and return a verdict. After the charge of the court is read to the jury, if any one of the jurors becomes unable to perform his duty, the jury may be discharged.

If nine of the jury can be kept together in a misdemeanor case in the district court, they cannot be discharged. If more than three of the twelve jurors are discharged, the entire jury must be dismissed. In the county court the verdict must be concurred in by each juror.

When jurors have been sworn in a felony case, the court may, at its discretion, permit the jurors to separate and go home after each day of court until the court has given its charge to the jury. After the charge, jurors may separate with the consent of the state and the defendant and the permission of the court.

Jury Deliberations and Penalty

Until they are ready to deliberate on a verdict, the jurors are not allowed to discuss the case with each other.

The jury in the justice of the peace and county courts determines matters of both fact and law. District-court juries determine only questions of fact. A unanimous verdict is necessary for a jury to reach a decision. In the event the jury cannot reach a verdict for either plaintiff or defendant, a "hung jury" exists. Under such conditions the jury is discharged, a new jury is impaneled, and a new trial is called.

The trial is divided into two separate hearings—one before the jury on the issue of guilt or innocence; if there is a finding of guilt, another hearing is held on the question of punishment. During this hearing the defendant's character, previous convictions, and some of his background can come before the jury or the judge. The judge will assess the penalty upon a finding of guilt by the jury unless the defendant requests that the same jury fix the punishment. This represents a departure from the common law under which the traditional function of the trial jury was to decide only the guilt or innocence of the accused person.

After the jury has brought in a verdict in a criminal case, but before the sentence has been pronounced by the judge, the judge may disregard the verdict and order a new trial if he thinks the jury has not done substantial justice.

Where the punishment is a jail (not prison) term, the court may permit the defendant to serve his sentence during off-work hours or on weekends.

The code of criminal procedure does not provide for suspended sentences, only probation for felony and misdemeanor cases. The jury, in felonies and misdemeanors, cannot grant probation; it can only recommend it where the punishment does not exceed ten years. If probation is recommended, the judge may not disregard it. The judge may grant probation whether or not the jury recommends it.

The Death Penalty. On June 29, 1972, by a 5 to 4 decision, the U.S. Supreme Court ruled that the death penalty, as it was administered at the time in the United States, was unlawful. For years, those opposed to capital punishment had argued that such laws violated the Eighth Amendment of the U.S. Constitution ("Excessive bail shall not be required, nor excessive fines imposed *nor cruel and unusual punishment inflicted*" [italics added].) The limitations of the Eighth Amendment was also a limitation on the states as a result of judicial interpretation of the Fourteenth Amendment (the doctrine or concept of incorporation). Also, many people believed the death penalty laws were discriminatory since persons of low income might have inadequate legal counsel and that the laws were applied in a capricious manner (whim, impulse, and unpredictability).

The death penalty laws in Texas limit the ultimate penalty to certain categories, including murder of law enforcement officers in the line of duty, murder for hire, and killings committed in the course of robberies, rapes, or kidnappings. The Texas criminal code provides as follows:

(a) Upon a finding that the defendant is guilty of a capital offense, the court shall conduct a separate sentencing proceeding to determine whether the defendant shall be sentenced to death or life imprisonment. The proceeding shall be conducted in the trial court before the trial jury as soon as practicable. In the proceeding, evidence may be presented as to any matter that the court deems relevant to sentence. This subsection shall not be construed to authorize the introduction of any evidence secured in violation of the Constitution of the United States or of the State of Texas. The state and the defendant or his counsel shall be permitted to present argument for or against sentence of death.

(b) On conclusion of the presentation of the evidence, the court shall submit the following issues to the jury:

(1) whether the conduct of the defendant that caused the death of the deceased was committed deliberately and with the reasonable expectation that the death of the deceased or another would result;

(2) whether there is a probability that the defendant would commit criminal acts of violence that would constitute a continuing threat to society; and

(3) if raised by the evidence, whether the conduct of the defendant in killing the deceased was unreasonable in response to the provocation, if any, by the deceased.

(c) The state must prove each issue submitted beyond a reasonable doubt, and the jury shall return a special verdict of "yes" or "no" on each issue submitted.

(d) The court shall charge the jury that:

(1) it may not answer any issue "yes" unless it agrees unanimously; and

(2) it may not answer any issue "no" unless 10 or more jurors agree.

(e) If the jury returns an affirmative finding on each issue submitted under this article, the court shall sentence the defendant to death. If the jury returns a negative finding on or is unable to answer any issue submitted under this article, the court shall sentence the defendant to confinement in the Texas Department of Corrections for life. The court, the attorney for the state, or the attorney for the defendant may not inform a juror or a prospective juror of the effect of failure of the jury to agree on an issue submitted under this article.[8]

The most serious thrust of the legal assault on the Texas law is the contention that the death penalty law gives jurors unconstitutional discretion to decide whether a defendant lives or dies, the same contention the U.S. Supreme Court invoked in striking down Texas's old death penalty law (that the law was capable of being applied in a capricious manner). It has been said that few psychiatrists could answer the three questions with any degree of reliability, and here a life hangs in the balance. Therefore, the law is said to be "standardless," and the three findings of the jury "highly subjective." This is a law that allows a jury discretion to assess death in one case and life in another with no difference *in the facts*.

On the other hand, the Texas murder law does not cover some of the more heinous crimes, for example, a father or mother who murdered their five children could not be given the death penalty under the law.

Charles L. Black, Jr. reminded his readers, "The Law of Moses is full of the death penalty. But as time went on the court in ancient Jerusalem, without of course touching one syllable of this law, devised procedural safeguards so refined, so difficult of satisfying, that the penalty of death could only very rarely be exacted."[9] By the very nature of the safeguards that evolved, the death penalty, at least to some extent, was considered an exceptional form of punishment—a "cruel and unusual punishment."

Mr. Justice Brennan of the U.S. Supreme Court expressed his views as follows: "We know 'that the words of the [Clause] [cruel and unusual punishments] are not precise, and that their scope is not static.' We know, therefore, that the Clause 'must draw its meaning from the evolving standards of decency that marks the progress of a maturing society.' "[10] In another case decided by the U.S. Supreme Court Justice Brennan observed, "This Court inescapably has the duty, as the ultimate arbiter of the meaning of our Constitution, to say whether, when individuals condemned to death stand before our Bar, 'moral concepts' require us to hold that the law has progressed to the point where we should declare that the punishment of death, like punishments on the rack, the screw, and the wheel, is no longer morally tolerable in our civilized society."[11] Yet, a large segment of the people of the United States do not agree with this view as the number of individuals murdered in the United States continues to increase at an enormous rate.

Charles L. Black, Jr. concluded, "Though the justice of God may indeed ordain that some should die, *the justice of man* is altogether and always insufficient for saying who these may be."[12]

The Courts

The state judicial system embraces not only the courts operating on a statewide basis (the supreme court and the court of criminal appeals) but those that operate in precincts, counties, and districts as well. From justice of the peace to the supreme courts (one civil and one criminal), all courts on all levels form parts of a single pattern, although in no way an integrated system.

Justice of the Peace Courts

The county commissioners court, as the governing body of the county, establishes the justice of the peace precincts in each county of the state. "In each such precinct there shall be elected one Justice of the Peace and one Constable, each of whom shall hold his office for four years and until his successor shall be elected and qualified; provided that in any precinct in which there may be a city of 8,000 or more inhabitants, there shall be elected two Justices of the Peace.[13] In some of the urban counties two justices of the peace are elected in one precinct (position 1 and position 2). Most counties have eight justices of the peace although the more populated counties may have nine or ten.

Counties of 18,000 to 30,000 may have as few as two justice of the peace precincts and no more than five. Counties of less than 18,000 may be designated as a single precinct unless the commissioners court found a need for more, but not more than four could be created.

The Texas constitution is silent on the matter of qualifications for justices of the peace.* Compensation varies from a few dollars a month in some precincts to several thousand dollars a year in other areas, depending upon the population of the precinct and the local salary law for precinct and county officials.

Justices of the peace have jurisdiction in criminal matters of all cases where the penalty or fine to be imposed by law may not be more than $200. Justice courts have original jurisdiction in civil matters of all cases where the amount in controversy is $1,000 or less, of which exclusive original jurisdiction is not given to the district or county courts. The justice of the peace courts may have other jurisdiction, both criminal and civil, as may be provided by law. Cases decided in the justice of the peace courts, where the judgment is for more than $20 exclusive of court costs, and in all criminal cases as may be prescribed by law, may be appealed to the county court.

Each justice of the peace in the state also presides as a judge of the small claims court that has concurrent jurisdiction with the justice of the peace court where the amount involved, exclusive of cost, does not exceed $1,000. Those who are in the business of lending money, as well as collecting agencies, may not bring action in the small claims court. If either party desires a trial by jury, a jury fee must be deposited with the court, at which point a jury will be impaneled as in other civil cases in the justice courts.

Creditors and persons seeking wages due, among other plaintiffs, may file in the small claims court by paying a modest filing fee. Hearings in the small claims courts are informal, and since no formal pleadings are required, one need not secure legal counsel. The justice of the peace renders judgment unless a jury is requested by either party. If the amount in controversy is more than $20, an appeal can be taken to the county court. Thus, an informal and inexpensive legal process is provided for hearing and settlement of small claims.

---

*Justices of the peace who are not licensed attorneys must take a forty-hour course in the performance of their duties and a twenty-hour course each year thereafter at an accredited state-supported school of higher education (Art. 5872, Revised Civil Statutes).

Many cases heard by justices of the peace, presiding over the regular justice of the peace court or the small claims court, involve consumer, landlord, and renter cases. Many small claims are filed by businesses. When the debtor learns that a suit for collection has been filed, the individual may pay the debt without appearing in court. Some individuals contend that businessmen should take full responsibility for extending credit and bill collecting and that local officials and tax money should be used for other purposes. The businessmen say that, since wages are exempt from garnishment (except for payment of child support), they need some inexpensive method of collecting small claims.*

Prior to the establishment of the small claims courts, one was hesitant about going to court with a claim because frequently court costs and the fees paid a lawyer amounted to more than the money in controversy. The small claims courts are designed to provide an inexpensive and expeditious method of settling claims that are not large enough to justify hiring a lawyer and filing suit in a higher court.

In Texas certain property of a family and of a single, adult person, not a constituent of a family is exempt, "except for encumbrances properly fixed thereon," from forced sale for payment of debts. Such property is the homestead, personal property not to exceed an aggregate fair market value of $15,000 for each single, adult person not a constituent of a family and $30,000 for a family, if included among the following: furnishings of a home, wearing apparel, tools, apparatus and books belonging to any trade or profession, current wages for personal services, various types and numbers of farm animals, and an automobile and other categories of travel.†

The courts in Texas have held that one truck and trailer are exempt from forced sale for debt under the provision exempting to the family "two horses and one wagon." A Ford truck, used on a farm, and serving the purpose of a farm wagon, there being no farm wagon on the farm, is a "wagon" within the meaning of the law. The exemption one carriage or buggy has also been construed to mean the automobile of a family, since "an automobile is a carriage."

Because of the exempt properties of the house and nonhouseholder, one might secure a judgment in the small-claims court but be unable to execute it. For this reason some debtors will tell their creditor, "You can only frighten and harass me. I have no money or property that can be taken." Frequently a person will pay his debt when threatened with legal action, despite the exemptions in the law. Once a judgment is obtained, the debtor's bank account can be garnished to satisfy the debt.

Justices of the peace perform a great variety of functions. They may conduct examining trials in criminal cases for grand jury action if evidence is sufficient, and may imprison for nonpayment of fine and costs, or for enforcement of their

---

*The Texas constitution provides that "no current wages for personal service shall ever be subject to garnishment [to attach] *except for the enforcement of court-ordered child support payments*" (Art. XVI, Sec. 28, author's italics). There may be garnishment of wages by contract if the contract is carefully drawn.

†Articles 3833, 3835, 3836, *Revised Civil Statutes.* A homestead in Texas is not protected from forced sale for nonpayment of notes for its purchase, taxes due, or for the cost of improvements. Also, no property is protected from the Internal Revenue Service for taxes or funds due the federal government.

authority. Peace bonds may be issued by justices of the peace to protect a threatened person's life or property. Search warrants are issued by justices of the peace and bonds in felony complaints are set and hearings held on those cases in which the amount of the bond is contested. The justice of the peace has power to take forfeitures of all bail bonds given for the appearance of any party at his court, regardless of the amount. In misdemeanor criminal cases, the majority of which are uncontested, the justice of the peace may assess a fine from $1 to $200. The justice of the peace also performs marriages.

If the county has no medical examiner, the justice of the peace holds inquests (acting as a coroner) and may order an autopsy to determine the cause of death in certain cases. It is the duty of the justice of the peace to hold inquests, with or without a jury, within his county, when a person dies in jail; when any person is killed, or from any cause dies an unnatural death (except under sentence of law), or dies in the absence of witnesses; when a human body is found and the cause of death is unknown; when the death of a person appears to have resulted from unlawful means; when any person appears to have committed suicide; and when a person dies without having been attended by a qualified physician (or when the attending physician is uncertain of the cause of death). If the attending physician, superintendent of the hospital or institution, or local health officer or registrar are uncertain as to the cause of death, they may request an inquest. The inquest will attempt to determine if death was caused by a criminal act. Also the inquest provides information for the local health officer (or registrar of vital statistics) to report the cause of death as required by the sanitary code of Texas.

Justices of the peace are not required to have any training at all in medicine and scientific crime detection. This seems unbelievable in an age of enlightened medical and scientific knowledge.

The commissioners' court of any county may establish the office of medical examiner. Two or more counties may enter into an agreement to create a medical examiners district and operate the office of medical examiner jointly. A countywide medical-examiner system, financed by the county, has been established in Bexar, Dallas, Galveston, Harris, and Tarrant counties. The medical examiner and his staff assume all death investigations (previously handled by justices of the peace) and perform autopsies. In those counties using the justice of the peace as a coroner, the county pays a doctor or hospital for each medicolegal autopsy.

The Texas Society of Pathologists, the Texas Medical Association, and other professional organizations have supported legislation to establish a statewide, state-financed, professional medical-examiner system with regional medical examiners in each of the thirty-one senatorial districts. As yet, the legislature has not shown much interest in the establishment of such a system.

County Courts

County judges, who need be only "well-informed in the law of the state," are elected in the county for terms of four years.* Vacancies in the offices of county judge and justice of the peace are filled by the commissioners' court until the next

---

*Most, or possibly all, judges of the county courts at law (statutory courts) must be licensed attorneys.

general election. Compensation of county judges varies in the counties and depends upon the local salary law.

The county court has original jurisdiction of all misdemeanors when exclusive original jurisdiction is not given to the justice's courts and when the fine to be imposed exceeds $200. The county court has concurrent jurisdiction with the justice of the peace court in civil cases when the matter in controversy exceeds $200 but does not exceed $1,000. Civil jurisdiction depends upon the amount of money involved in the controversy. County courts have appellate jurisdiction in criminal and civil cases (where the amount in controversy exceeds $20) originally heard in the justice of the peace courts. Cases may also be appealed from the municipal courts to the county courts. Appeals from the county courts are taken either to the court of appeals or the court of criminal appeals.

The county courts handle matters of probate. They probate wills (official proof of an instrument offered as the last will and testament of a person deceased); appoint guardians of minors, idiots, lunatics, persons non compos mentis (not of sound mind), and common drunkards; grant letters testamentary and of administration (appoint executors and administrators); settle accounts of executors; transact all business appertaining to deceased persons, minors, those of unsound mind, and to apprentice minors. Appeals in these matters are taken to the district court.

Under the mental-health code, any adult or the county judge may file an application for the *temporary* hospitalization of a mentally ill person for a period of ninety days.[14] The county judge schedules a hearing on the application and must appoint an attorney if the patient does not have legal counsel. Certificates of medical examination for mental illness must be filed by two physicians stating that the person is mentally ill and is in need of observation and treatment in a mental hospital. The hearing upon the application is informal and without a jury unless a jury is requested by the patient, his attorney, or the court.* In the event no one opposes the temporary hospitalization, the court makes its findings on the basis of the certificates of medical examination, whereupon the patient is committed to a mental hospital for a period not exceeding ninety days.

A person ordered committed by an order of temporary hospitalization may appeal his commitment. When an appeal is made, the county judge must stay the order of temporary hospitalization and release the proposed patient from custody, upon the posting of an appearance bond. This feature of the Texas mental-health

---

*In November 1956, the voters approved a constitutional amendment that added Section 15-a to Article I of the state constitution. It provided as follows: "No person shall be committed as a person of unsound mind except on competent medical or psychiatric testimony. The Legislature may enact all laws necessary to provide for the trial, adjudication of insanity and commitment of persons of unsound mind and to provide for a method of appeal from judgments rendered in such cases. Such laws may provide for a waiver of trial by jury, in cases where the person under inquiry has not been charged with the commission of a criminal offense, . . . and shall provide for a method of service of notice of such trial upon the person under inquiry and of his right to demand a trial by jury." The mental-health code was enacted by the legislature to carry out the above addition to the constitution. The constitutional amendment and enabling legislation were necessary, since the state supreme court had declared unconstitutional a 1913 statute in which the legislature substituted a commission of doctors in lieu of a jury to determine the question of lunacy (*J. A. White* v. *Lillie White*, 108 Tex. R. 570, 1917).

code permits a person adjudged mentally ill to remain free on bond set by the county court until the case is tried again in district court.

If the appeal provision of the code is interpreted to mean that the county judge has no discretion in the matter, it could set at large a dangerous person—someone obviously mentally ill. Such a person out on bond might take vengeance on his family or other persons who filed a complaint of mental illness; he then could not be held accountable because he had already been adjudged of unsound mind. However, the county judge could set a high bond for such a person and thereby make it impossible to secure bond.

A person may be committed *indefinitely* to a hospital for mental illness; however, within the previous twelve-month period, the person must have been in a mental hospital for at least sixty days under an order of temporary hospitalization. A petition for indefinite commitment may be filed with the county court by an adult or by the county judge in the county where the person is confined or in the county of residence. Prior to the hearing, a certificate of medical examination for mental illness, signed by a physician, must be filed with the court. At least two physicians who recently have examined the person must testify at the hearing. The mentally ill person is represented by a court-appointed attorney or by someone of his own choosing. The hearing may be before the county judge alone or the person may demand a trial by jury.

In the event an application for temporary hospitalization or a petition for indefinite commitment is pending in the county court, a physician may file a sworn certificate that the person is mentally ill and presents a substantial risk of serious harm to himself or others if not immediately restrained. The county judge may order any health or peace officer to take the person into protective custody and place him or her in a mental hospital or other suitable place pending a *probable cause hearing*. When an order for protective custody is signed, the presiding judge appoints an attorney if no attorney represents the proposed patient. If, after the hearing, the magistrate or master determines that no probable cause exists that the proposed patient presents a substantial risk of serious harm to himself or others, the individual is released. If it is determined the proposed patient presents a substantial risk of serious harm to himself or others, the person's detention in protective custody is continued and the magistrate or master must arrange for him or her to be sent to the mental hospital or other suitable place.

Unless there is also a finding of mental incompetence, mental illness or commitment, as judicially determined, does not abridge one's rights as a citizen, interfere with property rights, or affect legal capacity.

The mental-health code provides for the reexamination of mentally ill patients once they have been hospitalized to determine whether the person has recovered or still needs hospitalization. The patient, or someone acting on his behalf and with his consent, may petition the county judge of the county in which the patient is hospitalized.

If, after reexamination and hearing, it is found that the individual no longer needs hospitalization, the head of the institution must discharge the patient.

The mental-health code was designed to accomplish three basic objectives: (1) protect the civil rights of those mentally ill, (2) require medical testimony for commitment to a mental hospital, and (3) provide a waiver of the ordeal of a jury trial.

The code eliminates from the Texas law, unless trial by jury is requested by the patient or his attorney, the medieval concept that persons with mental illness are lunatics who must be "convicted of insanity" before being sent to a state mental hospital for observation and treatment. The code represents a positive State's rights program in action.

A county may have a single court that handles civil, criminal, and probate matters. In the more populated areas the legislature has provided various combinations of county courts. A county may have one or more criminal courts, one or more courts at law, a separate probate court, or a courtless judge who presides over the commmissioners' court. County courts at law may hear either civil or criminal cases or both. In most counties probate matters are handled by the regular county court rather than by a special county probate court. Appeals from the justice of the peace and municipal courts go to the appropriate local county court.

District Courts

The state is divided into a number of district court regions with one or more courts in each district. A single district court may handle both civil and criminal cases. Dallas, Tarrant, Bexar, and Harris counties have several civil district courts and criminal district courts, as well as domestic-relations and juvenile courts. If two or more counties compose the judicial district, the district judge presides at the regular terms of court at least twice a year at the county seat of each county.

A district judge, elected for four-year terms, must be at least twenty-five years of age, a citizen of the United States and the state, a resident of the district for two years next preceding his election, and a practicing lawyer or a judge in the state (or both) for four years preceding election. Salaries are fixed by the legislature and vary in the districts.

Vacancies in the supreme court, the court of criminal appeals, the courts of appeals, and district courts are filled by the governor until the next general election.

The district courts have original jurisdiction in all criminal cases of the grade of felony. Suits in behalf of the state to recover penalties, forfeitures and escheats, request for change of name, misdemeanors involving official misconduct, suits to recover damages for slander or defamation of character, suits for trial of title to land and for the enforcement of liens thereon, and contested elections come within the jurisdiction of the district courts. In civil action, where the amount in controversy is more than $500 but does not exceed $1,000, the district courts have concurrent jurisdiction with the county courts. If the amount in controversy exceeds $1,000, the district courts have exclusive jurisdiction. The district courts have appellate jurisdiction over probate matters originally heard in the county courts. Appeals from an order of the county commissioners' court may be taken to the district court.

Criminal cases tried in the district courts may be appealed to the court of criminal appeals by the defendant (the state has no right of appeal in criminal cases tried in any state court). Civil cases may be appealed from the district courts to the court of appeals and in some cases (exceptional) directly to the Texas supreme court.

Divorce cases, both contested and uncontested, continue to increase the workload of the district and domestic-relations courts. The grounds for divorce, as provided in the Texas family code (1969), are as follows:

1. *Insupportability.* On the petition of either party to a marriage, a divorce may be decreed without regard to fault if the marriage has become insupportable because of discord or conflict of personalities that destroys the legitimate ends of the marriage relationship and prevents any reasonable expectation of reconciliation.
2. *Cruelty.* A divorce may be decreed in favor of one spouse if the other spouse is guilty of cruel treatment toward the complaining spouse of a nature that renders further living together insupportable.
3. *Adultery.* A divorce may be decreed in favor of one spouse if the other spouse has committed adultery.
4. *Conviction of Felony.* A divorce may be decreed in favor of one spouse if since the marriage the other spouse (1) has been convicted of a felony; (2) has been imprisoned for at least one year in the state penitentiary, a federal penitentiary, or the penitentiary of another state, and has not been pardoned. A divorce may not be decreed under this section against a spouse who was convicted on the testimony of the other spouse.
5. *Abandonment.* A divorce may be decreed in favor of one spouse if the other spouse left the complaining spouse with the intention of abandonment and remained away for at least one year.
6. *Living Apart.* A divorce may be decreed in favor of either spouse if the spouses have lived apart without cohabitation for at least three years.
7. *Confinement in Mental Hospital.* A divorce may be decreed in favor of one spouse if at the time the suit is filed (1) the other spouse has been confined in a mental hospital, a state mental hospital, or private mental hospital for at least three years; and (2) it appears that the spouse's mental disorder is of such a degree and nature that he is not likely to adjust, or that if he adjusts it is probable that he will suffer a relapse.

A suit for divorce may not be maintained unless at the time the suit is filed the petitioner or the respondent had been a resident of the state for the preceding six months and a resident of the county in which the suit is filed for ninety days. A resident who has been absent from the state for more than six months in the military service may sue for divorce in the county where he resided prior to his entrance into the military service. A divorce may not be granted until at least sixty days have elapsed after filing for divorce.

Child support is a requirement in Texas; alimony is not. The father is primarily responsible for the support of his children until they reach the age of eighteen, regardless of whether the former wife has remarried or is working and supporting herself and children. A mother may file a support lawsuit even though she has not lived in the state for a long enough period to initiate a divorce action. Frequently the divorced mother will not inform the clerk of the district court (or domestic-relations court) that the ex-husband is in arrears with the child-support payments or is not making them, because she may have been intimidated in some way by the former husband. For example, he may have threatened to take the children. Hundreds of women in Texas are not receiving the child-support payments they are entitled to and, even though working long hours, have difficulty in earning enough to care for themselves and their children. The child-support laws need to be enforced and possibly strengthened, since there are administrative deficiencies.

Domestic-Relations Courts and Juvenile Courts

In urban counties, at the district-court level, there may be one or more domestic-relations courts and juvenile courts authorized by a local law passed by the legislature.

Depending upon the local law, a juvenile board, which may be composed of the county and district judges, may supervise the juvenile court and select the juvenile or probation officer.

Divorce cases, cases involving child custody, dependency, adoption, child support, as well as contempt matters growing out of failure to pay child support come within the jurisdiction of the district or domestic-relations court. Cases involving criminal acts committed by juveniles may be heard by the district judge or juvenile court if such a court has been authorized by a local law passed by the state legislature.

Administrative Judicial Districts

There is some flexibility in the state judicial system at the district-court level. The state is divided into administrative judicial districts and the governor designates one district judge to preside over each administrative area. If there are district judges in a particular administrative district who are overworked and behind schedule with their dockets, the presiding judge of the administrative area may temporarily assign any district judge in his administrative district to assist them. In the event no district judges in the administrative area are available, he may call upon the presiding judge of some other administrative district. The judge of one district court may be assigned temporarily to another district court in the administrative district because of the absence, disability, or disqualification of the judge in question. This transfer of available judges increases the efficiency of the judiciary in the district courts.

Courts of Appeals

Each of the courts of appeals is composed of a chief justice and associate justices elected for six-year terms by the voters in the respective supreme judicial districts. Judges of the courts of appeals must have the same qualifications as those of the supreme court. As their title indicates, the courts of appeals are appellate courts, since their jurisdiction is limited to cases on appeal. They have no original jurisdiction.

The courts of appeals may sit in sections as authorized by law. These courts have appellate jurisdiction of all cases in which the district or county courts have original or appellate jurisdiction. The appeal of all cases in which the death penalty has been assessed is to the court of criminal appeals. The appeal of all other criminal cases is to the courts of appeals as prescribed by law.

The supreme court may, at any time, order civil cases transferred from one court of appeals to another, when, in the opinion of the supreme court, there is good cause for such transfer. By the transfer of cases (courts of appeals) as well as judges (district courts), some judicial integration and coordination have been ac-complished in Texas. Texas has two "supreme" courts—the court of criminal ap-peals and the supreme court.

Court of Criminal Appeals

A presiding judge and eight other judges, elected statewide for six-year overlap-ping terms, sit on the court of criminal appeals in Austin. They must have the same qualifications as the Texas supreme court judges. The court of criminal appeals is authorized the use of three-judge panels to decide most appeals. However, the full court must act in all cases involving capital punishment and in such other cases as future legislatures may require by law.

Where three-judge panels are used, two judges constitute a quorum, and a two-member majority is required to support the decision. When the full court considers an appeal, five judges constitute a quorum, and the decisions require a five-member majority. Members of the court designate the presiding judge; this posi-tion is rotated among the members.

In matters of criminal jurisdiction, the court of criminal appeals is the highest court in the state. The Texas court of criminal appeals has only appellate criminal jurisdiction and hears cases that are appealed from county and district courts.

The Supreme Court

A chief justice and eight associate justices, elected statewide for six-year over-lapping terms, sit as the highest civil court in the state. The judges must be at least thirty-five years of age, citizens of the United States and residents of the state, and practicing lawyers, or both lawyers and judges of a court of record at least ten years prior to election.

The supreme court has appellate civil jurisdiction coextensive with the limits of the state. Its jurisdiction is defined both by statute and the constitution.

> Until otherwise provided by law the appellate jurisdiction of the Supreme Court shall extend to questions of law arising in the cases in the Courts of Appeals in which the judges of any Court of appeals may disagree, or where the several Courts of appeals may hold differently on the same question of law or where a statute of the State is held void.[15]

Appeals from the court of criminal appeals and the Texas supreme court go di-rectly to the U.S. Supreme Court.

Records of Cases Decided by Texas Courts

The cases decided by the Texas supreme court, the court of criminal appeals, and the courts of appeals (formerly the courts of civil appeals) may be found in the South Western Reporter (Texas Edition). The decisions of the Texas court of crim-inal appeals also are reported in the Texas court of criminal appeals report. How-ever, there is no separate report styled the Texas supreme court report.

Judicial Officials Other Than Judges

A constable is elected in each justice precinct and serves as executive officer of the justice of the peace court.* An elective sheriff and his deputies perform a simi-

*Precinct, county, and district officials are elected for four-year terms.

lar function for the county and district courts. They arrest offenders, take charge of prisoners, serve citations, maintain order in the court, execute court orders, and take charge of the jury.

Elective county and district clerks keep the records and collect the fees of their respective courts. The appellate courts appoint their own clerks. County and district attorneys, who are elected in the county or judicial district, serve as prosecuting attorneys in the county and district courts. County attorneys also may prosecute in the justice of the peace courts. The court of criminal appeals appoints its own prosecuting attorney.

Court reporters, who are attached to the supreme court and the court of criminal appeals, prepare the decisions of the state's highest appellate courts for publication. Reporters serve as an aid to the district courts.

Removal of Judges

Justices of the peace and county judges may be removed from office by the district court following a jury trial. District judges may be removed by the supreme court upon proceedings initiated by ten or more practicing lawyers in the judicial district. Appellate judges, as well as district judges, may be removed by impeachment and by the governor upon address of two-thirds of the house and senate.

On January 23, 1976, the Texas senate convicted state District Judge O. P. Carrillo of Duval County, removed him from office, and disqualified him from ever holding public office authorized by the state. Although the house approved ten articles of impeachment, Carrillo was convicted on only one of two charges considered by the senate. The article on which he was convicted in the senate charged that he conspired with others to collect money from governmental entities for rentals of equipment that did not exist and for rental of equipment that the governmental entities did not use. The Texas constitution (Art. XV) provides that "no person shall be convicted without the concurrence of two-thirds of the senators present." The senate voted 23 to 5 to convict.

State Commission on Judicial Conduct

The commission is composed of judges of designated state courts, some members of the state bar, and a limited number of citizens not licensed to practice law nor holding any salaried public office or employment. The commission, and the manner of appointing the members, are provided for in the Texas constitution.

Judges may be *removed* from office for willful or persistent conduct, which is inconsistent with the proper performance of judicial duties or casts public discredit on the judiciary or administration of justice. Also, a judge may be *censured*, in lieu of removal from office, or *suspended* from office with or without pay by the commission immediately on being indicted by a state or federal grand jury for a felony offense. Or the commission, after giving the person notice and an opportunity to appear before the commission, may recommend to the state supreme court the suspension of such person from office. The supreme court, after considering the record and recommendation of the commission, may suspend the person from office with or without pay.

The commission may receive complaints from any source and, after preliminary investigations, the commission may issue a private or public reprimand, or, if the situation merits such action, the commission may hold a formal hearing concerning the public censure, removal, or retirement of a judge. After formal hearing before the commission, the latter could refer the matter to the state supreme court for action. The supreme court, in an order for involuntary retirement for disability or an order for removal, may prohibit such person from holding judicial office in the future.

No judge may sit as a member of the commission in any proceeding involving his or her own suspension, censure, retirement, or removal. A recommendation of the commission for the suspension, censure, retirement, or removal of a member of the Texas supreme court would be determined by a special tribunal of seven court of appeals justices selected by lot.

The impeachment article of the Texas constitution (Art. XV) provides that the statewide elective officials (excluding the commissioner of agriculture), and the judges of the state supreme court, courts of appeal, and district courts could be impeached by the house of representatives and tried in the senate. Since the state commission on judicial conduct was established by constitutional amendment in 1977, the legislature may have believed the impeachment process was too time-consuming and too political for legislators.

14 Judicial Reform

IN THE STUDY OF the judicial system we have noted some improvements that have been made in Texas: creation of small-claims courts; passage of the Medical-Examiner Act; enactment of the mental health code; the transfer of district judges; and the authority of the supreme court to equalize the dockets of the courts of appeals. Other improvements have been made, some of which should be mentioned.

The Integrated Bar

The State Bar Act established the integrated bar in Texas.

> There is hereby created the State Bar, which is hereby constituted an administrative agency of the Judicial Department of the State, with power to contract with relation to its own affairs and which may sue and be sued and have such other powers as are reasonably necessary to carry out the purposes of this Act.
>
> All persons who are now or who shall hereafter be licensed to practice law in this State shall constitute and be members of the State Bar, and shall be subject to the provisions hereof and the rules adopted by the Supreme Court of Texas; and all persons not members of the State Bar are hereby prohibited from practicing law in the State.

As provided in the law, the state bar is composed of all the practicing lawyers of the state and is integrated with the judicial department of the state.

Under the State Bar Act the supreme court proposes rules and regulations for disciplining, suspending, and disbarring attorneys at law and for the conduct of the state bar, and it prescribes a code of ethics governing the professional conduct of members of the bar. Before these regulations become effective they must be submitted to, and approved by, the members of the state bar. In matters of policy-making, there is a degree of integration or interrelationship between the bar and the judicial department.

The rules, as amended, make up the bylaws or constitution of the state bar and provide for the organization, officers, and powers of the association. These rules set up a self-governing bar. Not only do the lawyers elect their own officers, set up committees, and hold annual meetings, but they have the right and duty to police their own organization.

Grievance committees of the state bar receive complaints of professional misconduct alleged to have been committed by members of the bar. If a majority of the committee hearing the evidence finds that a proceeding to disbar, suspend, or reprimand the accused member (for unethical, fraudulent, or dishonest conduct) should be instituted, a petition is filed in the district court.

Legal Advisors for College and University Students[1]

Colleges and universities have established student legal departments to protect and advise students in a variety of legal problems. One or more licensed attorneys are employed by the department, which may be funded in whole or in part by student services fees paid by the students.

Student legal advisors are confronted with a variety of problems, many of which involve legal considerations. Since large numbers of students live off campus, controversies between landlords and student tenants are inevitable. They may involve security deposits that have not been returned to students, broken leases, and failure to repair apartments. Another major problem for students is consumer protection. Many students are unaware of their rights as a consumer, which may be due in part to limited previous shopping experience. Other student legal problems involve traffic tickets, automobile accidents, insurance claims, breach of contract, stolen property, and physical violence of one type or another.

Students may consult legal advisors to avoid a variety of problems. For example, students may need advice on getting a passport or how to secure power of attorney (a document authorizing a person to act as attorney for the person signing the document). Frequently students need legal advice on charges of DWI (drinking while intoxicated).

Student legal advisors also may provide certain types of legal documents. For example, a student may wish to sell his or her motorcycle; the individual could obtain a release form from the legal advisor and thereby not be held responsible for those test-riding the motorcycle.

Legal advisors carefully screen cases before deciding to represent students, and for this reason student cases do not go to court unless the legal advisor believes the student has a substantial case and is likely to be successful in court. In controversies that involve $1,000 or less, the student could file in the justice of the peace or small claims court, regardless of whether or not the legal advisor was present. In such an event, the student would be responsible for the court filing fee.

Frequently, a student may tell the other party that he or she has consulted the campus legal advisor, and, as in the regular practice of law, this may encourage the party to drop the matter, or settle out-of-court by way of negotiation, the so-called informal method of settlement.

Student legal advisors cannot represent one student against another student, or a student against the university. In such situations, and those in which a large sum of money is involved, legal advisors will not intervene. They may suggest referral to a member of the county or state bar association.

Student legal advisors do not represent students in criminal violations. The advisors may informally consult with and advise a student as to a course of action and might suggest a referral to an off-campus lawyer.

Paralegals and Legal Assistants

Paralegals are extensively used in the East where the profession originated and in many states they are licensed after completion of their professional training and passing the licensing examination. As yet, a license is not required for paralegals in Texas (although it may be just a matter of time).

Paralegal training often is a two-year course. Southwest Texas State University in San Marcos offers an eighteen-hour graduate level lawyer's assistant program. Upon successful completion of this program, the student receives certification by the university as a paralegal. The requirements for admission are as follows: an undergraduate degree in any discipline; a 2.75 grade point average in the last sixty hours of undergraduate work; and an interview with the director. In addition to training in public institutions, there are private institutes which offer paralegal training.

Paralegals take over the attorney's routine tasks, thereby enabling him or her to do the more difficult work for which lawyers are trained. Paralegals are not trained to compete with attorneys and cannot make court appearances or do other work limited to licensed attorneys. They are not allowed to practice law, cannot give legal advice, and cannot represent a client in court.

On the other hand, paralegals can file pleadings, prepare interrogatories (examine by questioning), interview clients, arrange for hearings, take care of the more routine aspects of the law office, and perform legal research that can be quite time-consuming for an attorney who has many other things to do.

Much of the work of paralegals is similar to that done for years by law clerks, generally law students or law school graduates waiting to take the bar examination. The thing paralegals have to offer that law clerks usually cannot offer is permanency. Many law clerks eventually want to practice law.

Legal assistants may or may not have had prior paralegal training in a university or college, or in a private paralegal institute. A lawyer or law firm may provide the training for a legal assistant; however, paralegal training would, no doubt, be helpful. Legal assistants have been recognized by the Texas state bar—the legal assistant division of the state bar.

Rule-Making Power of the Supreme Court

According to the Texas constitution, the supreme court has the power to make rules of procedure for the courts of the state. The supreme court has power to formulate both civil and criminal rules of practice and procedure "not inconsistent with the laws of the state." Rules of procedure, or what is known as "adjective law," provide the machinery for hearing a case. This could have been a significant power of the supreme court if the legislature had not encroached upon the rule making of the court. However, by statute, the supreme court has been vested only with the rule-making power in civil practice and procedure. Once promulgated, these rules are effective unless disapproved by the legislature. Rules of criminal practice and procedure continue to be enacted by the legislature. The supreme court and the court of criminal appeals, if provided adequate staffs, are in a better position than the legislature to handle the rule making function.

The Texas Judicial Council

The judicial council movement has resulted in the establishment of public research agencies for the state courts. Such judicial councils are, in a sense, an arm of the courts and the legislature. In a more limited area, the judicial councils function somewhat similarly to the legislative councils.

The Texas judicial council is composed of judges, members of the legislature, lawyers, and laymen. It is the duty of the council to make a continuous study of the organization, rules, methods of procedure and practice, and accomplishments of the civil courts, to the end that procedure may be simplified, business expedited, and justice better administered. Once a year the council is required to make a report to the governor and supreme court of its proceedings and recommendations. Supplemental reports may be made as it seems advisable.

The increase in the size of the supreme court from three to nine members and the transfer of the power to make rules of civil procedure and practice from the legislature to the supreme court resulted, in a large measure, from the efforts of the Texas judicial council.

The Declaratory-Judgments Act

By an act of the legislature any person interested under a deed, will, written contract, or other writings constituting contract, or whose rights, status, or other legal relations are affected by a statute, municipal ordinance, or franchise may obtain a declaration of rights in the appropriate court. Such declarations have the force and effect of a judgment and may be reviewed as other orders and decrees. The act provides a form of preventive justice, since questions of construction, legal uncertainties, validity, and legal rights may be determined or clarified by the courts in advance of litigation.

The Removal and Retirement of Judges

Any judge in Texas may be removed from office for misconduct or retired on grounds of disability. Judges may be reprimanded (privately) or censured (publicly) in lieu of removal from office.

State Parole Officers

A division of parole supervision operates under the Board of Pardons and Paroles. More state prisoners have been released on parole and fewer have been returned to prison from parole since the establishment of the adult-parole system. Hence, the arrangement has proven beneficial to prisoners, their families, and the prison system.

Juvenile parole officers, authorized by the legislature, are supervised by the director of prevention and parole of the Texas youth commission; they supervise parolees from the state training schools.

Computerization

Computerization provides instant information as to the status of pending cases, length of time cases have been on the docket, their appeal status, and other pertinent facts.

Suggestions for Improving the Court System

Despite the improvement that has been made in the court system, much remains to be accomplished. The state bar, the Texas judicial council, newspapers, members of the legislature, and other interested groups have made various recommendations to strengthen the administration of justice.

Redraft of the Judicial Article of the Texas Constitution

Article V of the Texas constitution contains far too much statutory detail. The courts of the state and their jurisdiction are included in the article, as well as the term, qualification, and manner of selecting judges. A well-drafted judicial article—if one may take the federal Constitution as a model—should be general and brief, leaving to the legislature the implementation or filling in of details. Because of the statutory nature of Article V, changes in court structure would require constitutional revision or the fundamental law would have to be amended. Consequently, judicial reform in Texas is basically a constitutional problem.

Changes in Structure

Uncertainty, cost, and delay are the principal criticisms of the state judicial system. These shortcomings can be attributed to an ineffective organization that is outmoded in several respects.

1. Judicial provincialism—or the practice of each locality electing one or several judges—has a long tradition in the state.
2. The multiplicity of courts makes integration and coordination more difficult. The great number of courts are out of proportion to the amount of statewide judicial business and population.
3. Courts are organized along hard and fast jurisdictional lines; yet a considerable amount of concurrent jurisdiction results in needless jurisdictional controversies.
4. Judges without legal training may sit in the justice of the peace and county courts and thereby qualify—if they serve as judges long enough—for higher judicial positions.
5. There is a lack of proper coordination, as each court is more or less a separate entity.
6. The supreme court lacks adequate power to direct and control the system. A headless organization results from this deficiency.
7. Unnecessary trials *de novo* nullify judicial action and increase the workload of the courts. In some cases the whole judgment may be disregarded by filing an appeal bond. This makes for waste of money and time.
8. The courts are not organized into divisions, branches, or chambers. This fact accounts for some of the disintegration in the judicial department. Judicial integration would decrease the number of courts but increase judicial personnel in some courts.
9. Too much time of the courts is consumed with questions of practice when they should be investigating substantial controversies.

These and other weaknesses account for the disintegrated system of courts in the state. The disintegration and inefficiency are costly in money, in time, and in respect for law and are significant factors in the ever increasing crime rate. Out of every six offenses committed in Texas, only one person is convicted ultimately.

The Integrated-Court System

The integrated-court system makes it possible for the courts to function as a unit through the transfer of judicial personnel and cases, by vesting the rule making power in the courts, and by establishing an administrative and judicial head of the judicial department. The integrated form has been recommended by the Texas Judicial Council and a committee of the state bar. To establish the integrated court system in Texas would require a redraft of Article V of the Texas constitution.

An integrated-court plan might include a supreme court with civil and criminal jurisdiction, a court of appeals, district and county courts.

A court of appeals, with civil and criminal jurisdiction, would replace the courts of appeals. Divisions of the court of appeals could be established in the various appellate districts rather than having a separate court in each district.

The district courts might be retained as general trial courts. The supreme court could be authorized to establish specialized branches or divisions of any district court, determine the number of district-court regions and the number of district courts, as well as the times and places of their sitting. All judges could be assigned temporarily to other courts or divisions where the demands of judicial business might make such assignments advisable.

The county-court system could be revised to permit integration and the selection of more qualified personnel. Only lawyers could sit as county judges, and an adequate salary should be provided. The supreme court might be authorized to merge two or more counties into a county court district and might provide for part-time county-court judges. Such specialized divisions as probate, traffic, family, juvenile and domestic relations, and small cause might be made a part of the county court. This specialization would be particularly advantageous in the urban areas. Judges might be transferred from one court or division as the work of the district or county courts required.

Justice of the peace courts might be abolished and matters within their jurisdiction transferred to the small-cause, petty criminal, or traffic divisions of the county courts.

The supreme court would be administrative and legal head of the court system.

To become effective in Texas, an integrated-court plan would have to overcome serious obstacles, including securing an amendment to the Texas constitution, fear of delegating too much power to the state supreme court, lack of public support, and lack of support among the individual members of the state bar.

Selecting and Retaining Judges in Office[2]

It is not too difficult to agree that a judge should possess personal integrity, judicial temperament, and adequate legal training. Yet, there are considerable differences of opinion concerning the best method of selecting judicial personnel and the period of time judges should serve.

Popular Election

Popular election of judges is a phase of "Jacksonian Democracy" that has lingered far beyond the life of Andrew Jackson. With election of judges came the

short term, the object of which was to make possible the replacement of an unsatis-
factory judge with a minimum of delay.

A candidate for a judgeship can have no campaign policy other than his ability to
administer the law honestly and competently. Such a program does not attract
much voter interest. Popular election is an uncertain and haphazard method of
selecting persons for an office as technical as that of judge.

The political neutrality of judges is important. Their work should not be influenced by political alliances or political debts. Each time a person seeks election or
reelection to a judgeship he must contribute a considerable amount of his time,
money, and energy to his campaign. The elective system turns almost every
elected judge into a politician.

It is not the purpose of judges to give effect to the popular will on every occasion. At times the popular will may be vindicated by a court decree; however, it
may be that a decision or interpretation of a law may not be at all popular. The
courts should be independent of popular pressure.

Tradition and history offer support for election of judges; Texas and other states
have had considerable experience with this method of selection. Certainly the
courts—at least in part—operate within the framework of tradition. Because of
tradition, or lack of confidence in other methods of selecting judges, many lawyers favor a continuation of popular election.

Appointment

Appointment of judges by the executive, with senatorial confirmation, as employed by some states and the federal government, has its supporters. However, in
recent years there has been considerable criticism of the federal method of judicial
selection. Much of the criticism was evoked *after* some decisions in controversial
cases were announced by the U.S. Supreme Court.

Appointment of judges frequently is governed by political considerations, and a
person with proper political support, although lacking in judicial qualifications,
may receive the appointment in preference to a candidate better qualified legally
but less qualified politically. Judges, unless appointed for life, have no real assurance of security in office.

Unless a state has popular recall of judges, there is no way by which the people
might unseat appointive judges who are incompetent, although such judges might
be impeached. But impeachment is not a very practical method of removal. Although voters are usually at a loss to know which judicial candidates to vote for, if
a judge makes himself obnoxious, the people can oust him from office at the next
election. No comparable check exists with the appointive system.

The constitution of a state might provide that judges be appointed for definite
terms of office or hold office during good behavior. A combination of the two
methods might provide that judges of the supreme court be appointed for life during good behavior and all other judges appointed for definite terms.

The Missouri Plan of Selecting and Retaining Judges in Office

The Missouri or merit plan of selecting and retaining judges in office has been supported by some individuals in Texas.* To become effective, an amendment to Article V of the state constitution would be necessary. The merit plan might include all or some of the state courts and would combine the features of popular election and appointment of judges.

A key feature of the merit plan of judicial selection includes nomination of judges by a nonpartisan judicial nominating commission. Assuming the merit plan applied only to the Texas supreme court and the court of criminal appeals, a court nominating commission of five members might be established by constitutional amendment. The amendment might provide the members be selected as follows: two members to be appointed by the governor; one by the chief justice of the state supreme court; one by the presiding judge of the court of criminal appeals; and one by the president of the state bar—all appointees subject to confirmation by the senate. The regular terms of the members could be six years and until their successors had been appointed. No member would be eligible for reappointment or could be a holder of, or candidate for, any public employment or public office or be a party official.

When a vacancy occurred on the supreme court or court of criminal appeals, the court nominating commission would, by majority vote, submit to the governor three nominees with the qualifications provided by law. From the list of three nominees the governor would appoint one to fill the vacancy. The appointment by the governor would not require senate confirmation. If the governor failed to make an appointment, the appointment would be made by a majority vote of the justices of either the supreme court or the court of criminal appeals.

At the end of the six-year term of office, and prior to the general election, a member of the supreme court or the court of criminal appeals could file with the secretary of state a declaration of candidacy to succeed himself. If no declaration was filed, the office would become vacant. If such declaration was filed, the name of the applicant would be submitted to the voters of the state at a general election by a separate ballot or on the general ballot without a party designation. The justice would run against his record rather than against an opponent. The voters would vote on whether the justice should be retained in office. If a majority of those voting on the question voted against his retention, a vacancy would exist and would be filled by nomination and appointment as in the first instance. If a majority voted in favor of the candidate, he would remain in office for a term of six years.

In the event the merit plan included the judges of the state supreme court, the court of criminal appeals, and courts of appeals, a district nominating commission, as provided in the constitutional amendment, could be established in each supreme judicial district. Each of the district nominating commissions might be composed of five members: two lawyers residing in the district elected by members of the bar in the area, and three persons resident of the district, not licensed to practice law, appointed by the governor and senate. The district nominating commissions would nominate a list of three persons to fill vacancies in the courts of

---

*As provided in Article V of the Missouri constitution (1945), the plan is limited to certain courts: the supreme court, the courts of appeals, the circuit and probate courts within the city of St. Louis and Jackson County, and the Saint Louis courts of criminal correction. At any general election the qualified voters of any judicial circuit outside the city of St. Louis and Jackson County may, by a majority of those voting on the question, vote to come under the plan.

appeals, from which the governor would appoint one without senate confirmation. After six years in office, the voters of each court-of-appeals district would vote to retain, or not to retain, the judge in office.

Each district nominating commission could be authorized to select one of its own members to serve on the state nominating commission. When a vacancy occurred in the state supreme court or court of criminal appeals, the state nominating commission, by majority vote, would submit a list of three nominees to the governor who would make an appointment to fill the vacancy without senate confirmation. At the end of a six-year term of office the voters of the state would vote on the question of retention in office.

The district and county judges, as well as the justices of the peace, might continue to be elected by the people. If the plan were limited to only some judges, the constitutional amendment, by way of an optional feature, might permit other judicial districts to adopt the plan by a favorable vote in the district. On the other hand, the amendment might provide the extension of the merit plan by the legislature under such regulations and with such modifications as may be prescribed by law. An integrated-court system might or might not include the Missouri or merit plan of selecting and retaining judges in office.

Supporters of the Missouri plan contend it has a number of advantages over both election and appointment of judges. As a compromise between election and appointment, they point out that the plan utilizes the best features of both and provides safeguards which each lack.

The Missouri plan places considerable responsibility on members of the state bar. The bar must give information to the public concerning the record and qualification of judges when a vote is to be taken on their retention in office. If the organized bar believes the service of a judge should be continued, then the bar, rather than the individual judge, should conduct the campaign for retention, informing the public of the record of the judge involved.

Some who oppose the Missouri plan contend that it gives the local and state bar too much influence in selecting and retaining judges in office. Under the appointive and elective systems, however, the bar still has considerable influence, since it recommends persons to be appointed by the governor and senate as well as endorses judicial candidates seeking nomination and election. Others who oppose the plan say that the bar is a conservative force at best and that the Missouri plan will produce an ultraconservative or even a reactionary bench unable to meet the needs of the times. However, as in the election system, the voters may vote not to retain in office those judges who are endorsed by the bar.

The Missouri plan appears to work well in states that have adopted it. There has been little or no interest in returning to the former method of selecting judges.

The Jury System

In civil cases in the state district court where twelve-member juries are used, the decision may be by unanimous, 11 to 1, or 10 to 2 votes. In county civil cases where six-member juries are used, the verdict may be a unanimous or a 5 to 1 decision.

Should the requirement of a unanimous vote of the jury in criminal cases in Texas be continued? What questions should the jury decide? Should there be an alternate juror assigned to each case? Are too many excused from jury service?

In the majority of complicated civil cases it is probably unwise to use a jury. Under existing law in Texas, the defendant in a criminal prosecution of a noncapital offense may waive the right of trial by jury. Some feel the jury should be restricted to the more serious criminal cases.

Regarding the unanimity of the jury, it has been suggested that in trials of civil and criminal cases (below the grade of felony) in the district courts, nine members of the jury concurring could render a verdict; in county courts (in which six persons compose the jury) a verdict of five members concurring in criminal cases. Anything less than the unanimous verdict would be opposed as a departure from tradition.

The defendant in Texas can elect to have his punishment set by the same jury that found him guilty, or by the judge. The judge should have some discretion in assessing the penalty, and the trial jury should be limited to determining the guilt or innocence of the accused person.

The federal courts use the alternate juror as a replacement for any juror who, prior to the time the jury retires to consider the verdict, becomes unable to perform the functions of a juror. In the event the law were so amended, one additional peremptory challenge could be authorized against the alternate juror.

It is probably true that the most qualified people do not serve on juries. This is due in part to the practice of being rather lenient with those otherwise qualified for jury duty. Many people are not interested in serving because of the time lost from their work and the rather small remuneration jurors receive for their service.

Waiver of Indictment in Felony Cases[3]

Despite the Fifth Amendment of the federal Constitution, the U.S. Supreme Court, in the exercise of its rule-making power, has recognized the right of the accused to waive his right to be tried on an indictment and consent to be tried on an information filed by a prosecuting attorney. In Texas, the accused has the right to waive indictment by grand jury for noncapital felonies. On waiver by the accused (in open court or by written instrument), he shall be charged by information.

The requirement of indictment by grand jury in felony cases does have its defects, since it is a major cause for delay in criminal trials. If the grand jury is not in session when an offense is committed, the case must wait until the next term of court. If the district court is in session, the district judge may, if he thinks the situation so warrants, reassemble the grand jury after it has been discharged for the term. This delay frequently proves injurious to the state's case, due to the disappearance of witnesses and the fading of memories in regard to facts and is a major reason for the large number of no-true bills returned by the grand jury. Often, the grand jury does no more than rubber-stamp the opinion of the district attorney who has presented the evidence to the grand jury. The system as it exists is a burden on the witness who may have to repeat the same information three times (at the examining trial, grand jury, and trial before the jury).

The Medical-Examiner System

More counties should transfer the function of coroner from the justices of the peace to a medical examiner. A statewide, state-financed, medical-examiner system might be established.

The Civil and Criminal Codes of Procedure

Rules of civil procedure are made by the Texas supreme court and, although some improvements have been made, the rules need to be revised. Criminal rules of practice, pleading, and procedure are formulated by the legislature. The rule-making power in criminal cases might be transferred from the legislature to the court of criminal appeals or to the supreme court if an integrated- court system were established.

Justice for the Poor

In the federal and state courts indigent defendants have less chance of obtaining justice than wealthy ones—and still less chance of being free while awaiting a jury's action. In a sense, the problem is a phase of the war against poverty.

Federal and state court decisions have emphasized the constitutional obligation of the state to afford needy persons the assistance of counsel in criminal actions. In some counties the bar partially has met this obligation through creation of a non-profit organization, primarily financed by federal grants, which provides counsel; in others, volunteers from the bar donate their services to defend needy persons. And in other counties, the courts concerned appoint counsel.

Frequently court-appointed counsel for the needy is a young and inexperienced lawyer trying to get started in practice and therefore available. The fees allowed the court-appointed attorneys do not attract the well-established lawyer. The appointed counsel for defense must oppose a skilled and experienced prosecutor, with adequate staff, who has all the resources of the state government behind him. Also, the court-appointed attorney may lack both time and money to conduct the investigation and trial-preparatory work so necessary for an adequate defense of his client. There is little doubt that the existing practice lends itself to a serious miscarriage of justice on occasion.

The Public-Defender System

Especially in the metropolitan counties, the obligation to furnish competent counsel imposes a substantial burden on county financial resources. None of the alternative methods presently employed to furnish counsel has proven entirely satisfactory. A county-wide public-defender system may better satisfy the constitutional and statutory obligations for providing counsel for the needy accused.

The legislature passed a local law establishing the office of public defender in Tarrant County (Fort Worth). Each criminal district judge of Tarrant county is authorized to appoint one attorney to serve as a public defender and define his duties. The public defender serves at the pleasure of the appointing judge, and the salary is determined by the commisioners' court and paid from the appropriate county fund. The public defender may not engage in any criminal law practice other than that related to his office.

At indigent person charged with a criminal offense in a court in Tarrant County, or an indigent person in the county who is a party in a juvenile delinquency proceeding, shall be represented by a public defender or other practicing attorney appointed by a court. At any stage of the legal proceedings the court may assign a substitute attorney. The public defender may inquire into the financial conditions of any person he is appointed to represent, and the court may hold a hearing on the matter.

The legislature passed a local law authorizing the establishment of the public defender system in Wichita County (Wichita Falls). According to the law, the commissioners' court may appoint an attorney to serve at its pleasure as public defender; he or she may not engage in any other civil or criminal law practice in the county. The commissioners' court provides an annual salary for the public defender, who may employ, with the approval of the commissioners' court, assistant public defenders, investigators, secretaries, and other personnel. The public defender, or his assistant, may represent any indigent person charged with a criminal offense in the county and any indigent minor who is a party to a juvenile delinquency proceeding in the county.

Legislation should be passed authorizing the commissioners' court of any county to establish the office of public defender with adequate office and investigative staff.

The public-defender system has been opposed on grounds that it would increase the cost of county government and reduce the number of cases handled by private attorneys. However, many lawyers would welcome a system that would eliminate the court-appointed attorney. Nevertheless, other lawyers believe that the existing practice should be continued along with expanded legal-aid activities (aid to indigent persons) of law schools and the local bar associations. One may doubt if the court-appointed attorneys and the voluntary efforts offer an adequate solution to the problem. In any event, the public-defender system appears to operate satisfactorily in those states that use it.

Pretrial Release

Poverty may keep a poor man in jail when he is unable to post bail, whereas a wealthy suspect goes free because he is able to. This is a serious miscarriage of justice.

Hundreds of persons each year are charged with crimes of which they are not guilty. Between arrest and trial time, defendants unable to raise bail may spend months in jail and later, after trial, be acquitted. Such confinement is nonjudicial and does not constitute equal justice under law.

Bail Bond in Texas

According to the Texas code of criminal procedure, " 'bail' is the security given by the accused that he will appear and answer before the proper court the accusation brought against him." A "bail bond" is a written undertaking entered into by the defendant and his sureties for the appearance of the principal therein before some court or magistrate to answer a criminal accusation. A bail bond is known as an "appearance bond."

The bill of rights of the Texas constitution declares "All prisoners shall be bailable by sufficient sureties, unless for captial offenses, when the proof is evident."[4] Also the bill of rights declares "Excessive bail shall not be required."[5]

The judge, upon recommendation of the prosecuting attorney, may set bail so high that the person charged does not have sufficient funds to secure bail. If bond is refused, or is considered too high, council for defense may contest the action by *habeas corpus* proceedings—with the right of appeal to the court of criminal appeals in Austin.

In the Texas courts, as in the federal courts, a person may be released on bond in one of three ways:

1. By execution of a surety or bail bond. The bond attorneys or sureties obligate property equal in value to the amount of the bond. The usual fee of the sureties is 10 percent of the amount of the bond.
2. By execution of a cash bond in which the defendant may deposit funds with the court in the amount of the bond.
3. By execution of a personal bond (personal recognizance bond) in which the defendant is released without sureties or other security. The defendant must sign the following sworn oath: "I swear that I will appear before (the court or magistrate) at (address, city, county) Texas, on the (date), at the hour of (time, A.M. or P.M.) or upon notice by the court, or pay to the court the principal sum of (amount) plus all necessary and reasonable expenses incurred in any arrest for failure to appear."

It is within the discretion of the Texas courts to determine the type of bail available to a person.

There have been numerous unethical practices by bondsmen. They have falsely sworn that property on a bond belonged to the bondsman when the deed was in someone else's name. Few, if any, bondsmen have been prosecuted for false swearing. The same piece of property has been posted over and over again, often encumbering it for more than its value, and bond forms have been filled out incorrectly to render the bonds illegal and uncollectable. Bondsmen have sold the property after the bond was made and property has been sold or transferred after notice of the bond forfeiture has been received. In addition to these practices bondsmen give fees or a kickback to runners, young attorneys, law students, and law-enforcement officers for leads on bail-bond prospects. Persons arrested for the first time, who do not know a lawyer and are denied the right to contact one, pay exorbitant bond fees to secure release from jail quickly. Also, an attorney who makes bond for an accused person may represent his client in court, despite the conflict of interest.

If the bondsman's client fails to appear in court, as hundreds do every year, local judges frequently set aside the forfeiture of the bond and collect only a nominal sum in court costs. Hundreds of criminals escape trial each year and are free to continue their depredations. Furthermore, through failure to collect on forfeited bonds, the loss to local taxpayers amounts to several million dollars each year. With little or no risk involved with bond forfeiture, the bond fees are reduced, encouraging crime and undermining law enforcement. A limited number of bail bondsmen in the large cities enjoy a very lucrative business, which is, for all practical purposes, unregulated.

The Texas criminal code provides that any person who signs as a surety on a bail bond, and who is in default, is thereafter disqualified to sign as a surety so long as he is in default of the bond. The effectiveness of this provision of the law depends on whether the judges, prosecuting attorneys, law enforcing officers, and bondsmen fulfill their responsibilities under the law.

County bail bond boards have been established in all Texas counties having a population of 110,000 or more. These boards are composed of the county sheriff or his designee; a district judge; the county judge or a member of the commissioner's court designated by the county judge; a judge of a county court; and the district attorney or his designee. Persons engaged in the practice of law and who are members of the State Bar of Texas who personally execute bail bonds are not required to be licensed but are prohibited from engaging in the practices made the basis for revocation of license. However, other individuals who wish to act as a bondsman must secure a license from the county bail bond board.

The regulations relative to the making of bail bonds by bondsmen within the county are established by the county bail bond boards. Applicants for a bail bond license must list all nonexempt properties owned and rendered on the tax rolls of the county and certified by the county tax assessor-collector, along with a personal financial statement. If the application for a license is approved, a specified sum of money must be deposited with the county treasurer and held in a special fund called the bail security fund. Or the licensee may execute in trust to the sheriff a deed to nonexempt real property of the value, as determined by the sheriff, of not less than a specified sum of money. Such property could be sold—or funds withdrawn from the deposit—to satisfy any forfeiture of bonds after notice. When any sums are depleted from the deposit or trust to pay a judgment for forfeiture of bond, the licensee must, as a condition to continuing as a licensee, replenish the amount so depleted. Also, the law provides certain grounds for refusal to issue licenses, as well as the basis and procedure for suspension and revocation. The decision of the board may be appealed, by petition, to a district court in the county in which the board is located.

Despite the establishment of county bail bond boards in Texas, regulation of bondsmen is ineffective. Recommendations for improvement include the following:

1. The law should be broadened to include all (or more) counties.
2. Bail bond premiums should be paid only by cash, check, or money order; payment by chattels should be prohibited.
3. Attorneys who write bail bonds for persons charged with crimes should be prohibited from representing those persons in court.
4. No one should be allowed to issue a bail bond unless licensed by the state.
5. Attorneys should be prohibited from recommending bondsmen, and vice versa.
6. The state or county bail bond boards should be given authority to set maximum fees charged by bondsmen.
7. Sheriffs should have authority to require title insurance policies on real estate posted as security by bondsmen for bail, and such property should be appraised by a master appraiser or other qualified persons.

Judicial Reform and the State Bar

The courts in Texas have been subjected to a considerable amount of research and study. Much of the research has been done by committees of the state bar and individual lawyers. However, many lawyers have not supported reforms recommended by committees of the bar. Lawyers have not been very enthusiastic about establishing an integrated-court system, revising the civil code, improving the jury system, or changing the method of selecting judicial personnel. The lawyers themselves, aside from the constructive work done by the officers and committees of the state bar, must share a large amount of the responsibility for the inefficiency of the Texas court system.

The Overloaded Courts

Even though most cases never go to trial, since they are settled by the lawyers as a trial date approaches, nevertheless, both taxpayers and litigants suffer the expense of filings and counterfilings, interrogatories (formal questions or set of questions), responses, motions, countermotions, and the process of "discovery," by which lawyers probe through depositions (a written statement by a witness made under oath, to be used as testimony in court) for weaknesses in the opposition's case. In addition, there are many frivolous lawsuits that are filed primarily for their nuisance value. There have been occasions when an appellate court has ordered one litigous party to pay damages to the other party "for bringing a frivolous appeal." As a result of these and other considerations, the U.S. has more lawyers per capita than any nation in the world. Yet, a very large percentage of the population lacks sufficient funds to retain an attorney.

The Court of Common Pleas in Allegheny County, Pennsylvania, has had court-supervised arbitration for a number of years. A large percentage of all cases filed in that court are assigned to arbitration. The parties are given a certain period of time to settle their disputes and approximately half of the suits are thus resolved. If not resolved informally they go to arbitration. The average cost to the taxpayer for arbitration of each controversy is minimal as compared to trial in court. Litigants are generally satisfied with the Allegheny County system. Even though arbitrators' decisions are not binding, only about one-fourth of the awards are appealed and three-fourths of these are dropped or settled before trial. The plan has worked so successfully that the judisdictional limit on cases qualifying for arbitration was increased from $10,000 to $20,000 in 1983.

15 County Government

RESIDENTS OF TEXAS HAVE frequent contacts with county officials. Qualified voters secure their voter registration certificate from the county registrar of voters. By use of the mails (if out of the voting precinct or county) or in person, absentee ballots may be obtained from the county clerk's office. Voting precincts in which a voter votes are laid out and altered by the commissioners' court. Automobiles are registered with the county tax assessor-collector's office, and papers on automobiles are filed at the county court house. Birth certificates are filed with the county clerk and with the bureau of vital statistics in the state department of health resources, and county property taxes are assessed and collected by the county. The county clerk issues marriage licenses and records certificates of marriage ceremonies, and action for divorce may be instituted in the district or domestic relations court. Records of deeds and abstracts are filed with the county clerk. These and other services establish the counties as active units of government—all the more reason of the need for making county government more efficient.

Legal Position of the County

Counties possess only those powers delegated to them by the state constitution and general and local laws. Not only are they governments of limited powers, but the courts have construed rather narrowly the powers delegated to them. Hence, counties possess few or no implied powers. The counties do not possess the power to pass county ordinances. The county must seek legislative authorization before undertaking additional county functions. The taxing and financial powers of counties are limited by the constitution. County-state relations operate on a unitary basis, although local laws are passed by the legislature from time to time granting more powers to the counties.

The county is an administrative area for carrying out state functions. For example, the precinct and county election officials supervise state elections, the county tax assessor-collector levies and collects state taxes, justices of the peace, county, and district courts hear and decide cases involving state law, the county sheriff and his deputies enforce state law and preserve peace, and the inspections by the county health officer are an aid in the enforcement of the state health code. If the county did not perform these and other state functions, the state would be compelled to create other administrative areas or districts. Consequently, the county is part of the administrative machinery of the state government, and for this reason one might expect more state control and supervision over counties than municipalities.

The question involving the immunity of the county from suit, and the liability of the county is determined by the legislature. The state will not permit itself to be sued in its own courts without its consent. Consent to be sued is authorized by a law or concurrent resolution passed by the legislature. Since the county is an arm of the state, a suit against the county would be, in effect, a suit against the state, and would be prohibited under this rule—unless consent to be sued had been authorized by the legislature. As a general rule, unless tort liability (for a wrong or injury to person or property) is imposed by statute, counties are not liable for injuries that result from the negligence of county employees. To redress such a wrong or injury, the individual would have to institute legal action against the county employee (suit for damages) in his private capacity. In the event there was a criminal violation by the employee, the state could prosecute. There have been cases in which the courts have held the counties liable for breach of contract.

The Legal Framework

The legal framework within which counties operate is becoming more and more important. This is especially true when one considers the fact that some counties are rural, others urban, some industrialized, and the great variation in such matters as area, population, and assessed tax valuation.

In the urban areas, counties are performing more and more local functions and operate in many respects like municipalities. Obviously, with the population explosion and the expansion of governmental services, the metropolitan counties need adequate powers—especially of taxation and finance. The plight of the urban counties is indeed critical, much more so than the rural counties, many of which continue to lose in population. For the most part the rural counties merely carry out state functions. They do not find the centralized state-county relationship a serious problem.

The legal framework for county government was designed for rural counties. In the metropolitan areas, this jerry-built governmental system, which is a product of the eighteenth century, cannot adequately meet the challenge of twentieth-century living. For this reason the urban counties must constantly seek legislative authorization to perform local functions. Certainly the deficiencies of county government are compounded in the urban areas. The time will come when the pattern of county government will have to be altered in the heavily populated counties.

The Traditional Powers of Texas Counties

The statutes provide that the commissioners' courts shall:

1. Lay off their respective counties into precincts, for the election of justices of the peace and constables: fix the times and places of holding justices courts; and establish places in such precincts where elections shall be held.
2. Establish public ferries whenever the public interest may require.

3. Establish, change, and discontinue public roads and highways.
4. Build bridges and keep them in repair.
5. Appoint road overseers and apportion hands.
6. Exercise general control over all roads, highways, ferries, and bridges.
7. Keep in repair courthouses, jails, and all necessary public buildings.
8. Provide for the protection, preservation, and disposition of all lands granted to the county for education.
9. Provide seals required by law for the district and county courts.
10. Audit and settle all accounts against the county.
11. Provide for the support of paupers, idiots and lunatics that cannot be admitted into the lunatic asylum, residents of their county, who are unable to support themselves.
12. Provide for the burial of paupers.
13. Punish contempts by fine not to exceed twenty-five dollars or by imprisonment not to exceed twenty-four hours, and in case of fine, the party may be held in custody until the fine is paid.
14. Issue notices, citations, writs, and process as may be necessary for the proper execution of their powers.
15. And exercise all other powers and perform all other duties, as are now or may hereafter be prescribed by law.[1]

The legislature may confer additional powers upon counties by general and local law, for example, authorizing the county auditor in a particular county, upon order of the commissioners' court, to advertise for bids for transporting voting machines to the precincts in the county, or to purchase pickup trucks or fire-fighting equipment, or to loan road equipment to farmers. This type of county legislation illustrates the very limited powers of counties. In a sense state legislators are "ambassadors" from the counties, and the large volume of local laws passed each session of the legislature creates a spirit of localism in Austin.

Because the powers of a county are determined by the general, local, and special laws applicable to the county in question, they vary somewhat from county to county.

The Structure of County Government

Each county is divided into four commissioners' precincts. The voters elect one commissioner in each precinct for a four-year term. In case of vacancy, the county judge appoints some suitable person living in the precinct where the vacancy occurs to serve as commissioner until the next general election.

As a result of a U.S. Supreme Court decision in 1968, county commissioner's precincts in Texas had to be redrawn with approximately equal numbers of people in each precinct.* Thus the control of the county commissioners' courts was transferred to the residents of the major city in many counties. No longer could a city

---

*Avery v. Midland County, Texas et al., 88 S.Ct. 1114 (1968). According to the majority opinion of the court, the "Federal Constitution requires, with respect to development of arrangements of local government, that units with general governmental powers over entire geographic areas not be apportioned among single-member districts of substantially unequal population." U.S.C.A. Cons. Amend. 14.

have 75 percent or more of the total population of the county and only one representative on the county commissioners' court.

The four commissioners together with the county judge, compose the "commissioners' court," and the county judge, when present, presides. Any three members of the court, including the county judge, constitute a quorum for the transaction of any business, except that of levying a county tax. Regular terms of the court are held as specified by the statute and special terms may be called by the county judge or three of the commissioners.*

Besides the county judge and four commissioners who compose the commissioners' court, other elective and appointive county officials include the county judge, justices of the peace, constables, sheriff, county clerk, county treasurer, county tax assessor-collector, county auditor, county engineer, and county health officer.

The governmental structure of the urban counties is more complex than that of the rural counties. In the metropolitan areas the counties provide more services and must, of necessity, operate with a larger personnel and budget. In urban sections of the state there are more justices appointed by the commissioners' court. It is in these areas that special courts exist, as for example, juvenile courts and domestic-relations courts. In the urban counties there may be more programs operated jointly by the county and the major city of the county. Otherwise the basic structure of county government follows a common pattern in the 254 counties.

The County Commissioners' Court

The county commissioners' court is very active, especially in the urban counties. It is the policy-determining body of the county and as such adopts the county budget after it is prepared by the county judge or county auditor and, within certain limits, determines the county tax rate. The county commissioners' court lets contracts in the name of the county, and directs payment of all accounts against the county. Public welfare services of the county are administered by the court and the latter establishes and maintains county hospitals, libraries, parks, airports, and other public works. The court cooperates with Texas A&M University in providing demonstration work in agriculture and home economics. The maintenance of the county courthouse, jail, and other county buildings, the establishment and alteration of voting and justices of the peace precincts, and the construction and upkeep of county roads, bridges, and ferries come within the administrative duties of the commissioners' court. The county health officer and numerous other county officials are appointed by the court, which has power to fill vacancies in the various elective county and precinct offices. The persons so appointed hold office until the next general election. Because of these diverse duties and county services, the county commissioners in some of the metropolitan counties may approve a county budget calling for the expenditures of millions of dollars.

---

*A small, populated county in Texas may have only one county court. In addition to presiding at trials in the county court, the county judge also, if present, presides over the county commissioners' court. In counties that have more than one county court, one of the county judges only presides over the county commissioners' court and is referred to as the county administrative judge. The other county judges that may be elected in a county are law judges; that is, they preside over a particular court that hears cases.

In some counties the county judge, because of his long tenure and record, has become the unofficial head of county government. His responsibilities may approach those of a county executive, county manager, or county mayor, although by the constitution and statutes county government is headless.

The County Commissioners

Individually, the county commissioners serve as road commissioners in their road precincts. In this capacity they are responsible for building and maintaining county roads and bridges in the precinct from which elected. In some counties the commissioners' court appoints a county engineer, and he advises the commissioners and commissioners' court on matters of roads and carries out the road policy established by the commissioners. Some counties pool their road personnel and road equipment. This permits county roads and bridges to be built and maintained on a countywide rather than a precinct basis.

Each road commissioner hires road personnel and contracts for road materials and road machinery. The maintenance of roads and bridges may vary greatly from precinct to precinct. Politics can play a considerable part in the location of new roads, hiring of road personnel, and contracting or purchasing materials and equipment. By actual car count, it would be difficult to justify the *public* construction and maintenance of some roads.

Each year more and more miles of county roads are incorporated into the state highway system. The farm-to-market roads (or all-weather rural roads) that enable farmers and ranchers to move their cattle, produce, and products to market, are constructed and operated by the state. The county must provide a cost-free right of way for these roads and remove right-of-way obstructions such as fences.

Salaries of County Officials and Employees

Compensation of county officials and employees varies in the counties. With some exceptions, the county commissioners' court in each county determines the salary of the elective and nonelective county officials and employees. A person interested in county salaries in a given county should consult the current county budget, which may be obtained from the county judge or county auditor.

The Spoils System versus the Civil Service System

Texas counties with a population exceeding 300,000 may establish a county civil service system. According to the permissive state law, the commissioners' court may establish the system or call a county-wide election on the issue.

In the absence of a county civil service system, personal friendship and political considerations may influence employment and termination of employment.

Financing County Government

Each county in Texas has a countywide tax appraisal office to determine the current market value of real property subject to ad valorem taxes. The government of each county, and the municipal governments and school districts in each county are required to establish a single county tax appraisal office. The members of the countywide board are elected by the various taxing bodies (the county, municipalities, and school districts). The board employs a chief appraiser and assistants.

Votes on the board and cost of establishing the appraisal office are weighed according to the amount of tax revenues generated by the governmental entities.

The primary aim of the countywide tax appraisal office is to place one value on each parcel of property. While the various taxing units may mail out tax statements and collect property taxes, the taxing units do not use their own appraisers to determine values on property for tax purposes.

Other governmental units within the county, for example, the hospital district, the river authority, the community college district, and others, do not participate in the selection of appraisal district directors even though they must participate in the operations of the district. Although these special districts have no representation or vote on the countywide board, they are required to help finance the board's activities, and it is mandatory that these districts use the board's property assessments for their own tax purposes.

A provision of the Texas property tax code provides that citizens may petition for rollback elections if the effective tax rate exceeds 8 percent. If a rollback referendum wins voter approval, the tax rate is cut back to 8 percent. The law provides one way for taxes to be rolled back in school districts and another way for them to be rolled back in all other types of taxing units, such as cities and utility districts. For the first time, as provided in the code, Texas taxpayers may use the election process to reduce the tax rate of any taxing unit.

Taxes

The county commissioners' court determines, within certain limitations, the county ad valorem tax rate to be levied on each $100 assessed valuation of real property (fixed or permanent, as lands and tenements). The county commissioners' court is authorized by the constitution to levy an ad valorem tax rate not to exceed 80 cents on $100 valuation. Revenue from this tax source is distributed among the four constitutional funds of the county (the general fund, road and bridge fund, jury fund, and permanent improvement fund). Each year when the tax rate is levied, the county commissioners' court must set the specific rate for each fund. In addition, the qualified voters of the county may authorize a special levy not to exceed 15 cents on $100 valuation for road and bridge maintenance and a tax not to exceed 30 cents on $100 valuation for farm-to-market roads and flood-control purposes. The county may also levy such taxes as are necessary for interest and sinking-fund requirements on the bonded indebtedness that has been authorized by the voters of the county. The Texas constitution and statutes limit the amount of bonded indebtedness a county may incur.

Because of the county ad valorem tax structure, the county tax rate will vary somewhat in the counties of the state. Ad valorem taxes are the only taxes collected by the county for the operation of its government.

Cities and counties in which bars and clubs are located each receive 15 percent of the 10 percent state gross receipts tax on sales and service of liquor-by-the-drink paid by such businesses.

Fees and Licenses

Counties receive fees from the state for the service of assessing and collecting state taxes. In "wet" areas, the counties also receive fees from the state for their handling of wine, liquor, and beer licenses, trial and jury fees, fees for birth and death certificates, abstract costs, certificates of title fees, and all or some of the fees collected from the registration of motor vehicles.

Other Sources of Revenue

Other sources of county revenue include federal and state funds, fines, forfeitures, rental and sale of property, revenue from parks, oil royalties (in some counties), and federal revenue sharing.

Defects of County Government

County government has been attacked frequently by its critics, of which there is a growing number. However, there is some justification for this criticism, for county government is defective in both its structure and its operation.

Uniformity

Whether a county is urban or rural, industrialized or nonindustrialized, large or small in area, the basic structure of its government remains uniform throughout the state. This uniformity is established by the constitution. Yet counties in the heavily populated areas carry out many local functions and operate somewhat like municipalities. They are more than just administrative areas of the state. The constitution and statutes still continue the myth that they are convenient geographical areas for carrying out state functions. The uniform structure or pattern of county government places 254 counties in the same category, which appears unrealistic.

Legislative Supervision

The present arrangement requires too much supervision by the legislature, which is not a proper legislative function. It does not strengthen the will of the people to govern themselves efficiently at the local level.

Lack of Administrative Control

The numerous county elective officials are responsible to the people rather than to a chief executive within the system. Each official is much his own boss. State control is limited to legislative action. There is little or no state supervision over the assessment and collection of taxes. The accounting and auditing systems are established by local and county officials in accord with their own ideas of fiscal administration. When the county borrows money, through the sale of bonds, the state makes no investigation to determine the county's economic capacity to meet its financial obligations. This division of authority and lack of administrative control is a major defect of county government.

The Long Ballot

The election of many county officials is confusing to the voters and does not promote administrative control and responsibility in the county bureaucracy. Many of the elective officials who perform purely administrative functions could be appointed. Permanent employees—other than manual laborers and possibly technical personnel—should be selected and removed under regulations of the merit system.

The Spoils System

Employment may depend on whether or not one voted and worked for the successful candidate or knew the right person in the precinct or county. This is no guarantee that qualified persons will be selected to work for the county.

Low Salaries

Salaries for nonelective, as well as some of the county elective positions, are rather low. This makes it difficult for the counties to compete with business and other governmental units in selecting and retaining qualified personnel.

Housekeeping Functions

The purchasing, accounting, auditing, budgetary, property-control, filing, recording, and reporting systems are inadequate in many counties. One of the key officials concerned with the housekeeping functions is the county auditor. He prepares the county budget and presents it to the commissioners' court and audits the financial transactions of county and precinct officials. It is his responsibility to establish sound budgetary and auditing procedures as well as to make recommendations to county officials in regard to improving the operations of their offices. He may make specific recommendations concerning filing, recording, collection of fees, and so on. The auditor is an important county official, for he is one person that has an overall view of the operations of county government. Unfortunately some county auditors and county judges have not established or recommended adequate housekeeping procedures.

An inadequate system for collecting and recording fees has resulted in the leakage of public funds in some counties. Sound recording, accounting, and budgeting procedures would reveal such misapplication of public funds within a reasonable time.

Assessment and Collection of Taxes

Because of inadequate budget and staff in the county tax assessor-collector's office, or for other reasons, a considerable amount of property is not carried on the county tax rolls for county tax purposes. The author remembers all too well the paying of state and county ad valorem taxes in a Texas county over a period of years only to discover the property was not even entered on the county tax roll. One can speculate on what happened to the tax money collected under such conditions.

A More Efficient County Government

County government in Texas could be improved by various changes within the existing governmental framework. For instance, some departments and offices that are not established by the constitution could be consolidated. Personnel administration, accounting, auditing, filing, recording, purchasing, and budgeting systems could be strengthened.

Many county officials support this more moderate type of reform, although most county officials oppose any root-and-branch changes in the constitutional structure of county government. From the standpoint of local politics and the possibility of making the changes, there is much that can be said in favor of these internal reforms. The county auditor, county judge, or commissioners' court should recommend the necessary changes in procedures and see that they are carried out.

A County Civil Service System

Among the responsibilities of a county civil service commission would be the following: establishment and enforcement of rules relating to the selection and job classification of county employees; competitive examinations; promotions, seniority, and tenure; layoffs and dismissals; disciplinary actions and grievance procedures. Inadequate salaries, lack of job security, and the spoils system do not attract and retain qualified career personnel.

A Central Computer Service

The government of Dallas County has established a central computer service under the supervision of the county auditor. In many counties individual departments have some computer equipment or contracts for data processing service. Registration of voters, maintenance of the voter's list, jury selection, court dockets and records, assessment and collection of taxes, and expenditures, among other county functions could be administered by a central computer service.

Improve Road Administration

Many counties in Texas operate under local county road laws that authorize the commissioners' court to appoint a county road engineer. Under some of these laws the county engineer has been delegated rather broad powers, but there are counties that ignore the letter and spirit of the law. In such counties the engineer plays a secondary role. In order to retain more control over the road function, the commissioners do not want the engineer to exercise the powers authorized by law.

In those counties which have voted to come under the optional county road law, the commissioners' court is established as the county road department with power to formulate the road policy and appoint a qualified engineer to carry the policy into effect. Once a county has voted to come under the plan, the road personnel and equipment of the four road precincts are pooled and the county roads are built and maintained on a countywide rather than a precinct-to-precinct basis.

For this one county function—road administration—the law establishes the manager plan for the counties operating under it. The arrangement is a miniature of the administration of the state department of highways and public transportation. As far as the improvement of county government is concerned, the optional county road law was a significant step forward.

More counties would benefit by voting to come under the optional county road law. Those counties operating under individual road laws could strengthen such laws by conferring more powers upon the appointive county engineer. This might require amending or merely following the existing law.

County Home Rule

Home rule—either county or municipal—permits the local unit to operate under a locally drafted and approved home-rule charter. Whether authorized by the constitution or law, the local unit must take the necessary action. It must appoint or elect a charter-drafting commission, hold a public hearing on the charter so drafted, and submit the charter to the local voters for approval. Any form of local government may be incorporated in the charter but the latter must not conflict with the state constitution and laws. Home rule permits a considerable amount of flexibility in that a local unit may establish that form of government that the people want.

To make county home rule available to all counties, the state constitution would have to be amended and the necessary legislation passed. Some of the counties—especially the small populated rural counties—might wish to operate under the existing structure of county government, whereas some of the metropolitan counties might wish to operate under the county-manager form, county-administrator form, county-executive form, or some other variation as authorized in the county home-rule charter. Optional home rule for counties would provide some flexibility in the structure of county government and permit urban counties to operate somewhat like municipalities. Home rule has operated quite successfully in Texas cities. A municipality in Texas must have a population of more than 5,000 to qualify for home rule.

Alternative Forms of County Government

Alternative forms of county government have been suggested as a compromise between the existing county-government arrangement (which in Texas is uniform, rigid, and centralized) and home rule: for example, the county-manager, county-executive, or county-commission forms. Residents of a county would have the option of continuing the existing form of county government or voting to operate under one of the forms set up in the statutes passed by the legislature. A county voting to come under one of the optional forms of government provided by law, would operate under a legislative code rather than a locally drafted and approved charter (home rule).

The alternative- or optional-forms law is designed to provide the necessary flexibility in governmental structure and at the same time enable the state to retain adequate control over counties. State control would be exercised through the drafting of the alternative-forms law, which would spell out the structure and power of each form of county government to be made available to the counties. The legislature would have the power to repeal or amend the alternative-forms law.

If counties operating under the alternative-forms law were authorized to assume some of the duties and functions of municipalities (with approval of the qualified voters of the latter) as well as exercise broader powers in general, adequate financial powers would have to be granted to such counties. To operate as a municipal government, the county would need more power to tax and borrow money.

City-County Consolidation

City-county consolidation may take one of two forms—structural or functional consolidation. In the former, the government of the county would be merged with that of the principal city in the county, or one or more municipalities could be merged with the county government. Structural consolidation eliminates one or more governmental units in the county. Under functional consolidation one or more functions, such as health, roads, law enforcement, parks, water supply, sewage disposal, education, libraries, and public welfare would be consolidated either with the appropriate county department or with the appropriate department of one or more municipalities of the county.

Regardless of the type of consolidation, the government assuming more functions would need increased powers to tax and borrow money. In the matter of functional consolidation, the yielding governmental unit might make regular payments through the fulfillment of contractual obligations, or else the government assuming the function might levy the necessary tax in the yielding area.

As a result of a police pilot project, the police department of the city of Quanah was merged in 1971 with the sheriff's department of Hardeman County. Law enforcement was merged in a single agency supervised by a city-county board but directed by the sheriff of Hardeman county. The first arrangement of its type in Texas, the consolidation may provide a blueprint for more professional law enforcement in small cities. The consolidation was made possible by a grant from the Texas criminal justice council. Prior to the merger the taxpayers paid for two jails, two communications systems, two fleets of cars, and two sets of criminal records. Salaries were increased and law enforcement upgraded.

Improvement and Modernization of County Jail Facilities

In the 1970s, as a phase of the prison reform movement in the United States, the people of Texas became more aware of the serious deficiencies of county jail administration in the state. This public awareness was due, in a large measure, to newspaper accounts of reports made by county grand juries and the Texas legislative council; to statements made by environmentalists, employees of the state department of health resources and the state department of corrections, and the governor's criminal justice council; and to orders issued by the federal district court to improve county jail facilities. As a result, county judges and county commissioners, faced with the increased cost of county government, were confronted with an additional need for funds.

County jails in Texas were declared inadequate, outmoded, and lacking in minimum facilities and standards required by state law. In fact, it was reported that only five county jails were in compliance with the state standards; the state health officials who inspected jails had no authority to compel compliance. Some of the deficiencies included the following: (1) Thirty percent of the jail cells were not one-prisoner cells as required by state standards. One-prisoner cells provide for separation of certain types of prisoners and diseased prisoners. (2) Cells sleeping three or more prisoners had no access to a day room; this constitutes a violation of the state's safety and security standards. (3) Cells were overcrowded and could encourage or contribute to jailbreaks. (4) Plumbing was in disrepair. In addition, there were inadequate heating, lighting, and ventilation; excessive odors; and lack of outside exercise and recreational areas. (5) There was a lack of space for the proper interrogation of prisoners. (6) The county law officers were understaffed and had insufficient space and facilities.

The legislature created a commission on jail standards composed of nine members appointed by the governor and senate for a term of six years. It is the duty of the commission to establish minimum standards for the construction, equipment, maintenance, and operation of county jails; for the custody, care, and treatment of prisoners; for programs of rehabilitation, education, and recreation in county jails. The sheriff and commissioners of each county must make an annual report on the conditions of the county jails to the state commission. Employees of the commission must inspect county jails regularly to insure compliance with state law and commission orders. If the commissioners or sheriff of a county do not comply within the time granted by the commission, the latter may prohibit the confinement of prisoners in the noncomplying jail and designate another detention facility. The county responsible must assume the cost of transportation and maintenance of prisoners transferred. In lieu of closing a county jail, the commission may institute action to enforce or enjoin the violation of its orders. A county may appeal a commission order by filing a petition in a district court of Travis County.

16 Municipal Government

ONLY IN THE CITY does one find division of labor, specialization of talent, a large labor market, the productive machinery, commerce and finance, distribution, wealth, and rapid mobility of people and goods.

Mobility—especially as it relates to man—is the central fact of our existence. Rural people are moving into the urban areas by the thousands; urbanites are moving to suburbia; dissatisfied suburbanites are moving back into the central city. The twentieth century is characterized by greater mobility, restiveness, dissatisfaction, experimentation, planning, tearing down, and rebuilding of the city.

The activities of municipal government are broad indeed. Municipal officials make sure that the gasoline pump at the neighborhood service station is delivering a full gallon, that adequate sanitation measures are taken at the corner restaurant, that milk is pure and wholesome, that fund drives are bona fide and for a worthy purpose. Ineffective action in these and other areas may result in immediate problems of government being taken to "city hall," in the form of complaints about poor garbage service, failure to repair the street, poor utility service, and any number of other things.

Municipal-State Relations

In Texas, the state legislature involves itself to a considerable extent in the affairs of cities. In each regular session of the legislature a number of laws are passed regulating the affairs of cities.

Because of this legislative control, city officials and employees must lobby in Austin to secure more authority to perform local functions as well as to protect their own interests. Lobbyists from the municipalities and special districts are among the more active ones. Although it provides a number of services for city officials, the Texas municipal league looks after the legislative interest of municipalities.

Both general and local laws passed in Austin pertain to city management. Although many of these laws apply to general-law cities, some apply to home-rule cities. A few examples of local laws relating to matters concerning one or more cities may be noted.

1. Empowering city councils to levy additional taxes or provide tax exemptions.
2. Authorizing the governing bodies of cities and towns to fix rates and charges of certain persons, firms, corporations, and public-utility companies in the local area.
3. Providing benefits for firemen and policemen in some cities (hours of work, time off, vacations, pension system, civil service, and relief-and-retirement fund).
4. Validating acts of cities (validating bond issues and elections, tax levies, and the incorporation of cities).
5. Giving municipalities control over streets, alleys, and public grounds.
6. Regulating the bounds and limits of cities.
7. Permitting cities to create or abolish certain offices, and providing fees, allowances, and salaries of municipal employees.
8. Conferring the right of eminent domain upon cities for certain purposes.
9. Authorizing cities to disannex certain territory.
10. Permitting cities to purchase light and water systems.

Without question, the laws regulating cities, towns, and villages should be revised to grant broader powers to both general-law and home-rule cities.

Municipal-Federal Relations

Federal grants and assistance to cities run into millions of dollars. Urban renewal, planning, hospitals, airports, slum clearance, housing, and the school-lunch program are some of the areas in which Washington has intervened.

In order to qualify for funds, the cities must meet certain standards and requirements established by Congress and the federal agency administering the program. Also, they are subject to supervision and inspection by the appropriate federal officials. The federal lines of control are somewhat similar to those incorporated in the grant-in-aid programs to the states. As a result, Washington does exercise some control and supervision over the cities. For most federal grants to municipalities, the latter must provide part of the funds in order to qualify for federal aid. The financial formula, or matching arrangement, need not be on a fifty-fifty basis, as it depends upon the provisions of the federal law.

General-Law and Home-Rule Cities

Cities and towns having a population of five thousand or less may be chartered alone by general law. They may levy, assess, and collect such taxes as may be authorized by law, but no tax for any purpose shall ever be lawful for any one year which shall exceed one and one-half percent of the taxable property of such city.[1]

Cities with a population greater than 5,000 may either operate as general-law cities or draft and approve their own municipal home-rule charter. General-law cities do not operate under locally drafted and approved home-rule charters, but operate under the general and local laws of the state. They function under a legislative code instead of a local charter. General-law cities possess less local autonomy or local self-government than the home-rule cities, since the legislature has greater control over them. General-law cities are limited to the mayor-council, commission, and city-manager forms of municipal government. The taxing and annexing powers of general-law cities are more limited than those of home-rule cities.

A number of cities in Texas initially secured their charters from the legislature. Following the adoption of the municipal home-rule amendment in 1912, these cities had three options: (1) continue to operate under the special legislative charters, (2) draft and approve a new home-rule charter, or (3) locally amend the legislative charter. Some of the legislative charters continued in effect but were in time drastically altered by locally initiated and approved charter amendments. Where the special legislative charter has been so amended, the city is, for all practical purposes, a home-rule city. Otherwise, the city is said to be in the home-rule class if it has locally drafted and approved its own charter.

The Home-Rule Enabling Act of 1913, as amended, enumerates the powers of home-rule cities and provides the procedure for framing, approving, and amending home-rule charters.

In a sense, the home-rule charter is the constitution of the municipal government, although in case of conflict the superior law of the state will prevail. Several sections of the charter relate to city councilmen and the city council (selection, removal, term, salary, and qualifications of members of the city council; procedure for passing city ordinances; enumeration of the powers and limitations of the city council; and possibly provision for initiative and referendum). Other sections concern the mayor (powers, duties, manner of selection, term of office, salary, qualifications, and method of removal). If the charter provides for the city-manager form, sections will specify the manner of selecting the city manager, his powers, and relationship with the council. All or some of the departments may be established in the charter (finance and taxation, police, water, fire, parks, street, and so on). For those departments included in the charter, provision must be made for selecting and removing department heads, as well as defining their powers. Some sections concern the municipal judge, municipal court, and the city attorney. The manner of selection and duties of the city secretary and members of boards and commissions may be included in the charter. All city charters provide the procedure for annexing territory and amending the charter. The maximum tax rate, establishment of the civil service commission, and procedure for granting franchises might be included in the charter.

Types of Municipal Government in Texas

Mayor-Council

The weak-mayor and council form resembles the type of government that was predominant during the first eighty years of the American republic. One recalls the fear in this country of the strong executive type of government before and after the American Revolution. The weak-mayor and council form, as originally conceived, was in keeping with the philosophy that "the best government is that which governs least."

The most outstanding feature of the weak-mayor and council form is the long ballot which, along with the weak position of the mayor, shows the influence of the concepts of Jacksonian democracy. The mayor, councilmen, heads of departments, and members of boards and commissions, as well as other administrative officials, are elected by the people.

In an institutional sense (as regards powers and duties of the office), the mayor is weak and whatever powers he possesses or may exercise are largely of a residual nature. The accent is on the council, since it retains almost all the power over legislation and administration. The mayor can recommend and veto legislation, but the council may either ignore his recommendations or override his veto, usually by a simple majority vote.

The administrative powers of the mayor, in the weak-mayor and council form, are severely restricted. In both legislation and administration the mayor's power is proportionate to the success he has in persuading the council of the correctness of his position. Appointments made by the mayor must be confirmed by the council, and he has little or no power to remove public officials. Since heads of departments and other administrative officials, as well as members of boards and commissions, are popularly elected, they need not follow the lead of the mayor. In most cases, the initiative rests not with the mayor but rather with the elective administrative officials. The council, through committees, supervises administration.

The mayor may acquire some personal power and prestige if he is successful in persuading the council to accept his recommendations and advice. The institutional and human factors in government are interrelated and both must be considered in determining the effective power of public officials.

The weak-mayor and council form violates the administrative principle that power and responsibility are correlative in nature. The mayor is responsible for city government but does not have the power to govern. The same people who establish the legislative policies are responsible for executing them; hence, there is a combination, rather than a separation, of legislative and administrative powers. No single person is responsible for coordinating all the administrative activities. Finally, the absence of a strong executive makes it difficult to plan a long-range, coherent program for the city.

The emergence of the strong executive in this country during the latter half of the nineteenth century was due to a number of factors. The public became aware that the long ballot and the division of political power and responsibility did not ensure governmental efficiency and political accountability. Evolution of the large industrial corporations, with the concept of concentrated powers, had a tremendous impact upon the public mind. The appearance of complex urban problems was also a significant factor in the development of the strong municipal executive. These developments, plus the defects of the weak-mayor and council plan, created a rather widespread dissatisfaction with the city council both as an agency of legislation and administration. From 1870 onward there was popular demand for efficiency and economy in the management of public affairs. At the municipal level, this could best be accomplished, so it was contended, by concentrating both responsibility and commensurate authority in a chief executive.

In the strong-mayor and council plan the mayor exercises important legislative and administrative powers in addition to performing the customary ceremonial functions. He is—in both theory and fact—the administrative as well as the political head of the city. The mayor is elected at large by qualified voters. Members of the city council may be elected either at large or from districts.

The more important administrative powers of the mayor include the appointment and removal of most or all department heads with the approval of the council in most cities with this type of government. Thus, the short ballot is an important feature of the strong-mayor and council form. The chief budget officer and his staff prepare the budget after receiving the budgetary requests from the departments, boards, and commissions. Representatives from the budget office and agencies hold budget hearings and in due season the budget is submitted to the mayor who transmits it to the city council.

Since the population of cities continues to grow, more funds are needed to finance municipal services. Consequently, in the matter of developing new or expanding old programs, as well as in questions concerning the budget, tax rate, and bond issues, there is ample opportunity for conflict between the mayor and the city council. For this reason, the mayor and some of the candidates for the city council may campaign on the same program. Even if the "team" is elected, conflicts can, and often do, develop between the mayor and the city fathers (members of the city council). The voters, at the next election, may be called upon to resolve such conflicts.

Under the strong-mayor and council plan the mayor is expected to provide the legislative leadership, to present the legislative program to the city council. He may recommend hiring more firemen and policemen and an increase in salary for all or some municipal employees, or the expansion of airport facilities and other municipal services.

Members of the council may offer proposals at city council meetings; however, seldom can individual councilmen offer legislative leadership comparable to that of the mayor. It is only possible when the mayor has lost the support of the council or does not care to exercise the legislative powers of his office. In any event, it is the primary function of the council to consider all proposals and eventually determine the policy of the city.

The veto power, in the strong-mayor and council plan, originally was designed to protect the mayor against legislative encroachment but in time it came to be used as a device for influencing legislation. Usually the mayor's veto can be overridden only by an extraordinary majority.

In some strong-mayor and council cities, and especially the more populated ones, the mayor has been compelled to delegate functions to one or more assistants whom he appoints. Members of the so-called executive office of the mayor or the mayor's staff make it possible for him to devote more time to the broader aspects of policy, leaving to his assistants the supervision of the day-to-day affairs of the city. Assistants with ability and training, and an understanding of practical politics and public relations, can lighten the load of an overworked mayor in a large city.

The strong-mayor and council plan is no guarantee that the mayor will, at all times, occupy a strong position in the city government. Much depends upon the prestige and personality of both mayor and councilmen and whether the chief executive enjoys the council's confidence and support.

In some of the more populated cities with the strong-mayor and council form, steps have been taken to strengthen the managerial side of the mayor's office. This has been accomplished by authorizing the mayor to appoint a chief managerial assistant who sometimes has been referred to both as administrator and manager.

The chief administrative officer is usually appointed by and responsible to the mayor. Besides advising the mayor on matters of administration, he may assist in the preparation of the budget, develop a personnel system, and perform such other duties as may be authorized by the mayor. The assumption is that the mayor is just as capable as the council in selecting an efficient administrator; and responsibility is simplified, since a single person (the mayor) rather than a group (the city council) is accountable to the people.

Commission

The city of Galveston had a significant influence on the development of the commission form of municipal government in the United States. The hurricane of 1900 created urgent problems of relief and reconstruction in the city, and the existing mayor-council government failed to meet the challenge. As a result, a group of interested citizens were successful in securing legislative approval of a new charter. The charter provided that the city would be governed by five commissioners; three appointed by the governor and two elected by the people. One commissioner was designated mayor, although he served merely as chairman of the group. There was no separation of powers, since all executive, legislative, and administrative powers were concentrated in the five commissioners. Because of an adverse court ruling, the charter was amended in 1903 providing for the popular election of all the commissioners. It was not long until the Galveston plan spread to Dallas, Fort Worth, and many other Texas cities.

The commissioners are elected at large by majority vote. Collectively they constitute the legislative body of the city, and each commissioner serves as head of an administrative department, thus combining legislative and administrative functions. In some cities, individual commissioners campaign and are elected as head of a particular department, although it is rather common for the commissioners, acting as a body, to assign commissioners to departments. Usually the commissioner receiving the most popular votes is designated mayor by the governing body. Other than performing the honorary and ceremonial functions of the city, plus presiding over city council meetings, the mayor's position is similar to that of the other commissioners.

Commission government provides a rather direct and simple method of governing cities. Power is concentrated in five, seven, or more popularly elected commissioners whose responsibility to the public is maintained through nonpartisan elections, initiative, referendum, and recall. Yet, like all forms of government, it has weaknesses. For one thing, the combination of legislative and administrative functions does not, of itself, necessarily result in governmental efficiency. When people vote in commission cities, they do so to elect legislators rather than administrators, although the commissioners serve in a dual capacity. A successful vote-getter may not be an able administrator. Because of training and specialization, a qualified administrator may not be interested in seeking public office. Consequently, in matters of administrative qualifications and experience, an individual commissioner may be an amateur.

Despite the weaknesses of commission government, this type of municipal government may be found in both general-law and home-rule cities of Texas.

Council-Manager

Council-manager government evolved out of the commission form. The division of authority among the commissioners proved to be the outstanding weakness of the commission plan. To overcome this deficiency, some believed the council should delegate authority to a single professionally trained administrator. Once this idea was accepted, the council-manager plan emerged.

In 1907 the city council of Staunton, Virginia, made a study of the commission plan in Galveston and Houston. They recommended the appointment of a general manager. With the appointment of such an official the following year, a small first step was taken in the establishment of council-manager government.

The council-manager plan combines both an old and a new principle. The doctrine of councilmanic supremacy is a very old concept, whereas the emphasis upon professional management of municipal affairs—in place of the council-committee system—represents a new approach in municipal government.

The people elect members of the city council or commission who in turn appoint, for indefinite tenure, a professional or career administrator. It is the duty of the council members, as representatives of the people, to determine municipal policy and appoint and remove the city manager. The latter attends all council meetings, may suggest, recommend, or advise the council but has no vote. He may be called upon to give information to the council, as well as explain or defend his own actions and those of his assistants. Once policy is determined by the council, it is the responsibility of the manager to carry out the policy without alteration or change. If members of the council are dissatisfied with the way policy is executed, or dissatisfied with the manager in any way, they can remove him at any time. In other words, the council is the chief judge of the manager's administrative competency.

The manager appoints and removes the heads of departments, whereas most of the other municipal employees are appointed, promoted, and removed on the basis of civil-service regulations. Hence, the short ballot is an important feature of council-manager government. A direct line of responsibility is established. The heads of departments are responsible to the city manager; the city manager is responsible to the council; and members of the city council are responsible to the people. Insofar as the voters are concerned, the city council is responsible not only for municipal policy but also for the administrative record of the city manager. Therefore, ultimate supremacy rests with the people who elect the members of the city council. With this check by the people, the plan embodies both the principles of councilmanic supremacy and the professional administrator.

In the council-manager plan the council continues to occupy its original position of preeminence. Besides appointing and removing the manager, the council creates, reorganizes, and abolishes departments, boards, and commissions; approves the budget; sets the tax rate; authorizes the issuance of bonds (if previously approved by the voters in a bond election); provides for an independent audit; annexes and disannexes territory; amends or repeals sections of the health, fire, traffic, building, and plumbing codes; approves franchises; inquires into the conduct of any office or department; and makes investigations. Since the council has been relieved of the burden of administration (which it handled through the use of council committees), councilmen have more time to devote to policy matters. In brief, the council has two major functions; it supervises administration and formulates and approves municipal policy.

The city manager may head the finance and tax department. The budget is prepared by the budget officer and staff in this department, and the manager transmits it to the council for their consideration and approval. As head of this department, the manager is in close touch with the financial affairs of the city (the budget, tax rate, bonded indebtedness, bond issues, and so on) and is in a position to keep the council advised on the financial condition of the municipality. In addition to this important function, the manager negotiates contracts for the municipality subject to the approval of the council, makes recommendations concerning the nature and location of municipal improvements, sees that all terms of public-utility franchises or other contracts are carried out and reports all violations to the council. The manager makes reports to the council as requested by it and may make an annual report of his work for the benefit of the council and the public.

To win recognition as a successful city manager requires ability, training, and experience. An adequate understanding of public finance, public and personnel administration, public relations, and practical politics, as well as some knowledge of engineering, would be a great advantage for any city manager. Furthermore, the personal relationships of the manager are all-important. Regardless of training or experience, his success or failure frequently is determined by his personal relationship with his assistants, subordinates, and members of the council.

In the council-manager plan the mayor, manager, and members of the city council have a definite role to play. The council may designate one of its own members as mayor or the people may elect the mayor. Designation of the mayor by the council from its own membership is the more common pattern. The mayor presides over council meetings, participates in the determination of policy but has no power of veto, and represents the city on ceremonial occasions. In matters of administration the mayor is overshadowed by the city manager. On the other hand, the manager is in no sense the political head of the government and it is the council, rather than the manager, that receives credit for the effectuation of policy.

Although appointment and dismissal of department heads by the city manager usually require the approval of the council, neither the city council nor any of its members may use their influence in any way to secure the appointment or removal of individuals by the manager. Except for the purpose of inquiry, the city council and its members must deal with the administrative service solely through the city manager. This prevents the council or any of its members from giving orders to any subordinates of the city manager, either publicly or privately.

The occupation of city manager has undergone extensive professionalization. This is evident in increased training opportunities—many colleges and universities have introduced broad courses in city managing. Opportunities for advancement are excellent; a graduate might be appointed assistant city manager in a small city and in time—as his or her administrative record wins recognition—become manager of a larger city. Many city managers in Texas are members of the International City Managers' Association and the Texas City Management Association.

In the council-manager cities the managers are being retained for longer periods of service. In some cities the manager is entitled to notice and hearing before removal. The indefinite tenure, without any protection in the form of notice and hearing, has discouraged many qualified young men and women from entering the city-manager profession. The increasing number of qualified managers and the records they are making for themselves and the cities offer further evidence of a developing professional group.

The manager form has won many adherents. Hundreds of cities throughout the United States have adopted the form with considerable success. That the plan is popular and successful can be seen by the small number of abandonments in those cities in which it has been tried. In 1947, Houston abandoned the city-manager form and adopted the strong-mayor and council plan. Other than Houston and El Paso (mayor-council plan), the major cities in Texas operate under the council-manager system.

Forms of Government Available to General-Law Cities

Aldermanic or Mayor-Council

One of the three forms of government available to general-law cities is the aldermanic or mayor-council plan. The government may consist of a mayor, elected at large, and two aldermen elected from each ward, in addition to other elective or appointive officials. If the municipality is not divided into wards, the mayor and five aldermen are elected at large. In addition to the members of the city council (the mayor and aldermen) the general laws provide for the election or appointment of a secretary, treasurer, tax assessor and collector, city attorney, marshal, and a city engineer. All or some of these positions may be dispensed with by ordinance and their duties conferred upon some other person. For example, the council might designate the city secretary or city engineer as the chief administrative officer of the city and authorize him to handle the duties of treasurer, assessor and collector of taxes, and building inspector. Under such conditions the secretary or engineer would perform many of the duties of a city manager. Other persons appointed by the council might include the city judge, chief of police, fire chief, librarian, health officer, and city superintendent who directs all the city's outside projects, such as paving and street maintenance, garbage collection, and parks. Some city employees may be hired by the city secretary, city engineer, or department heads.

A limited number of official boards may be established by the council to assist in the performance of its duties, for example, a zoning commission that makes recommendations to the council on changes in the zoning ordinance; a board of adjustment that hears appeals on zoning action; and a traffic-safety commission that makes recommendations for decreasing the accident rate. Members of these and other boards, as well as most of the other elective and appointive officials, serve on a part-time basis.

There are variations in the aldermanic cities incorporated under general law. The basis for the differences is threefold. First, the general laws provide for the incorporation of "cities and towns" and "towns and villages," and the organization and powers of each class vary somewhat. Second, the council has considerable discretion in determining the number and type of offices, boards, and commissions. Third, the size and population of the aldermanic general-law city will influence the number of positions established by the council. In the small community most of the routine administrative work is handled by the city clerk or city engineer.

The aldermanic or mayor-council plan that is available to the general-law cities is the weak-mayor and council form. The emphasis is on the aldermen or city council and is quite appropriately referred to as the "aldermanic" form. If the mayor vetoes a city ordinance, it can be overridden by a simple majority of the aldermen. Since most officials and employees are either elected by the people or appointed by the council, city secretary, city engineer, or department head, the mayor has little or no appointive and removal power.

Commission

Under the general laws a city, town, or village may incorporate under the commission plan. The voters elect a mayor and two commissioners who sit as the governing body of the city. A clerk, who acts as treasurer, assessor, and collector of taxes, is appointed by the board of commissioners. Other officers considered necessary, as for example, a city attorney and police officers, may be appointed and discharged by the three-man governing body.

The general laws make it possible for a community that has incorporated under the mayor-council plan to adopt the commission form. The proposition must be submitted to the local voters and approved by a majority of those voting on the issue. Later, the voters, if they so desire, may vote to return to the original form of government.

City-Manager

A state law provides:

> Any incorporated city, town or village in this State incorporated under the General Laws, having a population of less than five thousand (5,000) inhabitants according to the last preceding or any future Federal Census, may vote upon the question of adopting a city manager plan of government as in this act provided.[2]

If a majority of those voting at such election favor the plan, the governing body of the city is authorized to appoint a city manager and fix his salary by ordinance. Once adopted, the city-manager plan may be abandoned by a vote of the local residents. The act is in the nature of a *legislative* charter of city-manager government for those cities of less than 5,000 population.

At one time only the aldermanic or mayor-council and commission forms were available to general-law cities; however, a number of them did provide for the manager form by ordinance. That is, before the law was passed, the council in a general-law city might pass an ordinance making the city secretary, city engineer, or some other official the chief administrative officer of the city who would perform many of the functions of a city manager. As a consequence, many general-law cities operated with the manager form—or at least something approaching the manager system—in everything but name. The law merely recognized the trend by permitting the voters of the local area to adopt the manager plan as provided for in the statute.

Incorporation and Disincorporation

If a community wishes to incorporate, a petition signed by the voters in the area must be filed with the county judge requesting him to call an election for the purpose of submitting the question of incorporation to a vote of the qualified resident electors.* Proof or evidence that the area contains the required population, together with the name, boundaries, and a plat of the proposed incorporated city, town, or village must accompany the petition. Assuming the petition is in order, the county judge will set the time and place for the incorporation election. At the election the voters will decide whether or not to incorporate, and the form of government (mayor-aldermanic or commission form). The voters may vote to incorporate and at the same or later election select the municipal officials. This is the process by which an unincorporated area may become incorporated. At a later date a majority of those voting on the proposition could vote to disincorporate, that is, return to an unincorporated status.

One incorporated area cannot annex another incorporated area. For this reason a community may incorporate to prevent being annexed by some other municipality. Some of the larger cities of Texas have objected to "bedroom" cities being organized in the fringe area beyond their boundaries. If a number of such areas are incorporated, it could stunt the growth of the central city by severely limiting the amount of additional territory it may annex. The race to annex and incorporate has produced some interesting legal battles in Texas and has been the source of considerable friction between powerful interest groups. Those living in an incorporated area may find it to their economic advantage to vote to disincorporate and be annexed by an adjoining municipality.

Annexation and Disannexation

General-Law Cities

The city council of general-law cities may, by ordinance, annex territory. However, there are limitations: the territory to be annexed must be contiguous to the city and be one-half mile or less in width, and a majority of the inhabitants qualified to vote in the territory must vote in favor of annexation. General-law cities with populations exceeding 5,000, according to the last preceding federal census, may annex territory up to one mile in width. There must be a petition from the residents in the area to be annexed and a favorable vote in the territory.

Fifty qualified voters living in an area that does not wish to continue as a part of

---

*A community that contains more than 200 and less than 10,000 people may incorporate as a *town* or *village*. For a town or village to incorporate under the mayor-aldermanic form, the petition must contain at least twenty signatures. A *city* or *town* containing 600 or more people may incorporate under the mayor-aldermanic form, in which case the petition filed with the county judge must contain the names of at least fifty qualified voters in the community. A *city* or *town* with a population of more than 500 and less than 5,000 and a *town* or *village* with more than 200 and less than 1,000 inhabitants may incorporate under the commission form. The petition filed with the county judge must be signed by 10 percent of the qualified voters in the unincorporated area.

the general-law city may petition for disannexation. Upon receipt of the petition, the mayor must order a city-wide election and if a majority of those voting favor disannexation, the area is separated from the city. There are limitations on the amount of territory a single city may disannex. The disannexed area is responsible for its pro rata (proportional) share of the city's debts. Until the disannexed area fulfills its financial obligations, the city council is authorized to levy an ad valorem tax each year on property in the territory at the same tax rate as that levied within the city.

Home-Rule Cities

State law and judicial decisions have given home-rule cities a broad grant of authority to annex. The city must follow the provisions of its charter and some part of the area to be annexed must be adjacent to the city. This annexing power, plus authority to levy a higher tax rate, has encouraged general-law cities with populations of more than 5,000 to become home-rule cities.

A charter may provide that the city may annex with or without the consent of the inhabitants in the territory annexed. And the charter may or may not require that an annexation petition be initiated by persons living in the unincorporated area.

Texas has had its share of incorporation and annexation wars. Cities have instituted annexation proceedings on first reading and by final passage of annexation ordinances to prevent incorporations, and to preclude other incorporated areas from annexing the land in question. Strips of territory have been annexed and cities have annexed circles around other incorporated places in order to limit the maximum growth of their competitors. One city may disannex a strip to open a hole for a friendly city to annex more territory, and such action may or may not antagonize a third city. A checkerboard pattern of defensive and competitive annexation and incorporation has resulted. These municipal activities offer ample evidence of the interrelationship between economic motivation, pressure politics, and the protection of self-interest.

Under the municipal annexation law a city may not annex territory in any one year in excess of 10 percent of the total corporate area of the city as it exists on the first day of the year. Excluded from the 10 percent are the following: territory annexed by the request of a majority of the qualified resident voters in the area and the owners of 50 percent or more of the land in the territory; and territory owned by the city, county, state, or federal government and used for a public purpose. In the event a city fails in any calendar year or years to annex the total amount of territory it is authorized to annex, the unused allocation may be carried over and used in subsequent years—although the city may not annex in any one year an amount in excess of 30 percent of its total area as it exists on the first day of the year. A city may annex territory only within the confines of its extraterritorial jurisdiction, but this limitation does not apply to the annexation of property owned by the city. Before a city may institute annexation proceedings, the city must provide an opportunity for all interested persons to be heard at a public hearing. To be valid, annexation must be completed within ninety days after a city institutes annexation proceedings.

The municipal annexation law provides that cities may exercise extraterritorial jurisdiction over surrounding unincorporated and contiguous areas, or "buffer zones," ranging from one-half mile for cities of less than 5,000 to five miles around cities of 100,000 or more population. Upon the request of property owners of contiguous territory, the extraterritorial jurisdiction of a city may be extended beyond its existing extraterritorial limits. When a city annexes additional areas, its extraterritorial jurisdiction expands in conformity with the annexation. One city's extraterritorial jurisdiction may not conflict with that of another. No city may impose any tax in the area under extraterritorial jurisdiction; however, the city may by ordinance extend its regulations governing plats (a map showing how land will be subdivided, or divided up, and built upon) and the subdivision of land in such an area.

No city may incorporate within the area of the extraterritorial jurisdiction of any city without the written consent of the governing body of that city. If the city refuses to grant permission for the incorporation of the proposed city, the resident voters in the territory may petition the city and request annexation. Refusal to annex the area constitutes authorization for the incorporation of the proposed city. Also, no special district, as a water district, may be created within the area of the extraterritorial jurisdiction of any city without the written consent of such city. Should the city refuse to grant permission, the voters of the proposed political subdivision may petition the governing body of the city and request the city to make available to the territory the water or sanitary-sewer service. Failure of the city and voters in the territory to execute a contract for such services constitutes authorization for the creation of the proposed political subdivision.

Cities may establish industrial districts in their buffer zones and exempt industries from annexation. Also, the municipal-annexation law provides for disannexation of any area in which a city has not provided services comparable to those in the annexing city within three years.

Many people are anxious to know the direction of future city growth. Homeowners, real-estate promoters and speculators, builders, contractors, businessmen, and others may buy in unannexed areas, wait a few months, and later resell the property at a nice profit following annexation and the extension of municipal services to the area. In a sense, the taxpayers are subsidizing these business ventures. These same groups use their influence to secure incorporation or annexation so that municipal services will be made available, for only in this way can an area be developed—unless arrangement is made for private concerns to supply basic services (water, sewage disposal, lights, garbage collection, and so on) or a special district is created to provide these services. In the matter of annexation, "inside information" on the direction of future city expansion could prove very beneficial, economically speaking. Members of the city planning commission, the city council, and the mayor usually have this information. Frequently it is a good investment to purchase land in or near the area where the developers have staked out a claim, although it may be several years before the area is annexed or incorporated.

Municipal Planning

In a municipality the members of the planning commission are appointed by the city council. The commission acts as an advisory board to the city council on all matters relating to planning, public improvements, and such other matters as the commission and council may deem beneficial to the city. Recommendations made by the planning commission may or may not be adopted by the city council.

The commission makes recommendations directly to the council on zoning changes, annexations, disannexations, subdivision development, capital improvements, public building sites, site planning, opening, widening and changing of streets, routing of public utilities, and all matters of long-range planning. In most cases the city planning commission will hold a preliminary hearing, after which it may recommend appropriate action to the council. The result may be the passage of an annexation, disannexation, or zoning ordinance. Frequently one will observe a degree of tenseness at a public hearing before the city planning commission as individuals (some with legal counsel) present their arguments for and against some proposed action by the city, for example, an annexation or zoning ordinance. Homeowners, real-estate promoters, builders, contractors, businessmen, and others may be vitally interested in the action the commission will take. Once recommendations have been made by the planning commission, the city council may hold a public hearing before voting on the city ordinance. Again, interested groups, with or without legal counsel, are given the privilege of presenting their case before the city council.

The long-term objective in city planning is to project the future growth of the city by a well-drawn master plan and thereby control the growth of the city in an orderly and intelligent manner. Too many cities grow and expand without the restrictions of some preconceived plan of future growth. Yet one must realize the pressures and obstacles under which city planning commissions and city councils operate.

Zoning

Zoning is designed to promote the public health, safety, order, convenience, prosperity, and general welfare. The city has the power, through the passage of zoning ordinances, to divide the city into zones or districts for the purpose of regulating and controlling the size, height, and use of buildings. Different regulations may be established for the various districts.

The city council may create and appoint the members of a board of appeals or review (adjustment). Anyone aggrieved by any order or decision of the city council concerning zoning may seek a hearing before the board of adjustment, and it may either recommend that the council modify the order or permit deviation from the zoning ordinance.

Zoning is an aid in stabilizing property value and prevents the formation of slums and low-value areas. After a public hearing before the city planning commission and city council, a zoning ordinance may be passed establishing certain areas as commercial or residential areas. One or more sections may be zoned for frame or brick homes of not less than a certain value. Other sections may be zoned for apartments, duplexes, one-story homes, and the like. When a residential area is rezoned for commercial purposes, property owners may suffer a substantial loss due to the devaluation of their property. In such a case, the interested property owners could present their case to the city planning commission and city council, and if unsuccessful before these bodies they might appeal to the board of adjustment and the courts.

Deed Restrictions

Individuals who plan to purchase a home, business property, or vacant land within a city should make inquiry concerning deed restrictions, a copy of which can be obtained from the county clerk's office. Deed restrictions include the reservations, restrictions, covenants, and easements that apply to the use of the property.

The deed restrictions might include the following:

1. *Architectural Control Committee.*

No building shall be erected or altered on any lot until the construction plans, and a plan showing the location of the structure on the lot, have been approved by the Architectural Control Committee as to proposed quality of building, harmony of external design with existing structures, and location with respect to topography and grade elevations. No fence or wall shall be erected, or altered, on any lot nearer to any street than the minimum building setback, unless similarly approved. The Architectural Control Committee is composed of three members whose names and addresses are as follows:

_____

_____

_____

In the event of any vacancy on the committee, the remaining members shall have authority to designate a successor. At any time, the then record owners of two-thirds of the lots shall have power to change the membership of the committee.

Before any lot owner in the subdivision shall erect any building, wall, fence, or other structure, such person shall apply in writing to the Architectural Control Committee for approval of such proposed structure. The Committee may institute suit to enjoin the construction.

2. *Land Use and Building Type.*

No plat shall be used for any purposes except single-family residential. Such residential homes shall consist of single-story brick homes of not less than 2,000 square feet or more than 3,000 square feet. The non-attached two-car garage and paved driveway, fences, walls, pools, terrace, and similar landscaping features shall be compatible with the residential structure.

3. *Lot Sizes.*

No building shall be erected on any lot having a width less than 65 feet at minimum building setback line or having an area less than 9,000 square feet.

4. *Dwelling Size.*

The heated floor area of the main residential structure, exclusive of open porches, screen porches, stoops (entrance to a house), and garage, shall not be less than . . .

5. *Materials Requirements.*

The main residential structure shall have no less than 51 percent of the exterior wall areas of brick or other wall masonry material. The architectural control committee may modify this requirement when the design and appearance as proposed are deemed to be of such nature as to be equally attractive and permanent.

6. *Easements.*

Easements for the installation and maintenance of utilities, and drainage, are reserved as indicated in the recorded plat.

. . . .

14. *Term.*

These covenants shall be binding on all parties for a period of forty (40) years from the date the covenants are recorded, after which time said covenants shall be extended automatically for successive periods of ten (10) years, unless an instrument signed by a majority of the current owners of the lots has been recorded, agreeing to change said covenants, in whole or in part. Each owner of one or more lots shall be entitled to one vote for each lot owned.

15. *Enforcement.*

Enforcement shall be by proceedings at law, or in equity, against any person violating, or attempting to violate, any covenant, either to restrain violation or to recover damages.

16. *Severability.*

Invalidation of any of the covenants, by court order, shall in no way affect any of the other provisions which shall remain in effect.

53695

DATE RECORDED _____

FILED AT _____ O'CLOCK _____

VOL. _____ PAGE _____

_____, COUNTY CLERK _____ COUNTY,

SIGNATURE _____

TEXAS

VOL. _____ PAGE _____

Deed restrictions should be drafted by a qualified lawyer in a clear or nonambiguous manner to protect the seller and purchaser of real estate within the city.

As a result of a special law passed by the Texas legislature, the city of Houston and other cities within Harris County may go to court to seek injunctions against deed restriction violations. They also may withhold building permits for construction that would violate the restrictions. Often the controversies are settled without court action. In fact, civic clubs, watching for deed restriction violations, are able to eliminate transgressions without city assistance. The city of Houston does not have zoning regulations, however, the legal department of the city has intervened, in selective cases, to enforce deed restrictions.

Sometimes in Houston it is simpler, and less time-consuming, to attack deed restrictions through other ordinances. For example, the deed restriction might prohibit commercial enterprises in a certain area. In such a situation, it might be more convenient to request that the police ticket an individual for violating an antinoise ordinance than to proceed against the individual for disregard of a deed restriction. City Public Works and Health Departments may unwittingly grant permits which violate deed restrictions, in which event the legal department would have the task of correcting the violations.

If breaches of deed restrictions are ignored and become widespread, the covenants may be invalidated in the eyes of the law.

An interesting legal issue may arise when a city council passes a zoning ordinance that is in conflict with an existing deed restriction. Such a situation involves both *legal* and *policy* conflicts. The following is quoted from the conclusion of a law review article.

The sole constitutional barrier to allowing ordinances to prevail over covenants is the requirement that property shall not be taken for public use without the payment of just compensation. Applying the two accepted modes of state action to the private covenant produces a rule that finds (1) a noncompensable taking within the police power when the covenant is merely regulated, and (2) a compensable eminent domain situation when the covenant is taken. It is suggested that in all cases, what is being "acted upon" by state action is not the covenant, but rights arising out of ownership generally. Therefore the determination whether a "regulation" or a "taking" has occurred must be made by comparing the total value of the landowner's rights before the governmental restrictions are imposed with the value after the restrictions are taken into account.

Under the present law this method of balancing interests generally is not followed. As a result governmental restriction is often obtained at a high cost that far overcompensates the private landowner for the amount of detriment actually suffered. If the gain to the public is small when compared to the hardship imposed upon an individual property owner, then there is no valid basis for a noncompensable taking. If it appears plainly, however, that the benefit to the public is substantial when compared to the detriment to the private owner, then courts should be able to authorize the imposition of the ordinance without the requirement of compensation despite violation of covenant rights. The better view seems to be that a covenant right is not a property right in the traditional sense of being something possessed by virtue of ownership, and it is clear that the zoning power cannot be impeded by such rights. It is suggested, however, that American courts find some element of value in these rights that must be thrown into the balance on the side of the landowner in determining whether an ordinance constitutes a taking.

The suggestions offered herein are directed toward finding techniques to insure a more equitable balancing of interests when the compensability of an ordinance restriction is in question. The problem whether compensation is required when deed covenants conflict with zoning ordinances or otherwise impede public planning is one with which courts will have to live for some time. It should be made clear, however, that there are few if any areas in which the weight of the public interest does not justify at least some noncompensable takings in a society in which private property rights have become so deeply interwoven in public planning and necessity.[3]

Those who purchase and sell residential and commercial lots and buildings within a city should determine if deed restrictions exist in a particular situation. The mayor and members of the city council may have little or no desire to become involved in legal action in the courts involving the infringement of deed restrictions. Such legal action could be time-consuming and costly, and the city might not be successful in the effort. Therefore, the city council might be very cautious, and possibly refuse to pass a zoning ordinance that would conflict with deed restrictions in a particular situation. However, the developer might believe the property owners adversely affected would not resort to court action because of the time and expense involved. Those that buy and sell real estate are interested in who will be elected mayor and members of the city council and may support certain persons that seek election to those positions. Or the city council may be more citizen oriented, in which case there could be more support for the interests of the citizens that might be adversely affected.

Housing Codes

The purpose of a housing code is to insure that housing does not endanger the health or safety of the occupants. Such a code may establish minimum standards for floor space, plumbing and sanitary facilities, heating, ventilation, electrical service, living space, safety conditions, lighting, insect and rodent control, garbage storage, and maintenance of all existing dwellings. The code may provide for inspectors and for a housing board to hear appeals and enforce the code.

A housing code applies to housing existing prior to its enactment as well as to buildings to be constructed and is designed to protect both renters and property owners. The code establishes minimum housing standards for those who rent and fines for those who destroy or damage rented property. Appropriate penalties are provided for failure to make repairs or rebuild.

An adequate housing code, properly enforced, is necessary for municipalities to receive federal grants under certain federal programs. Federal loans, not to exceed a specific maximum amount, with low interest rates, are available both to homeowners and those who rent property in order to make the necessary improvements.

Thousands of housing units in Texas and other states are substandard because the existing housing code is not enforced or is inadequate. The situation has contributed to the ghettoes, demonstrations, and violence in the cities. However, the solution of the housing problem is complex. If the housing unit is repaired or rebuilt, the rent may be increased to a level that a person with low income could not afford; or the property owner may refuse to make the improvements and rerent for fear of the destruction or damage of his property. Yet some progress has been made for the benefit of those who own or rent property, as well as considerable benefit for contractors and builders and for society in general. There is probably no instant solution to a problem that has evolved for many years.

Public Health

The municipal health departments of large cities of Texas are charged with the prevention of communicable diseases and enforcement of all state and city health ordinances. They work in close cooperation with the state department of health resources, medical societies, and school health officials.

The staff of a municipal health department records births and deaths (vital statistics), provides treatment for communicable diseases to those unable to afford medical care, examines and treats underprivileged children in well-baby clinics, examines food handlers, inspects restaurants and food-dispensing establishments, conducts schools on sanitation, and provides public-nursing and typhus-control programs. All local meat-processing plants are inspected by health department personnel. Dairies within the local milkshed—whether within or outside the city or state (as long as they provide the municipality with milk)—are inspected by the health department.

The Municipal Court and City Attorney

In the general-law cities the mayor may serve as city judge. The city judge and city attorney may be appointed (by the council) or elected by the people. In the home-rule cities the judge of the municipal court and city attorney are usually appointed by the city council.

The municipal court, sometimes referred to as the traffic, or city court, has jurisdiction within the territorial limits of the city in all criminal cases involving violation of city ordinances. It has concurrent jurisdiction with the justices of the peace (of the precincts in which the city is located) and county courts in other criminal cases (within the city) arising under the criminal laws of the state, where the punishment is by fine only and does not exceed $200. The court has no civil jurisdiction, except for the forfeiture and collection of bonds in proceedings before the court. Appeals from convictions in the municipal court may be taken to the county court (or county criminal court in some counties).

The court spends a considerable part of its time processing traffic violations. Most traffic violators pay their fines without asking for a trial. Nevertheless, in the larger cities there is a great backlog of pending traffic cases. This has encouraged more traffic violators to ask for a trial in order to delay or escape payment of the fine.

All cases brought before the municipal court are prosecuted by the city attorney or his assistants, and he represents the city in all litigation and controversies. The legal officer gives his opinion on proposed ordinances, drafts proposed ordinances granting franchises, inspects and passes upon all papers, documents, contracts, and other instruments in which the city may be interested, and serves as legal adviser to the mayor, city council, and other city officials.

Selection of Personnel

The selection and promotion of personnel on the basis of merit objectively determined is in operation in many cities in Texas. Members of the civil service board or commission are appointed by the city council. The classified service may include the competitive and noncompetitive classes. Included in the competitive class are all positions for which it is practicable to determine the fitness of applicants by competitive examinations. The noncompetitive class consists of all positions requiring peculiar and exceptional qualifications of a scientific, managerial, professional, or educational character, as may be determined by the civil service board. In cities which do not have a merit system, municipal employees are appointed by the city secretary, city engineer, and heads of departments.

Generally speaking, city staff turnover is a problem throughout the state. Other than illness, death, family responsibilities, and pregnancy, the principal reasons for leaving city jobs are better pay and opportunity for advancement. According to facts derived from exit interviews conducted by personnel officials, the largest turnover is in the ranks of the laborers and junior clerks, or clerk-typists, who are at the bottom of the pay scale.

Steps that are being taken in some cities to combat the recruitment and turnover problem include increased pay, expansion of fringe benefits, improved classification plans, job-evaluation programs, employee-orientation programs, expansion of the testing and service-award programs, quarterly reports on all probationary or first-year employees, and expansion of employee-safety and employee-relations programs.

Financing Municipal Government

Taxes

A number of sources supply municipalities with revenue. All cities levy an ad valorem property tax, the rate of which cannot exceed twenty-five cents for each $100 of assessed property valuation in towns or villages. In other general-law and home-rule cities the tax rate may not exceed $1.50 and $2.50 respectively on each $100 of assessed property evaluation. The city councils in the general-law and home-rule cities need not levy the full amount. Cities may also levy a tax on specified occupations not to exceed one-half of the rate levied by the state.

When the city council approves a franchise ordinance for such firms as Lone Star Gas Company, Southwestern Bell Telephone Company, power-and-light companies, taxicab companies, and city-transportation companies, such concerns have the exclusive right (or without competition) to operate in the city. For this privilege they are regulated by the city and must pay a gross-receipts tax. The council must approve the charges, fares, rates, schedules (for transportation companies), and extension and improvement of services. The city may have a supervisor of public utilities who handles matters relating to franchises. In any event, the granting of franchises provides an important source of revenue for Texas cities.

By majority vote of the local voters voting on the issue, cities are authorized to impose a local sales-and-use tax of 1 percent on those items taxable under the state sales-and-use tax (optional municipal sales tax). The state comptroller of public accounts is responsible for the administration, collection, and enforcement of the tax. A city may not pledge anticipated revenue from the tax to secure payment of bonds or other indebtedness.

Cities and counties in which bars and clubs are located each receive 15 percent of the 10 percent state gross receipts tax on sales and service of liquor-by-the-drink paid by such businesses.

Charges and Fees

Most cities own their water and sewage disposal plants and are able to collect water and sewer payments for each connection. Some cities own their own electric power plants and transportation systems; other cities operate parking lots and public marketplaces. These services provide revenue for the cities. Some cities charge a fee for garbage collection and most cities secure revenue from the operation of municipal swimming pools and golf courses.

Other Local Sources of Revenue

Municipal court fines, licenses, inspections, permits, rentals, parking meters, and miscellaneous fees are a source of municipal revenue.

Federal Grants

Federal grants for urban renewal, hospitals, airports, sewage disposal plants, planning, as well as for other local activities and federal revenue sharing have supplemented municipal revenues.

Municipal Borrowing

The municipal budget finances all regular operations of the city; however, it accounts for only a portion of the total expenditures for any given year. The remainder includes items financed by the issuance of bonds. Texas municipalities may issue two types of bonds—general obligation and revenue bonds. General obligation bonds, approved by a majority of those voting in the city, are secured by the full faith and credit of the city. Revenue bonds are payable from the revenues of the property. Revenue bonds may be used to construct or expand water systems, sewer systems, sanitary disposal equipment, swimming pools, and so on. Although not actually a part of the operating budget, the bond funds are very much in the budget picture. It is to the advantage of the city to maintain a good bond rate, which means selling the bonds at a favorable interest rate.

Most cities need additional revenue. The tax base of municipalities could be broadened by the legislature. Federal property located in cities is not subject to local taxation and for this reason some local officials believe that the federal government should make payments to the cities.

Municipal and County Industrial (Tax-Exempt) Bonds

As a means of attracting industry, the Texas legislature has authorized cities, counties, towns, and other units of local government in the state to establish non-profit corporations. Such corporations must be approved by the Texas Industrial Commission, which regulates the program concerned with increasing industry in Texas and providing more jobs. These corporations are permitted to sell special tax-exempt, industrial revenue bonds to finance projects attractive to industry. Billions of dollars in bonds have been sold to finance purchases of industrial sites, construct buildings and/or expand existing facilities. Projects cleared for funding have included expansion of a meat-packing company to finance construction of a distribution center, building a manufacturing plant, and constructing and expanding other types of industrial plants. The city council or county commissioners court may appoint an industrial development board to screen applications for the low-interest bonds or loans.

Under the program the nonprofit corporations of the local governments sell tax-exempt bonds to investors and then lend the money from the bonds to private companies. The bond investor (lending institution) benefits because he is not taxed on his investment, or any interest earned on the loan, and the borrower benefits by a low interest rate. Since the interest on industrial bonds is exempt from the federal income tax, the interest rates are lower than on private commercial loans. The bonds are paid off by the private commercial companies, and the local governments are not obligated to pay them off in case of default. This is provided for in the covenant or contract entered into by the local governments and private companies. Facilities built with the bonds' proceeds go on the property tax rolls.

The industrial revenue bond program has been criticized because: (1) it has reduced federal tax revenues; (2) questionable projects such as fast-food restaurants have been built under it; and (3) it competes with municipal bonds and provides a competitive advantage for the company receiving the bonds.

In decisions of the U.S. Supreme Court, a distinction was made between state functions that were "governmental" and those of a "business" or "proprietary" nature. Governmental functions were said to be immune from federal taxation, but when a state entered an ordinary business, as for example the liquor business, that state was not immune from the national excise tax on liquor dealers. This imposed on the Court the difficult task of determining in specific cases whether a particular function of a state was governmental or proprietary in nature. Does the creation of a municipal or county industrial corporation to promote various private business enterprises constitute a governmental or a proprietary function of the local government?

The federal Internal Revenue Service (IRS) and Congress have considered a change in tax policy; that is, the interest earned on state and local government bonds would be subject to the federal income tax. However, the lending institutions, as well as the state and local governments, and various business interests, can exert considerable pressure on Congress and the IRS to protect their own interests.

The promotion of economic growth could be considered a proper "governmental function" since the American Revolution. The national, state, and local governments instituted many programs over the years to accomplish this objective. Thus, should municipal and county industrial bonds be entitled to a tax benefit?

Municipal Elections

The federal civil rights law requires municipalities to secure preclearance from the U.S. Department of Justice for any action that has an impact upon voting and elections. For example, a city might annex an area which was predominantly a white residential area. Such annexation could dilute the voting strength of black voters. Or the election of all city council members by election-at-large might prevent the election of minority candidates to the city council—or at least prevent a fair representation of minorities on the city council.

The city council of San Antonio is considered a pure district plan of council representation since each of the ten members of the council are elected from individual districts, with the mayor elected from the city at large. On the other hand, the city of Houston has the mixed city council plan since nine of the fourteen members of the council are elected from individual districts, while the mayor and the remaining five council members are elected at large. The Houston plan has been upheld by the federal courts.

What has been the impact of the pure and mixed district plans upon minority voting? Some studies that have been made indicate there has been little or no change in the percentage of minority voting; that is, no great change in the percent of qualified minority voters as compared with minority voting in at-large city council elections. However, minorities have secured representation on city councils as a result of the pure and mixed-district plans of election and this alone justifies the termination of all members of city councils being elected at large.

The change from at-large election of city council members to the pure and mixed-district plans appears to have had little or no impact on budget allocations, the providing of municipal services, or the municipal bureaucracy in general. For example, in the low income sections of Texas cities there appears to be little or no improvement in police protection, roads, parks, and other city services.

The municipal reform movement of the progressive era had an important impact upon shaping the distribution of political power and authority in municipal politics. (The Progressive party was organized in 1912 by followers of Theodore Roosevelt with a program of direct primaries, extension of the franchise to women, the initiative, referendum, and recall. The National Progressive party was established in 1924 under the leadership of Robert M. LaFollette and the American political party by Henry A. Wallace in 1948.)

Among the structural reforms advocated by the leaders of the Municipal Reform Movement were nonpartisanship, at-large elections, smaller city councils, and council-manager and commission government. The concept of nonpartisanship advocated the elimination of state and national political parties from local politics. It was argued that the relevance of state and national parties to local politics was minimal and thus these organizations served only to confuse voters in making decisions regarding local issues and candidates. It was also argued that local party organizations facilitated the intrusion into local communities of national and state party corruption and graft which culminated in the establishment of party-dominated local political machines. . . .

The electoral base of the municipal reformers was not the ethnic voter who was the base of the political machine, but rather a coalition comprised primarily of elements of the upper class business elite, middle class entrepreneurs, small businessmen, and other elements of the middle classes.

The formal elimination of party organizations from local politics did not lead to the elimination of "all" organizations from local politics. In many communities there developed a political organization which serves many of the same functions as a traditional political party. Such organizations can be described as nonpartisan slating groups. A nonpartisan slating group (NPSG) is a voluntary political organization which recruits, nominates, finances, and campaigns on behalf of a "slate," i.e., group, of candidates for office in a nonpartisan electoral system. Of paramount importance is the function that the NPSG serves in providing this group of candidates an *organizational label* which links them to one another and especially identifies the candidates as a group to the electorate. In functioning as a local political party the NPSG has promoted the political interests of the members of the reform electoral base. The NPSG can then be understood as the formalization of the political power and political influence of the reform electoral base in such a way as to further guarantee the political dominance of this new political cleavage.

Although the presence of NPSGs varies nationwide, these organizations have dominated local [politics] in many cities. The cities of Dallas, San Antonio, Abilene, and Wichita Falls in Texas have each had such organizations operate as primary actors in municipal politics. The role of such groups in the distribution of political power and authority in local communities provides a new dimension through which the contemporary impact of the Municipal Reform Movement can be understood. It is evident that these organizations can be the most important actors determining both electoral outcomes and policy decisions in local communities.

However, the success of these groups has not been monolithic. Their success is enhanced and constrained by formal and informal characteristics of the communities within which they exist. A comprehensive understanding of the role of these groups in local politics can be gained by specifying the interaction of formal (nonpartisanship, structure of government), quasi-formal (slating group), and informal (class, race, ethnicity) characteristics of local communities. The variable rates of success of NPSGs can be attributed to the degree to which each of these factors and their interaction facilitate the predominance of such an organization, and therefore the political interests it represents, in local politics.[4]

In many Texas cities, a very small percent of the qualified voters actually vote in municipal elections.

17   The Metropolitan Problem

THE DISPERSAL OF PEOPLE and business, or the outward movement from the central city to the outlying sections, has been due to a number of factors. The automobile, highways, and improved commercial transportation, have played a vital role in the ever-increasing number of commuters. In some cases city dwellers followed the industrial plants as they left the city. The availability of land and lower taxes, the prestige of the suburbs, high cost of rebuilding in the city, unpleasant living conditions of the large urban center (congestion, blighted areas, small lots, excessive street traffic, and the increase in crime), and the desire to live in the country have encouraged the outward resettlement.

Some families that were caught in the suburban movement for some reason became dissatisfied with suburban living and returned to the city. For some it was urban life regained and a better understanding and appreciation of living and working in the city.

Because of the movement of people from rural to urban areas, and from cities to suburban sections, and from outlying places back to the city, the distinction between rural and urban life does not have the meaning it once had. Most Texans live either in central cities or in one of the satellites that form a part of the metropolitan complex. As in many other states, urbanization in Texas is proceeding at a rapid pace.

Many inhabitants residing in the satellites of the central cities have discovered that their habits, tastes, and attitudes are essentially urban. They look to the central city for employment, culture, and entertainment. In a political sense, the metropolitan area does not exist. It has no constitution, no officials, no boundaries, and no single areawide government. Hence, there is no coordinated approach to dealing with the pressing governmental problems of metropolitan areas.

The age of the suburban man—or the age in which large numbers of people work at places where they do not want to live and live at places where they do not want to work—has produced a serious financial issue. Many living in the suburban areas earn their living in the central city and enjoy the benefits of the city dwellers but assume none of the financial burden. The suburbanites pay municipal and school taxes, and possibly a special district tax, in the areas in which they live, but may pay no local property taxes in the central city.

Municipal Incorporation and Disincorporation

Sometimes a community will incorporate to prevent the area from being annexed by another municipality, or the people in the unincorporated area may see a chance to incorporate in order to secure taxes upon industrial or other property located beyond the boundaries of adjoining cities. It may be that business firms would support incorporation, since taxes in a smaller city might be lower than taxes in a larger annexing city. Supporters of incorporation may contend that such a step would prove profitable to the residents because of lower insurance and utility rates, increased loans on homes, lower taxes, and the availability, in a shorter time and at a cheaper rate, of basic services (water, sewage disposal, electricity, and garbage collection). Frequently a larger annexing city, because of rapid expansion and prior commitments, may find it impossible to extend basic services, as bus service, fire and police protection, street paving, and utilities to the newly annexed area as quickly as desired by the people living there. For these and other reasons the residents in the unincorporated area may believe it is to their advantage to incorporate.

The postincorporation period may reveal that incorporation and basic services come at too high a price, that the tax and utility rate, as well as the cost of operating government in general is more expensive than being annexed. Hence, there may be a vote to disincorporate in order to make annexation possible.

Growth of the central city in the metropolitan area may be limited by one or more incorporations near its territorial boundaries. These "island" or "bedroom" cities have caused a considerable amount of friction between the central cities and incorporated places. The multiplicity of governmental units, whether by municipal incorporation or the establishment of special districts, may hinder the overall metropolitan problem.

Annexation and Disannexation

Annexation and disannexation should be preceded by adequate planning. Many cities in Texas do not have planning agencies and in some cities where such agencies do exist they are not fully utilized.

Annexation is the most common device used in Texas to cope with the problem of metropolitanism. A number of factors enter into the economic aspects of annexation. For example, if special districts are to be annexed, one would have to consider the bonded indebtedness the city would assume under the annexation program. Annexation adds taxable property to the city tax roll. This fact, plus the normal tax-value increase in the annexing city, increases municipal revenues. Other than the matter of increased tax revenue, and the extent to which it will offset the cost of providing services to the annexed area, there are additional long-range factors to be considered. As the annexed area is built up, assessed property values increase and the expansion of business and employment, as well as the enlargement of the metropolitan market, tends to promote the economic well-being of the community.

Annexation may offer certain benefits to the people living in the annexed area.

In unincorporated areas rates and charges for various services may be considerably higher than in the annexing city because private companies may pick up garbage and operate the water and sewage systems. Electric and telephone rates may be lower once annexation is completed, and fire protection provided by the city should reduce the premium on fire insurance.

Cities continue to annex territory even though some are unable to meet current demands for fire and police protection, street maintenance and construction, health services, recreation, and other services within existing boundaries. Should a city take on additional burdens when it is experiencing serious difficulty in fulfilling existing obligations? The annexing city may feel that unless it continues to expand, new incorporations or annexation by other cities will prevent or limit future growth. So annexation continues despite the problem of providing services.

As observed earlier, the annexation procedure for home-rule cities depends upon the provisions in the charter. The decision to annex rests with the home-rule cities. This exclusive judgment and unilateral action has resulted in selective annexation. An area may not be annexed despite the fact that the fringe residents have requested to become a part of the adjoining city. If a fringe area lacks adequate taxpaying ability to finance a reasonable share of the cost of municipal services, there may be little or no interest in annexing it. To protect the health and social and economic well-being of the community, annexation may become necessary, although the immediate economic returns may not justify the action.

The desire to attract business and industry has contributed to selective annexation. Business firms may secure a guarantee from a city, before locating outside municipal limits, that a certain section will not be annexed within a given number of years, and the city may agree to annex a circle or buffer zone around the industry to prevent annexation by some other city. This immunity from annexation makes it possible for a firm to locate in the vicinity without paying city taxes until annexed.

A city may annex a strip of land between or around one or more cities to control their growth and thereby prevent any interference with its own expansion. The municipal-annexation law provides that cities may annex territory only within the confines of their extraterritorial jurisdiction. This limitation does not apply to the annexation of property owned by the city. Also the law provides "buffer zones" around cities. Therefore, a city may only annex unincorporated and contiguous territory within its own extraterritorial jurisdiction and outside the buffer zone of another city. Thus, a city has some protection against "strip" and "circle" annexation.

Smaller cities in the county may annex land far beyond present needs in order to prevent annexation by the central city with the probable increase in the tax rate and bonded indebtedness, depending upon the assessed valuation of the area annexed. There have been instances where some municipalities in the county have attempted to reach a "gentleman's agreement" in regard to future annexations. Such intermunicipal discussions have had little effect in resolving the annexation problem.

Annexation has not proved wholly adequate in providing a solution for the problems of metropolitan areas. Texas's annexation laws were designed principally to enable cities to cope with developing fringe areas contiguous to their boundaries.

Yet, developments in metropolitan areas seldom follow this simple pattern. An increase in population and industrial activity may take place in old or new communities several miles from the city's corporate limits and not contiguous to the city. The liberality of the laws under which a Texas community may incorporate makes the problem more difficult. One incorporated area cannot annex another incorporated area, and for this reason areas incorporate to prevent being annexed.

By ordinance a city council may vote to disannex territory. If the land detached is not annexed by some other city it may in time incorporate, provided it has a minimum population of two hundred. The area disannexed is responsible for its pro rata share of the city's debts. The city council that detaches an area may levy an additional ad valorem tax each year on property in the disannexed area at the same rate as that levied on property within the city, and such taxation may be continued until the area has paid its pro rata share of the city's indebtedness.

Special Districts

Many types of special districts, including conservation, drainage, navigation, water, and hospital districts have been created in Texas. These and other special districts represent another approach to the metropolitan problem in the state.

As a means of implementing the conservation amendments of 1904 and 1917, the legislature has authorized the creation of water districts. Water-control and improvement districts (WCID) may be organized for one or more of the purposes set forth in the conservation amendment of 1917. In addition to the water-control and improvement districts, the legislature has authorized the creation of fresh-water supply districts (FWSD) as agencies for securing and distributing water to domestic and commercial consumers. In certain of the larger urban counties, the water districts have assumed additional responsibilities such as sewage disposal, fire protection, and regulation of plumbing.

Whenever a water-control and improvement district has been organized by the granting of a petition by the commissioners' court or by the Texas water rights commission, and the directors of the district have qualified, an election is held in the district for the purpose of confirming the organization of the district by a vote of the qualified resident voters. Only a simple majority of those voting are required to approve the district and elect directors. In some cases the issue has been decided by as few as two persons voting. Fresh-water supply districts are created in a similar manner.

Since the fresh-water supply districts (FWSDs) are more rigidly controlled by the statutes, they are less popular than the water-control and improvement districts (WCIDs). In most cases the FWSDs are restricted to the two basic functions of a water district—providing water and sewer service. In general, the WCIDs are granted broader powers. They may pick up garbage, engage in flood control, and in some cases establish their own police force. The FWSDs cannot sell their bonds at discounts up to 10 percent as the WCIDs are permitted to do. The five elected supervisors in each FWSD must be both property owners and residents of the district. The five elected directors of a WCID must be property owners in the district but need not be residents (unless created by the Texas water rights commission, in which case at least three directors must be residents of the district).

Also, the legislature and the Texas department of water resources (TDWR) have authorized the establishment of municipal utility districts (MUDs) which have more expansive functions and thereby provide greater benefits for developers than either the WCIDs or FWSDs. In addition to drainage, water, and sewer facilities, MUDs may furnish fire-fighting services, solid-waste collection, and parks and recreational services.

These special purpose governments designed to facilitate land development by private interests have multiplied rapidly in Texas, especially along the upper Texas Gulf coast, and throughout the United States. As a result of providing housing for residents and essential services, the developers of these utility districts have contributed to the rapid economic growth in local areas. Needless to say, the utility districts, with some exceptions, have been very profitable for the developers.

Some of the special purpose governments were made operational by as few as two or three people approving a two or three million dollar bond issue; by a vote of the developer, his wife, and son or daughter. Also, in some cases relatives and employees of the district developer, as well as persons who served the developer in a professional capacity (lawyer, engineer, consultant, etc.), served on the board of directors or board of supervisors of the district. In some cases one or more members of the boards were party to a contract with the developer. And it is possible that district contracts were entered into with firms within a family circle. Finally, the legislature passed a law prohibiting relatives and employees of a district developer, as well as persons who serve the developer in a professional capacity, from serving as members of a water district board. Also, those party to a contract with the developer (other than a home purchase) are disqualified from serving on the board.

Since some districts were established in areas with few residents, the developer had no opportunity for broad participation in approval or disapproval of district bonds or the selection of persons to serve on the governing boards. In fact, most or all of the land in the prospective district may have been owned by the individual who desired to create the district. The creation of special purpose governments has been quite profitable for lawyers who may receive as legal fees a certain percent of the bond issue.

Various types of water districts have been created within unincorporated areas as well as within municipalities. An unincorporated area may incorporate as a water district rather than as a municipality; however, water districts do not have the same status as incorporated places. For one thing, water districts are organized for limited purposes and may be organized within, as well as annexed by, a municipality. Water districts perform many of the functions of cities, and for this reason they have been an aid to contractors and developers, especially in the unincorporated areas.

The water-district laws of Texas were conceived as a weapon to fight disease and discomfort. They were designed to help banish outdoor privies, septic tanks, and open water wells. However noble the purpose when the laws were passed, they have, on occasion, been distorted by land promotion schemes, private profiteering, and loose spending of public funds. On the other hand, many water districts have been created out of fear that the central city or some other municipality might take years to get service into the areas.

Municipalities have a vital interest in water districts created outside their territorial limits, for they in time may be annexed. An important question involved in the annexation of water districts is the matter of bonds. Bonds of WCIDs may originally be sold at a discount of up to 10 percent (or $900 for a $1,000 bond). Apparently the legislature provided the discount clause as an incentive to buyers of a sometimes risky venture when there was no city annexation. Because of the discount of bonds sold by WCIDs, and the favorable interest rate, water-district bonds are set up to yield a plump profit, at least on paper. However, there is always the chance that a water district will go bankrupt and default on its bonds. For this reason cautious bond buyers may not be eager to buy water-district bonds.

Annexation may transform risky water-district bonds into a blue-chip venture, since the financial resources of the annexing municipality stand behind the bonds. There have been instances where the sale of water-district bonds was contingent upon the district's annexation. When a water district and its bonded indebtedness are annexed, the water-district bonds may automatically jump to par value or higher. Such a situation may make it possible for bond speculators to reap a good harvest.

One of the reasons why special districts have been created in Texas is that financial limitations make it impossible for existing governmental units to undertake additional functions. Other special districts were created in order to permit the appointment of persons specially qualified for the tasks as directors and managers of the special districts. In some cases it was considered unwise to saddle county and municipal officials with additional responsibilities. In the case of school districts, tradition and a desire to disassociate them from county and municipal government politics account for their continuation as special districts.

The ease with which special districts can be established is a factor in their use; they are created under general or local law. From a legal point of view it is easier to create a special district than to abolish and consolidate governments. The special district approach is less comprehensive than most other methods, and for this reason it has wider appeal than either consolidation or federation. The fact that special districts are less comprehensive than some other approaches is one of the main reasons why local officials give their suport to the district idea. They regard other approaches as a threat to their governmental position. Few local officials favor the elimination or major alteration of local governments.

Municipal Consolidation

Cities incorporated under the general laws of the state may vote to terminate their corporate existence, and thereafter the disincorporated area may be consolidated with another city through the process of annexation. A vote to disincorporate is held on petition of one hundred qualified voters, and if a majority support dissolving the incorporation, the city ceases to exist as a corporate body. If the adjoining city with which consolidation is to be effected is a home-rule city, the annexation procedure is governed by the provisions of the charter; otherwise, if the adjoining city is incorporated under general law, the residents of the disincorporated area must petition for annexation. In either case, the city council makes the final decision, unless there is a court test, on the annexation ordinance.

State law also provides a method whereby municipalities that are contiguous may consolidate. If two adjacent cities are in the same county, they may amend their respective charters or articles of incorporation so as to permit consolidation under one government. As defined in the law, consolidation is the adoption by a smaller city (or cities) of the charter of the larger city and the amendment of the larger city's charter so as to include in its boundaries the territory of the smaller cities. There appears to be no legal procedure established for a home-rule city to abolish its existence other than by consolidation. One of the obstacles to consolidation by amendment of city charters is the provision of Article XI, Section 5 (the municipal home-rule amendment) of the Texas constitution "that no city charter shall be altered, amended or repealed oftener than every two years." The consolidated area takes the name of the larger city, unless otherwise provided at the time of consolidation, and the larger city takes over the books, records, assets, and debts of the entire area.

Nearly all municipal consolidations in Texas have taken place in the metropolitan areas of the state. The Baytown (Houston metropolitan area)-Pelly-Goose Creek consolidation was effected by ordinance, whereas the consolidation of Groves and Wesgroves (Beaumont-Port Arthur metropolitan area) was made possible by the dissolution of the corporate existence of Wesgroves. Apparently, the latter procedure (disincorporation-annexation) was followed in the consolidation of Preston Hollow with Dallas and Castle Heights with Waco. The cities of Velasco and Freeport voted to consolidate. The merger was approved by a five-to-one landslide in Freeport, but carried only by a narrow thirteen-vote margin in Velasco. The consolidated city is governed by Freeport city officials and under Freeport city regulations.

Extraterritorial Control by Municipalities

Cities sometimes exercise control over growth outside corporate limits with two objectives: to prevent premature or overambitious annexation programs of cities by giving them some control over the outlying areas and to provide a method whereby residents of the fringe areas are not required to pay city taxes until the area is completely integrated with the city and has access to all municipal services. The objectives, if realized, are designed to promote the interests of both the city exercising the extraterritorial control and the residents living in the fringe area.

Cities may exercise extraterritorial jurisdiction over surrounding unincorporated and contiguous areas, or "buffer zones," ranging from one-half mile for cities of less than 5,000 to five miles around cities of 100,000 or more population. Upon the request of property owners of contiguous territory, the extraterritorial jurisdiction of a city may be extended beyond its existing extraterritorial limits. When a city annexes additional areas, its extraterritorial jurisdiction expands in conformity with the annexation. One city's extraterritorial jurisdiction may not conflict with that of another. No city may impose any tax in the area under extraterritorial jurisdiction.

A city may by ordinance extend its regulations governing plats and the subdivision of land to its buffer zone. Whenever a tract of land within the area under extraterritorial jurisdiction is divided into two or more parts for the purpose of subdividing, or for laying out suburban or building lots, street, alleys, or parks, the city may require a plat of the subdivision. The city may require that the plat be approved by the city planning commission or by the city council in the absence of a planning commission. As a condition of approval, the city may insist that the proposed subdivision conform to the general plan of the city and its streets, alleys, parks, playgrounds, and public utilities, as well as comply with its regulations concerning health, safety, morals, and the general welfare.

Extraterritorial control of some cities in Texas is ineffective. Ordinances regulating plats and the subdivision of land within the city are inadequate and their extension to the buffer zone provides inadequate regulation in these areas. Some cities have not passed ordinances extending platting and subdivision of land regulations to their buffer zones. Subdividers have circumvented platting requirements by selling land by metes and bounds.* This practice is not considered "subdividing" and enables the developer to evade city regulations. Subdivision development beyond buffer zones, which is rather extensive in some areas, is not under the control of cities.

Cities also control growth outside corporate limits through agreements worked out with subdividers and water districts. The city does possess a certain amount of bargaining power. It may make annexation, approval of a plat, or the extension of municipal services dependent upon compliance with city rules and regulations. After all, a subdivider is under considerable pressure from various sources to request annexation by the neighboring city in order to develop and finance successfully a subdivision. To secure the cooperation of the city, the developer may be required to install sewers, water mains, pavement, curbs, gutters, and sidewalks. If the city does not have a refund policy, the subdivider may be required to provide all facilities at his own expense and later donate them to the city. Some difficulty has been experienced by cities in extending trunk lines where subdivisions have "leapfrogged," which results from the promotion of a subdivision in an area where land is cheaper than that adjacent to the city. This may mean the extension of utilities over undeveloped land, thereby tremendously increasing the cost of extending water and sewer lines to such areas. Some cities refuse to extend water and sewer lines to an area unless it is platted; consequently a developer must subdivide the property according to municipal regulations.

The legislature has delegated to the governing bodies of cities the authority to enact quarantine regulations to prevent the introduction of contagious diseases into the cities. These quarantine regulations may be enforced up to a maximum of ten miles beyond the city limits. The cities were also authorized to cooperate with the county commissioners' court in the various counties to establish joint sanitary regulations as might be necessary, and to arrange for the construction and financing of such improvements. The same article of the state law authorizes the governing body of the cities to provide water for the city and adjacent territory. As early as 1875, the legislature gave cities the power to "establish, maintain and regulate pest houses or hospitals at some place within or not exceeding five miles beyond the city limits."

---

*"Metes" denotes the measured distance; "bounds" denotes the natural or artificial marks that indicate their beginning and ending.

Municipal and County Planning

In the absence of a planning commission, the planning function is assumed by the city council and the city engineer. Planning commissions, at times, have not been fully utilized in studying individual annexations and planning for future growth of the city. Frequently, the city planning commission lacks adequate powers.

In some counties subdivisions in the unincorporated areas of the county are approved by the county commissioners' court upon the recommendation of the county engineer. The counties have power to adopt a county plan for roads and highways, and the commissioners' court may disapprove any proposed new plats and subdivisions that are inconsistent with the county road plan.

County regulations may stipulate that subdivision roads must have at least six inches of compacted base and a hard surface of either cement, asphalt, or black top, and that drainage ditches be sloped and cleared of debris in order that they drain properly. If subdivision roads and ditches do not meet these standards, the commissioners' court is not obligated to take them over for maintenance purposes. If the county should take over substandard subdivision roads, county tax dollars would be used to subsidize developers; otherwise, homebuyers would be caught in the lurch with badly deteriorating roads.

Some counties have adopted regulations governing the installation of privately owned sewer systems and the expansion of existing sewer systems. By orders of the county commissioners' court, the county health department may be authorized to issue permits for sewer facilities and to fine offenders. Anyone wanting to install a septic tank, chemical toilet, treatment tank or other sewage disposal system may be required to pay an inspection fee and construction may be required to follow standards established by state law. Percolation tests may be required by the county to determine if the soil can adequately absorb any effluents. No private sewer system may be installed within so many feet of an existing, publicly owned sewer system, and the lot or tract on which it is installed must meet minimum standards as to size.

As a result of a written agreement between Houston and Harris County, the city does most of the major planning for the entire metropolitan area. For the service, the county pays the city an annual fee. The agreement provides for the city to administer all subdivision control in unincorporated areas within five miles of the city limits; develop and maintain a major thoroughfare plan; make studies of the location of recreational areas; advise the county in its bond program for roads; and maintain statistics on population and growth.

Contractual Arrangements

There are many examples of contractual arrangements in urban counties as a partial solution to the metropolitan problem. Central cities may contract to provide basic services to areas beyond corporate limits. Certain joint programs, like city-county hospital and city-county welfare programs, are maintained, usually with much contention over the apportionment of costs, by contractual arrangement between the central city and the county. These and other contractual arrangements resulted from necessity or the inability of finding any other practical way of handling the functions. Such efforts are of limited application.

Informal Cooperation Between Government Units

Metropolitan areas in Texas and other states have found informal cooperation between governmental units useful. For example, municipal fire departments cooperate with each other in time of emergency inside and outside corporate limits. It is common for cities, as a means of protecting themselves, to provide some fire, police, and health protection beyond city limits. Municipal police departments may monitor the radio facilities operated by the county. In fact all governments, whether national or local, have found informal cooperation mutually advantageous.

Councils of Governments (COGs)

A council of governments (COG) or a regional planning agency has been established in the metropolitan areas in Texas under authority of state law. For example, the North Central Texas council of governments (NCTCOG—the Dallas-Fort Worth urban area and its environs) is a voluntary association of local governments represented by elected officials from counties, municipalities, school districts, and special districts in the North Central Texas region.

The organization of the councils of governments is not always the same. The general assembly of the North Central Texas council of governments is composed of elected officials, one representing each member government, and a number of citizen representatives. Each year the general assembly adopts an annual budget and determines membership dues based on current population; and these funds are supplemented by federal and state grants.

A state coordination agency—the division of planning coordination—was established in the governor's office. It makes state funds available to the councils of governments and regional planning commissions for specific programs. The councils of governments have no powers of taxation or enforcement; therefore they are not governments.

The councils of governments seek to resolve areawide problems through intergovernmental cooperation and coordination; to conduct and supervise metropolitan and urban-regional planning; and to provide a forum in which areawide problems can be discussed and resolved.

If a city seeks federal aid to build a sewage-treatment plant, a check must be made of the application to verify that the plant will not interfere with plans for a city park in another city. Pollution control and the design of highways and freeways throughout the urban area involve the need for coordinated regional planning. Local projects should conform to the overall needs and plans of the greater metropolitan area.

Many federal grants-in-aid to local governments require that their applications have the approval of a comprehensive planning agency. The North Central Texas council of governments has been designated as the areawide review agency. Applications by local governments for various federal loans or grants must be submitted to NCTCOG for review and comment.

Although the review and comment function is advisory, it tends to enhance the prestige of the regional planning agency, "for it is generally believed that a favorable review at the regional level is more likely to produce a more sympathetic and speedy response at higher levels.''¹ "The regional planning agency may take into account any violation of its regional plans in reviewing federal grant applications submitted by member governments, thus encouraging each member government to implement and enforce regional plans as those plans apply within its jurisdiction.''² Much depends on whether adequate regional plans have been formulated and approved and if such plans are a major consideration in approving or disapproving federal-grant applications.

Some of the councils of governments have made a survey of regional building, electrical, plumbing, and fire codes and development standards. There is a lack of uniformity in codes used in the various regions, as well as a shortage of qualified personnel to administer codes. This situation has created a serious problem for local governments; increased costs, confusion, and delays in the matter of codes. In time regional codes may be adopted.

The North Central Texas council of governments established a regional police academy and hundreds of police officers in the region have benefited from the academy's courses.

The councils of governments and regional planning agencies, with the encouragement of the federal government, have stimulated a greater interest in regional planning in Texas.

Other Approaches to the Metropolitan Problem

Many of the approaches to the metropolitan problem involve the consolidation of both governmental units and functions as well as the creation, reorganization, and strengthening of local governing authorities. Other approaches are concerned more with the physical features of cities. For example, all large urban areas in Texas are confronted with a traffic problem that requires the construction of expressways, freeways, and loops around cities for through traffic. Also, there are many different types of pedestrian-oriented schemes in operation or in the planning stage.

Suburban business and shopping centers are desirable and necessary as a part of the overall growth of urban places. Many businessmen feel this growth should not be at the expense of deterioration and blight in the downtown area, which traditionally has represented a high concentration of business activities and property and tax values. To discourage the "flight to the suburbs" by keeping the shoppers interested in downtown is one of the major objectives of these plans. They are an attempt to preserve the central business area of the city as the economic center of the community.

The Federated Metropolis

The federated metropolis has been suggested for urban areas that have a large number of incorporated suburbs. Under such a plan the suburbs would retain identity but would transfer certain powers that were of regional concern to a central government.

The federation plan would involve the establishment of a metropolitan government to handle metropolitan functions. Such an arrangement would require constitutional and legislative authorization. Besides this problem there would be the

matter of distributing the powers between the local units and the central government and providing local representation on the governing body of the metropolitan
government.

City-County Consolidation

The consolidation of city and county government is designed to eliminate duplication of governments within an area. It is difficult to devise an acceptable procedure by which consolidation may be carried out. Officials of the government to be
consolidated are not sympathetic, as a general rule, to consolidation.

City-County Separation

Under this arrangement the central city and adjacent urban areas may be separated from the rural part of the county, and the city and county consolidated in the
new city area. City-county separation divides the existing county without abolishing any existing governmental units. Taxpayers who object to the city assuming a
large share of the tax burden for the rural area may support city-county separation.
Since most of the taxable wealth may be located in the new city-county area, the
rural or rump county might run into financial difficulties.

As population spreads beyond the city-county limits, it may be difficult for the
consolidated unit to annex territory. Where population does spill over the city-
county boundary, a suburbanized rump county may develop and thereby somewhat relieve the tax problem of the county lying outside the consolidated area.

Traffic Management in Urban Areas

The Texas department of highways and transportation plays a major role in traffic management in urban areas. Through the joint efforts of the cities and the department, a number of techniques in the matter of traffic management have
evolved, some of which include the following: synchronization of traffic lights,
which permits a motorist to drive continuously through a series of green traffic
lights; sensitization, which keeps traffic moving through intersections until a motorist drives over the metal plate built into the side or connecting street; "contra-
flow" lanes for buses and other high-occupancy vehicles (at peak traffic periods
such lanes are reserved for buses and vans to move in an opposite direction to the
traffic); concurrent-flow lanes, referred to as "transitway" (such lanes do not affect the ordinary traffic flow and the middle lane is reserved for high occupancy
vehicles); double and triple overpasses for automobiles; high rise parking; underground parking; bypass highways that do not run through the central business district; and car-share and van-pool programs.

On some streets and highways where there is excessive traffic, cities have installed a signal preemption device for buses known as "opticom." The opticom
system can change a red light to green or prolong an already green light, giving a
bus time to move through an intersection. However, the signal will not change if
doing so would pose a safety hazard to pedestrian or vehicular traffic. A similar
system for trains at rail crossings has been in existence for some time. The opticom system works with the flip of a switch, which the bus driver manipulates from
a small box. A green light may be prolonged only for a given number of seconds.
Thus, only a short convoy of motorists may follow the designated buses through

the manipulated traffic signals. The light immediately changes once the bus is through the intersection. The device operates in any weather and at night. Buses approaching an intersection at the same time use the system on a first come, first served basis. However, pedestrians and cross-traffic have an opportunity to clear the intersection before the light changes. Some cities also use opticom for emergency vehicles such as fire trucks and ambulances.

A city may have a downtown tunnel system or underground walkways (as in the city of Houston). As it is good business to get connected to the system, a large number of buildings may be strung together by the underground walkway to form a continuous system through downtown. In the tunnel system major buildings and parking facilities may provide direct access to the various tunnel connections, and a number of shops and restaurants may operate at various points along the tunnels. Such a network takes some of the pressure off the street traffic, is safer and more convenient for the public, and provides protection in the event of a military emergency.

Bicycle traffic continues to expand in the urban areas and is an important component of traffic management. Some cities have constructed off-street bicycle lanes with a blacktop or concrete base, but this approach is quite expensive and land may not be available. Bicycle *routes* and bicycle *paths* have been established in the cities, and are so designated by an appropriate sign along the streets. Lanes are marked off that parallel the street curbs. The bicycle routes are reserved for those who ride bicycles, since one may not legally drive or park an auto within the area reserved for bicycles. If automobiles are parked within the bicycle paths, bicyclists are forced into the regular automotive part of the street; this can be dangerous for both bicyclist and motorist. Bicyclists and motorists must obey the traffic regulations and respect each other's rights; all too often this has not been the case.

The traffic problem in the metropolitan areas has encouraged cities to establish commuter express bus routes in the city and a metropolitan transit authority (MTA) which was authorized by the Texas legislature. The MTA is composed of the MTA board and a director. Cities within the metro complex, through action of their mayors and city councils, may join MTA. The cities are assessed a fee for the service and the individual commuters pay to help finance the organization.

A state law in Texas gives municipalities the right to withdraw from a taxing authority if 90 percent of its population live outside the boundaries of the authority's base county. Some cities that associated with the Houston MTA voted to withdraw from the organization. Various city officials believe the state law should be amended to permit any city that has a border outside the boundaries of the authority's base county to vote on leaving the MTA. Such an amendment to the law would, no doubt, create serious financial problems for MTA.

Various problems may arise once an MTA is operational; for example, the employment and retention of qualified directors; the purchase and repair of quality MTA buses; and most important, providing good service—at reasonable price—for the commuters in the metropolitan complex.

Garbage and Litter

As population and industry expand in the metropolitan areas, there has been a corresponding increase in the volume of garbage and litter, and environmental pollution. In fact, the saturation point has been reached in some areas.

The traditional landfill method of garbage disposal is no longer practical in some populated areas. This method requires deep trenches to be prepared by heavy equipment; the trucking of garbage to the disposal site; burning and covering over the remains with soil; and the re-use of the area after the lapse of a number of years. In some areas, the day of the landfill is nearly over, since environmental regulations increase operating expenses, and, most important, land is becoming more scarce, and landfill areas are located at great distances from the living areas of the cities. The main concern of municipalities is to dispose of garbage at the lowest possible cost. It is not a matter of recovering materials or even the production of energy. These things are important only insofar as they lower garbage disposal cost. Land once used for solid-waste landfill operations, or land set aside for such purpose, has become valuable real estate which has been added to the property tax base of the city.

In some cities tons of garbage have been transformed into fertilizer, low-grade fuel, and millions of kilowatts of electricity. The trend is towards the development of resource-recovery technology—high technology waste-to-energy systems which convert garbage into needed energy while providing an environmentally safe method of garbage disposal that eliminates the need for landfill operations. Not only have the new methods proven workable, they are rapidly becoming the only disposal methods open to municipalities in the densely populated regions. With "wall to wall people," resource recovery (or possibly some other technique) has become an absolute necessity for the overpopulated areas. Thus, one notes a growing interest in waste-to-energy generation. There is little wonder why solid-waste management is so important today, and in many areas regional disposal plans have or will replace local operations.

The New York and New Jersey legislatures approved legislation authorizing the port authority of New York and New Jersey to build industrial parks supplied by cheap, refuse-derived energy. Although the primary need for the area is waste disposal as landfills become scarce, the port authority's idea of linking industrial parks with disposal solutions also was designed to aid the manufacturing sector.

In some cities landfills have been established near, or above, underground or other sources of an area's water supply. Thus, there are risks of leaking dangerous pollutants into the water supply. Some of these are: methane (formed by the decomposition of vegetable matter); lead, arsenic (used in making insecticides, glass, and medicines); radioactive wastes or atomic garbage (capable of giving off energy in the form of particles or rays); insecticides (any substance used to kill insects); mercury (used in thermometers, air pumps, dentistry, pharmacy, etc.); zinc (used as a protective coating for iron and as a constituent in salt and medicine); cyanide (used in extracting gold from low-grade ores and case-hardening of steel); and fertilizers and bacterial toxins (produced by some microrganisms and causing certain diseases). As a result of the dangers involved, landfills have been closed—in some cases by federal court order.

However, the decision to establish resource-recovery facilities in an area also presents problems. Such facilities are a part of the expanding industrial society and may further endanger the environment unless the environmental regulations are enforced.

Some cities have contracted with private corporations to collect and dispose of garbage; nevertheless, the problems relating to the traditional landfills and resource-recovery facilities remain.

Litter has also created serious problems in all cities, regardless of size. Garbage is waste parts of food, as from a residence, market, or kitchen. Yet, garbage trucks pick up a variety of items in addition to food waste. On the other hand, litter refers to items scattered about in a careless manner and may include food waste as well as other items. Frequently, much of litter is uncollected garbage drifting about.

We live a throwaway lifestyle, as evidenced by the cartons, bottles, and other items that can be found almost everywhere—in residential yards and streets, on public school grounds and parks, at the zoo, around drive-in stores and large businesses, at filling stations, drive-in parks along the highways, and many other places too numerous to mention. The litter problem is everyone's problem, or should be. Unless a city or nation develops a strong tradition over a period of years for cleanness and pride, there is little chance that significant changes will be made. Various types of crash programs might well be only temporary in character. The increase in population and urbanization, along with more bottles, cartons, and throwaway items increases the possibility of more and more litter.

Part Three

Government Functions

---

18   Public Welfare

THE PROMOTION OF THE general welfare—or the welfare of the people—is as old as democratic government itself. However, as has been true of all government programs, the evolving social consciousness of government has witnessed greater expansion in some periods of history than in others. And some welfare programs have been terminated, modified, or expanded as the need arose which indicates the ever-changing nature or dynamics of democratically conceived programs enacted by popularly elected legislative bodies.

Over the years, public welfare has encompassed a great variety of programs, for example, government ownership and operation of highways, schools, colleges and universities, parks and playgrounds, museums and art centers, hospitals and clinics, libraries, and utilities at the local government level. In addition to these types of programs, there are various types of social insurance programs (Old Age, Survivors, and Disability Insurance; Medicare; Medicaid; unemployment insurance; and Workmen's Compensation); public assistance for the needy, the aged, dependent children, the blind, the physically and mentally handicapped, the orphans, and the totally disabled; and health care, food, and legal assistance for the needy. It is assumed that these and other types of government programs are necessary and desirable functions of governments.

There has been considerable diversity in financing welfare programs. Some have been financed entirely by the federal, state, or local governments. Others have been jointly financed by the federal and state governments, by the state and local governments, or by the cooperative efforts of all three levels of government. In some programs the financing is assumed by the employer and in other programs by the employer and employees.

The expansion of welfare programs has raised a number of critical issues and problems in the field of welfare management. What percent of public funds should be expended on various welfare programs? At what point should governments expand, halt, or cut back on welfare expenditures? What should be the welfare priorities? What is the impact of welfare spending, tax increases, and increase in wage deductions on economic growth? Also, there is the problem of abuse and mismanagement of the welfare programs. Rather than attempt to solve these and other problems, which are best left to the economists, legislative bodies, and administrators to ponder, we will focus our attention on the general aspects of welfare programs, many of which the student is familiar with.

The Social Security Program

Old Age, Survivors, and Disability Insurance (OASDI)

Under OASDI, which is administered by the federal Social Security administration, both employer and employee, if the firm or occupation is covered by federal law, pay a Social Security or withholding tax.

The original program has been enlarged by Congress to include benefits for wives and children of retired workers, for the survivors of deceased workers, and for disabled workers and their dependents. Besides additional dependents who have been made eligible, the program has been expanded to cover additional groups, and minimum monthly payments have been increased. Both men and women may retire at sixty-two (with benefits reduced 20 percent) instead of at the regular retirement age of sixty-five. When these changes were made, the law was amended to provide a schedule of increased contributions to cover the cost.

The contributions of employer and employee provide for the retirement benefits of the employee or survivors' insurance (upon death, before or after retirement, benefits accrue to survivors). Through the years the tax receipts in excess of current expenditures have been deposited in special trust funds at interest. These receipts and the interest completely finance the program, including administrative costs, without any subsidy from the general funds of the treasury. By law, these funds can be used only for Social Security purposes.

The only large group not eligible is the federal civil service, which has its own retirement system. There are, however, some 2 million employees of state and local governments who have not elected to be covered.

Old age assistance (OAA) is an outright monthly grant from federal funds to needy persons sixty-five years of age or over. For this reason, it is quite different from OASDI, which is a retirement program under Social Security in which contributions are made by the employer and employee. A person receiving OASDI is not necessarily disqualified from receiving OAA. In determining the need of the applicant for OAA, OASDI income is considered in the same manner as any other income or means of support.

Medicare

Medicare is a national program administered by the federal Social Security administration. It is a prepaid health insurance program for older people and is financed jointly by employer and employee contributions. Most individuals sixty-five years of age or older are eligible for benefits provided under the Medicare program.

Medicaid

Medicaid is a state program administered in Texas by the department of human resources. Persons of any age who are eligible to participate in the department's public assistance programs are automatically eligible for benefits under the Medicaid program. The needy recipients on the welfare rolls receive many of the same medical benefits as those received by the elderly under Medicare. The department also purchases, for old age assistance recipients, supplementary Medicare (medical insurance) benefits by paying the monthly premium of each recipient.

Payments for all Medicaid services, with certain exceptions, are administered through a contract with a private insurance firm. The department of human resources calls for bids on what may well be the largest single health insurance contract in the nation. The department pays premiums for health insurance for the needy, aged, blind, disabled adults, and dependent and foster-care children. The insuring agent in turn pays for health services for the welfare recipients. The department periodically renews its contract for administration of the program and solicits competitive bids.

Since the department of human resources pays the insurance premiums for Medicaid services, a limited type of socialized medicine has been established. In some countries, private individuals that are not classified as needy pay a certain amount each month for national health insurance, with considerable freedom to select their own doctors and hospitals. Or if an individual earns more than a certain income, he or she may have the option of being covered either by private or public health services. All democratic governments have provided some medical services to the needy, in one form or another.

Most physicians, hospitals, and nursing homes in Texas participate in the Medicare and Medicaid programs. The increased cost of medical and hospital care has created a serious problem in the administration of the two programs and only limited services are provided. There has been abuse of the programs—by patients, charges by doctors, hospitals, and nursing homes for services not rendered, and overpayment of services.

The Social Security Problem

Since 1937, when Social Security taxes on covered employers and employees were first imposed, the tax and the amount of money paid in benefits has increased considerably. A Social Security crisis evolved over a number of years and the only significant remedial action taken was to increase the tax—a short-range approach, which did not consider the actuarial implications. However, this approach was understandable because Congress wished to keep the tax as low as possible while increasing benefits and the number of beneficiaries. Members of Congress realized the political implications in their districts and states as a result of an increase in the Social Security tax, benefits, and number of beneficiaries—especially in light of the fact that 90 percent or more of the people of the United States are covered by Social Security.

The Social Security system and the U.S. economy are closely interrelated. Consequently, a deterioration or expansion of the overall economy creates serious problems for the nation's largest retirement system. An economic deterioration could require that Congress do more than simply authorize the Social Security retirement fund to borrow from the disability and hospital insurance fund.

In addition to the condition of the U.S. economy, a number of other considerations contributed to the Social Security crisis. For example, there have been unexpected changes in the population makeup, including increased life-span; inflation, which automatically increases the cost-of-living benefits for those receiving Social Security payments; and high unemployment, which prompts many workers to retire early at sixty-two (with benefits reduced 20 percent). These changes add to the demand for benefits while denying the system tax revenues paid by the employer and employee.

With the growth of the population, the number of Social Security recipients has increased. However, the population increase also has expanded the number of employers and employees contributing to the system. The increase in population has an offsetting quality. Yet, the funds of the contributors do not keep pace with the increased number of beneficiaries and the funds they require. A decline in the birth rate limits the number of contributors that would in time pay Social Security taxes.

Congress has expanded Social Security benefits, thereby increasing the expenditure of funds. Also, an increase in unemployment with a decrease in contributions paid by employers and employees has a considerable impact upon financing the federal Social Security system.

The "crisis" in Social Security is due, in large measure, to Congress and its committees, who have had the responsibility for reviewing the system since its inception in 1937. The general public cannot be expected to make a significant contribution to the Social Security problem—especially when Social Security economists and members of Congress find the matter overwhelmingly complex. Evidently many people believed they could pay a few hundred dollars a year for twenty-five to thirty years and then receive several thousand dollars a year for fifteen to twenty years during retirement. Even the miracles of compound interest could not have provided such a profitable investment.

Unless Congress finds a solution to the Social Security problem, retirement benefits may become so burdensome in the future (as the ratio of older workers to younger ones increases, forcing younger people to pay more) that the public at some point in time may refuse to pay the price. It is understandable that younger workers, who contribute to the benefits of the retired, are so concerned about Social Security.

No government program is any stronger than its efficient management. Considering the great magnitude of the Social Security program one would anticipate— even in the computer world—serious problems of administration. Nevertheless, the administration of the Social Security program has been inadequate. It has been revealed that Social Security benefits have been paid to people in the United States and abroad, but used for the benefit of others. Also, benefits have been paid to dependents who are "paper adoptions," as well as to deportees from the United States. There should be no room for cheaters, domestic or foreign, in a program so strapped for funds and so important for retired and other Americans.

Prior to 1983, federal law permitted hospitals, nonprofit organizations, as well as state and local governments, to withdraw their employees from the Social Security program if a comparable program was provided. However, two years' notice had to be given prior to withdrawal. Employees could not get back into the system once coverage was terminated. These were the only employers for whom Social Security was optional. As a result of economic conditions in the 1970s and 1980s, a number of employers of these groups did withdraw their employees from the system. This, among other factors, endangered the solvency of the Social Security system.

Throughout the history of the American Social Security system, comparisons have been made concerning the benefits of private retirement plans to those of Social Security. Various retirement plans may have certain advantages when compared with Social Security: they may maximize take-home pay; they may pay higher retirement benefits; they may allow earlier retirement; they do not reduce an individual's retirement benefit if one becomes employed after retiring; retirement date is voluntary; payments made to the private plan are tax deductible; and employees may put more of their money in the system for a greater return. However, many of the retirement plans that cities and counties prior to 1983 substituted for Social Security did not offer anything comparable to the disability and survivors' benefits or Medicare hospital insurance under Social Security. Also, many of the private and group plans do not increase benefits with the cost of living or give employees the same permanent pension rights known as "vesting" (to place authority, property rights, etc., in the control of a person or group), and cannot be transferred from job to job. Indeed, these features of Social Security were important considerations, for example, for some cities and counties that decided not to withdraw their employees from Social Security. Also, some labor union leaders and union members opposed withdrawing from Social Security after considering the advantages and disadvantages of the federal program.

In 1937, when the Social Security program in the United States became operational, there were considerable reservations by representatives of private insurance companies as well as many other individuals. Was insurance on a nationwide scale a proper program for the federal government? Would such a program be unfair for the private insurance companies? Should the national government undertake such a gigantic welfare program? Was it a move toward a more socialistic government?

After the Social Security program was established, private insurance companies continued to expand and diversify rapidly in this country. In fact, the nation became more retirement conscious, due in no small measure to the Social Security program. Many people purchased additional retirement insurance from private insurance companies, educational and other institutions, corporations, and labor unions. Other groups contracted with private insurance companies to provide a variety of retirement insurance programs. Thus, much of the early criticism and opposition to Social Security proved to be unfounded.

For many years few questions were raised publicly about the administration of the Social Security program. In fact, substantial surpluses were reported in the various funds of the system which were invested with interest. The money in the funds could not be transferred to other government funds since they were earmarked for specific purposes within the Social Security system. However, Congress provided more and more benefits under the program without an adequate increase in taxes, and there developed abuse and maladministration of Social Security.

As early as 1950 it became apparent to many qualified people that Social Security was not financially sound. The fear that Americans might lose their earned retirement benefits under Social Security was a significant factor in the conservative trend in the country and the antibureaucratic fervor that swept the United States in the 1970s and 1980s. As a part of this trend, many Americans—and people in foreign countries—believed the United States did not have the ability *to properly administer programs* enacted by Congress and implemented by administrative regulations. Interest groups secure advantages and loopholes in laws enacted by Congress and in the regulations of administrative agencies. The protection of self-interest, rather than statesmanship concern for the general welfare of the nation, is a serious problem of governments throughout the world.

In 1983, Congress enacted legislation in an effort to secure the long-term future of Social Security. The legislation was designed to ensure solvency of the system into the next century. The provisions of the law included the following: (1) postponing the scheduled July cost-of-living increases to January 1, 1984; (2) increasing the retirement age in the next century from sixty-five to sixty-seven years of age; (3) providing standby benefit cuts if Social Security reserves fall too low; (4) raising payroll taxes in 1984, 1988, and 1989; (5) placing a levy on benefits for affluent retirees; and (6) making Social Security coverage mandatory for *new* federal workers and employees of nonprofit organizations beginning January 1, 1984. Despite these and other changes in the Social Security system in 1983, further changes probably will be necessary in the future in order for the system to remain solvent and meet the needs of the people.

Unemployment Insurance

Unemployment insurance in Texas is administered by the Texas employment commission (TEC). The commission is composed of three members—a representative of labor, a representative of management, and a person who is impartial and represents the general public. The members are appointed by the governor and senate for a term of six years and no member may engage in any other business or employment. The impartial member acts as chairman and also serves as the executive director of all divisions of the TEC.

The unemployment insurance program is designed to aid those who lose their jobs through no fault of their own. It provides some financial assistance only until other work can be found.

The fund from which unemployment insurance, or unemployment compensation, is paid is provided by a tax collected from employers. None of the tax is paid by the worker. Unless exempted, employers who employ one or more persons for at least one day in each twenty weeks in a calendar year, or who have a payroll of $1,500 or more in a calendar quarter, must pay the unemployment compensation tax. Coverage has been extended to state employees and to employees of nonprofit organizations (except churches) that employ four or more workers on any day in twenty different weeks of a calendar year. Agricultural workers and domestics, under certain conditions, are eligible.

As is true of all the states, the Texas unemployment insurance program is related directly to economic developments in the state and nation. In the years past, the Texas unemployment compensation fund in the U.S. treasury had millions of surplus dollars and the interest on the fund increased by millions of dollars each year, which resulted in a minimal tax on employers. As a result of high unemployment in 1983, Texas found it necessary to borrow millions of dollars from the federal government, which had to be repaid with interest. In 1984, the tax on employers was increased considerably.

In 1983, the federal unemployment tax was 3.5 percent on the first $7,000 a year paid to each employee; however, the employer paid only .8 percent to the federal government. Out of the federal tax collections Congress appropriates funds for administration of the state laws and operation of the public employment offices. All taxes collected by the Texas employment commission provide a reserve fund, out of which unemployment-insurance benefits are paid.

Every new employer is required to pay a noncomputed tax of 2.7 percent of wages paid. This rate continues until the employer has established a qualifying period of at least one year of compensation experience during which his former employees, if unemployed and eligible, could have received unemployment benefits. Employers who maintain a good employment record are eligible for a reduced tax rate. Every employer's tax rate is computed each year in accordance with a formula and rate table in the law. The federal law does not contain variable tax rates, but it permits the states to adopt a system of variable tax rates based upon experience with unemployment.

An expanding Texas economy, a stabilized labor force, and an effective TEC job-placement service have saved Texas employers millions of dollars each year. When compared with employers of some other states, Texas employers are in a favorable position with regard to unemployment insurance.

In Texas the maximum regular duration for payment of unemployment insurance is twenty-six weeks in any twelve-month period. When regular benefits are exhausted, a maximum of thirteen weeks of extended unemployment benefits may be provided in times of high unemployment. Once unemployment compensation is paid for the entire period, benefits are exhausted for one year from the date of the initial claim. The claimant must have had some work since the establishment of the first benefit year in order to draw benefits in a second consecutive benefit year.

The total weekly unemployment insurance payment a person could receive in Texas in 1983 ranged from $37 to $168. Payments are based on a formula that considers previous earnings (over a base period) on work performed for a taxable employer. Claimants who secure part-time or occasional work must report their earnings and may qualify for reduced benefits.

Not all unemployed persons are eligible for unemployment insurance. Among other requirements, an individual must have earned a specified amount of money within a twelve-month period, registered for work at a TEC office, and be available for work. He or she may be disqualified from receiving part or all potential benefits if he or she left the last job without good cause connected with the work, if he or she was discharged for misconduct, or if he or she refuses to apply for or accept a suitable job. [1]

Also a person is not eligible for unemployment insurance if he is unemployed because of a labor dispute which he is directly or indirectly participating in or helping finance. For these and other reasons an employer may protest to the local employment-commission office that one or more individuals do not have a valid claim for unemployment compensation. Employers wish to maintain a favorable employment record in order to prevent an increase—or possibly a decrease—in their unemployment-compensation tax rate.

The TEC has entered into agreements with other states to process claims of individuals residing in one state who have earned wage credits in one or more different states. Thus, claimants may file claims in one state and claim benefits from the state in which they earned their wages. The law of the state in which the wages were earned is applicable in determining entitlement to benefits.

The Texas unemployment compensation fund is deposited with the U.S. treasury in accordance with the Internal Revenue Code. Revenue from state payroll taxes and interest on the fund are available for no other purpose than the payment of unemployment benefits to eligible claimants. All administrative costs of TEC are financed with federal funds.

TEC has a comprehensive system of fraud detection and individuals have been prosecuted for violating the law. Some employers have failed to pay the required tax and have ignored the requirement of making wage and tax reports. Some persons have employment and continue to receive unemployment compensation because TEC has not been informed of their reemployment. However, in view of the total program, fraud represents only a small percent of the funds administered.

The maximum benefit payable to the unemployed in Texas is below that of many other states. Since this limitation has not kept pace with increased wage levels in Texas, proposals have been made to raise the maximum benefit. In view of one of the program's major objectives—that of stimulating business or slowing a recession—it would appear desirable that the benefit approach the worker's normal wage. However, there are two important considerations: Would it reduce the worker's incentive to seek reemployment? Would it place an unfair burden on the employers at a time when they could least afford it? In determining what is an *adequate* benefit amount, the Texas Employment Commission takes the position that benefit payments cannot be based on *need*, as such. Rather, the TEC contends that this is an *insurance program*, and payments should be based on earnings of the worker, with certain limitations. To broaden coverage based on need alone would overburden most employers, who pay all the costs.

Since unemployment insurance is considered a weapon against the effects of *temporary* unemployment, should the maximum duration of unemployment-insurance payments (twenty-six weeks) be extended? If the existing maximum duration of benefits is adequate for the concept "temporary," then the responsibility of the employer terminates at this point, and it then becomes a problem for the community, state, or federal government to provide any additional financial assistance that might be needed.

There are considerable conflicts and politics as regards the Texas unemployment-compensation program. Leaders of organized labor have declared both the legislature and TEC (by a two-to-one vote on the commission) are sympathetic to business as indicated by the low unemployment benefits.

Supplemental Security Income

The federal supplemental security income (SSI) program, which is administered nationwide by the Social Security administration, became effective January 1, 1974. As a result of the legislation passed by Congress, the federal government assumed responsibility for financial aid to three adult welfare programs, formerly state administered, but jointly financed by the federal and state governments. The federal government assumed full financial responsibility for old age assistance (OAA), aid to the needy blind (ANB), and aid to the permanently and totally disabled (APTD). However, the states continue to provide medical and social services to those who receive SSI payments. Financial, medical, and social services for aid to families with dependent children (AFDC) is administered by the state, but jointly financed by the federal and state government.

Aid to Families with Dependent Children

The AFDC program in Texas is administered by the state department of human resources. A child must be deprived of parental support or care by reason of death of parents, continued parental absence from the home, or the physical or mental incapacity of the parents. He or she must have been deprived of the financial support of at least one parent. If the child lives with a working parent, the parent's income must be less than that needed to provide the child's basic needs.

The child must be living with father, mother, or some relative whose income or other resources are insufficient to provide a reasonable subsistence compatible with health and decency. Payments are made only for children under eighteen years of age—under twenty-one years of age if still in school. The law establishes a number of factors to be considered in determining need and the emphasis is on the family unit, not just on the child.

The amount of funds a family may receive each month is based on income, which includes money earned by working and funds received for child support, the number of persons in the family, and the needs of the individuals.

There has been a decline in AFDC rolls, due in part to the elimination by the department of human resources of cases with errors. Also, child support collection has been improved by a procedure devised to locate missing parents and charge them with the responsibility of assisting their children financially. Another reason is the department's continuing effort to provide a means through which the parent can obtain adequate income. An agreement between the department and the Texas rehabilitation commission provides work training and the purchase of day care services by local community groups.

The laws, customs, and practices in Texas relating to divorce, separation, desertion, and illegitimacy handicap the administration of AFDC.

Divorce

The district courts have power to enter a child-support order in a divorce proceeding involving children under eighteen years of age.

> While Texas has seemingly stringent provisions to insure support payments for minor children in divorces, custom and practice in the state in handling divorce cases has tended to minimize the effectiveness of such laws . . . mothers with limited income may find it more convenient to obtain a welfare grant than to force their ex-husbands to pay child support.[3]

Separation

If the husband and wife are separated but not divorced, Texas law permits welfare agencies to seek child-support payments. But frequently such support payments are not made.

Desertion

Under certain circumstances the department of human resources is responsible for locating fathers who desert their families and fail to support their children.

> Many times wives withhold information in the fear that locating the fathers would endanger their receiving AFDC. Charges filed in a district court or an indictment returned by a Grand Jury give fathers time to relocate and cause another search to be made. Because of such difficulties, many individuals are encouraged to desert their families to make the families eligible for AFDC.[4]

In the three types of family estrangements (divorce, separation, and desertion), the father is legally responsible for the support of his children. Yet, "These categories of family estrangement represent [a large] percent of all [AFDC] recipients in Texas."[5] Either existing child support laws in these categories should be enforced, or, if inadequate, additional legislation should be enacted.*

Illegitimacy

There has been an increase in the number of illegitimate children receiving AFDC.

> [Many] charges and counter-charges [have arisen] that the [AFDC] program encourages illegitimacy. Critics of the program have put forth ideas such as not permitting any mother who has a second or third illegitimate child to receive assistance grants. These critics do not explain how the children would be cared for or what would happen to them. . . . [Some] of these children are . . . not readily adoptable, [and] the problem is complex. Obviously, if a mother has more than one illegitimate child, the moral atmosphere is not of the quality the public assistance program seeks to preserve. The question, however, is what to do? If the mother is forced to support her children and is not equipped to take a job or cannot find one, she will increase her income through the attentions of men. This in time will result in more illegitimate children, and the cycle is started once again.
>
> Study after study has shown that girls who mother illegitimate children are emotionally unstable, have usually been deprived of a normal family life while they were growing up, and are seeking in promiscuous sexual relationships the attention and affection they have never had. To break this pattern will require something more than either taking away a monthly welfare payment or granting one. . . . In several states experiments have been conducted with unwed mothers to see if they would respond to skilled social work and related professional services. In such experiments progress has been made.
>
> There are better ways of attacking the problem of illegitimacy than simply removing the mother from the [AFDC] program. One of these methods is to pin down the responsible male and see that he pays child support. Too often in our society only the mother is blamed for an illegitimate child, yet it is also the responsibility of the father. By paying child support the father [might] be discouraged from engaging in other relationships, and some of the financial burden would be removed from government. . . .
>
> Under the common law originally neither parent was under any legal obligation to support an illegitimate child. In recent history this attitude has been modified. . . .
>
> This common law has been modified in all . . . states by legislative action [and court decisions] which imposes on both parents a duty to support their illegitimate children.[6]

---

*Art. XVI, Sec. 28, of the Texas constitution was amended in 1983 to read as follows: "No current wages for personal service shall ever be subject to garnishment (to attach), *except for the enforcement of court-ordered child support payments*" (italics added).

Many mothers who fail to provide proper parental care for their illegitimate children receive AFDC assistance. Legal action may be taken to have children declared dependent and neglected and eventually placed in an adoptive or foster home or, if necessary, in an institution. Since such programs and facilities for blacks are very limited in the state, the human resources department frequently must preserve a defective family situation, as it has no other choice. In such cases AFDC assistance is in the nature of a government subsidy for illegitimacy. With the aid of public funds the cycle of more and more illegitimate children is continued. The problem is deeper than monthly AFDC assistance.

Common-Law Marriages

Texas recognizes common-law marriages.

> Giving legal sanction to common-law marriage undoubtedly gives rise to a number of the children on [AFDC]. Common-law marriages are widely practiced . . . and are often used as an excuse for a couple living together with no intention of marriage. Many times the woman is told by her "husband" that it is a common-law marriage only to find out later that he has a family which he deserted, . . .[7]

A committee on domestic relations of the Texas Bar Association observed that,

> Common-law marriages in a modern state of modern society are too generally used to reduce the institution of marriage to the lowest common sexual denominator, or as a device to embarrass the estate of a descendant. When the preservation of the family is a subject of such great importance, this fossil of the frontier days lingers on and, as said by one authority, "supplies a means of defeating the marriage-law reforms. Premarital physical examinations are avoided by its recognition. It cheapens marriage and gives instability to the home. . . . The pioneer conditions which justified recognition of common-law marriage have disappeared. The Clerk's office is available to all, and none are beyond the sound of the church bells. If reason be the life of the law, it would appear to be wise and would abolish common-law marriages."[8]

Thus a large percentage of the AFDC cases in Texas reflect serious social problems that assistance grants alone cannot solve.

The state human resources department has a program—the father-finder plan—to locate and collect child support from fathers of children on welfare. Federal funds from the department of health and human services, law enforcement agencies, courts, and other agencies who help secure child support or establish paternity have greatly aided the program. The amount of child support collected from fathers of children on welfare has increased considerably, and the number of children on welfare has decreased.

As a result of a U.S. Supreme Court decision, a child born out of wedlock is entitled to the same child support from its natural father as a legitimate child; to discriminate between such children would violate the equal protection of the law clause included in the Fourteenth Amendment of the U.S. Constitution. The court decision has been an aid in child support collections.

The federal Social Security law requires a welfare applicant with dependent children to name the father of her children. And the mother is required by law to assist authorities in locating the father if child support is not being received. Much depends on locating the alleged fathers, proving paternity, and obtaining court orders for child support. If an alleged father denies paternity, refuses to pay child support, or ignores requests to discuss the matter voluntarily, a suit may be filed. Such paternity suits must be filed within four years of the birth of the child. Under the Texas family code, paternity suits require blood tests for the mother, children, and alleged father. In some cases, there may not be sufficient facts to proceed with paternity suits. Also, since many older children are on welfare, it may be difficult to determine the father in some cases.

Some fathers voluntarily agree to pay child support once they are located. A mother who does not cooperate in locating the missing father is denied support, but her children are not.

In Texas, a woman can legally record on a birth certificate as the father of her child only her legal spouse or the man who was her legal spouse ten months before the child was born. If she has been single for ten months prior to the birth of the child, the space on the birth certificate for the father's name must be left blank.

Under a provision of the Texas family code, the father of an illegitimate child may go to court and acknowledge paternity, after which child support can be collected on court order. There have been numerous cases of voluntary legitimization by fathers. The department of human resources also tries to legitimize children by establishing that a common law marriage did exist.

As the rate of divorce in Texas increases, so do the inequities of establishing child support. A number of changes in the Texas child support laws have been suggested, e.g., prohibiting suspension of support payments during an appeal of a judge's order; abolishing the statute of limitations on paternity cases; automatically increasing child support payments when there is a cost of living increase; and establishing court monitors to investigate and take enforcement action when child support is not paid. These and other proposals have been opposed by the Texas Fathers for Equal Rights as "incredibly blind and biased." Also, according to the association, divorce decrees involving children frequently provide only for "reasonable" or "mutual agreement" visitation rights. "This means that the noncustodial parent can be denied access to the children at the whim of the custodian. Parents who are not permitted to see their children often feel that withholding child support is the only weapon they have left." In addition, officers of the association have indicated courts provide free legal services for custodial parents who do not receive child support, but do not provide court-appointed attorneys to parents who are denied visitation rights.

Not only is there a problem of locating divorced fathers and enforcing child support payments, there is also the matter of determining child support payments that are both equitable and realistic for the parties involved. It is probably true that child support awards average far below the actual cost of raising a child. Awards may seldom exceed 10 to 15 percent of an absent parent's income. And despite the father-locator program, a large percent of the parents ordered by Texas judges to pay child support are delinquent in their payments. Should a support payment formula be established that would provide equally in all cases? Many fathers would oppose formula payments based on income. Should the earnings and more expensive standard of living of the mother be considered in determining the amount of monthly child support payments?

Child Welfare

The state department of human resources cooperates with the children's bureau of the U.S. Department of Health and Human Services in establishing and strengthening (especially in predominantly rural areas) public welfare services for the protection and care of homeless, dependent, and neglected children in danger of becoming delinquent. Those who operate homes for children, boarding homes, nurseries, orphanages, and child-placing agencies must secure a license to operate from the department. A director of licensed child-caring and child-placing institutions and agencies is available from the department.

As a result of the problems arising from neglect and exploitation of children, the state department of human resources devotes a considerable amount of time to casework. Agency services emphasize casework with the child's natural parents in an effort to strengthen and preserve the child's own home, provision for substitute parental care for children when removal from their own home becomes necessary, supervision of children in foster care, and direct services to children.

The department cooperates with local communities in establishing and maintaining local child-welfare units, recreational facilities, and youth centers for children.

Child Adoptions

As in other states, "black" and "gray" adoption markets exist in Texas.

Black market refers to an adoption situation where a baby is given to an adoptive couple for a sum of money that exceeds any legitimate fees. While the sum of money might vary, at least the person giving the child to the couple realizes a profit on the transaction. Gray market is a situation where a third party, usually an M.D. or an attorney, knows of the baby and of a couple who wants to adopt a baby and brings the two together. While this third person accepts a fee, it is usually only the professional fee he would charge for the legal or medical services he rendered; i.e., he does not make a "profit" on bringing the child and the adoptive couple together. The only direct advantage to him is the future good will of the adoptive parents. If, however, he charges a fee higher than the normal rate for the professional services rendered, then the situation would shade over into a black market transaction.[9]

At present many of the babies who are adopted without placement by licensed agencies are obtained directly at the hospital by the unlicensed person who takes the child directly to the adoptive couple. If a fee is paid, usually this person receives it. This person has worked out an agreement with the mother of the child prior to her entering the hospital (usually it is just with the mother, since the bulk of these babies are illegitimate) that the baby will be taken care of without her seeing it. Since this person is unlicensed, he is only concerned with delivering the baby to the adoptive parents and collecting a fee, if any, not with the finer points of whether this is a good adoptive home for the child, or if the child is in good mental and physical health.* Hospitals which allow this practice

---

*The attorney general has ruled that this type of child placing violates Article 695c of the Texas Civil Statutes. According to the attorney general "Parents may only delegate the right to place a child for adoption to a licensed child-placing agency as defined by statute and such an agency is the only one by statute permitted to give consent to adoption in place of the parents. One operating as a child-placing agency as defined by statute who does not comply with the provisions for license, violates the statute and is without authority to act" (Opinion No. WW 94, May 16, 1957).

are in danger of suit by the natural mother, since they release the child to an unauthorized person. . . .[10]

In general practice most hospitals require a person taking a child from the hospital to have some legal right by which they can take the child. Some hospitals insist that a dependency-and-neglect petition be filed and the court award custody of the child to a particular individual who may remove the child from the hospital. Some hospitals will release a child on the basis of a notarized waiver from the mother that she is releasing the child for adoption to a couple or an individual. In other hospitals it suffices for a person to say they have the right to take the child.

Sometimes children are adopted without a qualified person investigating either the child or the adopting family to ascertain their suitability to each other.

> Many adoptive couples want a baby so badly that they refrain from asking any questions about the child's background for fear that skilled adoptions casework will keep them from getting a baby. Some adoptive couples have tried to obtain a child from licensed adoptions sources, but have been rejected as not being potentially good adoptive parents (very frequently childless couples having domestic problems want a child to hold their marriage together). Thus they do not want any trained person involved in their adoption situation.[11]

Although preadoption investigations do delay adoptions, they should be required in every case as a means of protecting the interest of both the child and the prospective parents.

It is very difficult to find adoptive parents for Negro and Latin-American babies, as well as for older children of all ethnic groups. Since these children need good adoptive homes, a serious problem confronts the department of human resources.

The laws of the state make it difficult for the department of human resources to undertake an effective adoptive program.

> While the judge is required by law to "cause an investigation to be made," "such investigation shall be made by a suitable person selected by the court," no standards are established in the law as to the competency of the person making adoption investigations.
>
> Although the Department of Public Welfare [now Human Resources] by law, *may* make an investigation (in those cases in which the child was placed for adoption by a licensed child-placing agency in the state) and *may* appear in court if the best interests of the child are thus served, the department is not furnished with enough data on which to challenge an adoptions case. . . .[12]

A more effective adoption program in Texas would require adequately staffed and financed child-welfare units at the state and local levels.

Crippled Children's Services

The Social Security Act authorizes funds to help the states improve their health and welfare programs especially in rural areas. One section of the law provides for the allocation of funds to the states for the physical restoration of crippled children who meet eligibility requirements of the state laws governing such programs.

The problem of locating, examining, and physically restoring crippled children of the state is the responsibility of the division of crippled children's services, state department of health resources. A crippled child, as defined by state law, is:

. . . any person under twenty-one (21) years of age whose physical functions or movements are impaired by reason of a joint, bone, or muscle defect or deformity, to the extent that the child is or may be expected to be totally or partially incapacitated for education or remunerative occupation. To be eligible for rehabilitation service . . . the child's disability must be such that it is reasonable to expect that such child can be improved through hospitalization, medical or surgical care, artificial appliances, or through a combination of these services.[13]

The crippled children's division designates hospitals for the care of crippled children. Transportation, appliances, and braces may be in part or entirely provided by the division. As far as possible the patients are given a free choice in their selection of physicians and hospitals.

The parents of the child, or persons standing *in loco parentis* (in the place of a parent), must show that they are financially unable to provide necessary care and treatment, in which case the department assumes the balance of the necessary expenses.

Public Health

Local Health Services

Local health departments receive both consultative assistance and funds from the state Department of Health Resources. The advisory and consultative services offered local health-department units include assistance in their organization and operation, aid in recruitment, training, transfer, placement, and on-the-job training of local public-health personnel. The state Department of Health Resources also makes a scientific evaluation of local health programs.

Vital Statistics

Birth and death certificates are kept on file in the state Department of Health Resources. These records are available to prove age, parentage, citizenship, and for many other purposes.

Sanitary Engineering

The department makes investigations and collects evidence in connection with enforcing laws pertaining to safe water for the public. The sanitary maintenance of swimming pools and tourist courts, as well as the competency of water and sewage-plant operators, is certified by the department. Consultative service on public-health engineering matters is made available to local governments and other state agencies.

Veterinary Public Health

Veterinary public health includes such matters as investigating disease outbreaks among animals as they occur in all areas of the state, enforcing regulations governing meat and poultry plants under the state inspection program, and serving in a consultative capacity to the food and drug administration on activities related to meat, milk, and food programs.

Food Stamp Program

The Texas department of human resources determines who is eligible to receive food stamps and mails a card to all eligible persons each month, indicating the amount each recipient must pay for a specified number of stamps. Persons who earn less than a certain minimum income are eligible, and the number of stamps one may receive and the amount of money to be paid for them depend upon the income and size of the family. A person with a very low income may receive a certain amount of stamps free each month.

The department contracted with the post office to service each individual who must present the card, identification, and money for the food stamps. A person might pay $10 for stamps for which he could purchase $30 worth of nonexempt food items. The state assumes only the administrative cost of the program.

Food stamps may be used to purchase any edible food product other than imported items (exceptions are made for coffee, tea, bananas and other general-use products). Dietetic foods may be purchased, but not soaps, toiletries, alcoholic beverages, tobacco, household goods, paper products, and pet food. The food store may deposit the stamps at the bank as if they were money. Many persons who earn too much money to qualify for standard welfare benefits are eligible for food stamps.

19 Rehabilitation

It has been estimated that of those who commit serious crimes in America, only one in fifty will be sent to prison for their crime. Most crimes are not reported, and the police, for one reason or another, fail to arrest hundreds of those suspected of wrongdoing. Many individuals that commit crimes are repeaters. Serious doubts have been raised whether "correctional institutions" are truly correctional, or do they provide an environment that encourages crime.

Criminal activity in the world and in the United States is rampant. Prisons and correctional institutions are overcrowded, and legislative bodies are being pressured to appropriate more funds for the care of prisoners. Persons employed by the correctional institutions are, in many cases, underpaid and inadequately trained. Correctional institutions find it difficult to meet current expectations much less future needs.

The Texas Department of Corrections

The nine members of the board of corrections are appointed by the governor and senate for six-year overlapping terms. The board determines prison policy. The board, together with the director it employs, has complete supervision and control of the department of corrections. It is responsible for the proper care, treatment, feeding, clothing, and management of the prisoners confined in the department. The Texas department of corrections consists of the main prison plant at Huntsville (known as "the Walls") and a number of farms located in the southeastern part of the state.

In 1972 David Ruiz, a thirty-year-old inmate of the Texas department of corrections serving a twenty-five-year sentence for armed robbery in Austin, filed a class-action suit against the Texas prison system, charging it had violated the civil rights of the prisoners. Mr. Ruiz, and seven other inmates, requested U.S. District Judge William Wayne Justice to order Texas to overhaul its prison system, which inflicted "cruel and unusual punishment" upon its prisoners. The trial began in October 1978 and continued for 161 days—a trial in which Ruiz played a major part. Three hundred and forty-nine witnesses appeared in court, and 1,530 exhibits were entered into the evidence. The decision of the court came after months of study of all the evidence. The decision was, in a sense, an affirmation of the message Ruiz had been trying to communicate beyond prison walls for many years.

The federal district court ordered the U.S. Department of Justice to join the suit as a friend of the court in order to "investigate fully the facts alleged in prisoners' complaints. Officials of the Justice Department accused the Texas department of corrections of subjecting prisoners to cruel and unusual punishment for failure to provide for their personal security and safety, failure to provide decent medical care, and forcing the prisoners to live and work in unsafe conditions.

According to the order of the U.S. district court, the following areas of the Texas department of corrections were deficient:

Overcrowding—Virtually all inmates are exposed to, and many are victimized by, the concomitants of unguarded, overcrowded cells and dormitories—the ever-present risk of assaults, rapes and other violence—for every day of their incarceration at TDC.

Security and supervision—TDC has failed to furnish minimal safeguards for the personal safety of the inmates.

Medical care—Deficiencies in personnel, facilities and procedures combine to produce a system that persistently and predictably fails adequately to provide for the legitimate medical needs of the prison population.

Psychiatric care—Although a very large number of inmates have some character of mental disorder, few resources have been devoted by TDC to the provision of mental health services.

Special-needs inmates—Physically handicapped inmates must either manage as best they can, with virtually no special assistance, in physical environments which pose extreme difficulties for them, or spend their days vegetating, denied access to virtually all the programs and activities available to non-disabled inmates.

Disciplinary hearing procedures—TDC practices not only violate . . . minimum due process requirements . . . but also violate TDC's own written disciplinary procedures.

Solitary confinement—Although TDC regulations indicate that the punishment should be used sparingly, and then only when other less restrictive forms of punishment have been unsuccessful, solitary confinement is widely and frequently used throughout the TDC system.

Administrative segregation—The ease by which an inmate can be placed in administrative segregation, the lack of any formal process and the absence of accountability for administrative segregation decisions have allowed prison officials discriminatorily and illegitimately to subject writ writers and other disfavored inmates to segregative confinement.

Access to the courts—In light of TDC's past record, and evidence of its continuing unwillingness to respect plaintiff's fundamental right to meaningful, unimpeded access to the courts, a detailed order for relief in this area will be required.

When the federal district court decision was released to the press, many people in Texas were stunned by the reported deficiencies in the operation of the Texas department of corrections. For years there had been favorable reports on the prison system. However, these were self-evaluation reports made by TDC, rather than by a national or outside evaluation association or committee. Similarly, favorable reports and comments had been made by prison officials and private citizens from other states and foreign countries that visited the Texas prison system. There is no national accreditation agency to evaluate and rate prisons in the United States.

The matter of implementing the federal district court order created serious problems. For example, the TDC had to purchase more land on which new units of the prison system could be located, as well as provide temporary housing for prisoners until construction of more facilities could be completed. And the state, on occasion, sought delay in implementation of the court order since such massive changes were involved.

Rehabilitative Attitudes and Programs

The dark cell, the "window,"* and the practice of hanging in chains, among other methods of punishment, have been abolished. Better prisoner morale is evidenced by the decrease in escape attempts and the elimination of the practice of self-mutilation as a protest against intolerable prison conditions.

From the standpoint of rehabilitation, it is very important that those released from prison feel that the state and society care about their well-being and are willing to give them another chance. Various Texas department of corrections programs are designed to give prisoners this assurance and help them overcome an antisocial attitude. To stem the rising tide of crime, an effort is being made to reduce the possibility of a discharged prisoner's recidivism (return to criminal habits). This is the commitment of modern penology.

Prisons exist primarily to rehabilitate men and women and return them to society with a desire to live and work in harmony with their fellowman. This objective, and the improvements made in the Texas prison system, represent a healthy and vigorous aspect of a constructive states' rights program.

The diagnostic center at the Texas department of corrections' main Huntsville unit is the receiving center for the state's penal system. The various divisions of the center permit the separation of the young from the old inmates; the first offender from the recidivist; the strong from the weak; and the situational offender from the professional criminal.

New arrivals remain in the diagnostic unit approximately four weeks, during which time important data are collected on each individual. Various tests are administered, physical examinations are given, each person is fingerprinted and photographed, and the sociologists prepare admission summaries. This information becomes a part of the prisoner's record and serves as a guide in placing the inmate in the right unit and type of work. The classification committee interviews the inmates and assigns them to one of the units of the department of corrections. This testing, interviewing, counseling, and classifying is a far cry from earlier practice.

The educational activities of the department of corrections are an important phase of the rehabilitation program. An educational director, assistants, and a number of teachers are employed by the department. State law provides that all prisoners unable to pass a third-grade test must attend compulsory school. There are classes in various elementary and high-school subjects. Libraries assist in the educational program and provide extra recreational reading. By successfully pass-

---

*Prisoners were handcuffed to the bars over the prison window and were forced to stand on tiptoe to prevent cutting the wrists.

ing a series of tests, inmates may be granted a certificate of high-school equiva-
lency, which enables them to enter many colleges or universities. The Windham
independent school district is operated solely for inmates of TDC (a school district
within the penal system). The school district provides instruction in high-school
subjects, and TDC, with the cooperation of designated colleges and universities,
offers a program leading to a community college degree (associate degree) and a
four-year bachelor's degree through study at their assigned prison unit.*

A number of inmates take vocational correspondence courses, which are paid
for by the department. Vocational classes, which are correlated with on-the-job
training, are designed to provide some of the prisoners with a trade or skill in order
to make it easier to secure employment upon release from prison. The lack of such
trades or skills accounts for many persons being sent to prison in the first place.

About 25 percent of the inmates in the department of corrections are engaged in
the educational program, in one phase or another.

Paroled inmates who have completed high school may be eligible for vocational
rehabilitational services, in which case they may attend college and the TDC pays
for their education. TDC has parolees in many Texas colleges and universities.

The point-incentive program, which rates the inmates on such matters as work
habits, conduct and attitude, and educational and recreational participation, was a
logical outgrowth of the policy of the board and management and sets definite
goals toward which prisoners may strive. Under this system the individual starts at
a certain place on the prison ladder, so to speak, and can go up or down depending
upon his own efforts. An attempt is made to develop the total person. Work, conduct, attitude, and the point-incentive program are the cornerstones of the rehabilitation efforts.

When one completes the prison sentence, the Texas department of corrections
gives the individual money, new clothes, and a new pair of shoes. As a result of the
prerelease program an effort is made to give the released inmates something more.

The mandatory prerelease program is designed to make adjustment to normal
life easier and to aid one in living constructively in a free society, thereby reducing
recidivism. Among the subjects or topics included in the program are the following: personal habits and health, manners and courtesy, religion, the development
of good relations with the family and other members of society, and budgeting
money. Also included are how to secure and hold a job, purpose and function of
the law, wardrobe tips, the purchase and operation of motor vehicles, and Social
Security benefits. Teachers who are qualified in their fields donate their time to
help the inmates. Films on various topics are shown and each prisoner is given a
copy of the department's *Prerelease Manual,* which contains the basic information covered in the program.

During the time one is enrolled in the prerelease course, the inmate is given
several special privileges. For example, one is issued special clothing and shoes to
wear to classes, and family members may visit at the prison farm for picnic
lunches on Sundays.

Although not the sole contributing factor in a person's becoming a criminal,

*By act of the legislature in 1971, public junior colleges, by action of their governing boards, may be
re-designated community colleges.

physical defects may have serious effects on a person's personality and may limit or prevent job opportunity. For a number of years at the prison hospital in Sugar Land, residents in plastic surgery from Baylor University College of Medicine have corrected facial deformities—receding chins, grotesque scars, missing ears—of some inmates of the Texas prison system. In some cases parole was postponed in order that long-term reconstructive surgery could be completed. A survey of prisoners treated by the Baylor residents over a five-year period showed that 17 percent returned to prison compared to the 31.6 percent of the general prison population who did not receive similar treatment. Since the department of corrections has various rehabilitation programs, full credit cannot be given to plastic surgery, although it was probably an important factor.

Other phases of the improved program of the department of corrections include: adequate and proper diet, improved medical facilities, state approved trust system, spiritual guidance, mechanization of the farms, transportation to the fields in "troop carriers," clean clothing at the end of the day's work, television sets for all dormitories (one set for a certain number of cells for early-evening viewing), and motion pictures for both recreational and educational purposes. There are regularly scheduled league games in baseball and basketball. Each unit has its boxing team composed of all weight classes. The annual state-prison rodeo at Huntsville has become very popular as a result of excellent performances.

The net profits from the prison rodeo and commissary receipts go into the education and recreation fund, which provides for vocational education, music, library, motion picture, athletics, television, medical equipment, and a religious program. The salaries of persons who work for the rodeo are paid out of the fund. The tax dollar is not involved in these expenditures.

The department of corrections operates a number of industries—license-plate plant, mattress factory, canning plant, meat-processing plant, brick plant, broom-and-mop factory, and others. The department, at a considerable savings to the state, has provided much of its own food, clothing, and equipment. These commodities are also sold to other state agencies. Cotton is the only commodity grown or produced by the department that can be sold on the open market.

A pilot work-release program was authorized by the Texas legislature in 1969. Under the work-release program select prisoners may be permitted to work for private firms by day and return to the prison after each day's work. The prisoners wear nonprison clothes and travel by bus. Part of the regular wages earned by the prisoners are sent to their families, some of whom are taken off the welfare rolls; part of the money earned is deposited in a bank for the prisoner; and part is retained by the individual to pay personal expenses. The prisoners pay the department of corrections for transportation and room and board. Also the prisoners pay income taxes.

Paroled or discharged inmates have difficulty securing jobs, since employers are reluctant to hire them. Consequently, jobless former convicts may return to crime. As a result of the work-release program, an individual may have a job waiting for him after leaving the department of corrections. Also, the work-release program may help one overcome the problem of readjusting to normal living.

The work-release program supplements the department of correction's prerelease program in which persons with ninety days or less to serve in prison transferred to the prerelease center to be reoriented to society. Those in the work-release program go through the prerelease orientation.

The first prisoners that participated in the pilot work-release program were from the Houston area. In time, centers may be built or leased in various Texas cities, thereby reducing transportation costs.

The Correctional Ombudsman Concept

The ombudsman concept, which originated in Sweden in the early nineteenth century, was designed to place an official between the public and the bureaucracy. Some American states have established the office of correctional ombudsman to assist in handling problems between inmates and the prison staff. The ombudsman may be appointed by the governor or by the state legislature, and his power may be solely recommendatory with full access to the state's correctional institutions and their files. Neither the director of the state's prisons nor the wardens want to be overruled by the ombudsman. The fact that the latter office has been established has a positive influence on (and takes some of the pressure off) the director and wardens. Instead of an independent correctional ombudsman, the latter official in a state may operate under the director of the prison system or be a part of a state-wide ombudsman program.

A state may have a correctional ombudsman as well as direct grievance procedures. Some prison officials favor the ombudsman system because they realize the prison staff would not always be objective in matters involving inmates.

There has been, thus far, little interest in Texas for the establishment of the correctional ombudsman program. The grievance procedure in Texas follows the traditional pattern. Prisoners may take complaints directly to their immediate supervisor; any appeal beyond this individual would go to the warden of the particular unit, to the director of the department of corrections, or to the board of corrections. In Texas, attorneys are attached to each of the state's prison units and free legal aid is provided on all matters except possible civil rights violations. If a prisoner believes his or her civil rights have been violated, the state bar of Texas will provide free legal aid.

The fact that attorneys are available for the prisoners in each of the Texas prison units has made it possible for both the prisoners and the prison officials to better understand—and to appreciate—the problems of both prisoners and the prison staff. If prisoners rely solely on prison inmates or prison "writ writers" for legal aid, there is always the possibility that prison discipline may be undetermined by the influence of the inmate legal adviser.

Rights of Prisoners

Persons confined in prisons have raised a variety of legal issues during their incarceration, for example, the censorship of mail, refusal to allow obscene publications, denial of due process of law while in prison, and failure to furnish library facilities and legal assistance. In 1974, the U.S. Supreme Court decided *Wolff* v. *McDonnell* (418 U.S. 539), and the quotes below are from the decision of the court.

Lawful imprisonment necessarily makes unavailable many rights and privileges of the ordinary citizen. . . . But though his rights may be diminished by the needs and exigencies of the institutional environment, a prisoner is not wholly stripped of constitutional protections when he is imprisoned for a crime. . . .

Prison disciplinary proceedings are not part of a criminal prosecution, and the full panoply of rights due a defendant in such proceedings does not apply. . . . In sum, there must be mutual accommodation between institutional needs and objectives and the provisions of the Constitution that are of general application.

We hold that written notice of the charges must be given to *the disciplinary-action defendant* in order to inform him of the charges and to enable him to marshall the facts and prepare a defense. At least a brief period of time after the notice, no less than 24 hours, should be allowed to the inmate to prepare for the appearance before the Adjustment Committee.

We also hold that there must be a "written statement by the fact finders as to the evidence relied on and reasons" for the disciplinary action.

We are also of the opinion that the inmate facing disciplinary proceedings should be allowed to call witnesses and present documentary evidence in his defense when permitting him to do so will not be unduly hazardous to institutional safety or correctional goals.

Confrontation and cross-examination present greater hazards to institutional interests. . . . We think that the Constitution should not be read to impose the procedure at the present time and that adequate bases for decision in prison disciplinary cases can be arrived at without cross-examination. . . .

At this stage of the development of these procedures we are not prepared to hold that inmates have a right to either retained or appointed counsel in disciplinary proceedings.

As to the ability to open the mail in the presence of inmates, this could in no way constitute censorship, since the mail would not be read. . . . The possibility that contraband will be enclosed in letters, even those from apparent attorneys, surely warrants prison officials' opening the letters. . . . [italics added]

The outcome of prison disciplinary proceedings may affect "good time" earned for early release from prison, and the revocation of earned good time would be in the nature of a sanction. Therefore, the prisoner must be afforded some of the protections of due process of law.

When crimes are committed within the prison system, the individual is taken outside the prison for indictment and trial.

Juvenile Delinquency

Juvenile delinquency continues to increase throughout the nation. It is estimated that within a decade the number of Texas delinquents ten to seventeen-years-old will more than double. There appears to be no single cause of delinquency.

Many delinquents feel hostile toward society. For some reason they consider themselves to be left out and unwanted and think they are not receiving a fair deal. All seek acceptance. An adequate approach to the problem requires close cooperation between the parents, the community, the school, and the state.

The Texas youth commission administers the state's correctional facilities for delinquent children and provides a program of training aimed at rehabilitation and reestablishment in society of children adjudged delinquent by the courts of Texas and committed to the commission. The Texas youth commission consists of six members appointed by the governor and senate for six-year overlapping terms. Members are eligible for reappointment. A full-time executive director is employed by, and serves at the pleasure of, the commission.

The management and care of the state schools for delinquents are important responsibilities of the commission. The commission also has supervision over the state homes for neglected children, Corsicana State Home, and Waco State Home. The commission appoints a superintendent of each institution, and upon the recommendation of the superintendents appoints other officials, chaplains, teachers, and employees. The superintendents, with the consent of the executive director, may discharge any employee with good cause.

Every child committed to the youth commission as a delinquent, unless discharged at an earlier age, must be released from custody of the commission when eighteen years of age.

The juvenile court in any county can commit to the state school a boy or girl of at least ten and not more than seventeen years of age if it finds him or her to be a delinquent. A person can be adjudged a delinquent if he or she violates a felony penal law or any misdemeanor law for which the punishment prescribed may be confinement in jail, habitually commits finable misdemeanor offenses prohibited by state law or local ordinance, continually violates a compulsory school-attendance law, habitually acts to injure or endanger the morals or health of himself or others, or persists in association with vicious and immoral persons. The juvenile judge's finding in every case is that the boy or girl is a delinquent rather than a murderer or thief. Under Texas law, the hearing is a civil proceeding.

In Texas, the legal adult age is eighteen for boys and girls. The Texas court of criminal appeals held that a juvenile offender is put in double jeopardy if declared a delinquent by a court and later (upon reaching the legal adult age) tried and convicted for the *same offense*. When a serious crime such as murder or criminal assault is committed by a juvenile, he may be charged with a less serious crime pertinent to the act. If the juvenile is committed for the lesser offense, then he could be held there until he becomes an adult and tried for the more serious offense. In any event, no person who commits a crime before reaching the age of eighteen can be executed in Texas. Under such conditions one could be sentenced for any number of years in prison or receive a life sentence.

If a district attorney is of the opinion that a fourteen- or fifteen-year-old murderer should be prosecuted when he reaches the age of eighteen, he cannot produce the murder evidence in juvenile court to get the youngster adjudged delinquent during the original trial. If such evidence is withheld, and other evidence is insufficient, the juvenile court would have to release the person involved. If the district attorney presents the murder evidence to the juvenile court, he cannot use the same evidence in criminal trial when the youth becomes of legal age. When the youngster is legally responsible, three or four years after the crime was committed, it might be difficult to secure the necessary evidence. Because of these and other factors, law-enforcing officers and prosecutors are very critical of the existing juvenile laws.

Under the discretionary law, the judge of the juvenile court may transfer certain cases from the jurisdiction of the juvenile court to that of courts having jurisdiction over adults. Such transfer is at the discretion of the juvenile judge, and the juvenile offender must be sixteen years of age and must have committed an offense that would be a felony if committed by an adult. The regular criminal courts may refer such cases involving juveniles back to the juvenile court.

Those convicted under the discretionary law, and not previously placed in a juvenile school, may be sent to Ferguson Farm, which is under the supervision of the department of corrections and where first offenders under twenty-one years of age and convicted in the regular criminal courts are sent. The younger offenders are committed for definite terms and separated from the older and hardened criminals. Juveniles not indicted under the discretionary law may be sent to a state training school after a hearing in the juvenile court.

"Neither the Fourteenth Amendment nor the Bill of Rights is for adults alone," according to a decision of the U.S. Supreme Court, and "under our Constitution, the condition of being a boy does not justify a kangaroo court."[1] Therefore, juveniles, like adults tried in the regular courts, must be accorded certain constitutional safeguards, including notice of charges against them; legal counsel, appointed by the court if necessary, in any case in which the juvenile might be placed in custody; the right to confront and cross-examine complainants and other witnesses; advice of the privilege against self-incrimination; and the right to remain silent. The Court said "it would indeed be surprising if the privilege against self-incrimination were available to hardened criminals but not to children." However, the U.S. Supreme Court has held that juveniles accused of crime may be tried without juries. In Texas, a juvenile must sign a waiver of trial by jury. The High Court upheld the right of state courts to sentence juveniles to longer terms of confinement than they would receive for the same crime if committed as adults.

Many repeaters and hardened juveniles in the state schools continue their life of crime and in time end up at Huntsville, notwithstanding the efforts of the staffs at the state schools, and the local police and probation workers. Juveniles from the populous counties like Harris and Dallas have very little to learn in the way of crime. Those from the less populous counties can acquire quite a criminal education from these tough and experienced operators, because they were committed for less numerous and serious offenses than those of juveniles in the more populated areas. Rehabilitation at the state schools is doubtful for about 10 percent of those committed; these hardened individuals only tend to disrupt the rehabilitation program for those who can benefit from it.

The most extreme punishment a judge can give an underage boy or girl who has committed a serious crime is to send the child to a state school of correction. Under state law judges can sentence youths only to indeterminate terms; that is, the judge cannot say how long the youngster is to stay at the state school. The authorities at the school could release the youngster the day following arrival. Many people oppose definite commitments to the juvenile training schools because they believe such a policy would turn these schools into penal institutions.

A person with a record as a juvenile (age ten to seventeen), can, at age eighteen, request to have that record sealed (removed from his record) if, in the previous two years, he or she did not commit any unlawful acts. This is not done automatically but should be requested of the court with the assistance of a lawyer.

The liability of parents for damage caused by willful and malicious conduct of children and minors is limited to actual damages, not to exceed $15,000 per act, plus court costs and reasonable attorney's fees.

It has been suggested that the age of legal responsibility be lowered to fifteen or sixteen years. This recommendation has been supported by some county and district attorneys, among others. Both the Texas youth commission and the Texas board of corrections oppose lowering the age of legal responsibility. The board has declared that lowering the age of prosecution from eighteen to fifteen years "would involve turning the calendar of progress back." According to the board, lowering of the age limit would make it difficult for criminal courts to convict, because rules of evidence, clever defense lawyers, and oversympathetic jurors would result in overly lenient treatment of juveniles. Hence, "many a genuinely tough boy who would receive a commitment in a juvenile court would 'beat the rap' in criminal court." Another argument against the lowering of the legal age limit is that the number of inmates in the Texas prison system would increase, unless interim reformatories under the supervision of the Texas youth commission were established. The prison system has a serious problem of overcrowding under existing conditions.

The state must continue to expand facilities for the care of juvenile delinquents as the incidence of teen-age crime will continue to rise with the increase of population in the larger cities. Continued expansion of buildings and hiring of additional employees, plus better salaries for all personnel, are necessary if the state training schools are to carry out an efficient program of rehabilitation. If the state cannot or will not provide adequate facilities, the cities and counties may have to consider building or expanding their own correctional schools and institutions. The cities and counties, which are constantly expanding services and have limited taxing powers, may not have the financial resources for such an undertaking. Local taxpayers might object to being taxed twice to help support both state and local correctional schools for juveniles. The Harris County School for Boys at Clear Lake, which is financed by the county, cares for a limited number of boys under fourteen years of age. However, Harris County sends hundreds of juveniles to state schools each year.

Community Centers

It has been recommended that Texas dismantle its large reform schools for juveniles and send youthful offenders to community centers close to their homes for rehabilitation. Unless the community centers are established, rehabilitation of juveniles will be impossible. At present, little or nothing is done for juvenile offenders until they become hardened criminals, when, in most cases, it is too late for rehabilitation. Therefore, many interested citizens believe that local community facilities should replace the large, generally rural, institutions.

The newspapers of the state have reported what some state legislators and others have said about the operation of the juvenile program: that "staff brutality" at the institutions is ignored, and in some cases encouraged, by those in authority; that certain practices violate the dignity of the juveniles as individuals; that there exists a lack of adequate academic and vocational programs; that there is a need for bilingual education for Mexican-American juveniles; that there should be screening of prospective employees to eliminate persons unfit to work with children; that punishments of the juveniles are highly arbitrary and inconsistently severe; that tranquilizers are used on juveniles indiscriminately; and that the juvenile programs violate the right of children to be protected by the U.S. Constitution's guarantee against cruel and unusual punishment.[2]

The Texas youth commission has placed a large number of juveniles in community centers throughout the state, and it cooperates with local agencies and private groups in the rehabilitation of teenagers. However, juveniles with serious behavior problems must be kept in existing institutions under TYC administration. Nevertheless, new directions in administration and rehabilitation are being chartered to meet the ever-increasing challenge of a serious and complex problem.

Teen Juries in Municipal Courts

Some municipalities in Texas and other states have experimented with teen juries. Juveniles accused of misdemeanors such as traffic offenses and petty theft may ask to have their cases go before a teen jury, which is usually recruited from local high schools. If the judge approves, the jury hears testimony, arrives at a verdict, and assesses a fine or penalty or both. By law, judges must consider the verdicts and sentences of these juries purely advisory.

On occasion the municipal court judge has reduced sentence (usually a fine and teen jury duty), but rarely have teen verdicts been overturned. In some cases teen sentences were "on target" but too tough—the teen juries wanted their peers to learn their lesson. In many cases, the juries got what they wanted, the municipal judge accepted the sentence—*and* there have been very few repeat offenders.

Teen juries tend to give their peers respect; they perceive that adults do not do the same. If convicted, the teenager might hold a grudge against the municipal judge because the latter was an adult. In most cases, teenagers do not appear to hold grudges if judged by their peers. Experience with teen juries indicates that teens can handle the responsibility of being jurors. The teen system enables young Americans to demonstrate their ability to be responsible. Also, teen juries give the jurors a civics lesson they could not get in the classroom—and involve the community more closely in the judicial process. Courtrooms may be packed with students, parents, and interested citizens for teen-jury trials; thus, the trials are a civics lesson for individuals of all ages.

If the municipal court is a court of record, everything before the judge must be recorded. Cases decided by teen juries are not entered into the court record because the juries are not officially recognized by the courts.

In Retrospect

Rehabilitation and the right of legal counsel (before and after confinement) are major features of modern correctional practice. The emphasis is upon rehabilitation, rather than merely "warehousing" individuals for a period of time—a practice that encourages recidivism. Also, the federal courts have held that prisoners are entitled to legal counsel and the Texas department of corrections provides this service (financed in part by a grant from the Texas criminal justice council). Prisoners who act as lawyers may lack necessary legal training. Also, reliance on them could increase their influence and possibly undermine control by prison officials.

In the early history of the juvenile courts in this country, many juvenile judges had little or no legal training. In a sense the judge was a "substitute parent," in many cases presiding over an informal court. The concept of "substitute parent" has been modified—at least in theory—by federal court decisions. However, in actual practice many juvenile courts continue to function on an informal basis with a limited number of participants and others in attendance, despite the fact that juvenile jurisprudence is a specialized and complex field of law.

20 Public Education

THE AWARENESS OF THE need for equal educational opportunities has resulted in a movement to extend public education downward, upward, and outward. Many feel that public education should be extended downward to kindergarten and nursery school, upward through college and adult education, and outward to encompass more subjects. A fourth dimension of increased intellectual effort has taken on a new importance.

The public schools of the twentieth century, although in need of improvement, are far superior to those of the nineteenth. A rudimentary curriculum, ungraded schools, short school terms, the absence of compulsory school-attendance laws, poorly trained teachers, and inadequate school buildings were not uncommon during the last century.

Progress in education, as in other areas of American life, has not been without its controversies. Take, for example, the concept of "free" education. Those who opposed this revolutionary idea argued it would lead to social unrest, undermine the family, require an extensive bureaucracy, lead to mixing politics with the learning processes, and offer the government an opportunity to control the minds of young people. Many believed that those able to educate their own children in private schools should not be taxed to help educate other children whose parents were not so well-off. Or take the matter of "compulsory" public education. In the words of those opposed, should society, through the device of compulsory-attendance laws, force parents to send their children either to public or private schools? Was this not an undue interference with personal liberty by the state? In answer to these questions there evolved the concept that the liberty safeguarded by our constitutional system is "liberty within a social organization," meaning personal liberty may on occasion have to be restricted in the interest of society. Since the type of education society provides for the youth and adults is in a large measure the product of social forces and designed to serve social needs, controversial issues, pressures, and forces are bound to play an important role.

Today, as in the past, public education is confronted with important issues. Should there be more, or less, federal aid for public education? In this space age, should there be more emphasis on fundamental education, or should greater attention be given to general or progressive education? How many education courses should a teacher be required to take in order to qualify? Should sex education be taught in the public schools? Is it desirable that special classes be established for the exceptional students? What should the curriculum include? Should schools operate on a year-round basis? These and other questions confront the general public as well as school-board members and school administrators.

On numerous occasions American education has been revitalized by controversy and constructive criticism, both of which are essential ingredients for a healthy and mature school system. However, many a school community has been torn asunder by small, well-organized, and vocal pressure groups of various types, for example, anti-United Nations groups, pro-America organizations, and anti-Jewish groups masquerading behind some other organizations. Harassment by these groups has been an obstacle to educational progress and has not been in the best American tradition. Instead of group harassment, public education needs constructive criticism. Only a well-informed, interested, and vigilant citizenry can offer public education this vital service. Without the intelligent and continuing support of the general public, education in this country truly "stands on the razor-edge of danger."

Local School Administration

Types of School Districts

Independent School Districts. The school district, school board, school administrators, and teaching and nonteaching staff constitute a separate and distinct unit of government that is in no way integrated with municipal government. For this reason, these school districts, with their own governmental arrangement, are referred to as "independent."

Control of the independent school districts is vested in an elective school board of seven trustees; however, by special act of the legislature the Dallas independent school district has nine members on the school board. Nevertheless, the common pattern for independent school districts is a seven-member board. Members of the school boards are non-salaried and are elected for three-year terms (four- and six-year terms in some districts).

In some small independent school districts the school plant may consist of only one school building that provides classrooms for grammar and high school students. Such schools are under the immediate supervision of a superintendent, principal, and the classroom teachers. On the other hand, in the large urban districts one will find many elementary or grammar schools as well as junior and senior high schools and vocational schools, all under the supervision and control of a superintendent of schools and the local school trustees.

Some of the more important functions of the board are as follows: (1) selecting the superintendent (of schools in the urban areas) and approving contracts for the teaching and nonteaching staff; (2) accepting or rejecting the school budget; (3) approving contracts for the construction, expansion, repair, and maintenance of school buildings; (4) approving contracts for utilities such as gas, water, light, and sewage; (5) approving contracts for insurance and purchase of school supplies and equipment; (6) establishing a system of school transportation; (7) setting the dates for opening and closing the schools of the district; (8) arranging for an audit of school finances. Much of the work of the local school board is done upon the recommendation of the school superintendent.

Rural High School Districts. Contiguous independent districts (each having less than a specified number of pupils) may be grouped together to form a rural high-school district. Such districts are governed by a board of seven trustees, elected districtwide, although each of the original districts must have at least one member on the board.

Community-College Districts. In the total number of public community and junior colleges, Texas ranks second in the nation, exceeded only by California. In Texas they are locally owned and partially state-supported.

The Texas legislature has authorized the creation of *community-college* districts for the establishment of public-supported community and junior colleges. A petition for such a district, if approved by the coordinating board, Texas college and university system, must be submitted to the qualified voters of the independent school district or city, if the city has assumed control of its schools. The independent school district or city must have an assessed property valuation of not less than a specified amount or other income to meet the needs of the district, as well as an average daily attendance of not less than a specified number of students in its high school in the school year immediately preceding the petition.

There are various types of districts, for example, community and junior colleges that are units of the public schools; independent districts; union districts; and countywide and joint-county community-college districts.

All the public community and junior colleges in the state were established as tax-supported institutions through the initiative of local citizens and are locally controlled by elected boards of trustees or regents. Some have separate and independent governing boards; others are considered units of the public schools and are governed by the independent school-district board. They may have a governing board serving both the independent school district and the college district in a dual capacity. On the other hand, the trustees of an independent school district may appoint an independent and separate governing board for the college. Hence, there is considerable variation in the governmental arrangement of the community and junior college districts. The number, residence, and terms of the trustees who govern the colleges are determined by the type of district created and the number of counties included in the district.

Community and junior college districts receive state aid for each full-time student enrolled. Private individuals may contribute funds, land, and other forms of property.

Expenses during the first two years of college are usually lower if the student lives with his parents than if he goes away to study. Moreover, parents may feel it is desirable to keep their children near home. Of course, the business community and local chambers of commerce support educational expansion in the home town.

Transfer of Students

If high-school classes are not provided locally, pupils are transferred and the home district must pay the tuition required. For such a transfer of pupils to take place there must be a satisfactory agreement reached between the school boards of the districts concerned, since there is no law that requires a district to accept transfers from other districts. Frequently, if a district is overcrowded with pupils or lacks teachers and facilities, it may accept only a limited number of transfers or refuse them entirely.

It may be that the classes are taught in the home district, but for some reason the parents may wish to transfer their children to another district. Since such transfers are the responsibility of the parents, they are required to pay the tuition costs involved.

Decrease in Number of School Districts

School districts in Texas have decreased because cities have extended their boundaries to include an entire school district. There have been numerous elections to consolidate districts as well as the grouping of districts to form rural high school districts, and independent districts have been enlarged by the annexation of other districts. The liberality of the Texas law has encouraged school-district consolidation. There are approximately 1,150 school districts in Texas.

Regional Education Service Centers

The counties of Texas are grouped into regional education service centers that are supervised by the Texas education agency. The centers are financed by the state and by revenues from the services they provide, such as instructional media (film strips, overlays, and so on).

The centers assist the school districts with computer services and consultant programs and coordinate the disbursement of federal education grants by the Texas education agency.

Texas Education Agency (TEA)

The Texas education agency is composed of the state board of education, commissioner of education, and department of education. All public educational functions not specifically delegated to the TEA are administered by district boards of trustees.

The State Board of Education

The state board of education is also the state board for vocational education. Board members are elected for six-year overlapping terms by the voters in the congressional districts. The board selects, with the approval of the senate, the state commissioner of education to serve for a period of four years. It adopts policies and establishes general rules for carrying out the duties placed upon the board and the TEA by the legislature. It formulates and presents to the executive budget agency the proposed budget or budgets for operating the minimum foundation program of education, the TEA, and the other programs for which the board has responsibility. It adopts operating budgets on the basis of appropriations by the legislature and establishes procedures for budgetary control: expending, auditing, and reporting on expenditures within the budgets adopted. It submits biennial reports covering all the activities and expenditures of the TEA to the legislature. It regulates the accreditation of schools, purchases instructional aids, including textbooks, within the limits of authority granted by the legislature, and invests the permanent school fund, within the limits of authority granted by the legislature.

The State Commissioner of Education

The state commissioner of education is the executive officer through whom the state board of education and the state board of vocational education carry out their policies and enforce their rules and regulations. The state commissioner of education, among other functions, advises the state board of education, issues teaching certificates to public-school teachers and administrators, and vouches the expenses of the TEA according to the rules prescribed by the state board of education. The decisions of the state commissioner of education are subject to review by the state board of education. Parties having any matter of dispute arising under provisions of the school laws of Texas, or any person aggrieved by the actions of any board of trustees or board of education, may appeal in writing to the commissioner of education who, after due notice to the parties interested, must hold a hearing and render judgment without cost to the parties involved. Such action does not deprive a party of any available legal remedy.

The State Department of Education

The state department of education is the professional, technical, and clerical staff of the TEA. Directors of major divisions of the department and all other employees are appointed by the state commissioner of education under general rules adopted by the state board of education. The department aids local school districts in improving education through research and experimentation, consultation, conferences, and evaluation.

Public School Financing

In December 1971, a three-judge federal court in San Antonio ruled unanimously that the Texas system of public school financing—based in part on local property taxes—violated both the federal and state constitutions.* "The state may adopt any financial scheme desired, so long as the variations in wealth among the governmentally chosen districts do not affect the spending for the education of any child." The variations in the local school district ad valorem tax base, as the result of low and high property valuations in the school districts, violated the equal protection of the laws clause of the Fourteenth Amendment of the United States Constitution. In 1973, the U.S. Supreme Court, in a 5 to 4 opinion, reversed the federal district court decision and held that the Texas system of local ad valorem taxes for financing public education and the state's minimum foundation program did not work to the disadvantage of the poor or foster discrimination based on the rela-

---

*The Rodriquez case. The suit was instituted by fifteen parents in the Edgewood school district, a predominantly Mexican-American district in a poor section of San Antonio. They charged the state's system of reliance on local property taxes favored more affluent districts, as, for example, the Alamo Heights school district in San Antonio, and violated the equal protection requirements of the Fourteenth Amendment.

There are considerable variations in Texas school districts as regards the market or real value of property, the assessed valuation of property for ad valorem tax purposes, and the per-pupil expenditures in the districts.

tive wealth of families in any school district. Also, according to the Supreme Court, the Texas plan did not "impermissibly" interfere with the exercise of any fundamental right or liberty, since education is not within the limited category of rights recognized by the Court as guaranteed by the Constitution, and therefore is not covered by the Fourteenth Amendment.*

State Funds

The Permanent School Fund. The constitution of 1876 provided for a "perpetual public-school fund" composed of all funds, lands, and other property set apart for the support of public schools; all the alternate sections of land reserved by the state out of grants made to railroads or other corporations; one-half of the public domain of the state, and all money derived from the sale of such property. By action of the legislature the remaining public domain later was given to the permanent school fund. The landed endowment of the permanent school fund consists of several hundred thousand acres of unsold, surveyed school land. In addition to this there are several million acres in the mineral estate of the fund. Accruals to the permanent school fund from the landed endowment include bonuses, rentals and awards on mineral leases, oil and gas royalties, and principal on land sales. Investments held for the permanent school fund include U.S. treasury bonds and bonds of the state of Texas and its political subdivisions. Hence, the permanent school fund is composed of a landed endowment and an investment trust fund.

The interest earned on the investments of the permanent school fund is deposited in the available school fund and distributed to the local school districts each year on a per schoolchild basis. The income (interest) earned on the investments of the permanent school fund is used for operating the public schools.

The Available School Fund. Interest on the permanent school fund, one-quarter of the motor-fuel tax, occupational and severance taxes, grazing-lease rentals, interest on land sales, and other lesser sources, provide the revenue for the available school fund. The available school fund is distributed to all school districts on the basis of average daily school attendance during the previous year.

The Foundation School Fund. The minimum-foundation school program provides that all local school districts in the state must raise so many millions of dollars for public education purposes as a condition for receiving any state aid. Consequently, the financial ability of each school district to support the foundation school program must be determined. The formula employed is designed to indicate the extent to which one school district is financially able to support schools in relation to the other school districts in the state.

Funds from the available school fund may be insufficient for the district to operate a minimum program of education that meets state standards. In such event, the district may receive financial assistance from the foundation school fund. Payments from this fund are based upon "professional units," which are determined

---

*However, the Court warned officials in Texas and other states: "We hardly need add that this Court's action today is not to be viewed as placing its judicial imprimatur on the status quo. The need is apparent for reform in tax systems which may well have relied too long and too heavily on the local property tax. . . . And certainly innovative new thinking as to public education, its methods and its funding, is necessary to assure both a higher level of quality and a greater uniformity of opportunity."

by the average daily school attendance. The latter may be adjusted in the summer to make the attendance report more current.*

Federal Funds

Over the years Congress has passed numerous laws providing financial aid and other assistance to public education in the United States. Much of this federal funding is provided by Titles 1, 2, etc., of the Elementary and Secondary Education Act (ESEA) of 1965. Guidelines for the federally funded programs were established by the federal Department of Health and Human Services (HHS) and the Texas education agency (TEA). Federal funds have been disbursed to school districts to support a number of school programs, including the following: employment of counselors and special teachers for educationally handicapped students, regardless of family income; bilingual instruction for students with little or no command of English; purchase of audiovisual and other materials; and provision of clothing for students from low-income families. Federal funding for various public school programs has been terminated or reduced by Congress.

Selection of Textbooks

The state commissioner of education annually recommends to the state board of education the names of fifteen persons (no two of whom shall live in the same congressional district) for appointment to the state textbook committee. The board may approve or reject the committee nominations. Those named to the committee must be experienced and active educators engaged in teaching in the public schools of Texas.

The board of education issues a call for bids on textbooks in each grade and subject area for which contracts are to be awarded during a given school year. Publishers then submit sealed bids to the board describing textbooks offered by them for adoption, after which the state textbook committee conducts hearings and makes a detailed study of all of these books. By law the state committee is required to reduce each list to not more than five or fewer than three acceptable titles for each grade and subject area. The list is then mailed to every superintendent in the state on August 1 each year for critical evaluation. The list is made available for examination by any citizen. During the last two weeks in September of each year, members of the state textbook committee hear petitions of citizens in regard to textbooks. Not only are the books recommended by the committee critically evaluated by public school superintendents and private citizens, but the staff of TEA evaluate each recommended book with regard to presentation of factual information, treatment of controversial issues, and adherence to democratic principles.

By law the state board of education is required to provide rules that permit balanced input by Texans who wish to comment on textbooks under consideration for use in the state's public schools. At one time individuals were required to make detailed written statements to the board, and only negative comments could be

---

*The state does not provide monetary aid, textbooks, or transportation to parochial or private schools. Upon invitation, the Texas education agency examines for accreditation purposes the educational programs of parochial and private schools, in order that institutions of higher learning can determine whether graduates shall be accepted.

made concerning the books under consideration. The simplified rules make it easier for citizens to comment pro or con on proposed public school texts.

The board of education has adopted specifications for textbooks in various subject areas. For example, the board's written directive provides that world history texts "shall depict the role of the United States in world history in a positive manner." In the development of the twentieth century, publishers are required to explain "the positive aspects and effects of American capitalism upon the world" and the "hardships of life under both fascist and communist dictatorships." The board also ordered that the basics of grammar be emphasized in language and composition texts. These and other specifications are distributed to publishers.

The state textbook committee transmits the multiple-adoption lists to the commissioner of education, who in turn transmits the lists to the state board of education. Neither the commissioner nor the board may add titles to the lists, but both, by showing proper cause, are authorized to remove books from each list provided at least three titles remain on each list. Textbooks adopted by the board are placed on state contract.

Each school system has its own textbook committee that evaluates all textbooks on the statewide multiple-adoption lists and selects the textbooks to be used. Considering the large number of textbooks offered for adoption by publishers, it is necessary that the state reduce the number of books approved for each course and grade; otherwise the administration and distribution of the textbooks by the state would be difficult. The multiple-list textbook law established local choice (within the limitation of the multiple lists) as the basis for the selection of textbooks. This arrangement is a compromise between giving each school district complete freedom of choice in selecting textbooks and the state board of education specifying a single book for each course and grade. When a committee selects the textbooks from the approved list to be used in the local school system, locally designated textbook custodians obtain the books from TEA.

On occasion the charge is made that subversive textbooks are being used in the Texas public schools. The use of such textbooks in Texas schools is unlikely considering the numerous checks in the book-selection procedure. If textbook screening by the state textbook committee, commissioner of education, board of education, superintendents, private citizens, staff of TEA, and the local school textbook committees is inadequate in preventing the use of subversive textbooks in the public schools, it appears any additional checks would be useless also.

Also, in order to secure adoptions, authors, publishers, and editors of books strive to follow the specifications of the state board of education.

The School-Lunch Program

The school-lunch program is designed to furnish daily, well-balanced, nutritious lunches to children at a reasonable cost. In Texas, the school-lunch and special milk programs in the schools that elect to participate in the national school lunch program are administered by the state department of education. Both public and private schools of high-school and lower grades are eligible to participate in the national program, which is optional for the local schools. Federal funds are allocated to participating schools on the basis of the number of meals and amount of milk served. Some federal funds are used for direct purchases of commodities by the U.S. Department of Agriculture.

The federal government provides part of the funds for the school-lunch program; the remainder is paid out of local school funds and by parents. Free lunches for needy children, and in some schools free breakfasts, are provided by the local school district. To receive surplus commodities from the U.S. Department of Agriculture, a school district must provide free lunches for needy students.

The participating schools are required to file monthly reports of the number of meals and amount of milk served. These reports serve as a basis for establishing the amount of federal reimbursement. Such federal funds are an addition to the commodities the schools receive from the U.S. Department of Agriculture. This federal assistance interferes in no way with local control and operation of the schools. The program has been beneficial to parents and schoolchildren alike.

Problems in Public Education

Bilingual Programs

The 1980 census found that the Hispanics in Texas comprised 21 percent of the state's total population, and that Texas ranked second-highest in the country in number of Spanish-speaking inhabitants. Thus, there has always been a large number of students in the public schools who come from environments in which the primary language is other than English. Experience has shown that public school classes in which instruction is given *only* in English have often been inadequate for the education of these children. The mastery of basic English language skills is a prerequisite for effective participation in the state's public school educational program, regardless of whether students come from English- or Spanish-speaking backgrounds. Bilingual and special language programs, if properly organized and presented, can meet the needs of students from Spanish-speaking homes and facilitate their integration into the regular public school curriculum.

From the time Texas gained U.S. statehood (in 1845), thousands of students from Spanish-speaking backgrounds had been denied equal educational opportunities in the public schools. This was a serious detriment to their completion of a public school and/or university education, and jeopardized their chances of securing employment.

Prior to action in the federal courts, the Texas education agency mandated bilingual education from kindergarten through the third grade. A federal district court ordered Texas to implement a plan requiring that the state provide bilingual education for Spanish-speaking students at all grade levels. However, in 1982, the Fifth U.S. Court of Appeals held that legislation Texas enacted in 1981 providing a bilingual education program through the elementary grades was adequate to meet the needs of Spanish-speaking children.

Bilingual educational programs require qualified persons—individuals capable of teaching in both English and Spanish. In 1981, there was a serious shortage of such persons.

How bilingual courses should be organized and presented is crucial for Spanish-speaking students and their parents, as it will impact upon their ability to perpetuate their traditions and culture. The wrong approach to bilingual education could signal an end to the significant contributions in fields of literature, music, and art, (among others) that Spanish-speaking people have made.

Illegal Aliens

The problem of illegal aliens in Texas is related to the bilingual and special language programs required in the state's public schools. Despite the efforts of the federal border patrol, thousands of illegal aliens from Mexico have crossed the long border that separates Texas and Mexico. A federal district court held that illegal aliens in Texas of public school age are entitled to attend public school. The education of these individuals—especially in certain urban areas—has increased the cost of public education considerably.

The illegal aliens attending public schools, as well as their parents, pay a variety of state and local taxes; for example, taxes on automobiles, gasoline, sales taxes on various purchases, taxes on homes or property they own (or included in a rented apartment or house). By attending public school, and possibly a college or university, many Spanish-speaking individuals could be employed in better salaried positions and thereby pay more federal, state, and local taxes. Lack of adequate education or training has been an important factor in the number of citizens and aliens receiving welfare payments.

Aliens within the United States enjoy many of the privileges and immunities of American citizens. However, there are exceptions; for example, aliens cannot vote or hold public office, serve on a jury or grand jury, homestead on public lands, or secure an American passport. Nevertheless, the Fourteenth Amendment to the U.S. Constitution provides ''nor shall any State deprive *any person* of life, liberty, and property, without due process of law; nor deny to *any person* within its jurisdiction the equal protection of the laws'' (italics added). Both citizens and aliens, with certain exceptions, are *persons* within the meaning of the Fourteenth Amendment.

Married Students

Another problem in public education in Texas and the other states is the increase in the number of married and divorced students, as well as the increase in pregnancies of thirteen- and fourteen-year-old girls and upward. According to a federal court decision, married or divorced students in the public schools may not be prohibited from participating in extracurricular activities because such action violates the Equal Protection of the Law clause of the Fourteenth Amendment to the U.S. Constitution. Many public schools in Texas and other states either do not have professionally trained counselors or provide inadequate counseling services. Certainly, adequate counseling for an increasing number of public school students is necessary in the current school and social environment. In many localities, sex education in the public schools is either nonexistent or inadequate. This issue is highly controversial in many communities. In one form or another, young people will secure some type of information in this sensitive area.

Drugs, Alcoholism, and Absenteeism

Other problems in public education include drugs, alcohol, and absenteeism, which in some cases are interrelated. The problem of drugs and alcohol frequently involves the privacy of students. For example, a teacher or principal may believe a student has drugs or alcohol in his or her school locker. Physically, the school locker is a part of the school building and as such, is school property that is made available to students for school use. Rather than undertaking a "fishing expedition," in which drugs or alcohol *might* be found, public school teachers and administrators would justify the opening and examining school lockers on grounds of "probable cause" and "based on reasonable grounds to believe" the student has such items in his or her locker. Such a procedure is not as strict as that required of law enforcement officers under the Fourth Amendment of the U.S. Constitution (which also limits state policemen). The Fourth Amendment provides as follows: "The right of the people to be secure in their *persons, houses, papers,* and *effects,* against *unreasonable searches and seizures,* shall not be violated, and no warrants shall issue, but upon *probable cause,* supported by oath or affirmation, and particularly describing the place to be searched, and the persons or things to be seized" (italics added). Since public school administrators and teachers are not regular law-enforcement officers, no search warrant is required to examine school lockers. Nevertheless, public school personnel should limit themselves to "probable cause . . . based on reasonable grounds to believe" that a school locker or automobile contains either, or both, illegal drugs or alcohol, and a similar restraint should apply in questioning or searching a student elsewhere on school property.

A federal district court in Texas found the use of dogs by a school district "reasonable" in light of the "in loco parentis" doctrine under which school officials have some responsibility to act as students' parents during school hours. However, the U.S. Supreme Court agreed with an appeals court decision that school districts may not use drug-sniffing dogs to search students *randomly* for narcotics. Although the court held it was permissible to use dogs for investigating lockers and automobiles, it found the personal body sniffs more intrusive on privacy and declared they were constitutional only if there was "individualized suspicion" that a particular student had drugs. Therefore, the random sniffing of students by dogs is an unreasonable search. The sniffing of students' lockers and automobiles by dogs is not a "search" of the kind included in the Fourth Amendment of the U.S. Constitution. The use of dogs for such purposes is similar to their use at airports.

In some cases, the parents of public school students have been too protective of their children—even contending their children are not involved in drugs or alcohol. This compounds the problem for public school personnel.

A classroom teacher may send students with a drug, alcohol, or other behavioral problem to the school nurse for consultation. In severe cases, such students may be isolated from the other students for a time, or in more serious cases expelled from school for five to ten days or for the semester with loss of grades.

Absenteeism among public school students may, in some cases, be related to drugs, alcohol, or other behavioral problems. To manage this problem requires the coordinated effort of classroom teachers, school nurse, principal, and especially parents. Sometimes there is a lack of parental concern and cooperation, and the student ends up by being expelled from school with loss of grades or is in-and-out of school making low grades or failing. Truant officers (school officials who deal with cases of truancy) may get the students back to school or, under certain conditions, the parents may be fined. Classroom teachers report excessive absences to the truant officer, who in turn contacts the parents.

Curricula

The nature or content of the public school curriculum has been a continuing issue or problem throughout American history. Traditionalists advocate emphasizing and requiring *basic* subjects—reading, writing, math, grammar, literature, spelling, and science, to name a few. On the other hand, there are many supporters of a more liberalized curriculum, that is, certain required courses balanced with a number of nonrequired courses.

The Texas legislature amended the Texas education code in 1981 as relates to the required curriculum in the public schools.

> Each school district that offers kindergarten through grade 12 shall offer a well-balanced curriculum that includes: (1) English language arts; (2) other languages, to the extent possible; (3) mathematics; (4) science; (5) health; (6) physical education; (7) fine arts; (8) social studies; (9) economics, with emphasis on the free enterprise system and its benefits; (10) business education; (11) vocational education; and (12) Texas and United States history as individual subjects and in reading courses. . . . [The state board of education designates the essential elements of each subject listed.] In order to be accredited, a district must provide instruction in those essential elements as specified by the state board. . . . The State Board of Education shall provide for optional subjects in addition to those provided . . . as appropriate for districts that require choices in order to address unique local needs. . . . In addition, the Commissioner of Education may permit a school district to vary from the required curriculum as necessary to avoid hardship to the district.

Texas school districts may offer courses other than those required by the state legislature. For example, some districts offer courses in computer science, which are of considerable value for those students who plan to enter colleges and universities or possibly seek employment in various firms.

Despite the emergence of the word processor and other electronic machines to aid in word selection and spelling, there is certainly a need for correct spelling and proficiency in the English language. No matter how the world and society evolves in the future, such language ability will never be outdated.

However, the English language is difficult to master. "The Italian and Turkish alphabets each use *27 letters* to represent *27 sounds*, and German has *38 symbols* for *36 sounds*. In comparison, our *26 English* letters express at least *41 different sounds*, and those sounds have at least *561 different spellings*"[1] (italics added). Is it little wonder that many Americans are lost in the "horse latitudes" of grammar and spelling? Nevertheless, "the most important reason people top out in careers is their lack of facility with the language. They get to the point where they can't sell their ideas or write a really first-rate business letter."[2]

Some scholars believe the reform of the English language is an important aspect of the mastery of the English language and especially spelling. "The Soviet Union, Turkey, the Republic of China, Portugal and Holland are among the many countries that regularly sweep from their spelling systems the *entymological debris of past ages*"[3] (italics added).

Skills Test

High school students in Texas are required to take a skills test every year until they pass it, and school boards may make passage of the test a requirement for graduation. Also, high school transcripts must distinguish graduates who took advanced courses from those who took easier ones.

Higher Education

The state-supported colleges and universities in Texas are governed by boards of regents or directors, composed of nine members, appointed by the governor and senate for six-year terms. Some of the schools have separate governing boards, for example, the University of Texas and its branches (board of regents), and the A&M university system, among other schools.

Sources of revenue for the state colleges and universities include the biennial appropriations by the legislature, tuition and fees from students and professors (parking fees), federal contracts and research grants, and funds contributed by private individuals and groups. Income derived from the university permanent fund provides additional revenue for the University of Texas and Texas A&M. The university permanent fund, which was originally established by a grant of a million acres of land from the public domain, has been expanded considerably by additional grants and the discovery of oil and gas on the lands. Only the income from the fund may be expended for educational purposes (the university available fund).

The state-supported universities and colleges may issue bonds for building purposes. Income from the university permanent fund is used to retire bonds sold by the University of Texas and Texas A&M.

The coordinating board for state-supported higher education in Texas consists of eighteen members appointed by the governor and senate for six-year overlapping terms. The governor designates the chairman and vice-chairman of the board. Members of the board serve without pay but are reimbursed for their actual expenses incurred in attending meetings of the board or in attending to other work of the board. No member may be employed professionally for remuneration in the field of education during his term of office. The board appoints the commissioner of higher education who selects and supervises the board's staff and performs such other duties as delegated by the coordinating agency. The commissioner serves at the pleasure of the board.

The coordinating board has the authority to determine the role and scope of each public institution of higher education in Texas. Also the board may review periodically all degree and certificate programs offered by the public institutions of higher education to assure that they meet the present and future needs of the state. The board may order the initiation, consolidation, or elimination of degree or certificate programs. No new department, school, degree program, or certificate program may be added at any public institution of higher education in Texas except with prior approval of the board.

21 Business and the Professions

THE POWER TO PROTECT the health, safety, general welfare, convenience, and morals of the people, or what is known as the police power of the state, is the most important power reserved to the state by the Tenth Amendment of the federal Constitution. It is by virtue of this power that a state is entitled to regulate business, the professions, and labor. As is true of other state activities, there are limitations upon the exercise of the police power. There can be no deprivation of life, liberty, or property without due process of law, or denial of equal protection of the laws by the state. Hence, the Fourteenth Amendment of the U.S. Constitution places rather broad limitations upon the exercise of state powers. Business activities instituted by the national government, as well as those involving transactions in foreign and interstate commerce, are subject to federal regulation. Despite these limitations, state legislatures and regulatory agencies have passed hundreds of statutes and issued many administrative regulations under the police power. Several agencies in Texas regulate business and the professions.

Regulation of Business

Incorporation Under Texas Law

Many people who engage in business in Texas on a small or modest scale are not required to secure permission or authorization from the state to operate. Most medium-sized and large business concerns, which operate as partnerships or corporations, are, however, subject to state control. The formation and dissolution of partnerships and the rights and liabilities of partners are regulated by state law. Domestic corporations, namely those that are incorporated under Texas law, have no right to operate—or even exist—without a corporation charter issued by the state. Some corporations, for example national banks, are chartered by Congress; nevertheless, the majority of corporations secure their charters from the states.

Persons desiring to secure a corporation charter in Texas (with exception of a charter for a bank or insurance company) must file an application with the secretary of state. Besides the name of the corporation, the charter or franchise—if issued by the state—indicates the purpose for which it is formed, the shares and amount of capital stock, and other information that the secretary of state may deem necessary. Foreign corporations, or those incorporated under the laws of another state and wishing to do business in Texas, must file certified copies of their articles of incorporation with the secretary of state, after which permits to operate in the state may be issued. Before a charter or a permit is issued, the secretary of state must determine if the intended business operation is in violation of the state's anti-trust laws or other regulations. Besides state regulation, municipalities have considerable regulatory powers over corporations operating within their jurisdiction.

Many interstate corporations—those that do business in two or more states—secure their charters in New Jersey and Delaware because of the ease with which charters can be secured in these two states. However, if the existence of hundreds of corporations operating under state charters or franchises is a criterion, it does not appear overly difficult to incorporate in other states as well. In fact, the ease in which charters can be secured has encouraged the corporate form of doing business.

Securities

Regulating the sale of stocks, bonds, and other types of securities—as a means of offering some protection to investors—has long been considered an important activity of both the national and state governments. Vested with police power, all states have passed laws to regulate security issues. These laws, known as blue-sky laws, regulate and supervise investment companies. Through federal and state regulation the public is given some protection from investing in fraudulent companies. The laws are designed to prevent the sale of stock in fly-by-night concerns, imaginary oil wells, nonexistent gold and uranium mines, and similar fraudulent business undertakings.

In Texas, the securities board is composed of three persons appointed by the governor and senate for six-year overlapping terms. The board appoints a securities commissioner who serves at the pleasure of the board. Under the supervision of the board, the securities commissioner administers the provisions of the Securities Act.

Dealers, agents, or salesmen of investment companies who wish to sell securities in Texas must file certain detailed information with the securities commissioner. On the basis of this information the securities commissioner may issue them permits. Each corporation doing business in Texas and wishing to issue securities for sale in the state must file a complete financial statement with the securities commissioner. Among other things, the financial statement must reveal the assets and liabilities of the business concern and information on the securities to be sold. If the plan of operation and the securities intended for sale are approved by the securities commissioner, a certificate of permission to sell is issued. Without his approval, it is unlawful to offer or sell securities in the state. Hence, the permits and the registration of securities constitute an important feature of securities regulation in Texas.

Although regulation by the state, as well as by the federal government, is in itself not a guarantee of a fair return on an investment, such regulation is protection from investing in fraudulent companies. Once public information is released concerning the companies who offer lawful securities for sale, the decision to invest rests with the individual.

Enforcement of the State's Antitrust Laws

A business concern may attempt to prevent or lessen competition by controlling production, transportation, markets, or prices. These and other monopolistic practices are considered a combination or conspiracy in restraint of trade. Both federal and state antitrust laws are designed to prevent such unfair practices. The enforcement of Texas's antitrust law is a responsibility of the attorney general.

Federal antitrust laws cover corporations that operate in interstate commerce. The enforcement of the federal law by the U.S. attorney general and his staff provides the chief protection against monopolistic practices.

The Texas Truth-in-Lending Program

Inadequate regulation of consumer credit "imposes intolerable burdens on those segments of our society which can least afford to bear them—the uneducated, the unsophisticated, the poor and the elderly" (preamble, Texas consumer-credit code).

Consumer-credit regulation and consumer protection is of vital concern in Texas, where an estimated 25 percent of the people live in poverty. To what extent are interest rates on small loans (loans of $100 or less) a factor in poverty? Do such charges help cause or seriously aggravate poverty conditions? Although there are no definite answers to these questions, consumer-credit regulation is an important consideration in the general economy of Texas.

The small-loan industry is very competitive, but competition among companies is not sufficient to protect the public in payment of reasonable interest rates. Those who must secure small loans need additional protection against unscrupulous companies, which take advantage of persons in financial distress. On the other hand, there is considerable risk involved in making small loans, and for this reason it is unrealistic to limit the interest rate that loan companies may charge to 10 or 15 percent. If the maximum rate of interest that may be charged is too low, the loan companies will find ways to circumvent the regulation. For example, a small-loan company may collect brokerage fees. (A lending agent charges a brokerage fee for lending some other agency's money.) The company may require the individual seeking the loan to purchase a certain type of credit insurance. (A lender requires an individual to purchase an investment certificate from the company that is pledged as security for the loan. It is paid in full at the time the note becomes due. The loan company profits from both the interest on the loan and guarantee charges.) Carrying charges also may be assessed by the loan company. The brokerage fees, credit insurance, carrying charges, and other fees—all of which are interest charges—may make it possible for the lenders to collect more than the maximum percent of interest permitted by law. The question is, at what point does the protection of the public end and the legalization of usury begin?

The politics of small-loans regulation in Texas involves the interplay of various interest groups and includes the conflict in the legislature between the Texas and out-of-state loan companies, the conflict between the small- and small-small-loan companies, the lobbyists who represent the companies, the house and senate members that are retained by loan companies, the desire of Texas banks to increase the rate of interest on small bank loans, and the efforts of the Texas Consumers' Association to secure passage of more adequate laws regulating consumer credit. Therefore, the consumer-credit code, like all controversial legislation, was a product of compromise and pressure politics.

The consumer-credit commissioner of Texas is appointed by, and serves at the pleasure of, the finance commission. He is an employee of the finance commission, subject to its direction. The commissioner appoints and removes examiners and other employees.

The consumer-credit code—the Texas "truth-in-lending" regulations—governs all forms of consumer credit, that is all deferred-payment obligations that include a charge for the right to defer, incurred in the course of acquiring goods or services for personal or family use.[1] Banks, loan companies, credit unions, retail stores, home-improvement loans, and automobile installment sales are regulated by the code and the consumer credit commissioner and his staff.

No person may, without first obtaining a license from the consumer-credit commissioner, engage in the business of making loans with cash advances of $2,500 or less. An applicant for a license must file certain information with the commissioner and pay the required investigation fee. The commissioner may, after notice and hearing, suspend or revoke any license of a loan company, bank, savings and loan association, or credit union for failure to pay the annual license fee and for other violations of the code. Under certain conditions, the commissioner may reinstate suspended licenses or issue new licenses to those whose licenses have been revoked.

A law passed by the Texas legislature in 1981 permits the interest ceilings on most personal, automobile, and similar loans to rise to as much as 24 percent annually. Thus, the interest ceiling applies to most loans except home mortgages (whose interest is federally regulated) and to 28 percent for business, commercial, and investment loans of more than $250,000. Certain classes of loans by consumer finance companies could attract even higher annual percentage rates. Although maximum interest rates are prescribed by law, lending agencies may charge lower rates than the maximum allowed.

In financing a loan, an individual may pay only simple interest, but such interest is used only by a few lenders. One may pay a certain number of dollars per $100 per annum. This is "add-on" interest, since one pays on the full amount of the loan for the full term, although one does not owe the full amount if paying the money back in installments. Other forms of add-on interest may include brokerage fees, credit insurance, carrying charges, and other fees which make it possible for the lender to exceed the maximum percent of interest permitted by law.

The maximum legal interest rate is 240 percent. This rate applies only in limited cases, i.e., loans of less than $30 for a period of only a month. However, interest rates nearly as high apply to loans between $30 and $300.

Some consider the interest rates on loans of $300 or less an affront to the public conscience. However, the loan companies contend that the risk of repayment of these loans requires high interest rates, that small-small loans are the least profitable for the companies. The consumer-credit code greatly increased the interest rate banks may charge on loans of less than $300.

The disclosure provisions of the consumer-credit code give the lender an option in stipulating the rate of interest: as a total number of dollars (the method employed by almost all lenders) or as a simple interest rate. If a lender advertises the small-loan rates, he must state them as simple interest.

For loans of $1,500 or less, the loan period, as specified in the loan contract, may not exceed thirty-seven months; for loans in excess of $1,500, but not in excess of $2,500 the loan period may not exceed forty-three months.

Prior to enactment of the consumer-credit code, there was considerable dishonesty in home-improvement loans. Promoters made "misleading statements about the work to be performed, contracts and notes with the most vital sections [were] left blank, execution of few repairs, and substandard workmanship."[2] The code attempts to prevent some of these practices, since "its disclosure clauses applying to retail installment contracts also govern home-improvement transactions and require the contractor to submit an agreement specifying most significant items in advance."[3] Also, home-improvement lenders must secure a certificate of completion from the borrower thirty days afterward declaring the borrower is satisfied with performance on the contract. The purpose is to prevent unscrupulous contractors from selling the note and disappearing, leaving the borrower with no one to sue if the contract is not properly fulfilled.

Lenders and sellers on credit who charge more interest than is authorized, except through accident or error, must pay twice the interest or time price differential to the person who borrowed the money, as well as pay attorney fees. If they charge in excess of twice the interest that is authorized by law, they forfeit all principal and interest, plus any other charges, and must pay attorney fees.

The federal truth-in-lending law is primarily a disclosure law. A creditor must disclose to the consumer certain information concerning finance charges, annual percentage rates and other terms relating to consumer-credit transactions. Therefore, creditors in Texas must comply with the disclosure requirements of the federal law and, to the extent there is no conflict, they must also comply with the disclosure requirements of the state law. In addition, creditors must look to the state law for the allowable rates of finance charge; the federal law does not regulate the rates of charges for credit.

The federal truth-in-lending law contains a provision that permits a state to apply for exemption from federal regulation if the state law regulating credit transactions is substantially similar to the federal law. Since there are significant differences between the state and federal laws, Texas is not eligible for exemption from federal regulation.

Banking

In Texas the department of banking regulates state banks, state-chartered credit unions, and certain loan and brokerage companies, although the latter receive their charters from the secretary of state. State-chartered savings and building-and-loan associations are regulated by a separate department, the department of savings and loan. Both departments operate under general policy determined by the finance commission.

The powers and duties of the department of banking, banking commissioner, and the finance commission are included in the state banking code. The supervisory and regulatory functions of the banking commissioner and his staff include the examination of state banks and credit unions at stated intervals; approval of mergers and reorganization of state banks; the closing and liquidation of insolvent state banks; and removal of directors, officers, and employees of state banks for cause (malpractice or violation of state law).

The state banking board, consisting of one citizen of the state appointed by the governor and senate for a term of two years, the banking commissioner, and the state treasurer, considers applications for new banks and credit-union charters.

> The chartering of a credit union is not contested as a rule, since it is not competitive. Parties in favor of, and opposed to, the chartering of any state bank are notified by the board and have an opportunity to appear at a hearing prior to a charter's being granted or refused. In considering bank applications, the State Banking Board is charged by statute with determining, after hearing, whether: (1) a public necessity exists for the proposed bank; (2) the proposed capital structure is adequate; (3) the volume of business in the community where the proposed bank is to be established is such as to indicate profitable operation of the proposed bank; (4) the proposed officers and directors have sufficient banking experience, ability, and standing to render success of the proposed bank probable; and (5) the applicants are acting in good faith.[4]

Once a charter is granted it is the duty of the banking commissioner to see that the newly organized bank or credit union operates in accordance with state law. All companies regulated by the department are required by law to publish financial statements.

The closing and liquidation of banks, reopening of closed banks, reorganization of banks, and approval of amendments to the articles of association are considered by the board. It also serves as a board of appeals for directors, officers, and employees of state banks who are removed for cause by the banking commissioner. All decisions of the board are subject to review by the courts.

State law provides, "No state, national or private bank shall engage in business in more than one place, maintain any branch office, or cash checks or receive deposits except in its own banking house or through unmanned teller machines as authorized in Article 3A" (1983).

New banks continue to be opened in the populated areas of the state, with the greatest number in the suburbs as opposed to the downtown sections of the city. The population expansion to outlying areas and the resultant growth of new shopping centers and other businesses prompted this trend. Banks believe that the people will find a neighborhood bank convenient and will use its facilities in preference to a city bank. That this is the case is borne out by an increase in the percentage of deposits. Since Texas banks are not permitted to operate "branch" units, there is considerable competition between downtown banks to establish "affiliates" in the suburban areas. The increase in the number of applications for bank charters again illustrates the impact of developments in the metropolitan areas upon the political, economic, and cultural life of the state. It represents a phase of settlement and expansion on the metropolitan or suburban frontier.

Insurance

The state board of insurance consists of three members appointed by the governor and senate for six-year overlapping terms. The board appoints a commissioner of insurance as its chief administrative officer, who has primary responsibility for administering the provisions of the insurance code under the supervision of the board. He holds his position at the pleasure of the board.

The insurance industry is a major factor in the Texas economy. Therefore, adequate protection of policyholders and prohibition of unfair competition and deceptive practices are tremendously important. For this reason the commissioner of insurance (with his staff of insurance examiners and other employees) and the board of insurance have a large responsibility, along with the legislature (through strengthening the insurance code), in protecting the welfare of the state.

The board of insurance has broad regulatory powers. It incorporates, charters, examines, and issues licenses to companies operating under the Texas insurance laws. After proper investigation, insurance agents secure their licenses from the board. In case of insolvency or violation of the insurance code, the license of any company may be canceled or revoked. The commissioner of insurance may disapprove any life-insurance policy or withdraw any previous approval if "it contains provisions which encourage misrepresentation or are unjust, unfair, inequitable, misleading, deceptive or contrary to law or to the public policy of [the] State." Investigating agency violations, hearing complaints on claim matters, approving policy forms of underwriters, approving and determining insurance or premium rates, and supervising the setting up of reserves for payment of claims are important activities in the regulation of insurance. In the event an insurance company becomes insolvent and is placed in receivership by court order, the commissioner of insurance and the board of insurance must see that the assets of the bankrupt company are conserved and liquidated to the best possible advantage of the creditors and policyholders.

As for fire insurance, "Texas was the first state to adopt a 'schedule rating law,' now used by many states, based on a system of charges for hazards and credits for their removal, plus further credits for good experience records."[5] Under the "key rate schedule" cities and towns must be graded and rerated from time to time. This involves the investigation of the waterworks, fire department and equipment of municipalities, as well as the operation of regulatory city ordinances. The organization of the fire department, type of fire-fighting equipment, fire loss record, size of water mains, and the location and spacing of fireplugs, among other factors, are considered in determining a city's fire-insurance rate. The rating is based on a city's fire-loss record over a period of five years. A city with well-trained firemen, efficient equipment, and a good fire-loss record may be able to save the local residents thousands of dollars in fire-insurance premiums. The inhabitants of some cities in Texas would do well to take a hard look at the operation of their municipal fire department.

The insurance code requires applicants for charters and charter amendments to submit proof that they are acting in good faith. A negative finding on this point is sufficient for denial of a request. Every report or document required to be filed under the insurance code must be verified by a written declaration that it is made under the penalties of perjury.

Liquor

In 1970 the voters of Texas approved a constitutional amendment that authorized the state legislature to regulate the sale of mixed alcoholic drinks ("liquor by the drink"). A local election must be held and the voters must give their approval before mixed drinks may be sold in their community—the local-option feature. Private clubs continue to operate in Texas; however, many have converted to public bars.

Three members, appointed by the governor and senate for six-year overlapping terms, compose the Texas alcoholic beverage commission. Members of the commission appoint an administrator. Other than the determination of general policy and passing on rules and regulations, the commission has delegated most of its duties to the administrator.

Liquor permits and licenses are issued by the administrator and his staff; once issued they may be suspended or canceled for good cause after a hearing. In case of suspension or cancellation, the interested party has the right of appeal to the district court. Laboratory technicians analyze alcoholic beverages to determine the standards of quality and purity, and other staff members are concerned with the enforcement of proper labeling and advertising regulations. District inspectors investigate violations of the law regulating various phases of the liquor business and they may submit cases for action to the main office.

The liquor business conducted in interstate commerce is regulated by the federal government through the issuance, suspension, and revocation of federal permits, as well as the regulation of marketing, labeling, advertising, and selling practices. In certain areas, the Texas alcoholic beverage commission cooperates with federal agencies.

Moonshiners, or those engaged in illicit distilling, have operated in Texas since the days of the Republic. They operate without the required permits, and do not pay the federal and state taxes on liquor. Sometimes the constable, county sheriff, and federal-revenue agents will raid a still, arrest persons at the scene, and smash the still equipment. Moonshiners may be arraigned in either the county or federal district court, or in both. Despite the raids by the "revenooers," the illegal "corn-squeezing" operators, or the "Snuffy Smiths of Texas," continue to operate, especially in east and southeast Texas.

Transportation, Natural Gas, and the Oil Industry

The legislation creating the Texas railroad commission was patterned after the Interstate Commerce Act of 1887. Intrastate railroad regulation was placed under the Texas railroad commission, whereas interstate regulations were administered by the interstate commerce commission (ICC). John H. Reagan (then U.S. senator from Texas), who had a part in the establishment of both the federal and the Texas agency, resigned his seat in the U.S. Senate and became the first chairman of the Texas railroad commission.[6]

Composed of three members elected for six-year overlapping terms, the railroad commission is the most powerful regulatory agency in the state. One member of the commission is elected every two years and the chairmanship rotates among the members. By custom the chairman is the member next up for election.

Although the Texas railroad commission was originally created to regulate railroad rates and tariffs in Texas, prevent unjust discrimination, correct abuses, and enforce the state railroad laws, these matters are regulated by the federal interstate commerce commission.

When public buses and freight trucks became an important factor in the Texas economy, the legislature expanded the regulatory activities of the railroad commission to include truck and bus transportation. Probably the lawmakers thought all transportation should be regulated by a single commission, and since the railroad commission was already in existence the legislature merely expanded the commission's activities.

Applications for certificates of public convenience and necessity to operate truck and bus lines in the state must be filed with the commission in writing, accompanied by a filing fee and certain information required by law. Hearings are held by examiners and testimony is taken as to convenience and necessity. Court reporters take down the testimony at these proceedings and transcribe it into a record for the benefit of all parties concerned. Following the hearing on an application the examiner submits his findings to the commission, which may issue a permit to operate. If authority to operate is granted, the applicant must obtain acceptable insurance and pay the required plate and tax fees. It is through this procedure that the railroad-commission permits are displayed on the buses and trucks operating in Texas. Rate inspectors, stationed in various parts of the state, check bills of lading to determine if proper charges are made in rates.

Gas utilities are regulated by the railroad commission in an effort to establish and maintain fair and reasonable rates for the users of natural gas in Texas. All gas companies report to the commission the amount of gas sold, number of customers, and the rates charged. Whenever a city and a utility cannot agree upon a fair gas rate, the city authorities or the utility may appeal to the railroad commission for a hearing and examination of all facts, after which the commission may prescribe a fair and reasonable rate.

The railroad commission has broad regulatory and enforcement powers in the field of oil and gas conservation. Engineers, inspectors, and supervisors employed by the commission enforce the regulations that relate to the production of oil and gas in the state. It is the duty of the commission to ascertain the going market demand for Texas oil and see that production is kept at market demand because production in excess of market demand is wasteful, due to the evaporation of oil during storage. Today, conservation and prevention of waste in the production of oil and gas, and regulation according to market demand, are the major concerns of the Texas railroad commission.

The principal duties of the commission in regulating the production of oil and gas are as follows:

1. Issuance of drilling permits after a study of each application as to distance from property lines and producing wells, confiscation by drainage of adjacent properties, exploratory value, and other considerations related to conservation and prevention of physical waste.
2. Inspection at completion of each well as to equipment, safety, protection against water intrusion, ratio and volume of oil and gas, and other considerations relating to physical waste.
3. Regulation of production to conform to market demand, prevention of physical waste by orderly withdrawals designed to hold back undue water encroachment, prevention of isolation of oil pockets, maintenance of natural pressure, and use of all possible means of conservation and nonwastage.
4. Setting of allowables for each well in accordance with formulas prescribed in individual field rules or rules of statewide application, whichever are applicable. For each well, records are kept of crude-oil production.[7]

Monthly public hearings are held to determine proratable production for each oil well. Any producer, purchaser, or anyone else who has an interest in production may attend these hearings and present evidence to show that some change should be made either in the allowable or in the manner of operating the wells. Testimony at these open hearings is taken under oath. In making its regulations the railroad commission considers evidence submitted by the commission staff, operators, and other interested persons, as well as producers' and purchasers' requirements for oil and gas. Recommendations of the interstate oil compact commission and statistics made available by the U.S. Bureau of Mines are considered by the railroad commission. No doubt on occasion these public hearings are a formality, since the decisions have been made at a prehearing conference attended by the purchasers and producers of crude oil.

When the rate of flow of an oil well has been determined, the producer must comply with the system known as prorations. At one time proration orders issued by the railroad commission authorized the number of days each month wells were allowed to produce. The current practice of the commission is to place no limitations on production (as during an energy crisis) or to limit the flow to acertain percentage of production capacity. In the event a producer exceeds this allowable, the "hot" oil may be seized and sold at public auction and the money turned over to the state. Field and individual-well allowable are determined by the commission. Enforcement of the allowable prevents too rapid loss of pressure. Unless pressure is carefully controlled it is impossible to recover the maximum amount of oil from the earth.

One of the many factors that have made the regulation of oil production uniquely difficult is the "law of capture." Since oil can be drained from beneath one's land, a neighbor's well, by taking advantage of the law of capture, may deprive another landowner of a considerable part of his wealth. When "Dad" Joiner made his strike in the east Texas field in 1930 there was a frantic race to remove the black liquid gold from the earth. To prevent the loss of wealth through the law of capture, one well was drilled to offset another. In fact, wells were drilled in such close proximity that the legs of the superstructures were interlaced. In the matter of efficient recovery of oil, thousands of unnecessary wells—costing millions of dollars—were drilled in the east Texas field. Fortunately, the railroad commission has made considerable progress in establishing reasonable spacing requirements.*

To implement the state laws and regulations concerning the production of oil, Congress passed the Connally "Hot Oil" Act. This act prohibits the interstate movement of oil that is illegally produced.

The Politics of Oil Regulation ("Politics of the Umbrella"). The railroad commission provides an "umbrella" for the oil industry in Texas in order to stabilize

---

*Oil producers may make application to the railroad commission for approval of voluntary unitization agreements. Under present law, 100 percent of the working and royalty interests must agree to a unitization plan. If approved by the railroad commission, a single producer extracts the oil from the field, dividing the proceeds with royalty owners and working interests on the basis of the size of their holdings. It permits the use of repressuring techniques that cause oil to move about underground, techniques that could not be applied if each lease continued producing independently. Also, use of sophisticated secondary recovery techniques may increase considerably a field's lifetime production.

prices by keeping production in accord with market demand. Because Texas is such a large producer of oil, the extent to which the umbrella is maintained or tilted has a tremendous impact upon the oil industry in the United States. Oil developments in the other oil-producing states and foreign countries influence regulation in Texas. The "umbrella," however maintained, is of immediate concern to powerful interest groups—the producers and purchasers of oil. Considering the pressure and counterpressure that is brought to bear on the railroad commission, as well as the economic resources of the interest groups concerned, the "politics of the umbrella" is dynamic indeed, involving the interests of the major and the independent oil companies.

The Majors and the Independents. The distinction between the majors, as for example the oil empires represented by Humble and Standard Oil of New Jersey, and the independents is rather vague. Independents range in size from individual wildcatters to multimillion-dollar companies which, like the majors, operate their own refining and marketing facilities. In general, the independent is a producer who disposes of his oil to the majors. The bulk of Texas oil is purchased and marketed by the majors. Sometimes Texans use the terms *millionaires* and *billionaires* to distinguish between the independents and majors. In any event, the Texas Independent Producers' and Royalty Owners' Association (TIPRO), representing the independents of Texas, and the lobbyists and public-relations personnel of both independents and majors, make their influence felt in the legislative and administrative halls of Texas.

The power and influence of the majors and independents, as well as the conflict within the American oil industry, has made the regulation of oil production complex and difficult.

Sometimes the interests of the majors and independents are the same, yet there are conflicts at hearings before the railroad commission. They may differ on conservation policies. Considering the domestic and foreign oil investments of some of the majors, as well as their purchasing-marketing-pipeline-refinery tie-up in this country, there is a practical basis for their tremendous political power and influence.

In case of conflict of interest between independents and the majors, the railroad commission must hear the arguments of both parties before reaching a decision. At times the commission has been compelled to take decisive action in order to protect the industry and prevent waste. For example, when the east Texas field was discovered in 1930 it brought to the fore, for the first time in Texas, the problem of the independent in the oil industry. The discovery of the field ushered in the "golden age" of the wildcatters and shoestring operators. Wells were drilled and oil pumped as fast as possible with no regard for the consequences. The market was glutted and the price of oil dropped as low as ten cents a barrel. Oilmen refer to the development as the era of "ten-cent oil."

Although the majors had been able to control Spindletop (near Beaumont and discovered in 1901) and other fields, such was not possible in the east Texas field. The task was much too large for the majors. Hence, the railroad commission was forced to take action. Under the able leadership of Ernest O. Thompson, who had been appointed only recently to the commission by Governor Ross Sterling, the railroad commission took steps to put teeth in the state's statutes concerning waste of oil reserves, and to check the reckless and irresponsible exploitation of oil. The system of prorations guarantees the independents a proportionate share of the oil market.

Humble, in 1938, ordered price reductions in crude oil ranging from five cents to twenty cents a barrel, whereupon the commission ordered a fifteen-day shutdown of every field in Texas. In addition, the Texas commissioners prevailed upon four other major producing states to take similar action. Before the shutdown period had expired, Humble, with its stocks depleted, was forced to rescind the price cut, after which the railroad commission promptly allowed the fields to resume production.

Importation of Foreign Oil. Domestic crude oil must compete against vast quantities of foreign crude oil produced by some of the majors. For the independents, substantial importation of foreign oil from the Middle East and Venezuela has created a serious problem. As a result of oil developments abroad, the independents feel that the majors will show less and less interest in them as suppliers of crude oil. They have complained about the inability to secure pipeline connections as new wells are brought in and have denounced pipeline prorations that are cutbacks over and above the prorations set by the railroad commission. The pipeline prorations, applied from time to time by the majors, have been justified on grounds of insufficient storage capacity. The independents have charged that the foreign crude oil has been the real reason for the cutbacks and the delay in price increases. The refineries on the eastern seaboard processing oil from the Middle East and the tanker-construction program have caused grave concern among the independents.

Representatives of the major companies contend that the producers of domestic crude oil in the United States must find ways to reduce production cost in order to compete with foreign oil; that this is the real solution, not limiting the importation of foreign oil. On the other hand, representatives of the independents have declared the importation of foreign oil should be limited to a certain fixed percentage of domestic production.

Few independents feel there is enough industry statesmanship to make voluntary import controls on foreign oil workable; however, the majors, with vast oil resources in foreign countries, are not very enthusiastic about mandatory import controls enforced by the federal government.

Monopolistic Tendencies. To many independents, the majors constitute an international oil cartel that is able to manipulate the supply and prices of oil by playing foreign production and importation against domestic production and regulation. If this be true, the majors can manipulate the production and price of oil, both at home and abroad, to their own advantage. On occasion spokesmen for the Texas Independent Producers' and Royalty Owners' Association have charged that different prices are paid for the same oil in the same field in violation of the Texas laws covering purchases. These charges of price fixing may explain why the independents have shown some interest in federal control of the oil industry and prosecution of the majors under the federal antitrust laws.

Demand for an antitrust investigation or prosecution may result from the increase or decrease in crude-oil prices by the majors, as well as the increased importation of foreign oil. Under the U.S. antitrust laws the government has nothing to do with the level of prices, although the staff of the antitrust division of the Department of Justice may take steps to prohibit collusive action to control or manipulate prices. In the past such retaliatory action against the majors has not been very successful. In any event, there are those among the independents who doubt if the majors and independents operate under the same umbrella.

Also, independent oil producers believe that some of the major importing companies do the "homework" of some of the technical staff of the Texas railroad commission, thus encouraging the monopolistic tendencies within the oil industry.

Some independents believe legislation should be passed either to limit the powers of the railroad commission or create a new agency to regulate the oil and gas industry. These proposals indicate the independents believe the commission is more sympathetic to the interest of the majors. Considering the power and influence of the majors with the railroad commission and the legislature, it would be difficult to pass such legislation.

The Depletion Allowance. Prior to 1975, federal revenue laws permitted petroleum producers to claim a 22 percent deduction on their gross income on the theory that oil is an irreplaceable asset. In support of federal subsidization through tax immunity, the oil industry emphasized the waste involved in extractive as compared to nonextractive industries, increased expense in the search for new oil resources, and the need to encourage—rather than discourage—oil exploration. For years the major and the independent oil companies exerted their influence to prevent a reduction or termination of the oil depletion allowance. And, of course, they were in agreement on opposition to any increase of taxes on crude oil. However, in 1975 Congress passed the Tax Reduction Act which eliminated the 22 percent depletion allowance for the oil industry (except for operators producing less than two thousand barrels a day). Unless the act is amended, this tax benefit will be phased out by 1985. The impact of the change in the depletion allowance on the future price of gasoline is difficult to determine since there are other considerations involved.

Utilities

The purpose of utility regulation is to provide rates that are fair, just, and reasonable and services that are adequate and efficient. Both the state and the municipalities in Texas are concerned with the regulation of utilities. Private utility companies may operate in a city under a short- or long-time franchise or contract with the city. The contract may provide that the city may purchase, or cause a purchase of the property to be made, after a specified number of years. A power and light company may provide electric power for the city and operate without competition or as a monopoly. However, depending on the provisions of the franchise or contract, the company may be required to pay a certain percentage of its annual gross receipts to the city, as well as to secure city approval of rate charges, changes in services, and improvements that will cost more than a specified sum. The regulatory person or agency in each of the municipalities may be a public utilities director or a public utilities board or commission.

The state utilities commission is composed of three commissioners appointed by the governor and senate for six-year terms. It has original jurisdiction over electric, water, and sewer utility rates, operations, and services not within the incorporated limits of a municipality. Neither the state utilities commission nor the railroad commission (in the case of gas utilities) has power to regulate the rates or service of any utility owned and operated by any municipality within its boundaries. However, where a municipally owned or privately owned utility (electric, water, or sewer) extends services beyond municipal boundaries, the state utilities commission has jurisdiction over the operations beyond city or town limits. Also, subject to certain limitations imposed by law, the state utilities commission has original jurisdiction over the business and property of all telecommunications utilities in the state.

The railroad commission has original jurisdiction over the rates and services of gas utilities distributing natural or synthetic natural gas in areas outside the limits of municipalities, and over the rates and services of pipelines transmitting or selling natural or synthetic natural gas to gas utilities.

The governing body of each municipality has original jurisdiction over all electric, water, and sewer utility rates, operations, and services provided within its city or town limits. The governing body of a municipality may, by ordinance, elect to surrender to the state utilities commission its original jurisdiction over electric, water, or sewer utility rates, operations, and services, or to submit the question to the qualified voters of the municipality. A municipality that surrenders its jurisdiction to the state commission may, by vote of the electorate, reinstate the jurisdiction of the governing body of the city. The state commission has appellate jurisdiction to review orders or ordinances of municipalities as provided by law. Also, municipalities have original jurisdiction over all rates, operations, and services provided by any gas utility within their city or town limits. The railroad commission has appellate jurisdiction to review all such orders or ordinances of municipalities.

The state utilities commission and railroad commission may advise and assist municipalities upon request. Such assistance may include aid to municipalities with matters pending before the utilities or railroad commission, the courts, or before the municipal council. Staff members of the two state agencies may appear as witnesses and otherwise provide evidence for the cities.

Any party to a rate proceeding before the governing body of a municipality may appeal the body's decision to the state utilities commission or the railroad commission (in the case of gas utilities). Also, citizens of a municipality may appeal the decision of the governing body in any rate proceeding to the utilities or railroad commission by filing a petition for review signed by the required number of qualified voters of the municipality. Citizens and utility companies have the right to appeal rates set by the commission itself. Such appeal would be to the Texas supreme court.

In determining a fair rate of return to a utility company on its investment, Texas law provides for use of a combination of original cost of property and current replacement cost. This is what determines how much a utility company will be allowed to charge its customers. The rate base used by the state commission in determining a fair return to utilities is based on not more than 75 percent of original cost nor less than 25 percent of replacement cost. The commission *may* use a 60-40 percent base, thereby allowing itself some flexibility. The companies favor the use of replacement cost since it allows them to show a larger investment because of rising prices. The higher cost then may be used as a justification for rate hikes.

In utility regulation, the establishment of a rate base is complex and the guidelines to be employed are debatable. Some critics contend a reasonable balance should be given to original cost minus depreciation of the utility company's investment and to the current replacement cost minus an adjustment for age and condition. What are the measures of fair value? And what weight should be given to each? These are matters on which rate experts disagree.

Nursing Homes

Nursing home business has expanded as the population and life span in Texas has increased. With the need for more nursing home facilities, the public has become aware of inadequate regulation of the homes. Although many Texas nursing homes have been subject to little or no criticism, a number of critical incidents have been reported; for example, overcrowded conditions, the dispensing of wrong medications, unsanitary and roach-infested rooms, falsification of medical charts, inadequate security, improper and inadequate diet, little or no recreational facilities, lack of available medical personnel, the beating of a nursing home patient with a coat hanger (this incident sparked an investigation by an attorney general's task force), murder investigations of nursing home deaths, poor training and inadequate pay for nurses, aides, and other nursing home personnel, inadequate ratio of nurse's aides to patients, inadequate clinical record documentation, neglect, theft of personal property, misuse of patient funds, and psychological abuse. Other allegations against nursing homes include the theft of residents' money, either by someone managing to secure power of attorney over their estates or succeeding in becoming beneficiary of their insurance policies.

Nursing homes, like hospitals, have a routine: meals at a specified time, medication for some, bath for the residents, change of bed sheets, and, other than bedfast patients, some form of light exercise or movement, such as physical therapy, walking, or use of a wheelchair. While it is true that the residents of nursing homes, like other people, need and enjoy a certain amount of routine, mere routine is not enough for the more able residents who may be limited to viewing TV in their rooms, playing cards, or viewing TV in the lounge or reception room. For these people there should be other forms of recreation—a stroll in the nursing home flower gardens, bus tours in the community, concerts, exhibits, and movies, etc. Not all residents have relatives or friends that could provide this type of relaxation.

As a result of the age and illness of many persons in nursing homes, and the manner in which some homes are operated, it is understandable why people often experience feelings of depression during and after visiting a resident.

When nursing homes are segregated (as many are) from the mainstream of their surrounding communities, several problems may arise. Often, residents become alienated, the staff feels less accountable to the public, the public ignores conditions, and the overall care suffers.

Many residents of nursing homes are seldom visited by relatives, friends, or other individuals, except on a limited basis by ministers and priests. Relatives or friends may live in other communities or states. Hence, there is no close or interested person to check on the operations of the home and the needs of the residents. This is an important factor in the alienation of nursing home residents and the lack of patient-oriented homes. Thus, more supervision and control of nursing homes by the state and federal government is necessary.

Adequate regulation of nursing homes in Texas, as in some other states, has been difficult for a number of reasons. For one thing, the nursing home industry in Texas is a multimillion dollar operation, and many homes are owned by large corporations that have influence in Austin. The Texas Nursing Home Association, as a vested interest lobby, has been active in promoting the interests of nursing homes. And the fact that some Texas legislators own, or have an interest in, nursing homes has been to the advantage of the nursing home industry. The Texas Nursing Home Association has provided funds for the nomination and election of state legislators who use their influence to promote the interest of the nursing home industry.

The Texas department of health resources, the attorney general and his staff, and the state district courts have taken action on numerous occasions against nursing homes and their employees for violation of state law and administrative regulations. Several employees of a nursing home were indicted on murder charges for the deaths of eight residents. Some nursing homes were required to pay a certain amount of money in civil penalties to settle a lawsuit for violations of the Texas Nursing Home Act and the Deceptive Trade Practices and Consumer Protection Act. The district court issued a permanent injunction restraining future unlawful conduct, and the court ordered certain standards be met. The lawsuits were certified to the attorney general for filing by the department of health resources. A state district judge fined owners of a nursing home $10,000 for violating the state health code but agreed to return control of the facility to the owners with the understanding they would properly take care of the patients. The order was agreed to jointly by the owners and attorney general. The state took control of the home after state officials reported what they described as "abominable (nasty and disgusting) conditions."

Convalescent and nursing homes in Texas are licensed by the department of health resources, which may suspend a license or order an immediate closing of an institution, or part of an institution, if it is operating in violation of the standards prescribed by law. The licensing agency must provide for resident placement during the period of suspension to assure their health and safety. Inspectors are concerned that if they force the closing of a home the people being cared for will have no place else to go. Instead, they require that conditions be brought into compliance with state standards. The state has revoked a nursing home's operating license and removed the administrator, but did not close the home because many patients had nowhere else to go. However, the court did appoint a special administrator for the nursing home. One may assume the closing of nursing homes in the state will continue to be a rare thing.

State law requires at least two unannounced inspections of each nursing home each year; further inspections may be required by the licensing agency. "For at least two unannounced inspections in each year, the Licensing Agency shall arrange to invite in the inspections at least one person as a citizen advocate from one of the following groups: American Association of Retired Persons, the Texas Senior Citizen Association, or the Texas Retired Federal Employees, the Texas Department on Aging Certified Long Term Care Ombudsman, or any other statewide organization for the elderly.''

The licensing agency must hold at least one open hearing annually in each licensed institution to hear any complaints of substandard care or licensing violations. And it is the responsibility of the licensing agency to notify the institution, the designated closest living relatives or legal guardians of the institution's residents, and other appropriate state or federal agencies that work with the institution of the time, place, and date of the hearing. The institution's administrators and personnel may be excluded from the hearing by the licensing agency. The department of health resources is required to notify the institution of complaints made during the hearing and provide a summary of the complaints without identifying the source. The complainant must be notified confidentially of the results of the investigation.

Another provision of the state law provides that the department of health resources may cooperate with local public health officials of any county or incorporated city in carrying out the provisions of the law, and the department, at its discretion, may delegate to the local authorities the power to make the inspections and recommendations to the department in accordance with the provisions of the law.

The law also provides that any person, or any owner or employee of an institution who believes a resident of a nursing home has been abused or neglected by another person must report the matter to the department of health resources.

The department of health resources can recommend the withholding of state (Medicaid) and federal (Medicare) funds from nursing homes. The nursing homes have Medicaid contracts with the department of human resources. The state is also responsible for purchasing nursing home care for those who need it and qualify for Medicaid assistance. The department of health resources may put the nursing home on vendor hold, which means the home does not receive its Medicaid money until problems are eliminated. If that doesn't work, the department can decertify the home. This also stops the flow of Medicaid money. In time, the nursing home may be recertified, but it cannot recover the money lost while decertified.

From the time of the first nursing home in Texas, there has been a need for adequate state regulations to protect the nursing home residents and the nursing home industry. In 1981, the Texas legislature enacted legislation designed to strengthen the regulatory powers of the state. Some of the provisions of the 1981 law have been considered above. But a law or regulatory code is no stronger than its actual administration. All Texas nursing homes have four regular inspections yearly, at least one of which is unannounced. The department of health resources tends to embrace its role as a consultant to the nursing home industry, frequently exhibiting a protective attitude toward the industry. For the department to act as both policeman and consultant are not really compatible roles (there have been reports that the staff of the department of health resources has been informed not to write up homes for violations they observe when on a consulting visit). The staff of the department is instructed to bring the violation to the home's attention, give the latter adequate time to correct it, then make a follow-up inspection.

Nursing home officials often know in advance that an unannounced inspection is scheduled. By taking the necessary action in advance, the home is in a better position to secure a favorable inspection rating. Further, the department of health resources is a large department with many employees, and nursing home officials may have friends among the departmental staff. Thus, the potential for inspection leaks is great.

According to state law, the department of health resources must hold at least one open hearing a year in each licensed nursing home to hear any complaints of substandard care or licensing violations. This provision could be an important factor in regulating nursing homes, but much depends upon those who will attend the open meetings. Will enough interested persons attend? What kinds of comments will be made at such meetings? Will the statements be well prepared in advance? Will the nursing home take the corrective action that might be necessary? Will the department of health resources see that the necessary changes are made? Again, "bare bones" of the law is one thing, and its proper administration is something else.

Nursing home administrators and their supporting personnel have extremely difficult tasks, some situations and patients create almost unbelievable problems. Some nursing homes in Texas are praised by the inspectors, the patients, their relatives and friends, and due credit must be given those who serve their public well. Yet, in a nursing home, one always seems to hear the haunting cry, "Nurse, nurse, will somebody please help me?" When this matter is referred to the administrators, many profess helplessness by pointing to help shortages and increasing operating costs.

There is a need for more public interest in nursing homes and more public support for firm action by the state department of health resources. The conditions in all public institutions—at least to some degree—reflect public attitudes.

Regulation of the Professions

Protecting the health, safety, and welfare of the people provides the legal basis for regulating the professions in Texas. A number of the state's boards, for example, the board of pharmacy, the board of medical examiners, the board of law examiners, the board of morticians, the board of nurse examiners, and the board of dental examiners provide for the licensing and registration of various types of professional people. Except for the five members of the board of law examiners, who are appointed by the supreme court of Texas, members of these boards are appointed by the governor or by the governor and senate. With some exceptions, the boards consist of six members appointed for six-year overlapping terms.

State Board of Pharmacy

Applicants for a license to practice pharmacy in the state are examined by the board of pharmacy. Only graduates of a reputable college of pharmacy with not less than a four-year course are eligible to take the examination. These examinations serve as a basis for registering qualified pharmacists. Applicants must pay an examination fee and, if the license is granted, an annual renewal fee. Retail pharmacies and manufacturers of drugs and medicines must secure permits from the board that are renewable annually. Inspectors employed by the board inspect drugstores and enforce the state pharmacy law. There have been cases in Texas where the state board of pharmacy has put druggists on probation for employing nonregistered persons to compound prescriptions.

State Board of Medical Examiners

Another important agency in Texas is the board of medical examiners.

> The main function of the board is to license physicians to practice medicine in Texas, both by examination and by reciprocity with other states. The district courts of the state may revoke, cancel, or suspend the license of any practitioner for causes specified by law, and it is the duty of each county or district attorney, or the Attorney General if they fail to act, to prosecute such suits on application of the board.
>
> Each licensed practitioner must register annually with the board and pay a fee. In addition, every licensee must register with the district clerk's office of his county of residence and of every county in which he practices.[8]

Courses and equipment of the medical schools in the state must be approved by the board and the latter passes upon the entrance credentials of those who apply to enter medical school. The board also investigates complaints alleging malpractice and immoral or unethical practices and may, if the evidence so warrants, recommend that the county or district attorney initiate action in the district court to revoke, cancel, or suspend the license of a practitioner.

Unethical practice or conduct includes a number of things; for example, taking undue liberties with women patients, selling narcotics illegally, and treating a wanted criminal without reporting it. A complaint may be investigated by the county medical association, which might be followed by an investigation and hearing by a committee of the state medical board. Should a doctor be found guilty of unethical conduct by the county medical association he could be censured, suspended, or expelled from society membership. If expelled, he would be prohibited from practicing in area hospitals, which require that staff members be members of the medical society. In the event one's practice were impaired by expulsion, an appeal could be taken to the state district court. The county and state medical societies have important internal police powers.

In the event an individual suffers injury or dies because of malpractice, the person so injured or a relative (in case of death) may institute a suit for damages. In some cases it is difficult for the plaintiff to secure the necessary medical testimony and win his suit, as the medically trained do not care to testify against each other in the belief that any testimony adverse to a fellow doctor would undermine the public's confidence in the profession. Another obstacle is that as a result of previous decisions by the Texas courts one must prove that the malpractice is the *sole* reason for the injury or death and frequently this is impossible. Sometimes an out-of-court settlement may be reached in order to avoid publicity. In the last analysis, the best protection the public has against quacks and incompetents is vigilant county and state medical societies and the state board of medical examiners.

The increasing number of malpractice suits in the courts and the tremendous increase in the cost of malpractice insurance premiums paid by doctors, medical associations, and groups, have created a serious situation for the medical profession and the public.

22 Labor-Management Relations

IN 1899, THE TEXAS legislature recognized the right of workers to organize. The Texas law provided:

> It shall be lawful for any and all persons engaged in any kind of work or labor, manual or mental, or both, to associate themselves together and form trade unions and other organizations for the purpose of protecting themselves in their personal work, personal labor, and personal service in their respective pursuits and employments.[1]

Thus, the old common-law doctrine of "illegal conspiracies in restraint of trade" has been modified by statute, since the right of workers to organize is now recognized by all the states and the national government.

The rejection of the common-law doctrine of conspiracy, as well as such common-law defenses of "contributory negligence," "fellow servant," and "assumption of risk," encouraged the enactment of workmen's compensation and other laws favorable to labor. Nevertheless, the common-law doctrine of "illegal conspiracies in restraint of trade" continues to haunt the efforts of organized labor, since it influences the public, legislative bodies, and the courts when they have under consideration the matter of strikes, boycotts, and various other types of union activity. There have been many obstacles that have hindered or delayed the labor movement in the United States; not the least among these have been various common-law doctrines, which in time have been modified by legislative and judicial action.

As the economic system became more complex there developed a need for organized labor, that need being an organization that would enhance the bargaining power of employees. In an unorganized market labor is extremely competitive, with individual laborers in a much weaker bargaining position than employers. Still, quite naturally, the business community thought it should protect its bargaining power and vested rights; therefore, a conflict was inevitable between these two forces. The important question that remained unanswered was whether, through legislative and judicial action, a legal framework could be established in which conflicts between the contending forces might be resolved peacefully. In other words, certain "rules of the game" had to be established; otherwise physical force would be used by the parties.

The early 1930s were, in a sense, a period of adolescence in American labor-management relations, a period in which labor was experiencing growing pains, and management was attempting to protect acquired rights. It was natural that both groups developed rather extreme techniques to further their own interest. Management used various means to discourage labor from organizing and bargaining collectively, such as the use of industrial spies, inside and outside squads to check on union sympathy among workers and take whatever action necessary to discourage same, black lists, yellow-dog contracts, lockouts, shutdowns, company unions, firing and discrimination against employees who participated in union activities, and placing agitators in and around picket lines. These and other techniques, plus a press that was antilabor, resulted in rather strong feelings against the labor movement. Labor, not to be denied, developed its own weapons, such as the right to organize and bargain collectively, primary and secondary strikes, primary and secondary picketing, primary and secondary boycotting, the closed shop, featherbedding, the slowdown, and the freeze-out. Neither group appeared willing to use moderation, and both emphasized rights and said little or nothing about their obligations. "The end justifies the means" appeared to be the slogan of both groups. This period of immaturity in labor-management relations was to the disadvantage of both groups, as well as to the public. The struggle was transferred to the courts, where management sought writs of injunctions to prevent the use of certain labor techniques. The frequency with which such writs were issued caused labor to cry out "government by injunction." In time the struggle was transferred to the public arena to be fought out in elections and legislative chambers. The government was compelled to intervene as a neutral party. But in a democracy, where prolabor and antilabor people are elected to legislative bodies, as well as elected or appointed to serve in the courts, could the government long remain neutral? The government, at both national and state levels, intervened as a "third party" as a result of necessity.

No one appears anxious to exclude government entirely from labor-management relations, although the degree of government intervention varies from time to time. Nevertheless, over the years there has developed a legal order or framework, incomplete though it may be, within which the rights of labor and management may be protected. At the national level this is illustrated by the National Labor Relations Act of 1935 as amended in 1947 by the Taft-Hartley Act, as well as the passage of various other federal laws (and their interpretation by the courts) regulating management-labor relations. This legal order evolved through the modification of earlier judicial doctrines and statutes. Since both labor and management have an abundance of power, money, and organization, which to a degree enable both groups to check and balance each other, problems are being solved through the democratic processes in the United States. Labor-management relations are dynamic and for this reason there are no permanent or absolute solutions. On the other hand, intelligence and statesmanship in both management and labor are important factors in strengthening American capitalism.

As we approach a more mature labor-management policy in the United States, it is interesting to reflect upon the change of attitude. There is a considerable gap between the old common-law doctrine of "illegal conspiracies in restraint of trade" and the view of the U.S. Supreme Court in upholding the state of Washington's minimum-wage law for women and minors in 1937. Chief Justice Hughes, speaking for the Court, declared, "The Constitution does not speak of freedom of contract. It speaks of liberty and prohibits the deprivation of liberty without due process of law. . . . *But the liberty safeguarded is liberty in a social organization* which requires the protection of law against the evils which menace the health, safety, morals, and welfare of the people"[2] (italics added).

Corporations and Labor Unions (Labor Corporations)

Over the years corporations have provided numerous benefits for their employees, for example, paid vacations, holidays, bonuses, recreational facilities, investment counseling, sick leave, hospital and medical benefits, retirement programs, and opportunity for employees to purchase corporation stock, among other benefits. In fact, corporations have become welfare-minded in their competitive efforts to employ and retain qualified personnel. This has been good for business and society in general. It may be that many company employees look more to the corporation for benefits and protection than to labor unions, with the result that some contend this has weakened the power of labor unions in the nation. In any event, this phenomenon has placed labor unions and corporate management in a more competitive position.

Some benefits that corporations provide their employees may increase operating costs, part or all of which may be passed on to the consumer in the form of higher prices.

Those responsible for conducting the business of corporations include the president of the corporation, the corporate board, the attorneys and fiscal managers, and the stockholders. The decision-making power, for the most part, resides with the president of the corporation and members of the corporate board. Only a limited number of persons may attend, or participate in, meetings of the stockholders. One may assume most matters supported by the president of the corporation and the corporate board are approved at these meetings. When matters are submitted to the stockholders by a mailed ballot, the stockholders are informed of the yes or no vote favored by the corporate board on each issue. And again, one may assume that the majority of the stockholders voting (at least most of the time) follow the preference of the corporate board. Thus, corporations are not democratically managed. Since corporations operate in a very competitive environment, there is need for strong and decisive leadership and the ability to make decisions and adjustments as the need arises without undue delay.

In various ways, labor unions operate like corporations: they may own millions of dollars worth of property, borrow and invest large sums of money, manage various commercial enterprises, and concern themselves with the important matter of promoting the interest of the union members. Consequently, labor unions, by their very nature are, in a sense, labor corporations. Organizations come to resemble the organizations with which they are in constant conflict—the "Iron Law of Emulation."

Democratic trade unionism may not be feasible or practical in an industrial democracy. In the United States, considerable power is vested in the president and executive council of the AFL-CIO and the president and council of the state labor organizations. The presidents of the national and state organizations may hold office for life or a number of years, and at times this officeholding has some of the features of monarchism. Delegates from the various states attend national and state labor conventions and approve various resolutions. These meetings are planned in advance by the national and state presidents of the AFL-CIO and their executive councils, and these leaders play a dominant role in the organization and work of the various conventions. Local labor leaders are influenced by the program and decisions of the national and state labor organizations, and frequently only a small percent of union members attend the local meetings.

Codetermination

The Federal Republic of Germany has found a "third way," a "middle" course between unlimited capitalism and bureaucratic communism. The middle course, or third way, involves workers participating in private industry in both "saying" (codetermination) and "having" (capital sharing). This system has limited the extreme confrontation between management and labor in other countries. The large German coal and steel industry has had *equal* workers' representation on the supervisory board since World War II. Experience, however, has proved that key decisions have not been obstructed by parity; indeed the cooperation of workers has ensured that policy decisions are without confrontations and conflict.

In all German companies employing more than 2,000 persons, the supervisory board has proportional representation not only of workers, but also of middle management. The manner in which the latter representatives are nominated and elected to the supervisory board precludes them from merely supporting stockholders' or top management's interests. To avoid excessive trade union influence, one-third of the workers' delegates must be drawn from trade unionists not employed by the company, and selected by an employee vote.

The supervisory board selects the management and must approve investments. In a stalemate situation, shareholders have an advantage over workers' representatives since the chairman, who represents the shareholders, has a decisive vote when votes for or against a decision or a manager are equal. Since the vice-chairman must always be a worker, there has been a tendency toward agreement or compromise rather than decisive votes by the chairman of the supervisory board. Excessive decisive votes by the chairman could possibly undermine the arrangement of codetermination.

Capital-sharing is by no means as advanced as codetermination in West Germany, which includes individual coownership of workers in industry. Where this policy has been pursued, the workers and employees own (in shares and investment certificates) a certain percent of the value of the capital. The result has been, according to some businessmen, a decrease in worker absenteeism and an increase in personal interest in cooperation and productivity.

Laws Restricting Organized Labor in Texas

Texas does not have a modern labor-management relations code; instead the legislature, in piecemeal fashion, has enacted laws restricting labor and management. Some of the more important statutory restrictions on labor are noted briefly below.

Antistrike Law (The O'Daniel Antiviolence Law, 1941)

It is "unlawful for any person by the use of force or violence, or threat of the use of force or violence, to prevent or attempt to prevent any person from engaging in any lawful vocation within this state." Any person violating the O'Daniel Antiviolence Law is guilty of a misdemeanor. The right to strike exists but strikes must be conducted in a peaceful manner, since force and violence are prohibited.

Labor Union Regulatory Act (The Manford Act, 1943)

The preamble of public policy in the Manford Act declares "the right to work is the right to live," therefore, the workingman, both unionist and nonunionist alike, must be protected. To accomplish this objective the law provides for the regulation of the activities and affairs of labor unions, their officers, agents, organizers, and other representatives. Labor unions are required to file an annual report with the secretary of state indicating the name and address of the state, national, and international organization or union, if any, with which the union is affiliated. Each labor union must file with its first report duly attested copies of its constitutional or other organizational papers and records, and report thereafter any changes or amendments to such documents, papers, and records. These reports are open to grand juries and judicial and quasi-judicial inquiries.

Under the Manford Act all labor unions in the state must keep accurate books of accounts itemizing all receipts and expenditures, stating the sources and purposes. These books, records, and accounts of the labor unions are subject to inspection at all reasonable times by union members. Subject to the approval of the attorney general, any enforcement officer may inspect such books, records, and accounts. They are open also to grand juries, judicial and quasi-judicial bodies.

Labor unions may not collect any fee or assessment as a condition for the privilege to work from any person not a member of the union. This limitation does not prevent the collection of initiation fees. It is unlawful for any alien or person convicted of a felony (unless political rights have been fully restored) to serve as an officer or organizer of a labor union. The act further declares that it is unlawful for any labor union to make a financial contribution to a political party or to any person seeking public office as a part of the campaign expenses of an individual. Federal and state laws that attempt to prohibit or limit financial contributions of both corporations and labor unions to political parties and candidates are not very effective because the laws can be evaded by contributions being made by auxiliary committees or agencies. Political and financial neutrality of labor unions and corporations in Texas, as in other states, cannot be enforced.

The provisions of the Manford Act concerning filing of reports, bookkeeping, inspection of books, and election of officers reflect the distrust the legislature had for unions and their officers. The legislature must have felt that union leaders either were not capable or could not be trusted to manage the internal affairs of the unions in the best interest of the workers and the public. Since the internal controls did not apply to both labor and management, the legislature felt organized labor was in greater need of regulation and thereby made labor the villain in labor-management relations. As to be expected, labor took its fight to the courts, which have declared certain sections of the law unconstitutional.

Agrarian individualism and the corporate interest were largely responsible for the Manford Act. At the time the law was passed a majority of the legislators believed that unions and many of their officers were corrupt, power-mad, and irresponsible. There was a feeling in the legislature that organized labor in Texas was controlled by powerful out-of-state labor bosses. An antilabor press in Texas—especially the large dailies—kept these ideas before the public. The legislators felt that the state should intervene on the side of the workingman to protect him from the unions, thus the reasons for the detailed statutory regulations and limitations on organized labor.

The fear and suspicion of labor unions, antagonism to them, and the negative attitude toward labor-management relations, were formalized and legalized in the law of 1943. If at that time a more responsible and mature labor-management relations code could have been worked out, it would have been to the benefit of all parties, including the general public. Statesmanship, in both labor and management, was lacking in 1943 as is somewhat true today, and to some extent the "spirit" of the Manford Act is alive today in the state for it established a pattern in labor-management relations.

Organized labor in Texas has been very critical of the Manford Act. Labor contends that instead of protecting the workingman, the law was designed to severely limit the activities of labor unions.

Labor Union Dues—Withholding by Employer
(Anticheckoff Law, 1947)

Any contract that permits the retention of any part of the wages of an employee for the purpose of paying dues or assessments to any labor union, without the written consent of the employee (which must be delivered to the employer), is void and against public policy.

Contracts between unions and management with the checkoff stipulation authorize the employer to act as the collecting agent for unions in the collection of dues and assessments. Such a contract permits the employer to retain or withhold part of the wages of the union members for this purpose. This contractual arrangement, as far as labor is concerned, provides a convenient and sure method for the collection of union dues. It makes it easier for the unions to plan their financial operations. A contract with the checkoff proviso is permissible in Texas if the union members give their written consent.

Texas law prohibits any state employee payroll deductions not specifically authorized by the legislature. Union dues are among those deductions. The supporters of labor contend the measure does state employees an injustice by prohibiting them from making their own decisions as to what the state comptroller may withhold from their paychecks. The sponsor of the legislation in the House of Representatives said the bill was not "anti-union," but merely declared the state should not be in the business of collecting dues from unions or anybody else. However, it is rather common practice for private individuals and public officials to give their consent for salary deductions. For example, a school district in Texas may, with the consent of individual teachers, deduct funds from their monthly check to pay dues to the Texas State Teachers Association, make contributions to the United Fund, make payments to credit unions, etc.

Without the payroll deduction, or "checkoff," unions must hand collect their dues, thereby losing the financial stability they gain with the checkoff.

Right to Work—Closed Shop Outlawed (Anticlosed Shop Law, 1947)

State "right-to-work" laws came into vogue as a result of Section 14b of the federal Taft-Hartley Act, which gave the states the power (if they wished to exercise it) to legislate more restrictions on union security than existed in the federal law. Congress said in effect that the union shop was legal in terms of federal law but that the states could abolish it if they wanted to.

The term "right to work" is misleading, for it implies that a person has a right to work for any employer he or she chooses. This is, of course, absurd, because it would mean that no employer could refuse to employ anyone who wanted to work. A person has the right to work only if he wants and secures a job. In the absence of a contract, no one has the "right to work" for any specific employer.

The Texas right-to-work law declares that a person has the inherent right to work and bargain freely with his employer, individually or collectively, for terms and conditions of employment. This right may not be denied or infringed by law or by any organization. Therefore, no person may be denied employment based on membership or nonmembership in a labor union. Any contract between a labor union and an employer that would establish a closed shop is prohibited by the law.

The right-to-work law was amended in 1951 making it a "conspiracy in restraint of trade" for any employer and any labor union to enter into a contract whereby persons are denied the right to work because of membership or nonmembership in a union. In other words, a contract between a labor union and an employer establishing the union shop would be in violation of the state's antitrust laws.

The Texas right-to-work law prohibits various forms of union security.

1. Closed shop. Only union members may be hired. The closed shop is prohibited by the Taft-Hartley Act and state "right-to-work" laws.
2. Union shop. All workers must join the union—at least to the extent of paying dues—within a specified time after they are employed. The union shop is permitted by the Taft-Hartley Act but prohibited by the "right-to-work" law.
3. Agency shop. Employees must either join the union or, if they choose not to, pay to the union the amount of dues paid by union members. The agency shop is permitted by the Taft-Hartley Act but prohibited by the "right-to-work" law.
4. Maintenance of membership. Employees who are union members when the union-management agreement is signed, and nonmembers who join the union later, must remain members of the union for the duration of the contract. Maintenance of membership is permitted by the Taft-Hartley Act but prohibited by the "right-to-work" law.

If Congress repealed section 14b of the Taft-Hartley Act, the state right-to-work laws would automatically be voided in regard to enterprises covered by federal law (enterprises engaged in interstate commerce).

The repeal of 14b of the Taft-Hartley Act would not establish automatically the union shop in Texas. The various types of union security, other than the closed shop which is prohibited by the Taft-Hartley Act and state right-to-work laws, would have to be negotiated by representatives of management and labor. Union security is guaranteed by contract. Repeal of 14b of the Taft-Hartley Act would not void any section of the Texas right-to-work law with regard to enterprises not covered by federal law (enterprises engaged in intrastate commerce).

Peaceful Picketing Law (1947)

Pickets may not hinder the free ingress to or egress from an establishment. It is unlawful for any person, by use of insulting, threatening or obscene language, to interfere with or hinder any person from freely entering or leaving a strikebound establishment. Picketing that is accompanied by slander, libel, or the public display or publication of oral or written misrepresentations is prohibited, as is picketing to secure the disregard or breach of a valid labor agreement entered into by an employer and the representatives of employees.

Secondary Economic Techniques Prohibited (1947)

Organized labor may not employ secondary economic weapons or sympathetic actions, as secondary strikes and secondary boycotts, to accomplish its objectives. As regards striking, sympathetic or secondary actions differ from primary techniques. Assume the workers in plant A are involved in a labor dispute with their employer and call a strike. This is known as a primary action. The workers in plant B, not involved in a labor dispute with their own employer, nevertheless call a strike as a means of attempting to bring pressure against the employer of plant A. Such action by the workers in plant B would constitute a secondary strike.

The secondary boycott, which is prohibited in Texas, includes any combination, or agreement, by two or more persons to cause injury to any person or business for whom they are not employees by withholding patronage, labor, or other beneficial business intercourse; instigating a strike against such person or firm; refusing to handle, install, use or work on the equipment of such person or firm; interfering with the free flow of commerce.

Utility Antipicketing Law (1947)

Picketing the plant or premises of a public utility, with the intent to disrupt the service of such utility, is prohibited by law.

Damages for Breach of Contract (Equal-Responsibility Law, 1947)

A labor organization whose members picket or strike is liable in damage for any loss resulting to a person or firm in the event it is held to be a breach of contract by a court. The law applies only to those who commit certain illegal acts; hence, it does not extend to unions and union members involved in lawful strikes or picketing. If a court found that a union did breach or terminate its contract with an employer by calling a strike or establishing a picket line, the union would be liable for damages for any loss resulting to such person or firm. Both labor and management are equally responsible for breach of contract.

Public-Employees Loyalty Law (1947)

Officials of the state or of a county, municipality, or other political subdivision of the state may not enter into a collective-bargaining contract with a labor organization respecting the wages, hours, or conditions of employment of public employees. Public officials in the state cannot designate a labor organization as the bargaining agent for any group of public employees. However, if the voters of a city so approve in a referendum, firemen and policemen may bargain through their associations for increased salaries and improved working conditions. State district courts are the final arbiters in such wage disputes. Collective bargaining is based on the "prevailing local wage." In the absence of a referendum vote or due to a defeat of the referendum at the polls, firemen and policemen may present their requests only to the city council.

Despite the restrictions of state law in Texas, letters, memoranda of agreement, minutes of meetings, private conversations, and other techniques have been substituted for signed collective agreements in some political subdivisions in Texas. Governments such as cities and counties usually hear union views before setting pay rates and working hours and conditions. If the unions disagree with the local governments, the best the unions can do is to arouse public sentiment or to remind elected officials of the voting strength of the union. Yet, signed collective agreements or contracts are prohibited between most public officials and the representatives of public employees.

Those who work for the state or a political subdivision of the state may not engage in strikes or organized work stoppages against their employer. Any public employee who participates in such a strike forfeits his accumulated civil service, possibility of reemployment, and any other rights or benefits that he enjoyed as a result of his employment. As a result of this provision of the law, employees in the street, sewer, and sanitation departments of some Texas cities have been fired following a strike, and the same is true of bus drivers and mechanics employed by city-owned transit systems. Nevertheless, in some cases, as part of the agreement to terminate the strike the city agreed to reemploy all striking employees and permitted them to make up lost pay, in addition to an increase in wages and more satisfactory fringe benefits. In another instance, the city agreed to withdraw the decision that had caused strikers to leave their jobs and to pay strikers for time lost if they would return to work immediately. Obviously, some municipal officials in Texas ignore the state law and its penalties in order to resume normal operations, rather than dismiss the strikers and be confronted with the problem of replacing all or part of the particular work force. Some government officials in other states have reached the same conclusion.

The right of a public employee to cease work may not be abridged so long as the individual does not act in concert with others in an organized work stoppage. Public employees may present grievances concerning their wages, hours of work, or conditions of work, individually or through a representative who does not claim the right to strike. No person may be denied public employment by reason of membership or nonmembership in a labor organization. Thus, an individual may work for the state or one of its political subdivisions and be a member of a labor union, although the activities of his union would be restricted.

As the number of persons working for the many governments in the United States continues to increase, so will union activity among public employees. Consequently, the problem of unionization and collective bargaining in the public employment sector will become more important.

If public employees had the right to strike, the existence of the right—as well as its use—would enhance the bargaining power of public employee unions. Some have said "there is no difference between a strike of clerical employees of the county commissioners and employees of Ford Motor Company." Is this true? Should all—or none—of the public employees have the right to strike? Should the right of public employees to strike extend to all cases except where public safety and welfare are concerned? As Theodore Kheel has said, "our best chance to prevent strikes against the public interest lies in improving the practice of bargaining. In an environment conductive to real bargaining, strikes will be fewer and shorter than in a system where employees are in effect invited to defy the law in order to make real the promise of joint determination."[3]

Union Antitrust Laws (1947)

The Texas legislature considers unions as organizations that "affect the public interest and are charged with a public use," and should be regulated like corporations and other business concerns. With certain exceptions, labor unions have been brought under the state's antitrust laws.

A conspiracy in restraint of trade, as defined in the Texas antitrust laws, includes the following: (1) Where two or more persons or firms, engaged in buying or selling, enter into an agreement to refuse (or threaten to refuse) to buy from or sell to any other person or firm; (2) where two or more persons or firms agree to boycott or enter into an agreement to refuse to transport, assemble, or work with any goods of any other person or firm.

The laws do not affect the right of employees to engage in peaceful strikes against their immediate employer to secure better working conditions or more pay.

The law declares that a conspiracy in restraint of trade includes agreements between employers and labor unions that deny persons the right to work because of membership or nonmembership in a union. As noted previously, an agreement between an employer and a labor union establishing a union shop would be in violation of the state's antitrust laws.

Parkhouse-Spilman Acts (1955)

The Parkhouse-Spilman Acts restate the "right-to-work" principle, that is, the right of employment regardless of membership or nonmembership in a labor union. In addition, the acts make it unlawful to strike or picket in an attempt to force an employer to bargain with a labor union that does not represent a majority of the workers in the company. An election may be ordered by the trial judge to determine if the labor union represents a majority of the employees.

Disqualification for Unemployment Compensation Benefits (1955)

An individual is disqualified for unemployment compensation benefits when the Texas employment commission finds that total or partial unemployment is due to a stoppage of work created by a labor dispute at the establishment where the worker is or was last employed. This disqualification does not apply to those not a member of the labor organization involved in the labor dispute and to individuals who have made an unconditional offer to return to work. In other words, if the individual "is not participating in or financing or directly interested in the labor dispute which caused the stoppage of work,'' the disqualification does not apply. According to the legislature, the act was designed to limit "the payment of unemployment compensation benefits strictly to only those persons unemployed through no fault of their own and to have the state remain classless and observe a formal neutrality in matters of strikes or lockouts.''

Each statute restricting labor unions and their members provides sanctions and enforcement procedure in case of violation. The law may provide that any person guilty of violating the act is guilty of a misdemeanor or felony and, upon conviction, shall be fined not less nor more than a certain amount or be imprisoned not to exceed a certain amount of time or both. For some actions the labor organization may be liable or responsible instead of the individual. For example, the law may provide that the labor union shall be penalized civilly in a sum not exceeding a certain amount for each violation, to be recovered in the name of the state. Or a labor union may be liable for breach of contract. Other actions by the union may result in the forfeiture of its corporate charter and a fine, or the imprisonment of union officers. The statute may declare certain types of labor-management contracts void and contrary to the public policy of the state.

In some cases the state, through the attorney general or any district or county attorney, may institute suit in the district court to enjoin any person or labor union from violating the law. On the other hand, a person or firm subjected to certain types of labor action may seek injunctive relief in the district courts. Any person or a labor union convicted of violating a law may be liable for damages. Again, the type of sanctions and enforcement procedure depends upon the provisions of the particular law.

Restrictions on Management

There are a number of restrictions on management in the area of employer-employee relations. Among these restrictions are the following.

Discrimination Against Persons Seeking Employment

Those seeking employment may not be *blacklisted* by their former employer. Employers are prohibited from placing the name of any discharged employee, or any employee who has voluntarily terminated his employment, on any list with the intent of preventing the employee from securing employment with any other person or firm, either in a public or private capacity. This restriction does not apply if the former employee, or other person (or firm) to whom such person has applied for employment, requests in writing the reason for his discharge and why his relationship with his former employer was terminated. When such a request is made, either by the discharged employee or prospective employer, the former employer must submit the information in writing to the interested party or parties.

An employer may not discriminate against any person seeking employment on account of his having participated in a strike.

Coercion

An individual or company may not require an employee to purchase merchandise from a certain firm or store. Employees may not be excluded from work, punished, or blacklisted for failure to purchase from a designated establishment. If one were required to purchase at a company store, where credit was easy to secure and encouraged, a worker might be forced to continue his employment virtually in bondage to his creditor. The law is designed to prevent peonage or prevent a person being bound to service for payment of a debt.

Health, Safety, and Welfare Laws

A number of laws are designed to protect the health, safety, and welfare of the workers. Factories and other establishments in Texas are required to maintain sufficient air space for every employee and reasonable temperature. Unnecessary humidity which would jeopardize the health of employees is prohibited by law. All poisonous or noxious gases, and all dust, which is injurious to the health of the person employed, must be removed as far as practicable by ventilators or exhaust fans or other adequate devices. Other regulations are directed at the elimination of unpleasant odors.

Despite the regulations protecting the health, safety, and welfare of the workers, Texas does not have an effective industrial safety code comparable to that of some other states. From the standpoint of content, coverage, and enforcement, the regulations are inadequate. It has been conservatively estimated in dollar value that the cost of work injuries in Texas exceeds $500 million a year.

Some of the major industrial firms in Texas spend several times more money in a single month for industrial-accident prevention than the Texas state government spends in an entire year. Through the application of practical principles of safety engineering and education under their own safety programs, some of the major industrial firms in Texas have reduced their accidents by as much as 50 percent or more.

The Texas Industrial Safety Code

Occupational safety of employees is the major concern of the division of occupational safety and the occupational safety board in the state department of health resources. The board consists of three members, the commissioner of labor and standards, the director of the department of health resources, and a chairman appointed by the governor and senate for a term of two years. The board employs a state safety engineer who is director of the division of occupational safety. Also the board appoints a general advisory occupational-safety committee.*

The state safety engineer and his staff inspect plants to determine if the regulations of the occupational safety board are being violated. The county or district attorney, upon the request of the state safety engineer, may institute legal action against any person or firm violating the industrial safety code and regulations. Any person aggrieved by a regulation of the board may institute civil action in a state court in Travis County to set aside or suspend such rule or other action, with right of appeal.

Safety codes on various subjects, for example welding, woodworking machinery, fixed ladders, and abrasive wheels are approved by the general advisory

---

*The general advisory occupational-safety committee is composed of ten representatives of employers, ten representatives of employees, and the state safety engineer, who serves as chairman.

occupational-safety committee and recommended to the board which, after public hearings, may adopt them. With some modification, many states have adopted safety codes similar to those drafted by the U.S. Standards Institute, a nongovernmental organization. Uniform codes throughout the nation make it possible for a multistate firm to establish similar procedures in all of its plants. Safety-code writing is an endless job, since the codes must be changed frequently because of changes in industry and technology.*

Child-Labor Laws

Children under the age of fifteen years may not be employed to work in a factory, mill, workshop, laundry, or in messenger service in towns and cities of more than 15,000 population. No person under the age of seventeen years may be employed in certain hazardous occupations (any mine, quarry, or place where explosives are used).

Upon the application and sworn statement of a child, his parents or guardians, the county judge may issue a special work permit (for employment during the school term) to children over fourteen years of age whose earnings are needed to help support themselves and their families. To qualify for a special work permit, the child must have completed the seventh grade in public school or its equivalent and be physically able to perform the work as indicated by a certificate of medical examination issued by a licensed physician. Work permits may not be issued for a longer period than twelve months but may be renewed upon satisfactory evidence being produced that the conditions under which the permit was issued still exist. Such children may not be employed in any mill, factory, workshop, or other place where dangerous machinery is used, nor in any mine, quarry, or other place where explosives are used, nor where the moral or physical condition of the child is liable to be injured.

The child-labor laws prohibit any child under fifteen years of age from working more than eight hours in any one day or for more than forty-eight hours in any one week. Another limitation on the hours of minors makes it illegal to employ children under fifteen between the hours of 10:00 P.M. and 5:00 A.M.

Minimum-Wage Law

Those exempted from the law include the following: persons covered by the Federal Fair Labor-Standards Act (the federal minimum-wage—maximum-hour law) and employed in interstate commerce or work on projects financed with federal funds; persons whose employer does not contribute to the unemployment-compensation fund; and persons less than eighteen years of age who are neither high-school graduates nor graduates of a vocational-training program. The Texas minimum-wage law exempts many employees most in need of wage protection.

The law provides for employees to collect double the amount of wages owed them, plus attorney fees, in private lawsuits against employers who violate the law.

---

*The Federal Occupational Safety and Health Act of 1970 provides federal funds to the states where the state safety and health codes meet federal standards.

Workmen's-Compensation Insurance Law

The Texas workmen's-compensation law does not apply to domestic servants, or farm and ranch laborers.[4] The program is optional, rather than mandatory.

Under the Texas law, as in other states, the common-law doctrines of contributory negligence (that the employee was guilty of contributory negligence), fellow servant (that the injury was caused by the negligence of a fellow employee), and assumption of risk (that the employee assumed the risk of the injury incident to his employment) have been modified by statute. In an action to recover damages for personal injuries or death sustained by an employee in the course of his employment, the common-law rules may not be invoked as a defense for the employer. However, the employer may defend in such action on the ground that the injury was caused by the wilful intention of the employee to bring about the injury, or was so caused while the employee was intoxicated.

The workmen's-compensation law is administered by the industrial-accident board, which consists of three members appointed by the governor and senate for six-year overlapping terms. One member of the board must be an employee, one an employer, and one a lawyer who serves as legal adviser and chairman. Labor leaders have said that membership is two-to-one in favor of management.

The industrial-accident board determines the amount and duration of compensation (within the limits of the law) to be paid injured employees or their beneficiaries in case of death, and supervises the payment of claims. All compromise agreements between injured employees and an insurance company must be approved by the board. Records are kept of the employers who carry insurance, of all accidents reported, and the amount of money paid on each claim.

Upon payment of the necessary premiums, eligible employers may become subscribers to the Texas Employers' Insurance Association, which was created by the state. The association, rather than the employer, assumes financial responsibility for injuries or death of the members' employees. Insurance rates under the law are based upon the injury record of the employer.

Eligible employers are not required to join the association and pay insurance premiums. Yet, there are certain advantages in joining. (1) If the employer does join the association and pays insurance premiums, an injured employee may not institute a suit for damages against the employer for negligence. (2) An eligible employer who does not join the association may not invoke the three common-law defenses (contributory negligence, fellow servant, and assumption of risk) in a suit brought by an injured employee. Under such conditions, the person injured need only prove the employer was negligent. (3) There is always the possibility of large jury awards against the employer in a suit for damages for negligence. The latter are incentives that encourage employers to join the association.

The law covers on-the-job injuries and certain occupational diseases. If death results from an injury, the association must pay the beneficiaries a weekly payment equal to two-thirds of the employee's average weekly wage, but not less than the minimum weekly benefit ($16) nor more than the maximum weekly benefit ($70). The weekly benefits payable to a widow or widower are continued until the death or remarriage of the beneficiary. In the event of remarriage, a lump sum payment equal to the benefits due for twenty-four months (two years) is paid to the beneficiary. The weekly benefits payable to a child continue until the child reaches eighteen years of age, or beyond such age if actually dependent, or until twenty-five years of age if enrolled as a full-time student in any accredited educational institution. All other beneficiaries are entitled to weekly benefits for a period of 360 weeks.

The incapacity for work resulting from an injury may be total or partial, and the law provides that the association must pay the injured employee a weekly compensation. The basis for calculating the amount of compensation and the maximum period covered is provided in the law. Also, payments are provided for reasonable medical, nursing, and hospital care.

Lawyers who take workman's compensation cases may receive fees not to exceed a specified percent of the total award, whether the case is heard before the industrial-accident board or before a court. The percent of the total award constitutes maximum attorney's fees; a lesser amount could be set by the board or court.

The law provides for prehearing examiners to hold informal conferences in an attempt to settle claims amicably, without a hearing before the industrial-accident board or a court. This procedure is designed to expedite the settlement of claims.

If an employee who has suffered a previous injury suffers a subsequent injury which results in a condition of incapacity attributable to both injuries or their effects, the Texas Employers' Insurance Association is liable for all compensation provided by law. The association is reimbursed from the "second injury fund" to the extent that the previous injury contributes to the combined incapacity. The second injury fund is maintained in the following manner: "In every case of the death of an employee . . . where there is no person entitled to compensation surviving [the] employee, the association shall pay to the Industrial Accident Board the full death benefits, but not to exceed 360 weeks of compensation, as provided [by law], to be deposited with the Treasurer of the State for the benefit of [the] Fund."[5] The second injury fund makes it easier for persons previously injured to secure employment.

The industrial-accident board hears disputes over claims. Lawyers representing the association and other insurance companies, and lawyers who represent injured workers or beneficiaries are present at these hearings. Over two-thirds of the disputes heard by the board are appealed to the courts. Of the claims filed in court, only about five percent are actually tried, since settlements frequently are made out of court. A vast and complex field of workmen's-compensation insurance law has evolved. The Texas law, as amended, fills one whole volume of *Vernon's Annotated Civil Statutes*.

Boards of Arbitration

Any dispute between employers and employees may, upon mutual consent of all parties, be submitted to a board of arbitrators. Boards of arbitration consist of five persons: two members are designated by the employer and two members by the employees, either through their union or by a majority of the workers. The four arbitrators select a fifth person as arbitrator, who serves as chairman of the board. If the four arbitrators cannot agree upon a fifth arbitrator, the district judge of the district having jurisdiction of the subject matter, upon notice from either the arbitrators representing the employer or employees, designates the fifth person.

An award by a board of arbitration must be filed in the office of the clerk of the district court of the county in which the arbitration is held and is conclusive upon both parties, unless set aside for error of law apparent on the record. The award of the board continues in force as between the parties for a period of one year, and there may be no new arbitration upon the same subject between the parties until the expiration of the twelve-month period.

In submitting a dispute to arbitration, both parties agree in writing to execute the award of the board. The award itself may be enforced in equity and either party may appeal to the court of appeals from the order entered by the district court.

The industrial commission is composed of twelve members, appointed by the governor and senate for six-year terms. Few labor-management controversies have been referred to the commission.

Controversies between employers and employees may be referred to the commission by the governor. It is the duty of the commission, after making an investigation, to make a full report to the governor and legislature, setting forth the findings and recommendations.

In addition to its other duties, the commission is authorized to devise plans for attracting new industries to Texas. This appears to be the most important function of the commission.

The Promotion of Employment

The Texas employment commission administers programs of employment security designed to help stabilize the economy and mitigate the effects of unemployment. For carrying out this responsibility, the commission operates a system of public employment exchanges where employers seeking workers and workers seeking jobs are brought into mutually satisfactory contact. When this aim is not quickly achieved, eligible jobless workers may receive unemployment insurance payments.

The commission is also intrusted with the performance of farm-placement services, the collection of unemployment insurance taxes, and the dissemination of labor market information.

Employment Service

The employment service plays a major role in the employment-security program of the Texas employment commission (TEC). Service is available to all workers and all employers. Claimants are required to register for work as a condition of eligibility for unemployment insurance, and many thousands of nonclaimants register with the agency. All employers are urged to register their job openings with TEC in order that unemployed workers, including claimants, may quickly be placed in suitable employment to assure greater economic stability of workers, employers, and community alike. When an employer has a job opening, he may place an order with the commission, indicating the type of employee he needs. The commission screens the workers and refers one or more for interview and final selection. Hence, the agency provides an active placement service for both employees and employers.

More and more physically handicapped workers are being placed by the commission. Counseling, testing, and man-to-job comparison techniques are used to find suitable jobs for such persons. Many applicants are referred to the rehabilitation division of the Texas education agency, the Texas commission for the blind, or the Veterans Administration in order that vocational training and/or physical rehabilitation may be offered before job placement is attempted. Through the efforts of these agencies, and the governor's committee on employment of the physically handicapped, considerable progress has been made in promoting greater acceptance of physically handicapped workers in the state. This is an area where a continuous educational program, both for the handicapped workers and general public, is essential.

Employment counseling and guidance is an important activity of TEC as an aid in matching worker skills, abilities, and interests to jobs available. Frequently, before being referred to a job, individuals need guidance in choosing the type of work for which they are best suited. In this the general-aptitude test battery, which indicates basic ability in twenty broad fields, is used by the commission.

TEC assists in the channeling of youthful employees into the Texas labor market. This work often begins before students are out of school. A special effort is made to cooperate with the high schools and with other public and community service groups to place students who have not graduated in temporary summer jobs and in part-time jobs during the school term. By special agreement, a number of high schools avail themselves of the testing, employment counseling, and placement services provided by commission offices. These services aid graduating and terminating high school students in securing jobs.

The commission offers some industrial services to individual firms to cope with personnel and management problems that affect their ability to secure and retain qualified employees. These services include assistance in the developing of staffing or organizational patterns; assistance in studies of turnover or absenteeism; studies in personnel, job classification, training needs, and applicant testing and test development; assistance in conducting employee-attitude surveys, and the setting up of a system of exit interviews.

The farmers and farm workers receive assistance from TEC. Texas farmers need large numbers of workers for short periods because of the seasonal nature of farm work. These workers are provided by the referral of groups or crews of farmhands. A large number of citizen farm workers leave Texas temporarily each year to help harvest crops in other states. By arranging work schedules, in cooperation with other states, TEC endeavors to assure the departing workers jobs, not only on arrival at their first destination, but throughout their migration. TEC also attempts to assure the return of the workers in time for the harvest of crops in Texas. Through these work schedules and interstate cooperation, an effort is made to provide migratory farm labor a continuity of employment with a minimum of time lost during the farming season.

As a result of the urbanization trend, and with the resultant decrease in the available supply of farm labor, the farm placement operations of TEC for regular and seasonal farm activities have become more and more important.

Foreign Labor

Mexican nationals or braceros ("arm men" or "stoop laborers") who swim or wade across the Rio Grande River to work in Texas are referred to as "wetbacks." Most of these workers enter Texas illegally. They have been apprehended in Texas and flown deep into the interior of Mexico in the hope they would not flock to the Texas border in such large numbers, but these efforts have not been successful. The border patrol is responsible for enforcing the immigration laws along the Texas-Mexican border.

Frequently, the Mexican farm laborers in Texas have been paid wages below that of local laborers and housed in substandard buildings, as well as exploited in other ways. To combat the wetback problem and that of exploitation, the United States and Mexico found it necessary to take joint action.

Because of the unemployment, lower wages, and living conditions in Mexico, Mexican nationals are anxious to work in Texas and other American states. Since there is a shortage of domestic farm labor in the United States, farmers declare there is a need for these workers. Employers point out that, because it is to their advantage to accept wage, housing, and other conditions established by the governments of the United States and Mexico, the charge of widespread exploitation has been exaggerated and that most employers comply with the regulations.

Latin Americans who reside in Texas and are American citizens object to the employment of Mexican nationals in the United States, since they compete with them, thereby reducing wages and causing unemployment. Rio Grande Valley residents of Latin extraction cannot live on the low wages offered them by farmers. Every harvest season there is an exodus of native Texas workers from the valley and San Antonio to other states. Their organizations, G.I. Forum, Political Association of Spanish-Speaking Organizations (PASO), and the League of United Latin American Citizens (LULAC), have expressed their opposition to the employment of Mexican nationals on numerous occasions.

Leaders of organized labor declare the employment of Mexican nationals is detrimental to domestic workers by lowering wages and causing unemployment; that competitive forces do not operate in an economy where an employer can create a false labor shortage by offering unacceptable wages and then can employ foreign workers.

Texas labor unions oppose the "commuter" system in which residents of such border towns as Juarez, Reynosa, and Brownsville give a permanent residence address in the United States and commute daily from their homes in Mexico to work in Texas. The unions maintain that the commuter system gives employers all along the border an inexhaustible source of strikebreaking workers who have the low Mexican standard of living and earn Texas wages higher than those in Mexico, but lower than those American workers need to sustain themselves at the U.S. standard of living. The employment of Mexicans in Texas cities along the border tends to depress the local economy through lower wages and unemployment for American laborers. Also, the commuter practice makes it more difficult for the unions to organize plants along the Texas side of the Mexican border. If the commuter practice were terminated some business firms on the Texas side of the border would be hard hit, since they employ large numbers of Mexican nationals.

A U.S. court of appeals upheld a federal district-court decision that ruled against a Texas AFL-CIO charge that 50,000 Mexican nationals commute illegally each day to work in stateside border towns. In a suit filed against the U.S. attorney general and the immigration service, the union claimed the Mexican nationals entered on resident visas but were not U.S. residents. The attorney general's office and the immigration service argued that the visas allow, but do not require, permanent residence in the United States; that the Mexican nationals are free, under their visas, to reside either in Mexico or the United States. In the earlier stages of the dispute the U.S. State Department filed an affidavit warning that "a sudden termination of the commuter system . . . would have a serious effect on our relations with Mexico."

Thus, foreign labor involves a number of interested parties: the governments of the United States and Mexico, Mexican nationals, Spanish-speaking American citizens and their organizations, farm organizations, organized labor, and farm and ranch employers in the United States. The farm organizations, organized labor, and the organizations of Spanish-speaking Americans employ lobbyists to influence congressional policy.

Conclusion

Probably no other state has more restrictions on organized labor than Texas. These restrictions reflect an agrarian individualism in a state that has experienced difficulty in readjusting from a rural to an industrial society. In a sense the urban and industrial society that continues to evolve at an ever-increasing speed in Texas is more advanced in its *technological* than in its *psychological* and *governmental* aspects. The capacity or willingness to establish a modern labor-management code and to reorganize and strengthen the Texas department of labor and standards lags behind the forces that cause further expansion of the industrial society.

There has been some movement toward more mature labor-management relations in the state. In the 1930s in Texas some employers established "inside" and "outside" squads to find out which workers were sympathetic toward unions, and employees were intimidated, threatened, tarred and feathered, and beaten. On occasion professional wrestlers were hired to take care of those who supported organized labor. The newspapers of the state were antilabor and a person could not be elected to office if he had the support of labor. In short, it was a period of class warfare. Few, if any, would care to go back to the 1930s or even 1940s as regards labor-management relations.

As industrialization continues in the state, organized labor will become stronger, both in the number of union members and in political influence. More state legislators will be elected with the support of labor and labor and management will act as a check upon each other.

Under responsible and intelligent leadership, management and labor have vital roles to play in a democracy. They have a right to protect their own interests, but, nevertheless, they should become more concerned with the general welfare. Each could oppose the other on *specific issues* rather than along *class lines*. This applies to individuals who support or oppose either management or labor. Basing support or opposition on specific issues—rather than attempting to outlaw unions, as was the case in the 1930s—is a sign of maturity in labor-management relations. If such be the trend, the psychological and governmental aspects can move along with the advance in technology and industrialization.

23   The Environment

"ECOLOGY IS THE STUDY of living things in relation to their environment. The study of *ecology* is a significant change from the type of studies which have dominated science for years. Science for the most part has been concerned with altering or 'improving' the environment rather than trying to find ways of living with it. The problems we have today are an environmental backlash in part due to this 'subdue and conquer' approach to nature."[1]

Pollution is *observable* in various forms and combinations. It occurs in air and water, on land, or as smell and noise and "is the addition of substances into nature which have an adverse affect upon life."[2] Water and air are so polluted in some areas that these substances are beyond a usable level and beyond their capacity to purify themselves. This "overloading" of nature's purification level seriously alters the environment and disrupts the millions of relationships among living and nonliving things on earth. The alteration of the environment has been due largely to the population explosion and the technological revolution in the post-industrial world.

Water Quality Board

The Texas water quality board administers the provisions of the Texas Water Quality Act, which includes the establishment of statewide water quality standards. Local governments also are empowered to enforce provisions of the act, but the state must be a party to any suit instituted under the law.

As a result of federal law, the states were required to establish water quality standards by a given date. If adequate state standards were not established, federal standards would be applicable to the state. Texas water quality standards had to be approved by the federal government. Federal water pollution control functions are administered by the Environmental Protection Agency (EPA).

The Texas water quality board grants or withholds permits for waste discharge into Texas streams, lakes, and coastal waters. The board must determine the pollution load on a particular water resource based on so many pounds of biochemical oxygen demand (BOD) per day. BOD is a standard by which pollution is measured. It is the amount of oxygen required for decomposition of a given amount of waste. In 1972 the board established a quota system for discharge of wastes into the Houston Ship Channel that was designed to reduce the BOD load to a certain number of pounds per day. The quota was, in effect, imposed by the EPA. The board holds public hearings and employs hearing examiners to grant or withhold waste permits and establish a quota system for discharge of wastes.

The Texas attorney general's office voided a long-standing policy of immunity for governmental units by filing pollution suits against certain cities in Texas for dumping raw sewage into the coastal waters and rivers of Texas. This action set a precedent for possible prosecution of other cities for sewage disposal violations. Also, the state, by action of the attorney general, has filed suits for violations of air and water pollution regulations by various industries. At one time the state relied on local governments to initiate pollution suits. Such suits seek compliance with regulations of the water quality board and air control board, including failure to secure board permits.

The management of waste disposal into the streams, lakes, and coastal waters of Texas raises a number of political and economic issues. Conflicting interests exist among industry representatives, the environmentalists, federal, state, and local officials, chambers of commerce, health officials, and the general public. Such conflicts provide a basis for the politics involved and for the evaluation of the law of pollution control.

If pollution control measures are too strict there is a chance that industrial and municipal growth may be curtailed in some areas. As location of new industries in an area causes municipalities to expand, the quotas for discharge of wastes per industry must be reduced. The tightened quota standards might become prohibitively expensive for industry. Indeed, some industries have defied the quotas and other pollution regulations because of the huge company expenditures involved. Although more lakes may be built and lakes and streams may increase or decrease in water volume, the fact remains that the availability of water as a source of waste disposal does not keep pace with industrial expansion. Yet, despite the serious problems of industry there remains the need to protect the health of the people and to preserve marine life.

Occasionally doubts have been expressed about whether federal and state water quality standards are adequate or inadequate and, if inadequate, where the fault, if any, lies. Public agencies within a state may be in disagreement over standards. For example, the Texas railroad commission has approved waste discharge permits for oil producers to release oil slush and brine (salt water) into certain streams, whereas the granting of such permits was opposed by the Texas parks and wildlife department on the grounds that this waste is damaging to marine life. Other challenges are related to the size of an industry and the extent of its pollution. Texas dairies that milk more than fifty cows must have waste discharge permits to release their waste into the streams. Dairymen have complained that the regulations should apply only to large dairies. And considerable doubt may exist as to whether governmental agencies have enough reasonably unchallengeable scientific information on which to make decisions.

Politicians attempt to please the voting public by jumping on the "ecological bandwagon" while not alienating the business interests so dominant in the pollution problem and yet so essential to their political successes. For purposes of good public relations, politicians, individuals and industries may support pollution control but are unwilling to assume the added expense (both monetary and in terms of personal sacrifice or change of lifestyle) necessary to make major improvements in water quality.

As for the lakes of Texas, the Texas water quality board (TWQB) approved a consent judgment requiring one industrial firm to pay the cost of draining lakes contaminated with arsenic. According to the TWQB, wastewater from the manufacturing process had seeped into the lakes over a number of years, contaminating the sediments and degrading the water quality. Within a specified time, the company involved agreed to "dewater" the lakes and build storm-water diversion structures to aid the dewatering and prevent contaminated sediments from being washed downstream. The firm also agreed to dig a large pit, lined with compacted clay a foot thick, dispose of all arsenic-contaminated sediments from the lakes, and take the necessary steps to prevent further pollution of the lakes. Besides paying the cost of the cleanup, the firm had to pay the state a specified sum of money. The attorney general of Texas filed the suit to halt the arsenic discharges and force the cleanup of the lakes. The consent decree was approved by the board and the company, and the order was entered by the state district court.

Thus, through regulatory-judicial action, the state has made some progress in improving the quality of water, but much remains to be done. Indeed, clean water is a vital state resource.

Air Control Board

The air control board's main function is to prevent pollution of the state's air resources through enforcement of the Clean Air Act of Texas and the establishment of statewide air quality standards. Local governments also enforce the provisions of the Clean Air Act of Texas. However, the state must be a party to any legal action instituted by a local government under the law.

A major concern in Texas and the nation is the reduction of motor vehicle pollution. Under national air quality legislation, all states were required to submit a plan to reduce pollution to a level safe for public health. The air control board submitted plans to bring various urban areas into compliance with national standards. The EPA regional office may recommend that the Texas plan be rejected for lack of transportation controls and other reasons. Unless agreement is reached between Texas and the regional office, the latter may propose its own remedies and then hold public hearings. Although the staff of the TACB concludes that controls on industries and other stationary sources of pollution comply with national standards, EPA's consultants may not agree. Disagreement has resulted primarily from differing assumptions regarding the percentage of hydrocarbons that react with sunlight to produce smog. If the air quality standards can be met without controls, no drastic restrictions on motorists will be imposed.

Air and water pollution have been part of the price paid for achievements made in America's industrial technology. Of course, economic growth must continue but not without a serious commitment to the well-being of the existing and future society.

Atomic Waste

The increased use of atomic energy for domestic purposes in Texas and throughout the world has created the serious problem of the safe disposal of atomic waste. This radioactive supergarbage cannot be disposed of like regular waste. Thus, there has been considerable experimentation in methods of disposal. Proposed methods include burial in specially built containers on land, under mountains, or anchored to the ocean floor off the U.S. coast. Industry in Texas has contracted with private firms for the disposal of atomic garbage. Some has been disposed of off the coast of the state. Cities along the coast, fearful of the consequences, have protested to the U.S. senators from Texas and to members of the U.S. House of Representatives. Some of the disposal has taken place two hundred or more miles off the coast of Texas and is a matter of national and international concern.

Coastal Zone Management

Since Texas has 367 miles of coastline (2,498 miles of Gulf Bay and estuary shoreline), the matter of coastal zone management is of vital importance to the state and the nation. Like most modern problems, it involves the conflict of interests of various groups—environmentalists, coastal local governments, chambers of commerce, the business community, sports and recreational organizations, and the state and national governments.

The cleanliness and natural beauty of seashore areas, for both recreational enjoyment and the protection of marine life, is endangered by ocean dumping. Incoming and outgoing ships, oil spills, and the disposal of waste by industry and raw sewage by Texas cities into coastal waters threaten the shore areas. The concentration of industry along the coast has been a major factor in coastal air and water pollution. The overcrowding of the beaches in certain areas, especially during peak vacation periods, the excessive litter, the odor of dead fish and other types of marine life washed up on land, and at certain times the excessive amounts of tar and seaweed on the beaches hinder full enjoyment of the Texas coast. Also, the lack of adequate zoning, building, health, and sanitation restrictions on homeowners, eating establishments, rental housing, and other types of businesses, and the failure to enforce such restrictions when they do exist, have created serious problems along the coast of Texas.

To keep Texas beaches clean, policed, safe, and open for public use and to preserve something of their natural beauty will require considerable statesmanship and the cooperation among the federal, state, and local governments in Texas. Some international agreements or treaties may be necessary as well. Both the Texas legislature and the federal government have become more concerned with the coastal problem, and one would expect this joint effort to continue and to produce some positive results.

The Responsibility of Industry and Society

Although it is true that industry is responsible for an enormous amount of water, air, and sound pollution, millions of individuals in the United States must bear some responsibiity as well. Highways and other public and private places are littered with wastepaper, garbage, cartons, beer cans, and various other throwaway items left by careless and thoughtless persons. The warning signs indicating a fine of $100 or $250 for littering the highways are enforceable. Thus, the protection of the environment is a responsibility of society in general.

Epilogue

ACCORDING TO A PRELIMINARY press release from the advisory commission on intergovernmental relations in 1983, the states have, in recent years, resumed their pivotal role in American politics. However, some people consider the report somewhat overly optimistic as a phase of the so-called New Federalism—of transferring some existing federal responsibilities to the states. The federally sponsored panel of national, state, and local officials and private sector representatives indicated the final report will portray a "quiet revolution that has been occurring in state governments over the past two decades." The preliminary report contains a number of indicators. Individuals, of course, may agree or disagree with the existence or nonexistence of each indicator in particular states. There is considerable variation in this matter among the fifty states. The author has indicated whether he agrees or disagrees with the various indicators as they apply in Texas.

> Today, states, in formal representational, policymaking and implementation terms at least, are more representative, more responsive, more activist and more professional in their operations than they ever have been.'

Disagree. Lobbyists and political action committees (PACs) have tremendous power and influence in the Texas legislature as they do in Congress and the other state legislatures. In a sense, the Texas legislature approaches the corporate state with its tug-of-war in policy-making among economic groups. Maybe this is all that is possible in a modern and dynamic society unless the people's lobby becomes more numerous and better financed. Considerable progress has been made, however, in the operational aspects of the legislature in Texas, for example, the contribution of the Texas legislative council and its professional staff as a research arm of the Texas legislature and the improved staffing of legislative committees.

> They are better equipped to assume and fulfill their expanded roles as "middlemen" in the federal system.

Disagree. Like other states, Texas has a disintegrated legislative, administrative, and judicial system that makes it difficult to locate responsibility for action or inaction. The state tax system is disintegrated and regressive. And the many-splintered document, the state constitution, contains a limited amount of fundamental constitutional items, but an abundance of provisions that provide constitutional protection for various funds, boards, commissions, and offices, all of which makes it difficult, if not impossible, to secure a brief and well-written state constitution.

Legislative reapportionment, in the direction of "one person, one vote," has replaced the malapportioned legislative bodies of the past.

Agree. This development in Texas, as well as in other states, resulted largely from decisions of the U.S. Supreme Court and lower federal courts. For years malapportionment of seats in both houses of the Texas legislature was legalized in the Texas Constitution in favor of the rural areas of the state.

Four-fifths of the states have updated their state constitutions since mid-century.

Disagree. There is a difference between updating, which may mean amending a state constitution, and completely revising a state constitution. The Texas Constitution of 1876, a post-Civil War document, with numerous constitutional amendments added, remains the constitution of the state.

Thirty-six states have annual legislative sessions . . . compared with only ten with annual sessions in 1951.

Disagree. The Texas Constitution provides the state legislature shall meet for not more than 140 days every odd year. However, the governor may call one or more special sessions not to exceed 30 days in duration.

State lawmakers . . . have better and more professional staffs.

Agree.

All states require lobbyists to register.

Agree.

States also have moved to longer terms for governors . . . allowing most of them two or more terms.

Agree. The term of governor in Texas is four years, and there is no constitutional limitation on the number of terms a person may serve. This has increased the appointive power of the governor for each term of office and made it possible to hold the governor more responsible for administrative action or inaction.

All but nine states require financial disclosure by their lawmakers.

Agree. In addition to financial disclosure, Texas legislators are prohibited from using surplus campaign funds for personal use. The Texas financial disclosure law is administered by the secretary of state.

At least four-fifths of the states have adopted simplified and unified court systems over the last twenty-five years.

Disagree. The Texas legislature continues to create more civil and criminal courts, and the structure of the court system continues to become more disintegrated.

All states have open-meeting laws, while before 1967 no state had such a law.

Agree.

More minorities and women hold public office than ever before.

Agree. Progress has been made in Texas in regard to women and minorities holding public office, but more such persons should be appointed or elected to such offices.

States also have diversified their tax systems, provided equity features for the poor and elderly, and have indexed tax brackets.

Disagree. The Texas tax system is very regressive. Also, in 1983 the Conservation Foundation released its state-by-state rankings as part of a national report on environmental quality efforts. In its evaluation of state efforts to maintain environmental quality, the foundation considered the voting records of the state's congressional delegation, regulatory programs to protect the environment in the state, state spending, environmental quality, and twenty other factors. The state of Minnesota was ranked first in the effort to protect the environment for its citizens, and Alabama was last. Texas ranked ninth from the bottom of the list.

Notes

Chapter 1

1. See Joseph Milton Nance, *After San Jacinto: The Texas-Mexican Frontier, 1836–1841* (Austin: University of Texas Press, 1963). This study covers the period between the battle of San Jacinto and the Mexican capture of San Antonio in March 1842. Also see Joseph Milton Nance, *Attack and Counter-Attack: The Texas-Mexican Frontier, 1842* (Austin: University of Texas Press, 1964). This study begins with the Vasquez attack on San Antonio and ends with the return of the Somervell Expedition from the Rio Grande.

2. The material on the Mier Expedition was taken from *The Handbook of Texas*, Vol. 11, pp. 189–90, published by the Texas State Historical Assn., 1952. The account of the Mier expedition in *The Handbook of Texas* was written by Professor Joesph Milton Nance, Department of History, Texas A&M University.

3. V. O. Key, Jr., A History of Texas County Government, unpublished master's thesis, University of Texas at Austin, 1930, p. 37.

4. William B. Munro, *The Makers of the Unwritten Constitution* (New York: Macmillan, 1930), pp. 96–97.

5. Charles W. Ramsdell, *Reconstruction in Texas* (New York: Columbia University Press, 1910), pp. 59–61.

6. Ramsdell, *Reconstruction*, pp. 147–48.

7. R. Henderson Shuffler, director, Texana Department, University of Texas at Austin, "How Two Great Chiefs Became Political Pawns," *Houston Post* (Sunday) Magazine, July 17, 1966. Quoted with permission of the *Houston Post*.

8. See Edgar P. Sneed, "A Historiography of Reconstruction in Texas: Some Myths and Problems," *Southwestern Historical Quarterly* 72, 4 (April 1969):435–48; see also Ann P. Baenziger, "The Texas State Police During Reconstruction: A Reexamination," ibid.:470–91.

9. See Ramsdell, *Reconstruction*. See also S. S. McKay, *Texas under the Regime of E. J. Davis*, master's thesis, University of Texas at Austin, 1919.

10. Ramsdell, *Reconstruction*, p. 302.

11. E. W. Winkler, "Platforms of Political parties in Texas," *Bulletin of the University of Texas*, 53 (Sept. 20, 1916):126.

12. Roscoe C. Martin, "The People's Party in Texas: A Study in Third Party Politics," *University of Texas Bulletin*, 3308 (Feb. 22, 1933). The material in this section was taken from Professor Martin's study.

13. Ibid., pp. 258–59.

Chapter 2

1. See Arthur M. Schlesinger, *New Viewpoints in American History* (New York: Macmillan, 1922), pp. 220–43.

2. "Population" by R. L. Skrabanek, professor, Department of Sociology, Texas A&M University. The population analysis was written by Professor Skrabanek to be included in the *Texas Almanac*. The data on the 1980 census was taken from Professor Skrabanek's population analysis.

3. John Tebbel, "Rating the American Newspaper—Part 1," *Saturday Review*, May 13, 1961, pp. 59–62.

4. *Whitney* v. *California*, 274 U.S. 357 (1927). The concurring opinion of Mr. Justice Brandeis in which Mr. Justice Holmes joined.

5. *Cantwell* v. *Connecticut*, 310 U.S. 296 (1940).

Chapter 3

1. Charles W. Ramsdell, *Reconstruction in Texas* (New York: Columbia University Press, 1910), p. 302. Quoted by permission of the publisher.

2. Ramsdell, *Reconstruction*, p. 307. Quoted by permission of the publisher. This measure was vetoed by Governor Davis, but the legislature passed it over his veto.

3. Ibid., p. 309. Quoted by permission of the publisher.

4. S. D. Myres, Jr., "Mysticism, Realism, and the Texas Constitution of 1876," *Southwestern Political and Social Science Quarterly*, 9, 2 (Sept. 1928):166ff.

5. Opinion 2476, January 20, 1923.

6. Senate Concurrent Resolution No. 11, Thirty-Sixth Legislature, Regular Session, 1919.

7. *Acts, 1907*, p.328; Art. 3133, *Vernon's Annotated Revised Civil Statutes*.

Chapter 4

1. *Constitution of the State of Texas Annotated II* (Kansas City: Vernon Law Book Co., 1955), 341. Interpretive Commentary.

2. Senate Joint Resolution No. 7, Thirty-sixth Legislature, Regular Session, 1919.

3. House Concurrent Resolution No. 5, Thirty-sixth Legislature, Regular Session, 1919.

4. Article VI, Section 2, Texas constitution.

5. *Sergeant Herbert N. Carrington* v. *Alan V. Rash*, 378 S.W.2d 304 (1964).

6. *Sergeant Herbert N. Carrington* v. *Alan V. Rash*, 85 S. Ct. 775 (1965).

7. *Guinn* v. *U.S.*, 238 U.S. 357 (1915).

8. *Acts 1923*, Thirty-eighth Legislature, Second Called Session.

9. *Nixon* v. *Herndon et al.*, 273 U.S. 536 (1927).

10. *Acts 1927*, Fortieth Legislature, First Called Session.

11. *Nixon* v. *Condon et al.*, 286 U.S. 73 (1932).

12. *Grovey* v. *Townsend*, 295 U.S. 45 (1935).

13. *Acts and Joint Resolutions, South Carolina*, 1944, Sec. 2323, p. 2241.

14. Ibid., p. 2344.

15. *Elmore* v. *Rice et al.*, 72 F.Supp. 516 (July 12, 1947).

16. *Rice et al.*, v. *Elmore*, 165 F.2d 387 (Dec. 30, 1947).

17. 68 S. Ct. 905 (April 19, 1948).

18. *John Terry et al., Petitioners* v. *A. J. Adams et al.*, 345 U.S. 461. Mr. Justice Minton wrote a vigorous dissenting opinion.

19. Benjamin Miller, "Nonviolence and Ethical Ends," *Fellowship*, 23 (Mar. 1957):19.

20. *Harper* v. *Virginia State Board of Electrons*, 86 S. Ct. 1079 (1966).

21. *Seay et al.* v. *Latham, Secretary of State, et al.*, Supreme Court of Texas, 182 S.W. 2d 251 (Sept. 23, 1944).

Chapter 5

1. *Seay et al.* v. *Latham, Secretary of State, et al.*, Supreme Court of Texas, 182 S.W. 2d 251 (Sept. 23, 1944).

2. O. Douglas Weeks, *Texas One-Party Politics in 1956* (Institute of Public Affairs: The University of Texas, 1957), Public Affairs Series Number 32, p. 50. Quoted by permission of the author and the Institute of Public Affairs.

Chapter 6

1. *Colegrove* v. *Green*, 328 U.S. 549 (1946).
2. *Baker* v. *Carr*, 369 U.S. 186 (1962).
3. *Reynolds* v. *Sims*, 377 U.S. 533 (1964).
4. *Kirkpatrick* v. *Preisler*, 89 S. Ct. 1225 (1969). (See also *Wells* v. *Rockefeller*, 89 S. Ct. 1234 (1969).
5. *Avery* v. *Midland County, Texas*, 88 S. Ct. 1114 (1968).

Chapter 7

1. Bo Byers, "Legislators are getting tired of one-man control," *Houston Chronicle*, May 28, 1967.
2. William H. Gardner, "Committee System Is in Sad Need of Streamlining," *Houston Post*, Feb. 14, 1966.

Chapter 8

1. H.B. No. 169, 67th Leg., Reg. Sess., 1981. Art. 6252-9c, 3, *Vernon's* Texas Civil Statutes.
2. Opinion No. V-1254, August 25, 1951.

Chapter 9

1. *Commentaries*, Secs. 1419, 1424.
2. James Wilford Garner, *Political Science and Government* (New York: American Book Co. 1932), p. 680. Reprinted by permission of the publisher.
3. For a thorough study of the governor of Texas, see Fred Gantt, Jr., *The Chief Executive in Texas: A Study in Gubernatorial Leadership* (Austin: University of Texas Press, 1964).
4. Ralph W. Steen, "The Ferguson War on the University of Texas," *Southwestern Social Science Quarterly* 35, 4(March 1955):356–62.
5. See Frank M. Stewart, "Impeachment in Texas," *American Political Science Review*, 24, 3 (Aug. 1930):652–58. See also Felton West, "The Case Against 'Pa' Ferguson. The Texas Star," *Houston Post*, Dec. 26, 1971.

Chapter 10

1. *Buchanan* v. *Warley*, 245 U.S. 60, 81 (1917).
2. *Ex Parte Lefors*, 303 S.W.2nd 394 (1957).
3. *Frisbie* v. *Collins*, 342 U.S. 519 (1952).
4. *Walker* v. *Baker*, Chairman of Board of Control et al., 196 S.W.2d 324, 1946.
5. Fred Gantt, Jr., "The Governor's Veto in Texas: An Absolute Negative," *Public Affairs' Comment*, 15, 2(March 1969), University of Texas at Austin, Institute of Public Affairs.
6. Fred Gantt, Jr., *The Chief Executive in Texas: A Study in Gubernatorial Leadership* (Austin, University of Texas Press, 1964), pp. 188 and 191. Quoted by permission of the University of Texas Press.

Chapter 11

1. See A. E. Buck, *The Reorganization of State Governments in the United States* (New York: Columbia University Press, 1938).

2. Leonard D. White, *Introduction to the Study of Public Administration,* 3rd ed. (New York: Macmillan, 1948), p. 247.

3. The speaker of the house, the chairmen of the house committees on appropriations and revenue, the lieutenant governor, and the chairmen of the senate committees on finance and state affairs constitute the membership of the legislative audit committee.

Chapter 12

1. *Natural Resource Taxation,* Texas State Tax Study Commission, Report No. 7 (1958), p. 7.

2. *Taxes Paid by Business,* Texas State Tax Study Commission, Report No. 5 (1958), p. 17.

3. *Taxes Paid by Individuals, Texas State Tax Study Commission, Report No. 4 (1958), p. 1.*

Chapter 13

1. *Towne* v. *Eisner,* 245 U.S. 418, at p. 425 (1917).

2. Subsection (b) of Article 2.03, Texas Code of Criminal Procedure.

3. W. L. K. Preston, "The Validity of the 'Breathalyzer.' " *Medical Journal of Australia,* Feb. 8, 1969, p. 287. Also see, *Grey's Attorneys' Textbook of Medicine,* 1983, Vol. 4, pp, 133.73(1) and 133.74.

4. Article I, Section 10, Bill of Rights.

5. Article V, Section 17.

6. Article 2133, *Vernon's Annotated Revised Civil Statues.*

7. The material on the examination and selection of the jury was taken from an article, "What Happens When You Get a Jury Call," by Victor Junger which appeared in the *Houston Post,* April 12, 1959. Used by permission of Mr. Junger and the *Houston Post.*

8. Art. 37.071 (Procedure in capital case), *Vernon's Texas Code of Criminal Procedure.*

9. C. L. Black, Jr., *Capital Punishment: The Inevitability of Caprice and Mistake* (New York: Norton, 1974), p. 95. Quoted by permission of the author and publisher.

10. *Furman* v. *Georgia,* 408 U.S. 238 (1972), quoted from Justice Brennan's concurring opinion, pp. 269–70.

11. *Gregg* v. *Georgia,* 428 U.S. 153 (1976), Justice Brennan dissenting, p. 229. See Tao, "Beyond *Furman* v. *Georgia:* The Need for a Morally Based Decision on Capital Punishment," 51 Notre Dame Law. 722, 736 (1976).

12. Black, *Capital Punishment,* p. 96. Quoted by permission of the author and publisher.

13. Article V. Section 18, Texas constitution.

14. For an analysis of the code see Dick Smith, "Texas' New Mental Health Code," *Public Affairs' Comment,* 3, 6, Institute of Public Affairs, The University of Texas (Nov. 1957).

15. Article V, Section 3, Texas constitution.

Chapter 14

1. Some of the material on student legal advisors was provided by Ms. Leigh Forrest.

2. For an interesting case study of the selection of judges in Texas, see Bancroft C. Henderson and T. C. Sinclair, *The Selection of Judges in Texas: An Exploratory Study* (Houston: University of Houston Public Affairs Research Center, June 1965), Studies in Social Science, Vol. 1.

3. See Charles S. Potts, "Waiver of Indictment in Felony Cases," *Southwestern Law Journal,* 3, 4 (Fall 1949):437.

4. Article I, Section 11, Texas constitution.

5. Article I, Section 13, Texas constitution.

Chapter 15

1. Article 2351, *Vernon's Annotated Revised Civil Statutes.*

Chapter 16

1. Article XI, Section 4, Texas constitution.
2. *Acts 1943*, Forty-eighth Legislature, Chap. 356, Section 1.
3. Wade B. Perry, Jr., "Legal and Policy Conflicts Between Deed Convenants and Subsequently Enacted Zoning Ordinances," Vand. L. Rev. 24: 1031 0'71, pp. 1050–51.
4. The quoted material was taken from a summary prepared by Dr. Luis Ricardo Fraga based upon his dissertation, "Nonpartisan Slating Groups: The Role of 'Reformed' Parties in Substate Policy Making," Rice University, 1982.

Chapter 17

1. Stanley T. Gabis, "Public Planning and Changing Patterns of Authority," *Business and Government Review*, 9 (Mar.-Apr. 1968).
2. Philip W. Barnes, "Councils of Governments in Texas: Changing Federal-Local Relations," *Public Affairs Comment*, 14, 4 (July 1968), University of Texas at Austin, Institute of Public Affairs.

Chapter 18

1. *Let's Look . . . At TEC* (A Program Handbook for Employees), Texas Employment Commission, pp. 3–4.
2. J. J. Pickle, "The Texas Employment Commission: Progress and Problems," *Public Affairs Comment*, The University of Texas, Institute of Public Affairs (Mar. 1962), p. 4.
3. "Public Welfare: A Perspective," State Program of Aid to Dependent Children, Texas Research League, (Feb. 1960), Part 1, pp. 4 and 8.
4. Ibid., p. 5.
5. Ibid., p. 4.
6. *Children's Services of the Texas Department of Public Welfare. Findings, Conclusions, Proposals*, Report No. 1 (Dec. 1959) in a study of state welfare programs (Texas Research League), pp. 65–67.
7. Ibid., p. 70.
8. Ibid., p. 70.
9. Ibid., p. 129.
10. Ibid., pp. 139–40.
11. Ibid., pp. 132–33.
12. H.B. No. 268, 1965.
13. Ibid.

Chapter 19

1. *Application of Paul L. Gault and Marjorie Gault, Father and Mother of Gerald Francis Gault, a Minor*, 87 S. Ct. 1428 (1967).
2. *Alicia Morales et al.* v. *Dr. James A. Thurman et al.*, U.S. District Court, Eastern District of Texas, Sherman Division, Civil Action No. 1948, Aug. 31, 1973. *Findings of Fact and Order of the Court.*

Chapter 20

1. Suzanne Dolezal, "Do Yu Hav Trabul Speling? You're Justified, Says a Group Out to Reform Our English Spelling System," *Houston Post*, Sunday, Apr. 11, 1982, p. 4BB.

2. Ibid.
3. Ibid.

Chapter 21

1. Minor B. Crager, "The Texas Consumer Code: Consensus, Conflict, and Change," *Public Affairs Comment*, 14, 1 (Jan. 1968), The University of Texas at Austin, Institute of Public Affairs.
2. Ibid.
3. Ibid.
4. *Manual of Texas State Government*, Texas Legislative Council (Jan. 1953), pp. 56–57.
5. Ibid., p. 60.
6. For an interesting study of the Texas railroad commission see David F. Prindle, *Petroleum Politics and the Texas Railroad Commission*, (Austin: University of Texas Press, 1981).
7. *Manual of Texas State Government*, Texas Legislative Council (Jan. 1953), p. 71.
8. *Manual of Texas State Government*, Texas Legislative Council (1953), p. 103.

Chapter 22

1. Article 5152, Revised Civil Statutes, Acts 1899.
2. *West Coast Hotel Co.* v. *Parrish*, 300 U.S. 379 (1937).
3. Theodore W. Kheel, "Strikes and Public Employment," *Michigan Law Review,* 67 (Mar. 1969), p. 941.
4. Article 8306, Section 2, *Vernon's Annotated Civil Statutes of the State of Texas.*
5. Article 8306, Section 12c, *Vernon's Annotated Civil Statutes of the State of Texas.*

Chapter 23

1. "Learning New 'Environment' Terms Helpful," *Houston Post,* April 5, 1970. Quoted by permission of the *Houston Post.*
2. Ibid.

Index